An Introduction to the EU Legal Order

Carefully structured and supported with a wealth of examples, Elise Muir provides a clear, concise introduction to the EU legal order. Drawing upon her years of teaching experience, Muir outlines the history of the EU, its key actors, modes of action and its daily relevance. Offering students and instructors an up-to-date textbook, Muir pays attention to the latest developments, including the impacts of Brexit and the Covid-19 crisis. Written for students from a range of disciplines and levels of study, this book explains how the EU legal order works. Muir illuminates the complex and technical areas of EU institutional law through explanatory illustrations, schemes, and textboxes. With this engaging and accessible resource, students will be well-equipped to understand the fundamentals and functioning of the EU legal order.

Professor Elise Muir is Head of the Department for International and European Law of the Faculty of Law of KU Leuven, where she teaches introductory as well as advanced courses on the EU Legal Order. She is also a Visiting Professor at the College of Europe, Bruges. She has published extensively in the field of EU law, including *EU Equality Law: The First Fundamental Rights Policy of the EU* (OUP, 2018). Her research has received a Starting Grant from the European Research Council, as well as scientific prizes (Edmond Hustinx, 2012).

An Introduction to the EU Legal Order

Elise Muir
KU Leuven

CAMBRIDGE
UNIVERSITY PRESS

CAMBRIDGE
UNIVERSITY PRESS

University Printing House, Cambridge CB2 8BS, United Kingdom

One Liberty Plaza, 20th Floor, New York, NY 10006, USA

477 Williamstown Road, Port Melbourne, VIC 3207, Australia

314–321, 3rd Floor, Plot 3, Splendor Forum, Jasola District Centre, New Delhi – 110025, India

103 Penang Road, #05–06/07, Visioncrest Commercial, Singapore 238467

Cambridge University Press is part of the University of Cambridge.

It furthers the University's mission by disseminating knowledge in the pursuit of education, learning, and research at the highest international levels of excellence.

www.cambridge.org
Information on this title: www.cambridge.org/9781108485609
DOI: 10.1017/9781108757317

First published 2023

A catalogue record for this publication is available from the British Library.

ISBN 978-1-108-48560-9 Hardback
ISBN 978-1-108-70740-4 Paperback

Contents

Figures

Boxes

Preface

This book is intended to provide an accessible, yet solid introduction to the EU legal order. This legal order is understood as building on a number of foundational principles, fleshed out by a set of key actors, based on a sophisticated system of legal norms interacting intimately with national legal systems.

The European Union is hard work. It could be tempting, in a contemporary introduction to the EU legal order, to focus on the present and spare the reader the meanderings of a historical journey. Nevertheless, the EU is not a given. Its strengths and weaknesses can only be understood and critically examined when read in perspective, hence the attention paid to foundational principles developed over time (Chapter 1).

The European Union is alive. An approach to an introduction to EU law could have been to take the system of EU competences as the starting point, before setting out the institutional landscape. The approach chosen here instead looks at those who shape and flesh out the system of competences (Chapter 2), before insisting on the centrality of the principle of conferral and setting out the related system of EU norms (Chapter 3). This is because the boundaries and tools of EU law are ambitious, contested and subject to adjustments by key players.

Emphasis is placed on the main institutional features of the EU legal order, as well as the way it interacts with domestic legal systems in a unique fashion (Chapter 4), rather than on EU substantive law. My intuition is that the main institutional features remain insufficiently understood, and therefore focusing on the machinery of the EU and thereby setting the scene for a distinct study of EU substantive law is worth the time and effort. The extreme importance of the structures of EU law, and their relevance for our daily lives, is illustrated throughout the book, owing to multiple concrete examples of the relevant of institutional rules and their operation in context.

The approach chosen across all four chapters is decidedly legal. The text explicitly relies on concise direct quotes from primary sources of EU law and is supported with legal references. It is indeed addressed to those willing to gain familiarity with the legal specificities of the EU. The intention is to make the law accessible and to incentivise the reader to read directly from primary legal sources. Emphasis is on texts negotiated by Member States and the main EU political institutions, as well as on key samples from case law.

The selection of sources thus reflects the strengths and weaknesses of the system of checks and balances representing the plurality of interests and related actors engaged in European affairs.

The book is also an exercise of doctrinal legal analysis. While trying to keep the narrative simple – for instance, by limiting abbreviations and acronyms, and avoiding unnecessary EU jargon – it does not shy away from using traditional EU law terminology and categorisations. Even if at times contested and demanding for the reader, these are commonly relied upon in EU affairs; their understanding is thus both necessary to whoever wishes to understand the dynamics of EU law, and a precondition to any convincing critical analysis – and possible attempts at deconstructing and reconstructing – in more advanced academic scholarship.

The approach is purportedly contextual. The narrative often sets out how legal texts originate in, or are fleshed out by, legal practice and/or occur in response to a specific set of events. The choice has been made not to put forward specific theoretical arguments, and instead to seek to explain the main features of the mechanics of the EU legal order. The intention is not to replace, or even pretend to undertake historical work, nor to deny the importance of theories of European integration. It is rather to humbly point to the multitude of complex challenges that the EU construct seeks to address, often on a case-by-case basis and as a result of sensitive negotiations.

The book is cautiously normative, equally critical and openly forward-looking. The author believes that working towards a peaceful EU, focused on ensuring the well-being of its people, is worth a try; and also that such efforts can only have a chance of success if they are accompanied by a self-critical process, acknowledging that challenges must be addressed through deliberation, making space for doubts, experimentalism and nuance. With that purpose in mind, the choice has been made to point to key areas of controversy within the process of European integration rather than brushing them away, to identify the main components of the debate, and to let the reader make the final evaluation.

The text is fairly concise, while trying to equip the reader with sufficient knowledge to be able to engage with EU law and to develop critical analysis through future studies or professional experience. Cartoons and schemes may help the reader to navigate particularly technical elements of the text. Academic references are kept to a minimum, and are mostly intended to provide direction for more advanced reading. More exhaustive and well-updated accounts may be found in Lenaerts, Van Nuffel and Corthaut's *EU Constitutional Law* (2021) and Schütze and Tridimas's *Oxford Principles of European Union Law* (2018), volume I. The materials are updated, to the best of my knowledge and abilities, as of 24 February 2022.

Acknowledgements

This book, modest as it is, is the outcome of a long journey, begun upon my arrival at KU Leuven, a journey on which I have not been alone.

I am very grateful to Anjum Shabbir for language editing, Pascal Hansens (known as Malt) for most cartoons, Jean-Christophe Bousmar for the design of the maps and schemes, as well as Martina Guarracino and Alicja Slowik for their highly valuable research assistance in earlier stages of the project.

Although the usual disclaimer applies and any possible mistakes are only attributable to me, I am indebted to Bruno de Witte, Dominik Hanf and Antoine Bailleux for most valuable feedback on extensive excerpts from the manuscript. I am equally thankful to the many friends and colleagues who kindly agreed to share their views and suggestions on specific sections; many thanks in particular to Jonathan Bauerschmidt, Matteo Bonnelli, Pawel Busiakiewicz, Merijn Chamon, Francesco Costa Cabral, Richard Crowe, Diane Fromage, Gillian More, Andrea Ott, Eulalia Sanfrutos Cano and Jonathan Tomkin. I am grateful to Edouard Dirrig; I would not have engaged in this project without his support in the early stages.

This project would not have come to completion without the precious help of members of the Institute for European Law, in particular Pieter Aertgeerts, Caterina Molinari and Victor Davio, with whom I have exchanged views on certain aspects of the materials, as well as Sara Van Steyvoort, who helped me – always with calmness and kindness – to make connections with all those involved.

Amélie, Hania and Pawel may not realise how much this work, as well as I, owe them – allow me to remind them and to let you know at the same time.

Abbreviations

AFET	European Parliament's Committee on Foreign Affairs
AFSJ	Area of Freedom, Security and Justice
Brussels Treaty	Treaty of Economic, Social and Cultural Collaboration and Collective Self-Defence
BVerfG	German Federal Constitutional Court
CETA	Comprehensive Economic and Trade Agreement
CFEU	Charter of Fundamental Rights
CFSP	Common Foreign and Security Policy
Commission	European Commission
Coreper	Committee of Permanent Representatives
COSAC	Conference of Parliamentary Committees for Union Affairs
Council	Council of the European Union
CSDP	Common Security and Defence Policy
DG	Directorate-General
EC	European Community
ECHR	European Convention for the Protection of Human Rights and Fundamental Freedoms
ECON	European Parliament's Committee on Economic and Monetary Affairs
ECSC	European Coal and Steel Community
ECtHR	European Court of Human Rights
ECU	European currency unit
EEA	European Economic Area
EEAS	European External Action Service
EEC	European Economic Community
EFTA	European Free Trade Association
EMS	European Monetary System
EMU	Economic and Monetary Union
EPPO	European Public Prosecutor's Office
EU	European Union

EU Treaties	Treaty on European Union and Treaty on the Functioning of the European Union
Euratom	European Atomic Energy Community
Fiscal Stability Treaty	Treaty on Stability, Coordination and Governance in the Economic and Monetary Union
Frontex	European Border and Coast Guard Agency
GATT	General Agreement on Tariffs and Trade
GDPR	General Data Protection Regulation
High Representative	High Representative of the Union for Foreign Affairs and Security Policy
IGC	intergovernmental conference
JHA	Justice and Home Affairs
LIBE	European Parliament's Committee on Civil Liberties, Justice and Home Affairs
MEP	Member of the European Parliament
MFF (Regulation)	Multiannual Financial Framework Regulation
NATO	North Atlantic Treaty Organisation
NGO	non-governmental organisation
OECD	Organisation for Economic Co-operation and Development
OLAF	European Anti-Fraud Office
OLP	ordinary legislative procedure
Parliament	European Parliament
TCA	Trade and Cooperation Agreement
TEC	Treaty establishing the European Community
TEEC	Treaty establishing the European Economic Community (Treaty of Rome/EEC Treaty)
TEU	Treaty on European Union
TFEU	Treaty on the Functioning of the European Union
UK	United Kingdom
WEU	Western European Union

1

The Foundations of EU Law

The essential purpose of European Union (EU) integration is, as Article 1, paragraph 2 of the Treaty on European Union (TEU) makes clear, to create 'an ever closer union among the peoples of Europe'. The EU legal order is therefore shaped to support a dynamic process of European integration. Its legal construct relies on a number of foundational objectives, principles and values – such as equality between participating States and their peoples – that also act as compasses (Section 1.1). The ambitious nature of the process, going well beyond a simple form of economic collaboration among States, distinguishes it from other forms of regional integration while enabling multiple interactions with non-member States and other organisations (Section 1.2). This first chapter stresses that the legal specificities of the EU legal order are best understood in light of its ongoing process of change, constantly seeking to better match evolving political goals with an appropriate legal machinery (Section 1.3). The resulting decisive changes and predominant features of the EU legal order are first and foremost crystallised in the primary legal framework on which it relies, in the form of the two main treaties shaping the EU. This primary legal framework will be introduced subsequently (Section 1.4), before further elaborating on the actors of the integration process (Chapter 2), the system of legal norms (Chapter 3) and the unique nature of the EU legal order (Chapter 4).

1.1 EUROPEAN INTEGRATION: OBJECTIVES, PRINCIPLES AND VALUES

1.1.1 An Ever Closer Union

The objective of 'an ever closer union among the people of Europe', clearly asserted in EU law since 1957,[1] must be understood in light of post-World War II traumas. The founding Member States – the Benelux countries, France, Germany and Italy – agreed to engage in an

[1] TEEC, Preamble, Recital (1).

ambitious political and legal project, initially and primarily articulated in economic terms, with a view to reunifying the continent. The aim to create an ever closer union is sometimes mistakenly perceived as enabling a never-ending expansion of EU powers. It is actually a more nuanced – but no less ambitious – commitment to build a common future, which allows different paths to be chosen by agreement.[2]

1.1.2 Equality and Sincere Cooperation

This central objective builds on two indispensable principles. A first precondition for any serious attempt to pacify Europe was to avoid the mistakes of the past, such as humiliating a country or nation, and instead to postulate the equality of Member States. The EU must indeed respect the equality of Member States under the treaties on which it is founded.[3] Every single Member State that signs up to those treaties, no matter the size, economic or geopolitical power of that State, will be represented equally.[4] That equality between Member States also applies to the citizens of each Member State, all having been granted the status of 'European citizen' since the early 1990s.[5] The latter have been protected against discrimination on grounds of nationality, such as in the field of employment, since the early days of the project.[6]

There are settings in which intense negotiations on institutional rules have resulted in acknowledgement of the factual diversity and specificities of various Member States.[7] In an EU with an overall increasingly large number of members, and with ever wider fields of action, the legal presumption of equality thus comes with nuances. From the perspective of EU law though, these nuances do not call into question the fundamental premise: balance with a view to reunification can only result from the presumption of equality between Member States, unless otherwise carefully articulated within EU law.

Since 1992, the founders of the EU Treaties have deemed it useful to specify that the equality of Member States is combined with respect for 'their national identities'. The latter are understood to be 'inherent in [the] fundamental structures [of Member States], political and constitutional, inclusive of regional and local self-government'.[8] Multiple provisions of EU law, and examples of case law, illustrate deference to national organs for the

[2] On the possibility of reducing competences conferred on the EU, see for instance Art. 48(2) TEU; and for differentiated integration within EU law, see Art. 20 TEU. See further European Council, 'A New Settlement for the United Kingdom within the European Union: Extract of the Conclusions of the European Council of 18–19 February 2016', OJ C 69, 23.2.2016, p. 1, Section C.1; C-621/18, *Wightman*, EU:C:2018:999, paras. 61–67.

[3] Art. 4(2) TEU.

[4] See for instance the composition and functioning of the European Council, which has a key role in seeking to achieve consensus on most sensitive matters, Chapter 2, Sections 2.3.3.2 and 2.3.3.3.

[5] Art. 9 TEU. [6] See Art. 45 TFEU, and more generally the current Art. 18 *et seq.* TFEU.

[7] See for instance the composition of the Parliament, or the rules on the rotating presidency of the Council, Chapter 2, Sections 2.3.2.3 and 2.3.4.3. On the former, the German Federal Constitutional Court (BVerfG) noted that, '[a]s a representative body of the peoples in a supranational community, characterised as such by a limited willingness to unite, [the European Parliament] cannot, and need not, as regards its composition, comply with the requirements that arise at state level from the equal political right to vote of all citizens' (BVerfG, 2 BvE 2/08, Act Approving the Treaty of Lisbon, 30.6.2009, paras. 271, 279–280 *et seq.*).

[8] Art. 4(2) TEU. The concept was used for instance in C-208/09, *Sayn-Wittgenstein*, EU:C:2010:806, paras. 83, 92.

protection of sensitive interests.[9] While the advancement of the process of integration is inevitably both a response to and a driver for change, it is not intended to profoundly call into question the inherent specificities of each State. A delicate balance must be found, between national divergences and the general interests of the EU.

A second precondition for the European project to be successful is reliance on the principle of 'sincere cooperation'.[10] The EU and the Member States have always been expected to jointly contribute to achieving the objectives of the process of EU integration, as agreed upon in the EU Treaties. They must do so in full respect for each other, including in reciprocal relations between Member States.[11] On the one hand, Member States shall ensure the fulfilment of their obligations and facilitate the achievement of the EU's objectives. On the other hand, Member States shall refrain from any measure which could jeopardise the attainment of the EU's objectives. As for EU institutions, they are expected to practise mutual sincere cooperation[12] and act in line with the delicate balance of powers and interests that they represent at European level.

These two central principles of European integration: equal treatment among Member States and the principle of sincere cooperation, act as political compasses for the EU integration process. They also produce legal effects and may be used to shed light on compliance of actors with EU law.[13] This is intended to pave the way for a spirited collaboration between Member States, which is also sometimes referred to in terms of 'solidarity'.[14]

1.1.3 Founding Values and Mutual Trust

These principles, as well as the entire integration process, are themselves grounded in a set of values, common to the Member States and providing the foundations of the EU construct. These values have not always been explicitly asserted in the founding treaties, but can now be found in an important provision of the TEU, Article 2, according to which:

[9] See for instance the possibilities to derogate from the prohibition of restrictions to the free movement of goods (Art. 36 TFEU), or the rules on the interpretation of the CFEU (Art. 52(1) and (4) CFEU). Such a balancing is ultimately subject to judicial review by the Court of Justice of the European Union; for a recent example of acknowledgement of different national perceptions of animal welfare and freedom of religion see C-336/19, *Centraal Israëlitisch Consistorie van België et al.*, EU:C:2020:1031, para. 71.

[10] Art. 4(3) TEU.

[11] For a recent illustration, although it is not for the Court of Justice of the European Union to encroach upon the powers reserved for the Member States regarding geographical determination of their borders, Slovenia and Croatia, two of the latest States to join the EU, ought to 'strive sincerely to bring about a definitive legal solution consistent with international law, as suggested in the Act of Accession', to a related ongoing dispute between them in order to ensure 'the effective and unhindered application of EU law in the areas concerned' (C-457/18, *Republic of Slovenia* v. *Republic of Croatia*, EU:C:2020:65, para. 109).

[12] Art. 13(2) TEU.

[13] E.g. Case 39/72, *Commission* v. *Italy (Premiums for slaughtering cows)*, EU:C:1973:13, para. 24; see further Chapter 2, Section 2.3.1.2.

[14] For recent examples see: Arts. 3(3) TEU, 80 TFEU and related case law on the relocation of nationals of third countries in response to an emergency situation characterised by a sudden inflow into certain Member States (Joined Cases C-643/15 and C-647/15, *Slovakia and Hungary* v. *Council*, EU:C:2017:631, para. 252). See also: Art. 2 TEU, together with the provisions of Title II of Part Six of the TFEU on EU financial provisions and related case law where solidarity is understood to be given practical effect through the Union budget: Case C-156/21, *Hungary* v. *Parliament and Council (General Regime of Conditionality for the Protection of the European Union Budget)*, EU:C:2022:97, para. 129.

> The Union is founded on the values of respect for human dignity, freedom, democracy, equality, the rule of law and respect for human rights, including the rights of persons belonging to minorities. These values are common to the Member States in a society in which pluralism, non-discrimination, tolerance, justice, solidarity and equality between women and men prevail.

Because the EU legal order is based on the fundamental premise that its Member States share and recognise the founding values listed in Article 2 TEU, it is often said that there is 'mutual trust' between the Member States. That trust is understood to create a presumption that those values will be recognised by all Member States, and that EU law that implements these values will be respected.[15] Article 2 TEU has gained renewed attention in recent years due to vivid concerns expressed by selected European institutions about the risks of serious breaches of the rule of law, and the thorny question of how to sanction them, particularly in rule of law Poland and in Hungary.[16]

Although Article 2 TEU is of paramount importance for the EU, defining its key concepts is not an easy task. For instance, what is meant by 'rule of law' is not defined in the EU Treaties. The EU legislator recently stressed that respect for the rule of law is understood to be 'an essential precondition for compliance with the principles of sound financial management' in the EU.[17] In this context, it further specified that the rule of law includes the principles of legality, legal certainty, prohibition of arbitrariness of the executive powers, effective judicial protection, separation of powers, and non-discrimination and equality before the law.[18]

Guidance on other notions enshrined in Article 2 TEU is sparse in the EU Treaties themselves. By way of example, the TEU includes a number of provisions on 'democratic principles', such as the reference to 'representative democracy'[19] as the foundation of the functioning of the EU and the duty to take decisions 'as openly and as closely as possible to the citizens'.[20] The Treaty on the Functioning of the European Union (TFEU) prohibits discrimination among the nationals of the Member States.[21] Certain provisions of the treaties allow for the further adoption of EU legislation, giving flesh to some of the values listed in Article 2 TEU, such as the principle of non-discrimination, to which expression is given in several directives implementing the principle of equal treatment between persons irrespective of sex, racial or ethnic origin, religion or belief, disability, age or sexual orientation.[22]

[15] Opinion 2/13, Accession of the European Union to the European Convention for the Protection of Human Rights and Fundamental Freedoms, EU:C:2014:2454, para. 168. The implications and limits of the concept remain subject to much debate; see S. Prechal, 'Mutual Trust before the Court of Justice of the European Union', *European Papers*, 2 (2017), pp. 75–92.

[16] See Chapter 4, Section 4.3.2.1.

[17] 'Regulation (EU, Euratom) 2020/2092 of the European Parliament and of the Council of 16 December 2020 on a General Regime of Conditionality for the Protection of the Union Budget', OJ L 433I, 22.12.2020, p. 1, Preamble (7). Note that two Member States have requested the annulment of the regulation; the action failed; Case C-156/21, *Hungary* v. *Parliament and Council*, EU:C:2022:97.

[18] 'Regulation (EU, Euratom) 2020/2092 of the European Parliament and of the Council of 16 December 2020 on a General Regime of Conditionality for the Protection of the Union Budget', OJ L 433I, 22.12.2020, Art. 3(a); see further Arts. 3 (the following may be indicative of breaches of the principles of the rule of law) and 4(2) (breaches of the principles of the rule of law shall concern one or more of the following).

[19] Art. 10(1) TEU. [20] Art. 10(3) TEU. [21] Art. 18 TFEU.

[22] E.g. 'Council Directive 2000/43/EC of 29 June 2000 Implementing the Principle of Equal Treatment between Persons Irrespective of Racial or Ethnic Origin', OJ L 180, 19.7.2000, p. 22; 'Council Directive 2000/78/EC of 27 November 2000 Establishing a General Framework for Equal Treatment in Employment and Occupation', OJ L 303, 2.12.2000, p. 16.

Most of the guidance on the founding values is not actually found within the treaties, but elsewhere. Article 6 TEU acts as a bridge between the treaties and other sources of EU law.[23] In 2009 this Article granted the Charter of Fundamental Rights of the European Union (CFEU) the same legal value as the treaties, so that the Union now recognises the rights, freedoms and principles it contains. The European Convention on Human Rights (ECHR), a legal instrument belonging to a different legal order – that of the Council of Europe (which includes all the Member States, as well as other States) – also has significant influence on the definition of EU values. Finally, general principles of EU law, which have been developed through the Court of Justice's case law, and which are derived inter alia from the Member States' common constitutional traditions, also provide guidance on what the EU's key values are.

1.2 A UNIQUE FORM OF REGIONAL INTEGRATION

Building on this central objective, foundational principles and values, the EU was conceived, and further developed, as a unique form of regional integration. It differs from other models of regional integration because it encompasses a particularly ambitious range of policy areas, and deploys powerful tools so that its rules can be implemented.

1.2.1 An Ambitious Integration Process

Regional integration may vary in scope and range. Illustrating the starting point of economic integration between different States, somewhere at the bottom end of an 'integration scale' is the so-called free trade area. A free trade area is a group of two or more customs territories in which duties and other regulations having a restrictive effect on commerce – with exceptions – are eliminated on substantially all trade *between* the constituent territories in products originating in such territories.[24] It therefore ensures free trade between the contracting parties, in our case, the Member States of the EU. One may, for instance, buy a toaster made in Germany while shopping in the Netherlands, and take it to one's home in Belgium without having to pay customs duties.

More ambitious than a free trade area is a customs union, which is what exists in the EU. A customs union means there is a single customs territory instead of two or more customs territories. These territories not only benefit from a free trade area between them, but also apply substantially the same duties and other regulations of commerce to the trade of territories *from outside* the contracting parties.[25] By way of example, the Commission reported that in 2019 more than 3,699 firearms were seized at the external borders of the EU, along with over 400,000 pieces of ammunition and more than 7,500 explosives items. In doing so, customs officials from different Member States were applying common EU rules for the protection of consumers against illegal and dangerous goods entering the EU from third countries.[26]

The EU offers even more than a customs union: it seeks to establish its own internal market. This includes a customs union, which covers all trade in goods with free movement

[23] See further Chapter 3, Section 3.1.3.1.
[24] See General Agreement on Tariffs and Trade (GATT 1994), Art. XXIV(8)(b). [25] Ibid., Art. XXIV(8)(a).
[26] European Commission, 'Customs sees what you don't . . . and protects you', available at ec.europa.eu.

between the Member States, as well as a common customs tariff.[27] It also provides for a 'common market', in which the free movement of persons, services and capital is ensured, and where progress eliminating obstacles to movement leads to asserting the existence of an 'internal market'[28] in an 'area without internal frontiers', to which we return subsequently. For example, I am a national of a Member State of the EU (France), working in another Member State of the EU (Belgium), under the same conditions as the nationals of the host State. I benefit from the free movement of workers in the EU. This relies on a set of common rules facilitating the functioning of the internal market, such as those on the rights of family members of migrant workers. The EU also includes a large number of policies supporting the establishment of an internal market – such as a common competition policy, a common commercial policy, a common agricultural, environmental and transport policy. These policies allow the EU to develop tools for the achievement of common objectives in these fields, such as common requirements for the safe and efficient provision of air navigation services in the single European sky.[29]

Once again, the EU's regional objectives go a few steps further. This became particularly clear from the 1990s onwards. The EU allows the nationals of the Member States, who hold the fundamental status of EU citizens, to move and reside within the EU even if they do not engage in an economic activity – although carefully designed conditions apply.[30] The EU has a common economic and monetary policy, with a majority of Member States using a single currency (the euro); an Area of Freedom, Security and Justice (AFSJ) without internal frontiers, with a majority of the Member States having abolished internal border controls on persons (the Schengen Area), being part of a common asylum law system (the Dublin system), and with a policy on the prevention and combating of crime; as well as a Common Foreign and Security Policy (CFSP) with the progressive framing of a common defence policy among some of the Member States. The set of sub-objectives of the European Union, thereby summarised, is listed in Article 3 TEU.

As a result, the EU is a much broader economic, social and political project than those following traditional forms of regional economic integration. This is because, as noted already, the EU ultimately has a meta-objective to create a closer union among the peoples of Europe. The EU is a purposive project, constantly evolving to adjust to a rapidly changing domestic and international context. As a consequence, it is difficult to put a label on the specific type of regional integration that it represents without reflecting on the labels themselves.[31] Importantly though, this large scale project, the most advanced of its kind, remains limited by the fact that the EU can only be understood as a 'derivative' legal order.[32] As the last recital of Article 3 TEU clearly shows, '[t]he Union shall pursue its objectives by appropriate means commensurate with the competences which are conferred upon it in the

[27] Art. 28(1) TFEU. [28] Art. 26(2) TFEU.

[29] 'Regulation (EC) No. 550/2004 of the European Parliament and of the Council of 10 March 2004 on the Provision of Air Navigation Services in the Single European Sky', OJ L 96, 31.3.2004, p. 10.

[30] See further Chapter 2, Section 2.2.3.

[31] This would be beyond the scope of this book; see further: R. Schütze, *The Changing Structure of European Law*, vols. I and II (Oxford University Press, 2009, 2017).

[32] N. Walker, 'Human Rights in a Post-national Order: Reconciling Political and Constitutional Pluralism', in T. Campbell, K. D. Ewing and A. Tomkins (eds.), *Sceptical Essays on Human Rights* (Oxford University Press, 2001), p. 129.

Treaties'. The EU can therefore only exercise competences conferred upon it by its Member States, as will be further discussed in Chapter 3, Section 3.2.

1.2.2 A Regional Project that Interacts with Others

The EU is not the only form of regional integration in Europe, and it has a wealth of links with other organisations and European States. Several European States – which are today Iceland, Liechtenstein, Norway and Switzerland – have decided not to be part of the EU, but to create *among themselves* the European Free Trade Association (EFTA).[33] EFTA was initially created in 1960 in parallel to the early years of the European Economic Community (EEC) that has today become the EU. The objective of EFTA is to promote a continued and balanced strengthening of trade and economic relations with free trade in goods, progressive liberalisation of the free movement of persons as well as trade in services and of investment, providing fair conditions of competition, opening the public procurement markets and providing appropriate protection of intellectual property rights.[34] It is therefore a project that is more ambitious than a simple free trade area. Nevertheless, it remains primarily focused on the promotion of free trade and economic integration.

Most of the EFTA states (with the exception of Switzerland) are also part of the European Economic Area (EEA), created in 1994 to bring those EFTA States closer to the process of European Union integration, and its internal market in particular. The EEA aims to promote continuous and balanced strengthening of trade and economic relations between the EU and the EFTA States. To that effect, it entails the free movement of goods, persons, services and capital, a system ensuring that competition is not distorted, as well as cooperation in other fields, such as research and development, the environment, education and social policy.[35] The EFTA States engaged in the EEA also contribute to the EU budget for their participation in EU activities,[36] despite the fact that these States do not take part in all EU economic policies, such as agriculture and fisheries, the customs union and trade policy. Iceland, Liechtenstein and Norway have joined additional selected EU policies, such as the Schengen Area (in which there are no internal border controls) through ad hoc agreements with the EU.[37] Nevertheless, the cooperation in the context of the EEA remains primarily focused on economic forms of cooperation. Overall, the EFTA States are not developing common policies with the EU in fields such as the monetary union, most aspects of Justice and Home Affairs (JHA; other than the Schengen Area) and CFSP.[38]

Two of the EFTA States stand out in terms of the nature of their relationship with the EU. Norway, on the one hand, is an EEA partner that has a set of additional ad hoc arrangements with the EU going beyond mere economic forms of integration, for instance, in the fields of

[33] See further Chapter 2, Section 2.1.1.

[34] Convention Establishing the European Free Trade Association, Art. 2.

[35] 'Agreement on the European Economic Area', OJ L 1, 3.1.1994 (consolidated 15.3.2021), Art. 1.

[36] Ibid., Art. 82.

[37] E.g. 'Agreement Concluded by the Council of the European Union and the Republic of Iceland and the Kingdom of Norway Concerning the Latter's Association with the Implementation, Application and Development of the Schengen Acquis: Final Act', OJ L 176, 10.7.1999, p. 36.

[38] More information on 'What Is the EEA Not?' at www.efta.int/eea/eea-agreement.

JHA and CFSP.[39] Switzerland, on the other hand, is not an EEA State, but has developed a very close relationship with the EU owing to a multitude of bilateral treaties that are largely comparable, in terms of their content, to the EEA.[40] Switzerland is also now a member of the Schengen Area.[41]

These close partners of the EU are expected to accept a set of rules for international cooperation and to ensure the smooth functioning of the internal market. For instance, seven bilateral agreements between the EU and Switzerland were concluded together in 1999, with a clause specifying that all would cease to apply if any of them was terminated (a 'guillotine' clause).[42] Furthermore, it is often argued that the EFTA States, and Norway in particular, must comply with many EU rules (as a consequence of either the EEA Agreement, or further ad hoc international treaties) without actually taking part directly in the drafting and negotiations of these EU rules. One ought to keep in mind therefore that much of what is discussed in the remainder of this book may be relevant outside of the EU, for countries such as the EFTA States.

These are points that have been particularly vividly debated in the context of the negotiations on Brexit, and the negotiations to design a new relationship between the EU and the United Kingdom (UK).[43] The UK left the EU on 31 January 2020.[44] After a transition period which expired on 31 December 2020, EU law ceased to apply to that State unless otherwise provided. Specific provisions of the Withdrawal Agreement between the UK and the EU are intended to ensure an orderly withdrawal by requiring certain EU rights to continue to apply. Some of these rights relate to customs and the free movement of goods in relations to Northern Ireland.[45] Others seek to ensure a level of continued protection of EU citizens and UK nationals, and their respective family members – but only those who exercised their free movement rights before the end of 2020.[46] In addition to the provisions

[39] E.g. 'Convention on Jurisdiction and the Recognition and Enforcement of Judgments in Civil and Commercial Matters', OJ L 339, 21.12.2007, p. 3.

[40] E.g. 'Agreement between the European Economic Community and the Swiss Confederation', OJ L 300, 31.12.1972, p. 189; 'Agreement between the European Community and Its Member States, of the One Part, and the Swiss Confederation, of the Other, on the Free Movement of Persons: Final Act', OJ L 114, 30.4.2002, p. 6; 'Agreement between the European Community and the Swiss Confederation Concerning the Criteria and Mechanisms for Establishing the State Responsible for Examining a Request for Asylum Lodged in a Member State or in Switzerland', OJ L 53, 27.2.2008, p. 5. An attempt to have an Institutional Framework Agreement, intended to enhance and develop EU-Swiss bilateral relations for the future, failed in 2021 after the Swiss Federal Council took the decision to terminate the negotiations with the EU.

[41] 'Agreement between the European Union, the European Community and the Swiss Confederation on the Swiss Confederation's Association with the Implementation, Application and Development of the Schengen Acquis', OJ L 53, 27.2.2008, p. 52.

[42] 'Agreement between the European Community and its Member States, of the One Part, and the Swiss Confederation, of the Other, on the Free Movement of Persons', OJ L 114, 30.4.2002, p. 6, Art. 25(4).

[43] E.g. House of Lords, European Union Committee, 'Brexit: the options for trade', HL Paper 72, 13.12.2016, pp. 22–23.

[44] See Chapter 2, Section 2.1.3.

[45] 'Agreement on the Withdrawal of the United Kingdom of Great Britain and Northern Ireland from the European Union and the European Atomic Energy Community', OJ L 29, 31.1.2020, p. 7, Protocol annexed to the EU Treaties on Ireland/Northern Ireland, Art. 5.

[46] 'Agreement on the Withdrawal of the United Kingdom of Great Britain and Northern Ireland from the European Union and the European Atomic Energy Community', OJ L 29, 31.1.2020, Part II. The provisions of this Agreement and the provisions of EU law made applicable by this Agreement shall produce in respect of and in the United Kingdom the same legal effects as those which they produce within the EU and its Member States. 'Agreement on the Withdrawal of the United Kingdom of Great Britain and Northern Ireland from the European Union and the European Atomic Energy Community', OJ L 29, 31.1.2020, Art. 4(1); see also Part II and Art. 158 on citizens' rights.

Map 1.1 The EU, the EEA, Switzerland and the UK

on separation and the protection of acquired citizens' rights, a new Trade and Cooperation Agreement (TCA) was agreed in December 2020, with a view to establishing 'clear and mutually advantageous rules governing trade and investment'.[47] It builds on the assertion

[47] 'Trade and Cooperation Agreement between the European Union and the European Atomic Energy Community, of the One Part, and the United Kingdom of Great Britain and Northern Ireland, of the Other Part', OJ L 149, 30.4.2021, p. 10, Preamble recital (4); other agreements may also be concluded, e.g.

that both sides will ensure a level playing field for open and fair competition, with non-regression clauses on matters such as labour and social standards, or environmental protection, thus expecting the UK not to back track from its earlier commitments under EU law in these fields. As noted in the TCA, the new relationship with the UK is primarily (although not exclusively) narrowed down to a focus on trade in goods, and the EU seeks to establish 'an area of prosperity and good neighbourliness characterised by close and peaceful relations based on cooperation'.[48] At the time of writing, there remain tensions in the implementation and compliance with the agreed provisions.

Along with its privileged links to the EEA States, Switzerland and the UK, the EU thus interacts with a broad range of other international organisations and third States, as illustrated by the customs union with Turkey or the ambitious free trade agreement with Canada.[49] Furthermore, the Member States of the EU may develop various forms of cooperation in the form of international agreements between them, including to achieve further progress in reaching the objectives set out in EU law.[50]

1.2.3 A Powerful Set of Tools for Integration

The political ambition of the EU integration project is not only illustrated by the broad range of the areas of common policies that it has implemented, intends to develop and at times shares with other States or organisations. The EU also comes with an exceptional set of tools for doing so in a more effective way than in more classical forms of international cooperation. Agreements between States are traditionally concluded at international level by representatives of the governments of the contracting parties. The implementation of most agreements of the sort is then commonly ensured through equally 'intergovernmental' methods primarily reflecting the interests of each individual State, requiring, for instance, consensus of State representatives within the given governing body, and creating obligations on them rather than rights and obligations for individuals.

While the international treaties on which the EU is founded have primarily been adopted through such intergovernmental techniques, the legal effects that derive from these treaties largely depart from this approach. The governance model on which the EU relies is often said to be 'supranational'. Such a system of governance acknowledges the importance of the interests of each individual State party to the organisation. Yet the system *also* makes space for the representation of other interests, such as those of the citizens of the State

'Agreement between the European Union and the United Kingdom of Great Britain and Northern Ireland Concerning Security Procedures for Exchanging and Protecting Classified Information', OJ L 444, 31.12.2020, p. 14.

48 'Trade and Cooperation Agreement between the European Union and the European Atomic Energy Community, of the One Part, and the United Kingdom of Great Britain and Northern Ireland, of the Other Part', OJ L 149, 30.4.2021, Art. 1.

49 'Decision No. 1/95 of the EC–Turkey Association Council of 22 December 1995 on Implementing the Final Phase of the Customs Union', OJ L 13, 17.1.2014, p. 74; 'Comprehensive Economic and Trade Agreement (CETA) between Canada, of the One Part, and the European Union and Its Member States, of the Other Part', OJ L 11, 14.1.2017, p. 23.

50 See Chapter 2, Section 2.1.1 and Chapter 3, Section 3.5.1.2.

parties, as well as for the idea of a 'common good' – or 'a measure of 'aboveness'[51] – going beyond the mere addition of the interests of each individual State party.[52]

Reference is often made to the 'community method' that characterises the particular dynamics of decision-making within the EU since its early days, under the umbrella of what was then called the European Economic *Community* – hence the name of the method. The community method is the one that prevails in the current daily functioning of the EU. This approach consists of empowering institutions at supranational level to balance the various interests identified previously, and to work towards the general interests of the EU. The evolution of the status of each institution, the composition of these institutions, their rules on internal decision-making and the relationship between them is thus at the core of the assertion of the increasingly sophisticated nature of the EU legal order.

To briefly illustrate the point: it is common that the adoption of EU legislation only requires support from a (qualified) majority of the Member States, gathered in an institution – named the Council of the European Union (the Council). The adoption of such a legislative act also requires support, in principle, from an institution composed of directly elected representatives of citizens – the European Parliament (the Parliament). An independent institution promoting the general interest – the European Commission (the Commission) – must have autonomously decided to initiate the decision-making process. The Commission also monitors implementation and compliance with acts thereby adopted. Another institution, also acting independently of the Member States – the Court of Justice of the European Union, ensures judicial review.

The supranational approach thus relies on a particularly powerful set of institutions, taking into account States' interests, but also putting flesh on an ambitious common project. There is more to the supranational nature of the process of European integration. This extraordinary institutional setting offers a fertile nest for the development of a vast array of legal norms that are integrated in domestic legal systems. EU law prevails over domestic law – by virtue of the principle of primacy – and has a number of other characteristics (to which we will return later)[53] contributing, on a daily basis, to the good operation of European integration. This overall process, in which law plays a vital role, has been coined 'integration through law'.[54] It is sometimes feared that this approach to Europeanisation does not result from enough political debate and support, both at Member State level and within the Member States.[55] I hope to give the readers of this book enough materials to come to their own opinion.

The supranational nature of the process of European integration hereby defined does not negate the existence and importance of dialogue between representatives of the Member

[51] For a more in-depth discussion of how the concept may be usefully articulated: J. Weiler, 'The Community System: The Dual Character of Supranationalism', *Yearbook of European Law*, 1/1 (1981), p. 268.

[52] See further K. Lenaerts and P. Van Nuffel, *European Union Law* (Sweet & Maxwell, 2011, 3rd ed.), pp. 16–19, 25.

[53] See Chapter 4, Section 4.1.

[54] M. Cappelletti, M. Seccombe and J. H. H. Weiler (eds.), *Integration through Law*, 5 vols. (de Gruyter, 1986); see also Section 1.4.2 and Chapter 4, Section 4.1 on primacy and direct effect.

[55] On the purported 'democratic deficit' of the EU, see for example, V. Schmidt, *Democracy in Europe: The EU and National Polities* (Oxford University Press, 2006), chs. 3 and 4; J. H. Weiler, 'In the Face of Crisis: Input Legitimacy, Output Legitimacy and the Political Messianism of European Integration', *Journal of European Integration*, 34 (2012), pp. 825–841; A. Follesdal and S. Hix, 'Why There Is a Democratic Deficit in the EU: A Response to Majone and Moravcsik', *Journal of Common Market Studies*, 44 (2006), pp. 533–562.

States at European level on interests that they deem to be of particular importance to them. Such examples abound. One of the clearest examples of heavy reliance on an intergovernmental logic at EU level is to be found in the context of the CFSP of the EU.[56] Often, we also see solutions to crises – the euro, refugees, COVID-19 or the Russian military aggression against Ukraine, to name but a few – being addressed by an emergency gathering of the representatives of the governments of Member States within the EU institution that represents them at the highest level.[57]

The EU has grown to be increasingly supranational overall, with greater emphasis on the main features of today's version of the community method over time. Simultaneously, the EU has unquestionably asserted itself as a forum where responsibility is organised and

Box 1.1 **Rough guide to the EU institutions**

Parliament (Art. 14 TEU)

- Its members are directly elected by EU citizens.
- It co-decides on the EU budget and is normally a co-legislator. It also exercises political control on other institutions.

European Council (Art. 15 TEU)

- It is composed of the Heads of State or Government, it has a President who is *not* one of the Heads of State and Government, and also includes the Commission's President.
- It provides impetus for development, and defines general political direction and priorities.

Council (Art. 16 TEU)

- It is made up of the representatives of the Member States at *ministerial* level.
- It co-decides on the EU budget and is a (co-)legislator; it is also in charge of policy-making and coordination.

Commission (Art. 17 TEU)

- It is made up of independent members, promoting the general interests of the EU.
- It initiates legislation by making proposals that the co-legislators decide on, and ensures the application of the EU Treaties and derived law.

Court of Justice of the European Union (Art. 19 TEU)

- It is made up of independent members.
- It ensures that, in the interpretation and application of the Treaties, EU law is observed.

56 Title V TEU.

57 On the difficulty of distinguishing between Member States acting jointly and in their sovereignty on the one hand, and action of their representatives as part of an EU institution on the other hand, see Chapter 2, Section 2.1.1; on the role of the European Council as an EU institution contributing to responses to crises, see Chapter 2, Section 2.3.3.

decisions are taken by the Member States to act jointly.[58] The distinction between the logic of a supranational approach, relying on a powerful common institutional framework complemented by a set of integrated legal tools, and that by which Member States create a 'sphere in which to do things together' through intergovernmental dialogue is not black and white; both exist side by side.[59] While there may be tensions between the two logics, they primarily complement each other in the EU legal order.

The key institutional players, to which we will return in Chapter 2, are briefly introduced in Box 1.1.

1.3 EVOLUTION

The most visible expression of integration through law is the centrality of the EU Treaties in the process of European integration. The main features of the legal order under scrutiny in this book are encapsulated in the said Treaties, which are sometimes referred to as the 'basic constitutional charter' of the EU by the Court of Justice of the European Union.[60] How did we go from the Treaty establishing the European Economic Community to the current version of the EU Treaties?[61] A few words of explanation are necessary before the historical overview.

1.3.1 Introduction to Treaty Change

The European Economic Community (EEC) was created by an international treaty, entitled 'Treaty establishing the European Economic Community', signed in Rome in 1957 by the six initial Member States (often referred to as TEEC, or Treaty of Rome). Subsequent changes were most often introduced by new international treaties signed in different places across Europe. They are therefore also commonly referred to in association with the name of the relevant city, such as the most recent Treaty of Lisbon, with twenty-seven current participating States.

The Treaty of Rome has been subject to several amendments adjusting the political ambition, the material scope of action and the tools for integration. Overall, treaty reforms to date have pushed towards a deepening of the integration process, a broadening of the scope of intervention of the EU and more supranational as well as more democratic tools for integration. This is reflected in the fact that they led to the European Economic Community becoming the European Union as we know it today.

These types of treaty amendments must be distinguished from another important series of treaty amendments intended to enact accession of new Member State.[62] This second category of treaty change, which will be discussed in Chapter 2, broadens the geographical

[58] Paraphrasing L. van Middelaar, *Alarums and Excursions: Improvising Politics on the European Stage* (Agenda Publishing, 2019), p. 167.

[59] Ibid., pp. 165–166. [60] Case 294/83, *Les Verts*, EU:C:1986:166.

[61] For a recent insightful analysis of the history of the EU, see K. K. Patel, *Project Europe: A History* (Cambridge University Press, 2020). Please note that several of the historical documents referred to in this section are made available by the Institute for Contemporary History of the University of Luxembourg at www.cvce.eu.

[62] A chronological overview of amendments having adjusted the material and geographical scope, as well as tools for the process of European integration is available at http://eur-lex.europa.eu/collection/eu-law/treaties/treaties-overview.html.

ambit of the process of European integration and makes the necessary technical arrangements. In contrast with the first type of treaty amendments that we will now discuss, and although enlargement of the EU is an important political decision, the second category of treaty changes does not in principle modify the material scope of action or the tools for integration.

1.3.2 From Zurich to Lisbon

This book does not aim to give an exhaustive historical overview of European integration. I only flag up a number of landmark stages in that process, shedding light on and outlining developments that contribute to our understanding of the current institutional design of the EU.[63] The main developments surrounding the changes of name to the legal order, from the EEC to the EU, will be used to structure this historical overview; the related treaty changes are put forward to illustrate adjustments in the ambition of the project.

A number of changes will also be deemed to be of 'structural importance', and thus outlined subsequently, even though they do not relate to formal treaty change. This allows for the painting of a more dynamic, as well as more accurate, picture of the process of European integration than that emerging from a view that is limited to treaty changes. With a view to shedding light on contemporary EU law and policy, I highlight key dynamics in three policy areas that have come to take centre stage in EU affairs, along with the foundational project of market integration: monetary policy, home affairs and foreign affairs. As will be explained subsequently, these are currently reflected in the Economic and Monetary Union (EMU), the AFSJ and the CFSP, respectively. The transversal question of the EU budget will also be given specific attention.

Due to limited space, the focus is on themes that have crystallised and continue to epitomise fundamental features of the system of checks and balances between Member States and the EU, as well as among EU institutions. It is acknowledged that these choices result in other important EU policies, such as agriculture, the environment or consumer protection, being subject to less attention.

1.3.2.1 Towards the European Economic Community

We start with the famous speech given by Winston Churchill, former British Prime Minister, in Zurich in 1946. He called for 'a kind of United States of Europe'.[64] In the aftermath of World War II, several initiatives were taken at the European level to stimulate cooperation among European States. The aim was to work towards the economic and political reconstruction of the continent, as well as to counter the growing influence of the Soviet Union. Certain initiatives allowed a defence alliance to be developed[65] that led to the creation of the well-known North Atlantic Treaty Organization (NATO, 1949).[66] Others intended to support the economies of European States. The US-sponsored Marshall Plan (1948–1951),

[63] This is intended to set the foundations not only for this book, but also for further study of EU law.
[64] Address given by Winston Churchill, Zurich, 19.9.1946.
[65] Treaty of Economic, Social and Cultural Collaboration and Collective Self-Defence (Brussels Treaty), 17.4.1948.
[66] North Atlantic Treaty, Washington, 4.4.1949.

in particular, paved the way for the Organisation for Economic Co-operation and Development that still exists today (OECD, 1960).

Common Concerns and Realising Human Rights

At the Hague Congress, in 1948, a federalist movement called for the creation of structures to support more ambitious and political forms of cooperation. This progressively led to the creation of the Council of Europe among ten European States in 1949.[67] The Council of Europe, not to be confused with the Council of the European Union or the European Council,[68] hosted a Committee of Ministers as well as a Consultative Assembly that could be understood to be the very first parliament of modern Europe,[69] with its seat in Strasbourg. The aim of the Council of Europe (made up of forty-seven participating States at the time of writing)[70] is 'to achieve a greater unity between its Members for the purpose of safeguarding and realizing the ideals and principles which are their common heritage and facilitating their economic and social progress'. It shall do so through 'discussion of questions of common concern and by agreements and common action in economic, social, cultural, scientific, legal and administrative matters and in the maintenance and further realisation of human rights and fundamental freedoms'.[71]

Soon after its creation, the Council of Europe agreed the European Convention for the Protection of Human Rights and Fundamental Freedoms (ECHR, 1950). It is currently interpreted by the European Court of Human Rights (ECtHR), also based in Strasbourg. The participating States undertake to abide by the final judgment of the ECtHR in any case to which they are parties. Although the Council of Europe with its Parliamentary Assembly, and the ECtHR that can be seised by private parties, had – and still have! – features of a supranational legal system, this was not considered to be sufficient to 'make' Europe.

A Community for Coal and Steel (1951)

In an important speech inspired by Jean Monnet (a senior French civil servant), Robert Schuman (the French Foreign Minister of the time) observed on 9 May 1950 that the *rassemblement* of European nations required the elimination of the age-old opposition of France and Germany. With a view to achieving that aim, his central and foundational idea was to pool the resources of France and Germany, and to place them under the authority of an independent supranational institution. Key elements of his speech are reproduced here:

[67] Belgium, Denmark, France, Ireland, Italy, Luxembourg, the Netherlands, Norway, Sweden and the United Kingdom.

[68] The Council and the European Council are two institutions of the European Union (Chapter 2, Sections 2.3.3 and 2.3.4), which is a distinct legal organisation from the Council of Europe.

[69] C.D., 'Europas erstes Parlament', *Die Zeit*, 18.8.1949, p. 1.

[70] This includes all EU Member States, as well as many others, such as Turkey and the Russian Federation, although the latter is unlikely to remain a member after the military aggression against Ukraine.

[71] Statute of the Council of Europe, London, 5.5.1949, Art. 1(a) and (b).

Erfinderstolz:
„Hoffentlich entwickelt sich das Ding besser als die Sicherheitsnadeln."

'The pride of the inventor: Let's hope that the thing develops better than the safety pins.'[73]

> Europe will not be made all at once, or according to a single plan [. . .]. It will be built through concrete achievements which first create a de facto solidarity. [. . .] The solidarity in production thus established will make it plain that any war between France and Germany becomes not merely unthinkable, but materially impossible. [It] will lay a true foundation for their economic unification. [. . .T]here will be realised simply and speedily that fusion of interests which is indispensable to the establishment of a common economic system; it may be the leaven from which may grow a wider and deeper community between countries long opposed to one another by sanguinary divisions.[72]

Robert Schuman suggested proceeding incrementally, starting with coal and steel, with a view to rebuilding the economies of the States concerned as well as overcoming their historical antagonism, by making space for and building up mutual control and trust. This would also act as a counterweight to the growing influence of the Soviet Union. The collaboration would be open to all European States, but agreement was initially secured in utmost secrecy, and with the support of the United States. Today, in memory of the foundational statement quoted previously, 9 May is known as Europe Day; it celebrates peace and unity in Europe.

The Schuman Declaration was soon followed by the Treaty establishing the European Coal and Steel Community (ECSC, 1951) signed by France and Germany, as well as Italy and the Benelux countries. It created a common market for coal and steel among these countries and established a yet more supranational set of institutions than those of the Council of Europe and the ECtHR: an independent High Authority responsible for assuring the fulfilment of the said Treaty, a Council composed of representatives of the Member States' governments, an Assembly composed of delegates from the parliaments of each of the Member States (or elected by direct universal suffrage, depending on the Member States), and an independent Court of Justice. These constituted the first steps towards the institutional design of the EEC, and later the EU, as we shall see. In 2002, the ECSC Treaty expired. Its main provisions have today been integrated in mainstream EU law.[74]

[72] Excerpts from the Schuman Declaration, Paris, 9.5.1950.

[73] © Klaus Pielert (Künstler); Haus der Geschichte, Bonn.

[74] Protocol on the financial consequences of the expiry of the ECSC Treaty and on the research fund for coal and steel (Treaty of Nice, 2001).

No Community for Defence (Yet?)

Despite these important steps forward, an initiative to establish another sectoral European community, in relation to defence this time, resulted in failure. The creation of a European army was foreseen that could include German units. The proposal for a European Defence Community received support from many countries, but the French National Assembly rejected it in 1954. This made space for a softer form of intergovernmental collaboration with Germany's accession to NATO (1955), and the complementary creation of the Western European Union (WEU) on mutual assistance in resisting any policy of aggression among ten States on the continent (1955).

The WEU was closed in 2011 and its tasks were taken over by the CFSP of the European Union that will be introduced subsequently.[75] We have seen in recent years a renewed interest for the establishment of a Common Security and Defence Policy (CSDP) in the form of a 'permanent structured cooperation' anchored in the EU legal order.[76] This new policy increases investment and enhances cooperation in developing defence capabilities among EU States on a voluntary basis. It is not, at this stage, a form of military integration as hoped for by some in the 1950s.

A European Economic Community (Treaty of Rome, 1957)

Despite the failure of the project for a European Defence Community, the Foreign Ministers of the six Member States of the ECSC met in Messina in 1955 to relaunch the European integration process. They created an intergovernmental steering committee chaired by Paul-Henry Spaak, Belgian Minister for Foreign Affairs and former President of the Consultative Assembly of the Council of Europe, entrusted with reflecting on how to 'further progress [. . .] towards the setting up of a united Europe by the development of common institutions, the gradual merging of national economies, the creation of a common market, and the gradual harmonization of their social policies'.[77]

This led to the drafting of the well-known Spaak Report,[78] which provided a blueprint for discussions on what became the Treaty establishing the European Economic Community or 'Treaty of Rome', signed in 1957, and which entered into force in 1958. The Treaty of Rome laid down the essence of what was necessary for the European Union as we know it today to develop. It created a general common market, thus looking beyond specific sectors (unlike the ECSC), and was intended to progressively approximate economic policies.[79] The common market, with free movement of goods, persons, services and capital, was supported by a number of flanking policies ensuring undistorted competition and common policies on trade, agriculture and transport, for instance.[80] The EEC was already uniquely ambitious in its scope, and built on the same

[75] Statement of the Presidency of the Permanent Council of the Western European Union on behalf of the High Contracting Parties to the Modified Brussels Treaty – Belgium, France, Germany, Greece, Italy, Luxembourg, the Netherlands, Portugal, Spain and the United Kingdom, Brussels, 31.3.2010.

[76] 'Council Decision 2017/2315 of 11 December 2017 Establishing Permanent Structured Cooperation and Determining the List of Participating Member States', OJ L 331, 14.12.2017, p. 57.

[77] Resolution adopted by the Foreign Ministers of the ECSC Member States, Messina, 1–3.6.1955.

[78] Report of the Heads of Delegation to the Foreign Ministers, Brussels, 21.04.1956. [79] Art. 2 TEEC.

[80] Art. 3 TEEC.

type of supranational institutional framework as the ECSC: with a Council, an Assembly, a Commission (reflecting some of the main features of the High Authority of the ECSC) and a Court of Justice.

A Community for Atomic Energy (1957)

The Spaak Report also served as a basis for the creation of a new sectoral community, along with the ECSC, with a narrower focus than that of the EEC. It was set out by the Treaty establishing the European Atomic Energy Community (Euratom, 1957, also signed in Rome). That Treaty on Euratom had, and *continues* to have, the goal of contributing to 'the development of relations with the other countries by creating the conditions necessary for the speedy establishment and growth of nuclear industries'.[81] It created a 'nuclear common market'[82] focused on civil nuclear energy.

A Single Institutional Framework for Three Communities

In light of the establishment of three parallel communities, one for coal and steel, one for atomic energy and one for the creation of a common market, the participating States soon deemed it necessary to merge the relevant institutional frameworks. This resulted in the creation of a single Council, with representatives of the governments of the participating States, and a Commission of the European Communities with one to two independent members per State.[83] As noted previously, this trend towards greater unity has resulted more recently in the ECSC being fully incorporated in mainstream EU law, as well as Euratom and the EU now having a full set of common institutions.[84]

1.3.2.2 Towards the European Community within the EU

A Bumpy Start for the EEC

The most ambitious part of this set of initiatives intended to further European integration was unquestionably the EEC, on which I focus in this book. The first few years after the entry into force of the Treaty of Rome were promising: the abolition of customs barriers, the adoption of a common external tariff and the introduction of a common agricultural policy. In the mid-1960s, however, President Charles de Gaulle adjusted France's approach to the process, vividly resisting the move towards supranationalism. The French authorities refused to attend meetings and thereby blocked decision-making, in the context of the so-called 'empty chair crisis' (1965).[85] They also opposed accession by the United Kingdom.[86]

[81] Treaty establishing the European Atomic Energy Community (Euratom, 1957), Art. 1.

[82] Ibid., Arts. 92–100.

[83] Treaty Establishing a Single Council and a Single Commission of the European Communities (Merger Treaty), OJ L 152, 13.7.1967, p. 2.

[84] See also, as regards Euratom, the institutional changes introduced by the Treaty on European Union, OJ C 191, 29.7.1992, p. 1, Art. I.

[85] Councils of the European Communities, Communiqué issued after the French decision, 6.7.1965. See further: B. Schoenborn, 'VII. La Crise de la chaise vide (1965–1966)', in B. Schoenborn, *La mésentente apprivoisée: De Gaulle et les Allemands, 1963–1969* (Graduate Institute Publications, 2014), pp. 200–213.

[86] On the procedure for accession, see Chapter 2, Section 2.1.2.

'On the way to a common market: Missing a wheel'[87]

The crisis came to end when the participating States agreed to the 'Luxembourg compromise' (1966). It provided that:

> [w]here, in the case of decisions which may be taken by majority vote on a proposal of the Commission, *very important interests* of one or more partners are at stake, the Members of the Council will endeavour, within a reasonable time, to reach solutions which can be adopted by all the Members of the Council while respecting their mutual interests and those of the Community.

Furthermore, 'the French delegation consider[ed] that where very important interests are at stake the discussion must be continued until unanimous agreement is reached'.[88]

The empty chair crisis, and the related Luxembourg compromise, should not be mistaken for mere historical anecdotes.[89] With the process of European integration becoming increasingly supranational, and with heavier reliance on the 'community method', Member States have often been concerned that their important interests should be protected; even when EU law allows for the adoption of legislation by qualified majority voting among participating States. As noted already, the supranational nature of the process of European integration ought *not* to negate the need for Member States to be able to draw attention to interests that they deem very important.

Today, functional equivalents of the Luxembourg compromise are the rules on calculation of blocking minorities in decision-making at the Council, as well as

[87] © Hans Geisen, Cartoonmuseum Basel, 2021; Sammlung Karikaturen & Cartoons.
[88] Council, Final Communiqué of the extraordinary session, Luxembourg, 29.1.1966. Emphasis added.
[89] See further J. P. Jacqué, 'Le vote à la majorité qualifiée', in J. P. Jacqué, *Droit Institutionnel de l'Union Européenne*, 9th ed. (Dalloz, 2018), p. 380 *et seq.*

'emergency brakes' enshrined in the TEU and TFEU.[90] The latter, in particular, allow Member States to express specific concerns in particularly sensitive areas of EU law and thereby to slow down, or block, EU decision-making in the field.[91] The European Council, in its contemporary form, is the natural forum for discussion on such sensitive matters; the leaders gathered therein act as the 'impasse breaker'.[92]

Strengthening the Initial Design in the 1970s

One of the aspects of EEC intervention that triggered friction with President De Gaulle related to the financing of the common agricultural policy. It was decided in 1970, to change the system of resources of the EEC.[93] The existing system of financial contributions by individual Member States had made the EEC budget too dependent on national actors.[94] Instead, the EEC would now be allocated resources of its own, drawn from the revenue accruing from external customs duties, agricultural levies, as well as the application of a uniform rate to the value added tax collected in the Member States, with a view to ensuring budgetary balance. Two new treaties were subsequently signed to amend certain budgetary provisions of the initial Treaty of Rome, in 1970 and 1975.[95] These amendments increased the influence of the Assembly, alongside that of the Member States gathered in the Council, on decisions relating to the EEC budget. The involvement of the Assembly was then deemed a necessary guarantee to accompany the establishment of the EEC's system of own resources.

This also illustrated a broader reflection on the status of the Assembly in the process of European integration. In 1976, the Member States' representatives gathered in the Council decided that the representatives of the peoples, gathered in the said Assembly, shall be elected by direct universal suffrage.[96]

[90] See Chapter 2, Section 2.3.4.4, Qualified Majority Voting.

[91] E.g. Art. 48 TFEU as regards the adoption of EU legislation in the field of social security as may be necessary to ensure free movement for workers.

[92] van Middelaar, *Alarums and Excursions*, p. 180.

[93] 'Council Decision of 21 April 1970 on the Replacement of Financial Contributions from Member States by the Communities' Own Resources (70/243/ECSC, EEC, Euratom), OJ L 94, 28.04.1970, p. 19.

[94] The introduction of a system of own resources was already envisaged in Art. 201 TEEC; see further C.-D. Ehlermann, 'The Financing of the Community: The Distinction between Financial Contributions and Own Resources', *Common Market Law Review*, 19 (1982), pp. 571–589.

[95] Traité portant modification de certaines dispositions budgétaires des traités instituant les Communautés européennes et du traité instituant un Conseil unique et une Commission unique des Communautés européennes, Treaty Amending Certain Budgetary Provisions, OJ L 2, 2.1.1971, p. 1; Treaty Amending Certain Financial Provisions of the Treaties Establishing the European Economic Communities and of the Treaty Establishing a Single Council and a Single Commission of the European Communities, OJ L 359, 31.12.1977, p. 1.

[96] Act concerning the election of the representatives of the Assembly by direct universal suffrage, 20.9.1976, Art. 1.

EU elections: the little seed that grows?[97]

The first elections took place in 1979 and, although the role of the Assembly in decision-making procedures did not immediately change, this paved the way for its ongoing strengthening, which has continued to the present day. From the first subsequent major Treaty reform, the Single European Act, the Assembly would become known officially as the European Parliament – which is still the current title – to reflect its newly gained democratic credentials.

In conjunction with the increasing emphasis placed on the representatives of the people of Europe in the form of a parliamentary assembly, greater attention was also drawn to the political guidance of the Heads of State and Government, assisted by foreign affairs ministers. They started meeting on a regular basis, several times a year, in parallel to the gatherings of their governmental representatives in the context of the Council. They discussed topical or urgent matters at the highest political level. These meetings were soon to be referred to as gatherings of the *European* Council (1974),[98] to be distinguished from the lower level of formal Council meetings. The European Council was to become a formal institution four decades later, in 2009.

In the meanwhile, with enlargements to include Denmark, Ireland and the UK (1972), the size of the formal institutions of the time – not only the Assembly, but also the Council, the Commission and the Court of Justice – grew, thereby putting pressure on the earlier modalities of decision-making and paving the way for further institutional reform that would come with the Single European Act in the 1980s. As we shall see in subsequent chapters, the case law of the Court of Justice also gained importance in asserting the unique nature of the new legal order thereby developing.[99]

Parallel Developments: Foreign Affairs, Monetary Policy and Home Affairs

The progressive development of the supranational dimension of the EEC, intended to strengthen the initial framework established by the Treaty of Rome, was accompanied by the emergence of advanced forms of coordination on a number of specific themes at the edges, or outside, the scope of the initial Treaty of Rome. I highlight here three sets of developments that are particularly vividly discussed in contemporary European affairs.

First, the EEC became an important actor on the international stage. A form of coordinated foreign policy emerged, supported by the Tindemans report.[100] It was called for by the

[97] Malt © Pascal Hansens, Brussels, 2021.
[98] Déclaration du Président Giscard d'Estaing à la presse à l'issue de la réunion des chefs de gouvernement de la Communauté européenne à Paris, 10.12.1974.
[99] See Chapter 4, Section 4.1.
[100] L. Tindemans, Report on European Union, 29.12.1975; see also the earlier Rapport Davignon, 27.10.1970.

newly created European Council: full advantage should be taken of possibilities for cooperation between the governments in the field of foreign policy to pioneer the development of a common external policy.[101] As will be further explained below, today, the EU has a developing CFSP, covering all areas of foreign policy and questions relating to the EU's security, including the progressive framing of a common defence policy.[102]

Secondly, Member States took preliminary steps towards the creation of an EMU, which is the backbone of today's euro area and its common currency – the euro. The Treaty of Rome included provisions on the free movement of capital and on the coordination of Member States' economic policies.[103] Yet the latter had not been on the agenda much until then.[104] In 1972, a 'European currency snake' was created,[105] establishing margins – measured against the dollar – to limit fluctuations of exchange rates of participating States, as well as a European Monetary Cooperation Fund,[106] to increase cooperation between Member States in the field. While the Fund was to progressively become what is known today as the European Central Bank, the European currency snake failed to convince in the context of the first oil crisis. In 1978, Member States decided on the creation of the European Monetary System (EMS), with a view to establishing a 'durable and effective scheme' for a 'zone of monetary stability in Europe'.[107] The said system would provide stability to exchange rates between the currencies of Member States, and exchange rate policies vis-à-vis third countries would be coordinated. The European currency unit (ECU) would be at the centre of the system being used as a means of settlement between monetary authorities of the EEC.

Thirdly, the common market as it developed in the 1970s, based on the free movement of factors of production, could not be fully dissociated from cooperation in the field of police, security and justice. There were no competences to address such questions through the tools of the EEC at that time. Solutions therefore developed in parallel to the Treaty of Rome, which itself called, among other things, for cooperation among Member States on the simplification of formalities governing the reciprocal recognition and enforcement of judgments of courts or tribunals.[108] This resulted in the Brussels Convention on jurisdiction and the enforcement of judgments in civil and commercial matters.[109] A practice of cooperation, with senior police officers alongside ministers meeting to discuss counter-terrorism and coordinate policing, also developed under the umbrella of the so-called TREVI Group as from 1976.[110] Concerns to coordinate action on migration control and asylum would soon follow, as we shall see.

[101] European Council Conclusions, The Hague, 29–30.11.1976.
[102] Art. 24(1), subpara. 1 TEU. See more at https://eeas.europa.eu. [103] Arts. 67–73, 103–109 TEEC.
[104] P. Werner, Report to the Council and the Commission on the realization by stages of economic and monetary union in the Community, 8.10.1970.
[105] Council, Resolution on the application of the Resolution of 22 March 1971 on the attainment by stages of the economic and monetary union in the Community, 21.3.1972; Central Banks of the Member States of the Community, Agreement on the Narrowing of the Margins of Fluctuation between Community Currencies (Basle Agreement), 10.04.1972.
[106] 'Regulation (EEC) No. 907/73 of the Council of 3 April 1973 Establishing a European Monetary Cooperation Fund', OJ L 89, 5.4.1973, p. 2.
[107] Presidency Conclusions, European Council, Bremen, 6–7.7.1978; Resolution of the Brussels European Council on the establishment of the EMS, Brussels, 5.12.1978.
[108] Art. 220 TEEC. [109] See consolidated version: OJ L 299, 31.12.1972, p. 32.
[110] T. Bunyan, 'Trevi, Europol and the European State', in T. Bunyan (ed.), *Statewatching the New Europe: A Handbook on the European State* (Statewatch, 1993), p. 15.

The Single European Act (1986)

In the early 1980s, the trends initiated in the previous decades deepened in terms of both institutional design and thematic focus, supporting a sense of growing trust between Member States. To start with the design, the first directly elected Assembly took office in 1979, strengthening that institution's claim to power at European level and the notion of a community of people belonging to a common citizenry.[111] The most influential work of the Adonnino Committee further contributed to the move towards a 'people's Europe', with 'realistic' initiatives intended to be of 'direct relevance to Community citizens', such as enhancing recognition of diplomas to facilitate free movement.[112] The Committee also suggested involving citizens in European decision-making, for instance through a more uniform procedure for elections for the parliamentary assembly,[113] and developing students' mobility as well as common symbols.[114]

Some of these concepts sound very familiar today, if one thinks about the Erasmus student exchange programme, thirty years of which were celebrated in 2017, or the European flag showing a circle of twelve golden stars on a blue background, which is a symbol shared with the Council of Europe.[115] In the meantime, the Heads of State or Governments continued to meet in the context of the European Council, an entity that confirmed its function to provide 'general political impetus to the construction of Europe'.[116] The size of the formal institutions continued to grow, with enlargements to include Greece (1981), Spain (1986) and Portugal (1986).

In terms of thematic focus, the Member States agreed to strengthen and develop European political cooperation in the area of foreign policy and to continue to progress towards a European monetary union.[117] It was also forcefully observed that, in the context of the recession, more effort was needed to continue work to improve the functioning of the common market, if it was to be turned into a fully 'single integrated internal market'.[118] Furthermore, enlargements to less industrialised and more agricultural countries in the south of Europe called for a reflection on how to address economic and social discrepancies between the various regions and to deal with the related budgetary implications.

These institutional and thematic dynamics resulted in the signature of the Single European Act in 1986 (entered into force 1987).[119] That international treaty was the first major text amending the Treaty of Rome since it had been signed. It made two main categories of changes. First, the Single European Act reformed the institutional framework

[111] Assembly, Draft Treaty establishing the European Union (Spinelli Plan, 14.2.1984), *Bulletin of the European Communities*, February 1984, No. 2, p. 8, point 3.

[112] Report on a People's Europe, 29.3.1985. [113] See Chapter 2, Section 2.3.2.2.

[114] Committee on a People's Europe, Report submitted to the European Council, Milan, 28–29.6.1985.

[115] E.g. 'Resolution on the Adoption of a Flag for the European Community', OJ C 128, 16.5.1983, p. 18. Although the symbols are not mentioned in the EU Treaties as such (see Chapter 1, Section 1.3.2.3), they are in use by application of other instruments, see for instance: Parliament, 'Rules of Procedure' (9th parliamentary term, as last updated January 2021), Rule 238 and Declaration 52 by Member States annexed to the TEU and TFEU.

[116] Heads of State or Government of the Member States of the European Communities, meeting within the European Council, Solemn Declaration on European Union, Stuttgart, 19.6.1983.

[117] E.g. Heads of State or Government of the Member States of the European Communities, meeting within the European Council, Solemn Declaration on European Union, Stuttgart, 19.6.1983.

[118] See, in particular, Commission, White Paper, 'Completing the Internal Market', COM(85) 310 final, 14.6.1985, point 4.

[119] Single European Act, OJ L 169, 29.6.1987, p. 1.

of the EEC, as it resulted from the Treaty of Rome, with a view to ensuring greater efficiency in decision-making, allowing for the creation of a Court of First Instance (today known as the General Court) to alleviate the work of the Court of Justice,[120] as well as greater involvement of the Assembly, renamed the European Parliament (here, referred to simply as Parliament).[121] Second, it extended the range of common European policies in areas such as research and environmental policy that had already been touched upon by earlier legislation through incidental law-making for the good operation of the common market.[122] It also created a new EEC policy on '*Co-operation* in Economic and Monetary Policy (Economic and Monetary *Union*)'.[123] It also formalised 'European Co-operation in the Sphere of Foreign Policy', which stood alongside the EEC.[124]

The effort towards greater institutional efficiency was intended, most importantly, to speed up the completion of the internal market with the aim of achieving it by the end of 1992.[125] The Single European Act is most often alluded to with reference to one more set of institutional changes allowing much greater reliance on qualified majority voting among the Member States gathered in the Council.[126] This change in voting threshold eliminated some of the burdens resulting from earlier voting arrangements for decision-making set out in the Luxembourg compromise.[127] The Single European Act also added the concept of an 'area without internal frontiers in which [. . .] free movement [. . .] is ensured'.[128] The idea, which remains extremely powerful today, is that along with granting the *right* to cross-border movement of goods, persons, services and capital, European law shall aim at 'getting rid *entirely* of physical and other controls between Member States'.[129]

With the emphasis placed on the 'area without internal frontiers' by the Single European Act, and thus the removal of (physical) border controls, the need for cooperation on matters of police, security and justice, as well as asylum and migration control, became more pressing. Yet that took place externally to the legal framework provided for by EEC law that continued not to cover these fields. The Schengen Agreement of 14 June 1985 on the gradual abolition of checks at their common borders developed outside of the legal framework of the EEC.[130] From the late 1980s, further agreements and conventions were concluded between the Member States, with a view to contributing to the joint objective of building an area without internal frontiers, but their ratification was delayed. For instance, the Dublin Convention of June 1990, on determining the State responsible for examining

120 Single European Act, Art. 11, on Art. 168a TEEC; see further Chapter 2, Section 2.3.6.2.
121 E.g. Single European Act, Art. 6 on the newly created cooperation procedure for the adoption of new acts.
122 See further Chapter 3, Section 3.2.3.3.
123 Single European Act, Art. 20. Emphasis added to show ambiguity in the nature of the policy.
124 Single European Act, Art. 30. It should be noted that the article does not amend the TEEC; it created a self-standing common European policy, anchored in the Single European Act itself.
125 L. W. Gormley, 'Some Reflections on the Internal Market and Free Movement of Goods', *Legal Issues of Economic Integration*, 16/1 (1989), pp. 9–20.
126 The most common example is the insertion of a new Art. 100a TEEC.
127 In practice, the Luxembourg Compromise is said to have effectively died with the Single European Act. A. L. Teasdale, 'The Life and Death of the Luxembourg Compromise', *Journal of Common Market Studies*, 31 (1993), pp. 567–579, at 575.
128 Single European Act, Art. 13.
129 Commission, White Paper, 'Completing the Internal Market', COM(85) 310 final, 14.6.1985, point 12 (emphasis added).
130 See Chapter 1, Section 1.4.3.1.

applications for asylum lodged in one of the Member States of the European Communities, ultimately only entered into force in 1997.[131]

A second point only partially addressed by the Single European Act related to social policy.[132] The Heads of State or Government of most Member States, with the exception of the UK, solemnly proclaimed the Community Charter of the Fundamental Social Rights of Community Workers (1989).[133] Although it did not have legal effects, it was accompanied by a social action programme issued by the Commission[134] that resulted in the adoption of several important legislative instruments, such as the Working Time Directive,[135] in the years that followed. Furthermore, this Community Charter has come to feature prominently in the current version of the EU Treaties.[136]

A third matter that was not addressed by the Single European Act as such was the question of the EEC's budgetary difficulties. In the 1980s, the system of own resources established in the previous decade was put under pressure by increasing expenses resulting, in particular, from the agricultural policy and enlargement to the south. As well as the three own sources of funding initially identified,[137] the EEC and the Member States needed more and more often to artificially keep the budget within the ceiling. The Single European Act added to the financial needs of the EEC, with the creation of a new European policy on 'economic and social cohesion'.[138] The Assembly, or (European) Parliament, was also delaying the adoption of the budget more frequently to assert its position on the inter-institutional stage.

These budgetary matters were ultimately dealt with through important developments, in parallel to the entry into force of the Single European Act. Together with his institution, Jacques Delors – then President of the Commission – proposed reliance on a new (fourth) type of resources that would be provided by a contribution based on each Member State's Gross National Product.[139] This resource, which was de facto a national contribution rather than a 'genuine' own resource, was then intended to be residual and only called upon when necessary to keep revenue and expenditure in balance, after all other revenue has been taken into account. It was also decided that the EEC's budget would be planned on a multiannual basis (four years at the time), owing to an inter-institutional agreement.[140] Furthermore, the possibility of ad hoc corrections was introduced, as illustrated by the UK's rebate as from 1985,[141] to allow lower contributions to the EU budget for selected Member States.

[131] See also, for another example, Convention between the Member States of the European Communities on the Enforcement of Foreign Criminal Sentences (1991).

[132] It should be noted, however, that the Single European Act allowed for the adoption of measures to protect the health and safety of workers by qualified majority voting at the Council (Single European Act, Art. 21).

[133] Published in Commission, Directorate-General for Employment, Industrial Relations and Social Affairs, 1 (1990), *Social Europe*, p. 45.

[134] Commission, Communication, 'Action Programme Relating to the Implementation of the Community Charter of Basic Social Rights for Workers', COM(89) 568 final, 29.11.1989.

[135] The current version is 'Directive 2003/88/EC of the European Parliament and of the Council of 4 November 2003 Concerning Certain Aspects of the Organisation of Working Time', OJ L 299, 18.11.2003, p. 9.

[136] Preamble of the TEU and Art. 151 TFEU.

[137] See Chapter 3, Section 3.6.3.1.

[138] Single European Act, Arts. 21, 23, 25, respectively.

[139] Commission, Communication, 'Making a Success of the Single Act: A New Frontier for Europe', COM(87) 100 final, 15.2.1987, p. 18.

[140] E.g. 'Interinstitutional Agreement on Budgetary Discipline and Improvement of the Budgetary Procedure', OJ L 185, 15.7.1988, p. 33.

[141] European Council Conclusions, Fontainebleau, 25–26.6.1984.

The EC within the EU (Treaty of Maastricht, 1992)

The Single European Act had created the possibility to further develop economic and monetary policy as part of the EEC legal framework. It enabled Member States and the Commission to submit proposals for institutional change to the Council, with a view to further developing economic and monetary policy through Treaty change, thereby paving the way for the upcoming Treaty of Maastricht.[142] There was, however, much disagreement on how to make progress on economic and monetary policy.

As Commission President, Jacques Delors once again tabled a most influential report[143] and proposed the three-step approach that was ultimately to be followed.[144] He understood the European monetary union as implying, next to the completion of the internal market that was already the quest behind the Single European Act, 'irrevocably fixed exchange rates between national currencies and, finally, a single currency'. Such a union would represent 'the final result of the process of progressive economic integration in Europe'.[145] From the early days it was noted that monetary union without a sufficient degree of convergence of economic policies was unlikely to be durable and could be damaging. Parallel progress in that latter field was needed 'in order to avoid imbalances which could cause economic strains and loss of political support'.[146]

In a first stage, which began in 1990, Member States sought greater convergence of their economic performance by strengthening their economic and monetary policies. For instance, all currencies joined the EMS, created in the 1970s. In a second stage, the basic organs and structure of the EMU would be set up through the creation of a European System of Central Banks. It was seen as a preparatory stage leading to collective decision-making, while the ultimate responsibility for policy decisions would remain with national authorities. The third and final stage would see the move to irrevocably locked exchange rates and the attribution to European-level institutions of monetary and economic competences. National currencies would eventually be replaced by a single one.

Before fast-forwarding to the adoption of the euro, the single currency as we know it today in the participating Member States (or euro area), it should be recalled that the Single European Act already envisaged further institutional change to lay down the subsequent stages. The context was marked by the position of the UK Government on the project, which resonates particularly strongly with recent developments at EU level. John Major, Chancellor of the Exchequer of the Thatcher Government at the time, preferred to 'concentrate on developing a yet closer partnership, of individual nation states, and achieve in that way the objectives upon which we are all agreed', rather than 'moving towards a federal Europe'.[147] As a result, the UK Government fundamentally objected to stages 2 and 3 of the Delors step-by-step approach.

Despite opposition from the UK, but with the 'necessary majority', the Heads of State and Government did convene an intergovernmental conference (IGC), with a view to shaping the

[142] Single European Act, Art. 20.
[143] Committee for the Study of Economic and Monetary Union, Report on economic and monetary union in the European Community, 12.4.1989. This built on the Werner Report; see Chapter 1, Section 1.3.2.2, note 104.
[144] European Council Conclusions, Madrid, 26–27.6.1989.
[145] Committee for the Study of Economic and Monetary Union, Report on economic and monetary union in the European Community, 12.4.1989, point 16.
[146] Ibid., point 42.
[147] J. Major, Economic and Monetary Union, *Hansard*, HC, vol. 159, 30.10.1989–10.11.1989.

'final stages' of the Economic and Monetary Union (EMU).[148] In parallel, another IGC was called for, this time focusing on the 'Political Union'.[149] This second IGC echoed the Parliament's call 'rapidly to transform the European Community into a European Union of federal type and going beyond the single market and economic and monetary union'.[150] It furthermore reflected concerns from key political leaders to move towards greater unity in response to German reunification.[151]

The outcome of these efforts was the signature of the Treaty on European Union (often referred to as TEU or the Treaty of Maastricht, signed in 1992).[152] The Treaty of Maastricht acted as major step towards the EU as we know it today. Not only was it the second main treaty reform after the Single European Act, but it was the first genuine attempt to institutionally bridge the purely intergovernmental nature of several policies developed outside of the Treaty of Rome since the 1970s,[153] and what would become the more sophisticated nature of these EU policies as we know them today. The challenge was tremendous, due to the highly sensitive nature of the related policy fields for domestic sovereign States. As a consequence, the institutional design negotiated to construct the said bridge has been remarkably peculiar.[154] It relied on a single institutional framework, that of the newly created 'European Union', but was composed of different legal regimes, as will now be explained. As a result, the legal structure created by the Maastricht Treaty is commonly referred to as the three-pillar structure, reminiscent of a Greek temple (see Figure 1.1).

The first pillar of the Union included an amended version of the EEC. This was the main pillar of the Greek temple, thereby reflecting the central role of the EEC in the process of European integration. In more precise and technical terms, the first pillar was composed of the 'communities' (thereby meaning the treaty provisions of the EEC, the ECSC and Euratom), as developed since the 1950s and updated by the Treaty of Maastricht itself in 1992.

The economic dimension of the EEC project (in the first pillar) naturally remained present, but the supranational ambition would reach beyond the confines of economic integration and become more explicitly political; hence the change of name from the European *Economic* Community to the European Community (EC). The main changes made by the Maastricht Treaty to the EEC, as from then EC (and thus enshrined in the TEEC as renamed 'Treaty establishing the European Community', TEC), related to: (i) increasing democratic legitimacy (creation of European citizenship for nationals of the Member States, with a limited number of new rights, and a greater role for the Parliament in decision-making procedures[155]); (ii) institutional

148 European Council Conclusions, Strasbourg, 8–9.12.1989.

149 Presidency Conclusions (Part 1), European Council, Rome, 14–15.12.1990.

150 Parliament, 'Resolution on the Intergovernmental Conference in the Context of Parliament's Strategy for European Union', OJ C 96, 17.04.1990, p. 114, point B.

151 E.g. Joint message from François Mitterrand and Helmut Kohl, Paris, 18.4.1990. It was decided that the territory of the German Democratic Republic would be integrated into the European Community unlike for other States from the former Soviet Union (Presidency Conclusions, European Council, Dublin, 28.4.1990).

152 OJ C 191, 29.7.1992, p. 1.

153 See Chapter 1, Section 1.3.2.2.

154 See the proposals enshrined in the draft Treaty on Union proposed by the Luxembourg Presidency, Luxembourg, 18.6.1991.

155 Creation of the co-decision procedure for the adoption of new acts by the Council and the Parliament jointly (Art. 189b of the amended EC Treaty). The Parliament would have a term of the same length as that of the Commission (five years). The Parliament would also be consulted by the governments of Member States for the nomination of the President of the Commission, and give its consent to the nomination of the Commission as a body (on a

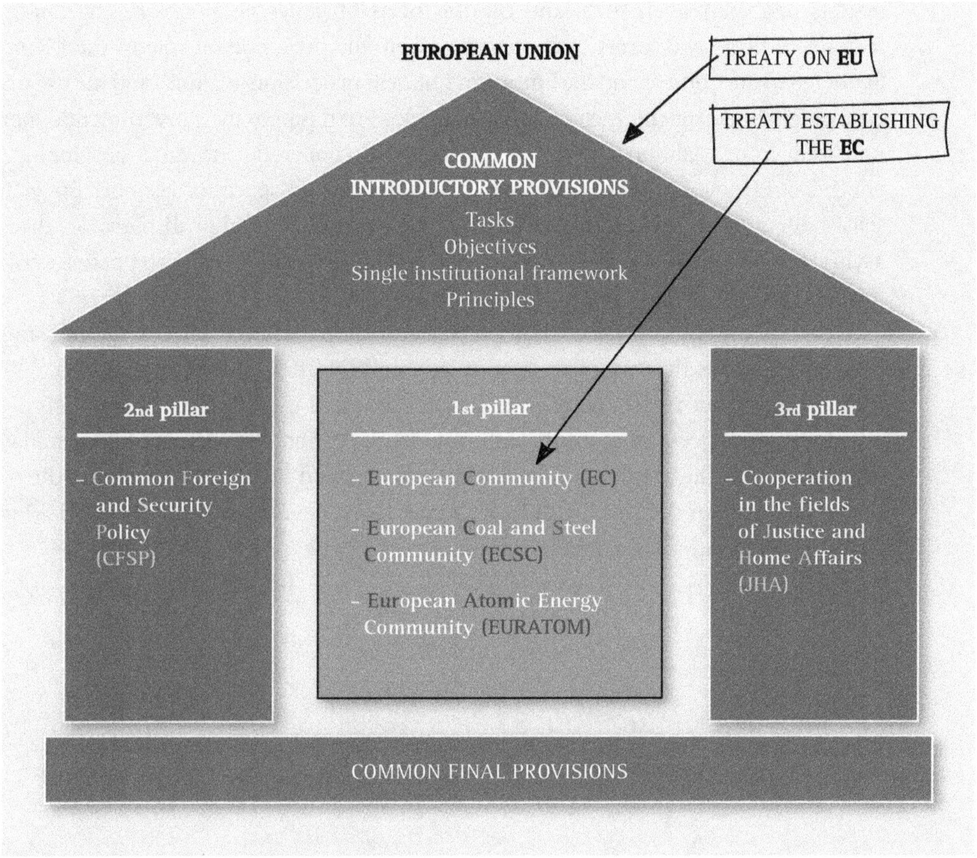

Figure 1.1 The three pillars of the EU (Maastricht, 7 February 1992)

effectiveness (growing importance of the European Council[156] and of qualified majority voting – to the detriment of unanimity – at the Council); and (iii) the creation of new competences for the EEC, such as in relation to consumer protection, and in the context of the EMU. The EMU would come to rely on close coordination of Member States' economic policies, as well as the progressive fixing of exchange rates that would lead to the introduction of a single currency several years later.[157]

The first pillar was supplemented by two main forms of 'cooperation'[158] at EU level: the 'second pillar' on the Common Foreign and Security Policy (CFSP), and the 'third pillar' on cooperation in the fields of Justice and Home Affairs (JHA). The CFSP aimed, in particular, to safeguard the common values, fundamental interests and independence of the Union on the international stage, to strengthen the security of the Union, preserve peace and strengthen international security. . Cooperation in the field of JHA covered matters such as asylum, border control, migration policy towards third country nationals,[159] judicial cooperation in civil

proposal by the governments in consultation with the President-nominee for the other members) before final appointment by common accord of the governments of Member States (Art. 158 of the amended EC Treaty).

[156] E.g. Treaty of Maastricht, Art. D. [157] Ibid., Art. G, creating a new Art. 3(a)(1–2) TEC. [158] Ibid., Art. A.

[159] Note that rules on visas could be set as part of the first pillar of the EU, e.g. Art. 100c TEC.

matters and criminal matters and certain forms of police cooperation. The main common features of these two forms of cooperation were the predominant role of the Member States (gathered in the Council and the European Council) in decision-making, and the use of a distinct type of legal instrument, thereby remaining close to a purely intergovernmental logic.[160] The transition from traditional forms of international cooperation towards developing common policies at EU level in these fields, while leaving enough space for Member States to protect sensitive interests (as remains relevant in the context of current disputes on the European asylum law system, or 'Dublin' system), were already present when the competences of the EU in this field were created.

In reality, the setting was even more complex than the three-pillar structure suggests, for two main reasons that are often used to exemplify 'differentiated integration'[161] in the EU legal order. To start with, within the first pillar – and the EC, more specifically – the EMU relied on a very peculiar institutional framework,[162] and two Member States had expressed reservations on the progress of the EMU. Denmark and the UK both reserved the possibility not to take part in the third, and final, stage of the development of the EMU which would result in the creation of a single currency.[163]

Maastricht Treaty: the rise of differentiated integration[164]

[160] In contrast, supranational organs such as the Commission and the Parliament were left with a very marginal role in these areas, if any role at all, as for the Court of Justice of the European Union. The supranational approach was defined previously; see Chapter 1, Section 1.2.3.

[161] See Chapter 1, Section 1.4.3. [162] See Chapter 1, Section 1.4.3.2.

[163] Treaty of Maastricht, Protocol on certain provisions relating to the United Kingdom of Great Britain and Northern Ireland, Point 1; Protocol on certain provisions relating to Denmark, Point 2.

[164] Malt © Pascal Hansens, Brussels, 2021.

Next, eleven (out of twelve) Member States were authorised by the Treaty of Maastricht to use institutions, procedures and mechanisms of the EC to adopt and implement decisions on the social rights of workers. This authorisation, and the related enabling provisions, were enshrined in a Protocol and Agreement among the eleven Member States on social policy. This was a response to the opposition of the UK Government to the development of competences for the EC on social questions, already observed in relation to the Community Charter of the Fundamental Social Rights of Community Workers from 1989.[165]

These ad hoc adjustments, as well as making explicit references to compliance with the principle of subsidiarity[166] and respect for national identities,[167] were intended to assuage concerns voiced in reaction to the progress towards a more politically ambitious union. Nevertheless, the Treaty of Maastricht could only enter into force after ratification at national level, which ultimately happened in late 1993. That proved difficult. These difficulties already signalled, as may be natural, that with the greater politicisation of the process of European integration would come a higher likelihood of challenges. For instance, in Denmark, two referenda and reassurances on the special status of Denmark were needed to obtain approval.[168] In France, a referendum took place in a highly sensitive context and resulted in a narrow positive outcome.[169] In the UK the political context was also quite sensitive, there being a rebellion from a number of members of the Conservative Party; ratification resulted from a vote in the House of Commons, in which many members of the Labour Party obeyed the order to abstain.[170] In Germany, several cases brought before the Constitutional Court delayed ratification.[171] On the other hand, in countries such as Ireland, Belgium, Spain, Luxembourg, Greece, Portugal and the Netherlands, ratification was fairly straightforward.

Once again, in parallel to these Treaty negotiations and ratification processes, the way to approach the budget evolved. Under the leadership of Jacques Delors, the Commission issued a second Communication on the budget.[172] It built on the principles established in the 'Delors I' package introduced previously. The ceiling on Community resources would be increased to match the new ambitions of the integration process, in particular for regional policy. The contribution from the fourth type of resources, introduced in the late 1980s and

[165] See Chapter 1, Section 1.3.2.2, note 133.
[166] Maastricht Treaty, Art. G, on Art. 3b TEC; see also Chapter 2, Section 2.3.4.1. [167] Ibid., Art. F.
[168] Presidency Conclusions (Part B), European Council, Edinburgh, 11–12.12.1992, 'Denmark and the Treaty on European Union'.
[169] C. Goybet, 'Le oui à Maastricht … et après?', *Revue du Marché commun et de l'Union européenne*, 361 (1992), p. 681.
[170] P. Wynn Davies, 'Tory MPs in Record Revolt: Lamont Leaves Door Open for ERM Re-entry', *The Independent*, 20.5.1993.
[171] BVerfG, 2 BvR 2134/92, 2 BvR 2159/92, Decision on the Treaty on European Union, 12.10.1993.
[172] Commission, Communication, 'From the Single Act to Maastricht and Beyond: The Means to Match Our Ambitions' ('Delors II' package), COM(92) 2000 final, 11.2.1992.

calculated with reference to the Gross National Product of each country, would grow in importance. Furthermore, the inter-institutional agreement on multiannual financial perspectives was extended to a seven-year period, which is the time frame that still applies today.[173]

1.3.2.3 Towards the European Union (Only)

A First Revamp of the Treaties on the EC within the EU (Treaty of Amsterdam, 1997)
The Treaty of Maastricht already envisaged that a conference of representatives of the governments of the Member States was to be convened in 1996 to consider treaty change.-[174] That year corresponded to a deadline for the reassessment of the possibility to move to the third stage of the creation of the EMU.[175] The Maastricht Treaty also allowed the Member States, gathered in the Council, to decide to apply a more supranational governance method to decision-making in several of the fields covered by the third pillar of the EU on JHA – this type of facilitated, or anticipated, change is known as a passerelle clause today.[176] It was therefore anticipated in the early 1990s that further structural change would be needed.

In the meantime, countries from Central and Northern Europe showed interest in the single market. The States of EFTA and the EC moved towards the signature of the EEA Agreement that entered into force in 1994.[177] Several of these States, as well as others, also applied for accession to the EC (or to the EEC, as it was called before the Maastricht Treaty): Austria, Sweden, Finland, Switzerland and Norway.[178] Although the application by Switzerland was withdrawn,[179] and Norway ultimately rejected accession further to a referendum,[180] the other three countries became members of the EC following expedited negotiations.[181]

This enlargement process transformed the EU of twelve into an EU of fifteen, triggering important changes to the functioning of the institutions.[182] The changes were intentionally left for discussion until after the entry into force of the Maastricht Treaty and agreement on the new financial perspectives, thereby confirming the extreme importance of these budgetary negotiations.[183] The necessary institutional changes ultimately entered into force in 1995, together with the accession treaties for Austria, Finland and Sweden. It was also decided that the 1996 IGC would have to further examine a number of institutional questions.[184]

[173] 'Interinstitutional Agreement on Budgetary Discipline and Improvement of the Budgetary Procedure', OJ C 331, 7.12.1993, p. 1.
[174] Maastricht Treaty, Art. N(2). [175] Art. 109j TEC.
[176] Maastricht Treaty, Art. K.9; see also Chapter 1, Section 1.4.4.2.
[177] See further Chapter 1, Section 1.2.2.
[178] Austria's application for accession to the EEC: 14.7.1989; Sweden: 1.7.1991; Finland: 18.3.1992; Switzerland: 20.5.1992; Norway: 24.11.1992.
[179] Swiss Government's letter on the withdrawal of Switzerland's membership application to the EU, 27.7.1996.
[180] In 1994, according to the Norwegian Ministry for Foreign Affairs, a majority of Norwegians (52.2 per cent) rejected EU membership in a referendum.
[181] Presidency Conclusions, European Council, Brussels, 29.10.1993, point III.
[182] European Council Conclusions, Brussels, 10–11.12.1993, pp. 31–35.
[183] European Council Conclusions, Lisbon, 26–27.6.1992, point I.1.
[184] In particular, the legislative role of the Parliament, the number of members of the Commission, the weighting of the votes of the Member States in the Council, any measures deemed necessary to facilitate

Pending the reform, the Member States deemed it necessary to adjust institutional practice. The concerns behind the 'Luxembourg compromise' that had allowed Member States to be reassured in the early days that their important interests would be protected, even for the adoption of measures by qualified majority voting (thus not requiring unanimity) among their representatives,[185] were revived.[186] The new 'Ioannina compromise' indeed established that, if a specified number of States indicate their intention to oppose the adoption of an act,[187] the Council – composed of representatives of the Member States, 'will do all in its power to reach [...] a satisfactory solution'.[188] Such a solution would have to be supported by a greater number of States than formally required under the Treaty rules on qualified majority voting.[189]

In parallel to these institutional reflections and after a bumpy start,[190] the EMU entered its second stage in 1994, as provided for by the Maastricht Treaty. The Member States were then concerned to reduce their budgetary deficits to meet the criteria to be able to continue to prepare for the single currency. They also worked towards the creation of the European Central Bank,[191] which, as part of the European System of Central Banks,[192] is an EU institution primarily responsible today for ensuring price stability.[193] A legislative framework was developed, referred to as the Stability and Growth Pact,[194] to enhance budgetary discipline.[195] This Pact is still used as a yardstick – sometimes deemed to be too weak[196] – to assess Member States' compliance with the founding principles on which the single monetary union is based.

the work of the institutions and guarantee their effective operation. Presidency Conclusions, European Council, Brussels, 10–11.12.1993, joint declaration, Annex III.

185 The Luxembourg compromise was mostly used from the 1960s until the new voting arrangements for qualified majority voting at the Council were introduced by the Single European Act; see further Jacqué, 'Le vote à la majorité qualifiée', p. 380 *et seq.*

186 Letter to the Parliaments of Europe, 'The new "Luxembourg compromise"', *Crocodile* (March–April 1994).

187 As noted in ibid., it was no longer necessary that the matter relate to 'very important interests'.

188 'Council Decision of 29 March 1994 Concerning the Taking of Decision by Qualified Majority by the Council', OJ C 105, 13.4.1994, p. 1 (adjusted version in OJ C 1, 1.1.1995, p. 1).

189 This may be compared to the current rules on the calculation of the so-called blocking minority in decision-making at the Council; see Chapter 2, Section 2.3.4.4, Qualified Majority Voting.

190 Finance Ministers and Central Bank Governors of the Member States of the European Community, Communiqué on the EMS (2.8.1993), *Bulletin of the European Communities* 7/8, 1993, p. 21.

191 Protocol 18 annexed to the Treaty establishing the European Community by the Treaty on European Union, 7.2.1992.

192 It includes national central banks, together with the European Central Bank.

193 Art. 127 TFEU; see also Chapter 2, Section 2.3.7.

194 'Resolution of the European Council on the Stability and Growth Pact Amsterdam', 17 June 1997, OJ C 236, 2.8.1997, p. 1.

195 A soft method of governance, the 'coordinated strategy for national employment policies' echoing the freshly drafted provisions of the Treaty of Amsterdam, was also developed to address employment matters alongside economic governance. Presidency Conclusions, Extraordinary European Council, Luxembourg, 20–21.1997.

196 For more on this: A. de Gregorio Merino, 'Legal Developments in the Economic and Monetary Union During the Debt Crisis: The Mechanisms of Financial Assistance', *Common Market Law Review*, 49 (2012), pp. 1613–1646; note that this field is undergoing important institutional mutations in the aftermath of the COVID-19 crisis.

'The Euro Balancing Act'[200]

The latter, which marks the third stage of the EMU, was launched in 1999 among eleven Member States, then known as constituting the euro area, through the irrevocable fixing of conversion rates among the currencies of participating countries and against a single currency. The newly described euro was then used in commercial and banking transactions and, from 2002, euro notes and coins entered into circulation.[197] The Ministers for Economy and Finances of the eleven Member States started to meet informally to share responsibility for the single currency,[198] thus paving the way to what has become known as the Eurogroup.[199]

Compared to the EMU, which was part of the first pillar of the EU since the Treaty of Maastricht, the main innovations introduced by the second pillar had a (much) slower start. The CFSP was in search of its common agenda,[201] with the weakness of the Member States' joint diplomatic efforts being particularly painfully illustrated in the context of the humanitarian crisis in the former Yugoslavia. In the field of JHA (the third pillar), the Member States' desire to move towards greater integration was more visible. A number of important features of this policy date back to that period. This is the case, for instance, of the European Police Office,[202] or Europol, designed to improve the cooperation of national authorities in preventing and combating terrorism, unlawful drug trafficking and other serious forms of international crime. The European Council also soon welcomed the completion of the ratification of the Dublin Convention, determining the State responsible for examining applications for asylum lodged in one of the Member States.[203] Although the Dublin system originated from outside the EU legal system, it has been incorporated and reformed since then, and came to take centre-stage in contemporary European politics.

In this context, the main features of the Treaty of Amsterdam that resulted from the long anticipated 1996 IGC are perhaps unsurprising. The new Treaty reform, which was signed in 1997 and entered into force in 1999, hardly touched the institutional design of the EMU that

[197] Presidency Conclusions, European Council, Madrid, 15–16.12.1995.

[198] Presidency Conclusions, European Council, Luxembourg, 12–13.12.1997, para. 44; and Helsinki, 10–11.12.1999, para. 32.

[199] See Chapter 2, Section 2.3.4.7.

[200] © The Hague, KB, National Library of the Netherlands 5142075. All efforts have been made to contact the widow of the deceased author, Behrendts.

[201] E.g. Parliament, 'Resolution on the Intergovernmental Conference in the Context of Parliament's Strategy for European Union', OJ C 96, 17.04.1990, p. 154.

[202] Council, 'Convention Based on Article K.3 of the Treaty of the European Union, on the Establishment of a European Police Office' (Europol Convention), OJ C 316, 27.11.1995, p. 1.

[203] European Council, Amsterdam, 16–17.06.1997. The Convention was ultimately published in the Official Journal - OJ C 254, 19.8.1997, p. 1.

developed within the framework established by the Treaty of Maastricht. Similarly, the second pillar on CFSP was subject to fairly minimal reforms. It remained primarily intergovernmental, with the noticeable intention to work towards 'the progressive framing of a common defence policy',[204] as well as the creation of a High Representative for the CFSP.[205] This High Representative, who was then supposed to assist the rotating Presidency of the Council of ministers in the field, has since become a prominent symbol of the policy.

The main changes brought in by the Treaty of Amsterdam were concerned with reasserting a number of values, and taking one stage further the decisive steps initiated by the Maastricht Treaty. First, it was made explicit that the Union 'is founded on the principles of liberty, democracy, respect for human rights and fundamental freedoms, and the rule of law, principles which are common to the Member States'.[206] Furthermore, the 'existence of a serious and persistent breach' of these principles may have institutional implications.[207] These were the precursors of the current Article 2 TEU with which we started this book, as well as the warning and possible sanctioning mechanisms having being triggered against rule of law Poland and Hungary at the time of writing.[208]

Second, the Member States wished to further strengthen the position of the Parliament in decision-making in the first pillar of the EU, within the European Community in particular. The procedure for the adoption of acts with the involvement of the Parliament became more common. The Parliament would also give its approval on the appointment of the President of the Commission, resulting in the latter being strengthened politically.[209] Meanwhile the range of policy areas covered by European law continued to broaden. In the late 1990s, with the arrival of a new Labour Government in the UK, it was possible to bring within the first pillar the former Protocol and Agreement on social policy that had been annexed to the Treaty in Maastricht, and to apply its provisions to that country. This was accompanied by the development, or strengthening, of a number of other policies within the first pillar of the EU.[210]

Thirdly, the Treaty of Amsterdam replaced the notion of JHA that had been used to describe the content of the third pillar after the Maastricht Treaty with the notion of Area of Freedom, Security and Justice (AFSJ) that remains in use today. This relabelling conveyed an important message, furthering the idea of 'an area without internal frontiers':[211] the Member States seek to 'facilitate the free movement of persons, while ensuring the safety and security of their peoples, by establishing an area of freedom, security and justice'.[212] This came with important institutional changes.[213] The fields of asylum, border control, migration policy[214] and judicial cooperation in civil matters were brought within the scope of the first pillar. This allowed the integration into the first pillar of the Schengen acquis abolishing border checks at the common borders of the Member States, which is so dear to the daily comfort of many of us living in Europe, as painfully recalled in the context of the COVID-19 crisis.[215]

[204] Treaty of Amsterdam, Art. 1.7, on Art. J.7 TEU. [205] Ibid., Art. 1.10, on Art. J.8.3 TEU.
[206] Ibid., Art. 1.8, on Art. F TEU. [207] Ibid., Art. 1.9, on Art. F TEU. [208] See Chapter 4, Section 4.3.2.1.
[209] Treaty of Amsterdam, Art. 2.40.
[210] E.g. non-discrimination, employment, public health, consumer protection and environment.
[211] This expression had been introduced by the Single European Act.
[212] Treaty of Amsterdam, Art. 1.3, modifying the preamble of the TEU.
[213] A helpful schematic overview of the three-pillar structure of the EU after the Treaty of Amsterdam is available at www.cvce.eu/obj/en-ca13c018-6997-4c94-80e6-77ee99e9aa9f.
[214] Treaty of Amsterdam, Art. 2.15, on Art. 73(i) *et seq.* TEC.
[215] Protocol integrating the Schengen acquis into the framework of the European Union.

The change is much more than symbolic. Law-making was thereby brought significantly closer to (although not yet fully in line with[216]) the traditional approach of the community method that characterises the governance applicable in older areas of European law, such as the internal market. This is why countries that were opposed to deepening integration on certain of these matters, such as the UK, Ireland and Denmark, obtained the carving out various derogation regimes that permeated through time.[217] In contrast, police and judicial cooperation in criminal matters was left in the third pillar of the EU, subject to more intergovernmental law-making;[218] yet with an embryonic effort to involve supranational institutions[219] and a new tool called 'framework decisions'.[220] The latter is the type of instrument subsequently used to create the European arrest warrant,[221] which often appears on newspaper headlines such as those concerning the Catalan leader residing in Belgium at the time of writing, Carles Puigdemont Casamajó. These institutional changes were soon turned into a set of concrete legal initiatives resulting from the political impulse given by the special meeting of the European Council in Tampere in 1999, to discuss the creation of an 'area of freedom, security and justice'.

Finally, the Treaty of Amsterdam is known for having introduced a procedure allowing the development of 'enhanced cooperation' within European Union law, by opposition to outside EU law.[222] The controversies surrounding the creation of this possibility for differentiated integration, allowing a group of Member States to further integrate (while allowing others to join later), illustrated the fact that within an enlarged – and enlarging – EU, decision-making was increasingly difficult. At that point in time, though, no agreement could be reached on broader institutional change: the composition of the Commission – where some Member States still had more than one Commissioner – and the voting arrangements within the Council. Both aspects of the institutional framework remained too closely connected to vested interests of the Member States. The matter was left, as had often been the case in the past, for discussion at a future IGC.[223]

A Second Revamp of the Treaties on the EC within the EU (Treaty of Nice, 2001)

Since the late 1980s, and the fall of the Berlin Wall, it had been clear that a whole group of new States from the former Soviet Union might soon be knocking at the doors of the EU. These States were engaging in an ambitious process of economic and political transition. The challenge involved with making the accession of an extraordinary large number of States possible was discussed by the Heads of State or Government in a European Council

[216] In particular, there was a five-year transition period for several policy areas, reserves of competences for the Member States and derogatory provisions on the jurisdiction of the Court of Justice of the European Union: see Treaty of Amsterdam, Art. 2.15, on Art. 73(i) *et seq.* TEC.

[217] See Chapter 1, Section 1.4.3. [218] Treaty of Amsterdam, Art. 1.11, on Art. K.1–14 TEU.

[219] E.g. The Commission gained the right of legislative initiative, along with the Member States; the Parliament gained consultation powers; and the Court of Justice began to exercise a level of scrutiny. Treaty of Amsterdam, Art. J.18 on Title VI TEU.

[220] Treaty of Amsterdam, Art. 1.11 on Art. K.6(2)(b) TEU.

[221] This is a judicial decision issued by a Member State with a view to the arrest and surrender by another Member State of a requested person, for the purposes of conducting a criminal prosecution or executing a custodial sentence or detention order. '2002/584/JHA: Council Framework Decision of 13 June 2002 on the European Arrest Warrant and the Surrender Procedures between Member States: Statements Made by Certain Member States on the Adoption of the Framework Decision', OJ L 190, 18.7.2002, p. 1, Art. 1.

[222] Treaty of Amsterdam, Art. 1.12, on 'closer cooperation' (which was the initial name of the procedure); see also Chapter 1, Section 1.4.3.4.

[223] Protocol on the institutions with the prospect of enlargement of the European Union.

meeting in Copenhagen in 1993.[224] The EU would support this process through funding instruments, as well as special partnerships called 'Europe agreements', with 'associated countries', intended in particular to progressively open up trade with these countries. The associated countries in Central and Eastern Europe were told that, if they so desired, and as soon as they could satisfy the economic and political conditions outlined at the Copenhagen meeting, they could become members of the EU.[225]

A decade later, as the Treaty of Amsterdam was being finalised, enlargement to Central and Eastern European States was getting closer. This involved intense exchanges with twelve States,[226] and would have significant institutional and budgetary implications. The institutional questions left open by the Treaty of Amsterdam would have to be addressed. Furthermore, the pre-accession strategy to help future Member States to prepare for, and process, accession would inevitably have to be discussed alongside agricultural and structural policies in the negotiations for the next seven-year financial framework beyond 1999.[227]

The new President of the European Commission, Jacques Santer, proposed a package referred to as Agenda 2000.[228] The resulting agreement on the 2000–2006 multiannual financial framework led to a new increase of the fourth resource introduced in the 1980s, based on the Member States' Gross National Product (and later on Gross National Income))[229] – ultimately contributing more than 70 per cent of the budget's resources today. This brought the financing of the EU budget one step further away from the idea of 'own resources' introduced in the early 1970s, as this marked a powerful return of national contributions. This is why, still today, negotiations on multiannual financial frameworks remain so intense, difficult and immensely important. They crystallise the relationships between the Member States and between EU institutions, various sets of actors often being deemed to be unequal in this context. They must also balance the relative importance of various EU policy objectives each time.

As the Agenda 2000 was being transformed into the new budget for the next seven years, inter-institutional tensions were building up. The Parliament was displeased with the Commission's report on the implementation of the Community budget.[230] The Commission was also under severe criticism due to accusations of maladministration by Commissioners, and in particular a clear case of favouritism.[231] This resulted, in January 1999, in a first – and almost successful – attempt by the Parliament to vote a motion of censure against the Santer Commission. In light of the failures of individual Commissioners, of the Commission as a body, as well as of the mounting threat of a second vote on a motion of censure,[232] the Commissioners collectively resigned in March 1999. This institutional crisis triggered the

[224] Presidency Conclusions, European Council, Copenhagen, 21–22.6.1993, point 7.

[225] See Chapter 2, Section 2.1.2. [226] This included Cyprus and Turkey.

[227] European Council, Amsterdam, 15–16.6.1997.

[228] Commission, 'Agenda 2000 – For a Stronger and Wider Union', *Bulletin of the EU*, 5/97, 13.7.1997.

[229] Presidency Conclusions, European Council, Berlin, 24.–25.3.1999, p. 1.

[230] Parliament, 'Resolution on the Postponement of the Discharge in Respect of the 1996 Financial Year', OJ C 138, 4.5.1998, p. 1.

[231] Commissioner Cresson was reported – and later found responsible – for having wrongfully appointed one of her close acquaintances, a dental surgeon, as a 'visiting scientist', C-432/04, *Commission* v. *Cresson*, EU:C:2006:455.

[232] Committee of Independent Experts, First report on allegations regarding fraud, mismanagement and nepotism in the European Commission, 15.3.1999, point 9.3.

need 'to reinforce the political and democratic dimension of the EU', in particular by 'strengthening the accountability of the Commission to Parliament and by offering the chance to build a new, strong, politically responsible and efficient Commission'.[233] Individual Commissioners would, as a result of future reforms, be made more accountable on an individual basis,[234] and the Commission's reflection on its own culture of financial management resulted in the creation of the European Anti-Fraud Office (OLAF).[235]

It is in this context that the question of the representation of up to twelve new Member States, bringing the EU from fifteen to twenty-seven members, in the institutional design of the EU, as well as the overall efficiency of the system, had to be discussed in the IGC called for by the Treaty of Amsterdam. The latter was convened in early 2000[236] and worked during the year that followed. Despite suggestions for ambitious change,[237] the choice was made to focus on important technical adjustments, strengthening the 'legitimacy, effectiveness and public acceptability of the institutions' and enabling 'the Union's firm commitment to the enlargement process to be reaffirmed'.[238]

Rather than a deep reflection on the process of integration, the adjustments made by the Treaty of Nice were of a technical nature, as made particularly salient by their incorporation in a protocol intended to address the consequences of the upcoming enlargement. Several institutional arrangements were inserted to reflect the growing number of Member States, as well as concerns to ensure an effective functioning of the system.

First, there would be a new calculation for the number of persons elected in each Member State to become Members of the Parliament.[239]

Secondly, the votes of the State representatives at the Council would be given an adjusted weight. Moreover, the premises of a system of double majority were introduced – bridging towards the one that we know today – combining the pre-existing idea of qualified majority with weighting of the votes of each State representative, with the new possibility for a State to request verification that the votes in favour of the adoption of an act represent at least 62 per cent of the population of the Union.[240] The new weighting was deemed to be less favourable to populous States, but the 62 per cent threshold allowed a degree of rebalancing in their favour.

Thirdly, the Commission would be composed of one Commissioner per State, thus meaning that larger States gave up on having a second Commissioner. The possibility remained to modify that number, with a view, in a Union of twenty-seven States, to have even less than one Commissioner per State.[241] Learning from the Santer crisis, the President was also granted more authority on individual Commissioners.[242]

[233] Parliament, 'Resolution on the Resignation of the Commission', OJ C 177, 22.6.1999, p. 19, point 5.

[234] Ibid., points 6 and 7; see also Chapter 2, Section 2.3.5.

[235] The office carries out external administrative investigations for the purpose of strengthening the fight against illegal activities adversely affecting common financial interests: 1999/352/EC, ECSC, Euratom, 'Commission Decision of 28 April 1999 Establishing the European Anti-fraud Office (OLAF)', OJ L 136, 31.5.1999, p. 20 (last amended 2015).

[236] European Council, Cologne, 3–4.6.1999.

[237] See, in particular, R. von Weizsäcker, J.-L. Dehaene and D. Simon, Report to the Commission, 'The Institutional Implications of Enlargement', 18.10.1999.

[238] Presidency Conclusions, European Council, Nice, 7–9.12.2000, point 4.

[239] Protocol on the enlargement of the European Union, Art. 2. [240] Ibid., Art. 3. [241] Ibid., Art. 4.

[242] Note also that the President of the Commission became nominated and appointed by the Council voting by qualified majority (instead of unanimity, as previously; new Art. 214(2) TEC).

Fourthly, the EU judiciary was reorganised to handle a growing caseload. It was made possible, for instance, to create specialised judicial panels,[243] a possibility that was used in 2004 to create the Civil Service Tribunal – resolving disputes between the EU and its staff (the Civil Service Tribunal was dissolved in 2016[244]).

Remaining Treaty changes focused on making it easier to use the warning and sanctioning mechanisms for breaches of EU foundational principles, such as the rule of law,[245] as well as the tools for enhanced cooperation.[246] Although these changes were overall rather technical, most had been the subject of heavy political negotiations at the highest level, with a particularly tangible difference of approach between France and Germany. Time was pressing as the enlargement process was moving forward. It was thus decided to postpone decisions on a deeper reflection on the future of European integration.

Despite a difficult start, with a first negative referendum in Ireland, the process leading to the ratification of the Nice Treaty by all Member States went rather smoothly, and it entered into force in 2003. The concern for the efficiency and legitimacy of the European construct, however, was not fully addressed. Reflections on the substance of the European integration project, such as the shape of economic governance and its relationship to social policy, or European defence policy, had been left out of the Nice Treaty negotiations.[247] Furthermore, deep interrogations on the future directions of the project had been raised, attracting an increasing level of public attention, and left unanswered. This last point was particularly well illustrated by work taking place in parallel to the negotiations and drafting of the Nice Treaty.[248]

The Charter of Fundamental Rights (Charter of Nice, Proclaimed in 2000)

The Charter of Fundamental Rights of the Union (CFEU) was officially proclaimed by the presidents of the Parliament, the Commission and the Council, just before the opening of the Nice European Council. It was the outcome of a new type of law-making at EU level, departing from the IGCs traditionally leading to treaty change. The body that drafted the CFEU became known as a 'Convention'. It consisted of one representative from each EU country, the President of the Commission, and members of the (European) Parliament (sixteen) and national parliaments (thirty).[249] Representatives of the Court of Justice of the European Union, as well as the Council of Europe, participated as observers. Representatives of the Economic and Social Committee, the Committee of the Regions and the Ombudsman would be invited to give their views. Applicant States would exchange views, as would other bodies, social groups and experts. In principle, hearings and documents submitted at such hearings were public.

In many ways, the CFEU was a natural complement to the developing Area of Freedom Security and Justice that had grown out of the third pillar of the EU created by the Treaty of

243 New Arts. 215 and 217 TEC; Arts. 220 and 225a TEC.

244 Its competence was merged back into the work of the General Court as it stands today.

245 Art. 7 TEU was amended to allow for a 'clear risk of a serious breach' by a Member State of the principles listed in Art. 6 TEU to be identified.

246 See in particular the new Art. 43 TEU *et seq.*, as well as Art. 11 TEC *et seq.*

247 Presidency Conclusions, European Council, Nice, 7–9.12.2000.

248 Presidency Conclusions, European Council, Helsinki, 11.12.1999, paras. 14–19.

249 Presidency Conclusions, European Council, Cologne, 3–4.6.1999; Presidency Conclusions, European Council, Tampere, 15–16.10.1999, Annex.

Maastricht to deal with Justice and Home Affairs, including the rights of asylum seekers or persons concerned by a European arrest warrant. Increased legal intervention in the sensitive field of rights called for a corresponding level of protection, and required more principled assertions of rights than those developed by the Court of Justice of the European Union until then.[250] The joint text agreed upon showed the resolve to share a 'peaceful future based on common values',[251] and built on the idea of a common EU citizenship that was gaining salience in the 1990s and early 2000s.

The rights and principles are structured in six chapters in the CFEU. The first three, 'Dignity', 'Freedoms' and 'Equality', are illustrative of a rather traditional approach to fundamental rights law. The fourth, 'Solidarity', sought to engage with a new generation of social fundamental rights, but was particularly difficult to draft due to divergent approaches, and is thus formulated in general terms. The fifth chapter, 'Citizens' Rights', focuses on EU citizens, while the sixth, 'Justice', contains the much-used provision on the fundamental right to an effective remedy.[252] Importantly, the final provisions clarify the link between the CFEU and other instruments of EU law, as well as other sources for the protection of fundamental rights.

The decision on the legal effects of the CFEU was left for future discussion.[253] In its early years, and unlike today, the CFEU could therefore derive no legal effect from the EU Treaties. Indeed, in the period surrounding its proclamation and the drafting of the Treaty of Nice, there was no agreement on the key directions for the future of European integration. That deep reflection called for and left open-ended in the early 2000s, as well as the methodological experiment of the Convention for the drafting of the CFEU, paved the way for a decision to convene a yet more ambitious Convention on the Future of Europe.

A Draft Constitutional Treaty (2004)

In an annex to the Treaty of Nice, Declaration 23 on the future of the Union made clear that the Treaty of Nice opened the way for enlargement. Indeed, in 2003, ten new States from Central and Eastern Europe signed Accession Treaties: the Czech Republic, Estonia, Hungary, Latvia, Lithuania, Poland, Slovakia, Slovenia, Malta and Cyprus. They joined in 2004, thereby largely reuniting the continent through the most expansive enlargement in the history of the EU.[254] This was a highly symbolic success for the European integration process; yet it also raised fears in terms of loss of efficiency of the institutions and ability of the twenty-five Member States to jointly design the future of Europe. Two more countries, Bulgaria and Romania, also signed a Treaty of Accession in 2007.

Declaration 23 called for a 'deeper and wider debate about the future of the European Union' and encouraged 'wide-ranging discussions with all interested parties'.[255] The European Council, at its meeting in Laeken in December 2001, was tasked with following up on the initiative. Accordingly, the resulting Laeken Declaration[256] called for the gathering of a new Convention to make a proposal for the IGC scheduled to take place in 2004.

[250] See Chapter 3, Section 3.1.3. [251] CFEU, Nice, 7.12.2000, preamble (1). [252] Art. 47 CFEU.
[253] Presidency Conclusions, European Council, Nice, 7–9.12.2000, para. 2.
[254] There were then three other candidate countries: Bulgaria, Romania and Turkey.
[255] Treaty of Nice, Declaration No. 23.
[256] Presidency Conclusions, European Council, Laeken, 14–15.12.2001.

The Convention on the Future of Europe had a similar composition to the Convention that had drafted the CFEU, with representatives of the Member States, the Commission, the (European) Parliament and national parliaments. It also involved a number of other actors, such as accession candidate countries, of which there were many.[257] The four key objectives of the Convention were to work towards: (i) a better division of competences; (ii) simplification of the Union's instruments of action; (iii) increased democracy, transparency and efficiency; and (iv) a Constitution for Europe's citizens. The latter included a reflection on the legal effects of the CFEU.[258]

The idea of having a 'Constitution' for Europe was not new, as illustrated by the Spinelli draft from 1983,[259] but it had never been addressed on such a scale. The term is highly symbolic and had been discussed, alongside other references to a 'confederation' or a 'federation', to describe or identify new directions for European integration. No prior treaty reform had relied upon such an ambitious and open reflection process, well beyond traditional intergovernmental negotiations, as the one proposed by Declaration 23 and the Laeken European Council. Several ambitious plans for reform of the legal framework for the European Union, including a restructuring of the EU Treaties, would be discussed.[260]

The Convention was not a constituent assembly as such; it merely proposed a text to the IGC that followed: a full Draft Treaty establishing a Constitution for Europe that was deemed to constitute 'a good basis for starting in the Inter-governmental Conference'.[261] It took several months before the Heads of State or Government reached a final agreement. Among other reasons, less populated States and medium-sized States were reluctant to lose some of the benefits of the Treaty of Nice on institutional arrangements. Yet in 2004 the European Council could ultimately assert that:

> The Treaty establishing a Constitution for Europe is an historic step forward in the process of integration and cooperation in Europe. Based on the work of the Convention, the Constitution establishes an efficient, democratic and transparent framework for the future development of the Union. It completes the process which began when the Treaty of Rome established the basic framework for European integration. Like the Treaty of Rome, it will serve for many years as the foundation of a Union at the service of its citizens.[262]

The Treaty establishing a Constitution for Europe[263] – despite its tortuous itinerary, as will be explained, but thanks to its innovative drafting process – has had an important influence on the current shape of EU institutional law. It merged earlier treaties into a single one, under the name of 'Union', thus leading to the formal elimination of the three-pillar structure inherited from the Maastricht Treaty, as well as of the reference to the

[257] These States were 'fully involved' and represented in the same way as the current Member States, without, however, being able to prevent any consensus which might emerge among the Member States.

[258] For an overview of the thinking at the time, see B. De Witte, 'Simplification and Reorganization of the European Treaties', *Common Market Law Review*, 39 (2002), pp. 1255–1287.

[259] Parliament, 'Resolution on the Draft Treaty Establishing the European Union', OJ C 77, 19.3.1984, p. 33; see also, inter alia, F. de Menthon, Draft Federal Constitution for a United States of Europe, June 1948.

[260] E.g. von Weizsäcker et al., 'The Institutional Implications of Enlargement'.

[261] Declaration of Rome on the occasion of the opening of the intergovernmental conference, 4.10.2003.

[262] Presidency Conclusions, European Council, Brussels, 17–18.6.2004.

[263] Treaty establishing a Constitution for Europe, OJ C 310, 16.12.2004, p. 1.

'Community'. It incorporated the CFEU and gave it legal effect. It aimed to clarify the system of allocation of competences between the EU and the Member States, and the typology of instruments adopted by EU institutions. It better integrated the contribution of the citizens of the Member States, and their representatives, in the institutional design of the EU, seeking to enhance parliamentary involvement.

Perhaps precisely because public opinion was involved to a much greater extent than in the past in the reflection on the future of the European project, and was asked to answer difficult questions on complex matters, the Treaty establishing a Constitution for Europe triggered vivid and contrasting reactions. In the summer of 2005, the Heads of State or Government of the Member States took stock: ten Member States had successfully ratified the Constitutional Treaty, but the outcome of referenda in France and the Netherlands were negative. The Heads of State or Government considered that 'these results do not call into question citizens' attachment to the construction of Europe. Citizens have nevertheless expressed concerns and worries which need to be taken into account.' It was decided to enter a period of reflection 'to enable a broad debate to take place in each of [the] countries, involving citizens, civil society, social partners, national parliaments and political parties'.[264] In the meantime, the Parliament gave its support to the Constitutional Treaty.[265]

Breakdown of constitutional reform[266]

[264] Declaration by the Heads of State or Government of the Member States of the European Union on the ratification of the Treaty establishing a Constitution for Europe, European Council, Brussels, 16–17.6.2005.

[265] Parliament, 'Resolution on the Treaty Establishing a Constitution for Europe', OJ C 247E, 6.10.2005, p. 88.

[266] Malt © Pascal Hansens, Brussels, 2021.

The European Union (Only) (Treaty of Lisbon, 2007)

After a couple of years, the European Council agreed that the period of reflection had provided time for 'wide public debate and helped prepare the ground for a solution'.[267] It was decided to convene an IGC that was given a very specific mandate. It would draw up a treaty amending existing treaties, Treaty on European Union and Treaty establishing the European Community, as they resulted from the Treaty of Maastricht and had been amended in Amsterdam and Nice. Unlike what had been foreseen by the Draft Treaty establishing a Constitution for Europe, the concept of a single text called a 'Constitution', as well as the reference to the symbols of the Union in the text of the Treaties themselves, were abandoned.[268] The name of 'laws' for EU instruments was not to be used, and the CFEU would not be formally incorporated in the new EU Treaties.

Yet it was also agreed at the outset that several key innovations resulting from the Convention and the subsequent 2004 IGC would be introduced into the existing Treaties. The Treaty on European Union kept its name, but the Treaty establishing the European Community was renamed the Treaty on the Functioning of the European Union. The term 'Community' was to be replaced by 'Union'; the Union was given a single legal personality; and the three-pillar structure inherited from the Treaty of Maastricht was formally eliminated.[269] The CFSP of the EU was thereby strengthened; the High Representative for the CFSP was given the broader mandate of High Representative for Foreign Affairs and Security Policy, and would receive the support of a European External Action Service. The institutional framework of the AFSJ was largely brought closer to mainstream EU policies. The CFEU was published along with the Treaties, instead of as part of them, and was given legal effect.

Furthermore, there was a clear effort towards bringing clarity to the system of allocation of competences between the EU and the Member States, as well as to the typology of instruments adopted by EU institutions. The European Council was at last acknowledged as an EU institution, with a stable President. There was a further assertion of the supranational nature of EU law-making with the expansion of the procedures allowing the Parliament to act as a co-legislator, or at the very least to have a say in EU decision-making procedures – for instance, in relation to external relations – as well as the redefinition and extension of decision by qualified majority voting at the Council. Citizens (through the European Citizens Initiative[270]) and national parliaments (using yellow and orange card warnings for threats to the principle of subsidiarity[271]) would also be more involved in EU decision-making.

Within a few months, the Heads of State or Government signed the Treaty of Lisbon and called for its prompt ratification. After another round of difficult experiences, in particular with a first negative referendum in Ireland, the Treaty of Lisbon, which constitutes the latest major treaty reform, entered into force on 1 December 2009. We will come back to its main features subsequently.

[267] Presidency Conclusions, European Council, Brussels, 21–22.6.2007, point 8 and Annex 1.

[268] They were not fully abandoned though; see Chapter 1, Section 1.3.2.2, note 115.

[269] In practice, and as will be illustrated subsequently, the CFSP has continued to have an overall atypical institutional design; and the AFSJ is still characterised by a number of features that sit uncomfortably with a genuine supranational logic, in particular in so far as police and justice cooperation in criminal matters is concerned.

[270] See Chapter 2, Section 2.2.2. [271] See Chapter 3, Section 3.4.1.

The Treaty of Lisbon in action[272]

1.3.3 When History Merges into the Present

1.3.3.1 Key Challenges since Lisbon

Although there have been no large-scale reforms of the EU Treaties since the entry into force of the Treaty of Lisbon, a number of developments have influenced the remainder of this book, along with two political mandates of the Parliament and the Commission (2009–2014; 2014–2019).

To start with, several crises have had a particularly severe impact on the EU. The economic and financial crisis in the EU that followed the collapse of Lehman Brothers bank in 2008, as well as the refugee crisis that resulted at least in part from a humanitarian crisis in Syria in 2015, have received responses that mobilised the Member States and their representatives. This often took place outside of the legal framework provided for by the EU Treaties, as best illustrated by the creation of a European Stability Mechanism[273] to provide financial support to Member States of the euro area. Another example is the Joint Statement between leaders of EU Member States and Turkey (sometimes referred to as the EU–Turkey deal)[274] as an effort to address the refugee crisis.

[272] Malt © Pascal Hansens, Brussels, 2021.

[273] Treaty Establishing the European Stability Mechanism, Brussels, 2.2.2012.

[274] The precise legal nature of the deal remains unclear; see T-192/16, T-193/16 and T-257/16, *NF, NG and NM* v. *European Council*, EU:T:2017:128. An appeal against the ruling by the General Court before the Court of Justice was dismissed on procedural grounds, but substantive legal questions could be presented before that higher court again.

The measures were adopted in a context of – at the very least – perceived extreme urgency. They have been and remain controversial. They raise multiple questions. How can these approaches be articulated with EU law? How does the exercise of authority at the outer limits, or even at the periphery, of EU law ensure the protection of fundamental rights, as well as democratic and judicial accountability? How can the EU or its Member States express solidarity through the pooling of financial resources? Similar questions have arisen in the context of the COVID-19 crisis, as this book was being drafted, and are freshly unfolding in the context of the Russian military aggression against Ukraine, as this book goes to print.

The foreign affairs of the EU, as well as those of its Member States, were strongly impacted by the Arab Spring (2013), Russia's attack on Ukraine's sovereignty and territorial integrity (in Crimea, 2014; and, more broadly, 2022), the transition between the Obama (2009–2017) and the Trump (2017–2020) leadership in the United States, to give but a few examples. These developments called for joint responses at the European level, highlighting again the role of the Member States and their representatives in the context of EU's CFSP.

Within the EU, a number of events affected the European construct. In 2013, Croatia became a new Member State. The subsequent years have been marked by the bitter debate on Brexit: following the outcome of a referendum in support of leaving the EU in 2016, the UK did withdraw on 31 January 2020.[275] Meanwhile, other States – in the Balkans, as well as elsewhere, perhaps, too (e.g. Ukraine?) – are knocking at the EU's doors, seeking accession.

On a different front, selected EU institutions asked the Council to determine that there is a clear risk of a serious breach by Poland (Commission, 2017) and Hungary (Parliament, 2018), respectively, of the values on which the EU is founded and that are common to the Member States, as identified in Article 2 of the TEU.

These developments also raise fundamental questions: How can the EU reconcile its mandate to ensure unity and stability and protect common values on the continent, with calls for diversity and respect for national identity? This list of challenges is not exhaustive. It only serves to remind the readership of the extremely dynamic and immensely challenging environment in which the process of European integration continues to evolve. Across this book, we will return to the questions raised.

1.3.3.2 Terminology and Numbering

As emerges from this historical overview, the name of the legal order to which this book is devoted has evolved (see Figure 1.2). This deserves clarification. Three expressions have been used: (1) European Economic Community (EEC), when discussing developments predating the signature of the Treaty of Maastricht in 1992; (2) European Community (EC), when discussing developments postdating the Treaty of Maastricht, but predating the signature of the Treaty of Lisbon in 2007; and (3) European Union (EU), when discussing developments since the Maastricht Treaty and until today. The expression 'European Union' is the one currently in use.[276] It will be used to capture all legal developments related to the legal order under examination in this book, unless otherwise specified.

[275] See Chapter 2, Section 2.1.3.
[276] According to Art. 1 TEU, the 'Union' shall replace and succeed the 'European Community'.

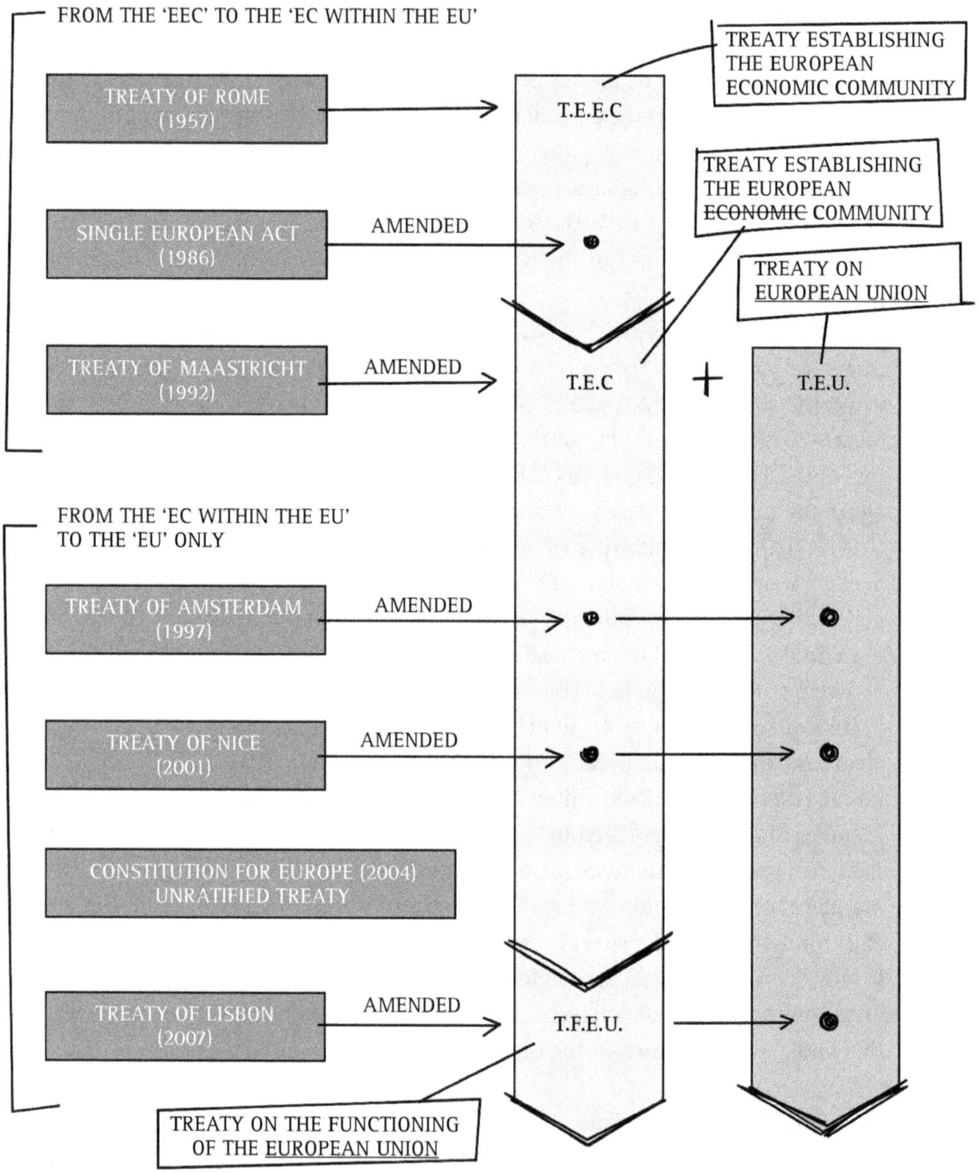

Figure 1.2 From the EEC to the EU: A succession of treaties

As a consequence of multiple amendments to the Treaties on which the European (Economic) Community and European Union have been based, the numbering of the various provisions of the founding Treaties has also evolved. Tables of equivalences between new and old treaty numberings are available in an annex to the consolidated version of the TEU and TFEU after the entry into force of the Treaty of Lisbon (for a pre-/post-Lisbon comparison), as well as in an annex to the Treaty of Amsterdam (for a pre-/post-Amsterdam comparison).[277] The current text of the Treaty of Rome, originally signed in 1957, and of the TEU, originally signed in 1992, and each modified several times to result respectively in the TFEU and the TEU, would be unreadable if one needed each time to look at all successive amendments. Instead, so-called 'consolidated' versions of the Treaties are available and incorporate all earlier changes into a single legal text. At the time of writing, the latest consolidated version of the EU Treaties dates back to 2016, so as to reflect Croatia's accession.[278]

1.4 THE PRIMARY LEGAL FRAMEWORK

1.4.1 A Legal Order Defined by the EU Treaties

The centrality of the Treaties signed by Member States to shape the European Union and the process of European integration was made clear in the previous section. The legal order of the EU, as it stands today, is encapsulated in two treaties: the TEU and TFEU referred to jointly as EU Treaties.[279] These treaties have been signed and duly ratified in accordance with domestic constitutional requirements,[280] by all the Member States who reciprocally agreed that the Treaties would apply to them.[281] Both Treaties have been concluded for an unlimited period of time,[282] illustrating a commitment to a process of creating an 'ever closer' union among the peoples of Europe.[283]

The two Treaties have the same legal value.[284] There is therefore no hierarchy between them. All versions in one of the twenty-four original languages of the EU are also of equal value.[285] The relationship between the TEU and the TFEU is defined by their substantive focus: on the one hand, by the Treaty on European Union, the Member States establish the EU on which they confer competences to attain objectives they have in common; on the other hand, as its name indicates, the Treaty on the Functioning of the European Union 'organises the functioning of the Union and determines the areas of, delimitation of, and arrangements for exercising its competences'.[286] In very broad terms, the Treaties shall therefore be understood as complementary, with the TEU setting the key structural features of the system and the TFEU specifying the substance of the project, as well as putting flesh on key technicalities.

[277] All available on the EUR-Lex website: https://eur-lex.europa.eu.

[278] Full text available at: https://eur-lex.europa.eu/collection/eu-law/treaties/treaties-force.html. All references in this book are related to this version of the EU Treaties unless specified otherwise.

[279] The Euratom Treaty will not be further discussed here; see Consolidated version of the Treaty establishing the European Atomic Energy Community, OJ C 327, 26.10.2012, pp. 1–107.

[280] As requested by Art. 54 TEU and Art. 357 TFEU. Domestic requirements are diverse; it is not uncommon for treaty ratification to require a referendum, as illustrated in Chapter 1, Section 1.3.2.3.

[281] The two Treaties apply to the Member States, with some specific arrangements for certain territories (Art. 52 TEU, Art. 355 TFEU). The territorial scope of the Treaties corresponds to the combined territorial scope of each Member State, as defined by each of them in accordance with international public law (C-111/05, *Aktiebolagetn NN*, EU:C:2007:195, para. 54; see also Art. 77(4) TEU). Specific rules exist for certain overseas countries and territories (see Arts. 198–204, 349, 355 TFEU). In case of a dispute between Member States on their respective borders, this is 'without prejudice to any obligation arising from Article 4(3) TEU to strive sincerely to bring about a definitive legal solution consistent with international law, as suggested in the Act of Accession' (C-457/18, *Slovenia* v. *Croatia*, EU:C:2020:65, para. 109).

[282] Art. 53 TEU, Art. 356 TFEU.

[283] Preamble, Recital 13, Art. 1, para. 2 TEU. Contrast with the ECSC; see Chapter 1, Section 1.3.2.1.

[284] Art. 1 TEU, Art. 1 TFEU. [285] Art. 55 TEU. [286] Ibid.

The internal structure of the EU Treaties, as is visible from key elements of its early provisions and table of contents, provides a useful preliminary introduction to the main features of the related legal order. To help the reader grasp the relative importance of these features, the page references as they are provided in the Official Journal of the European Union have been included in Box 1.2.

Box 1.2 **Rough guide to the EU Treaties, Protocols, Annexes and Charter**

Treaty on the European Union (TEU)

By this Treaty, the HIGH CONTRACTING PARTIES establish among themselves a EUROPEAN UNION, hereinafter called 'the Union', on which the Member States confer competences to attain objectives they have in common. [. . .]

The Union shall be founded on the present Treaty and on the Treaty on the Functioning of the European Union [. . .] (Article 1 TEU)

Treaty on the Functioning of the European Union (TFEU)

This Treaty organises the functioning of the Union and determines the areas of, delimitation of, and arrangements for exercising its competences. (Article 1(1) TFEU)

[287] The various titles herein relate to the internal market (with provisions on the free movement of goods, agriculture and fisheries; free movement of persons, services and capital); the AFSJ (with provisions on border checks, asylum and immigration; judicial cooperation in civil matters and in criminal matters; police cooperation); transport; common rules on competition, taxation and approximation of laws; economic and monetary policy; employment; social policy; the European Social Fund; education, vocational training, youth and sport; culture; public health; consumer protection; trans-European networks; industry; economic, social and territorial cohesion; research and technological development and space; environment and energy; tourism; civil protection; administrative cooperation.

(cont.)

Protocols & Annexes

The Protocols and Annexes to the Treaties shall form an integral part thereof. (Article 51 TEU)

Charter of Fundamental Rights of the European Union

The Union recognises the rights, freedoms and principles set out in the Charter of Fundamental Rights of the European Union [. . .] which shall have the same legal value as the Treaties. (Article 6(1), paragraph 1 TEU)

As can be seen from this overview, taken in conjunction, the two Treaties constitute a remarkably long, and therefore also detailed, text of reference at the highest level in EU law. It is significantly longer and more technical than traditional constitutional texts at domestic level. This explains why the fundamentals of EU law are often perceived as uniquely complex and opaque. Furthermore, a vast number of political choices in the Treaties, for instance on the key tenets of the internal market and economic integration, which prevail over national laws, place these choices above the realm of daily politics.[288] This feature of the EU Treaties is therefore sometimes criticised for hampering debate on important societal choices. There is much legitimacy in both sets of concerns. Yet what may be perceived as significant weaknesses of the EU Treaties also sheds light on the delicate compromises reached by the Member States, over more than half a century, in their quest to (re)unify the peoples of Europe.

Box 1.2 highlights the need to introduce two nuances to the rough description introduced previously of the relationship between the TEU, as establishing the system, and the TFEU, as fleshing it out. To start with, the TEU allows for the creation of enhanced cooperation between Member States who wish to advance EU objectives.[289] Safeguards seek to ensure a smooth relationship between these forms of cooperation, and the standard policies developed on the basis of the TFEU.[290] Furthermore, by way of exception, the TEU provides details on one substantive area of EU law: the CFSP, including a Common Security and Defence Policy. Safeguards also exist here to ensure a sound coexistence between the implementation of the CFSP and that of standard EU policies.[291] The specific design of the CFSP is best understood in the light of its historical trajectory, as illustrated by the creation of the second pillar of the EU with the Treaty of Maastricht; it emphasises the strong intergovernmental character that continues to distinguish this policy from other areas of EU law.[292]

[288] See Chapter 3, Section 3.1.1. [289] See Chapter 1, Section 1.4.3.4.
[290] Art. 20 TEU, Arts. 326–334 TFEU; see also Chapter 3, Section 3.1.1.2. [291] Art. 40 TEU, Art. 275 TFEU.
[292] See Chapter 1, Section 1.3.

Turning to the TFEU itself, the third Part is the bulkiest, on 'Union policies and internal actions'. It sets the stage for the majority of EU substantive law.[293] This includes the rules on the internal market, which have largely remained unchanged since the Treaty of Rome. It also includes the provisions on the EMU, and those on the AFSJ. The latter were progressively transformed from the initial third pillar of the EU introduced by the Treaty of Maastricht that was primarily intergovernmental, into what is today a largely supranational policy.[294] The second most detailed part of the TFEU relates to institutional and financial provisions. Together with the first and final provisions of each Treaty, as well as of the main aspects of the TEU, these institutional provisions are the main subjects of attention in this book.

The Treaties are accompanied by a number of documents of equal legal value. The CFEU, to start with, is attached to the TEU and TFEU.[295] The said Treaties are further accompanied by thirty-seven Protocols, two Annexes and sixty-five Declarations. Their importance must not be underestimated. Protocols and Annexes form an integral part of the EU Treaties;[296] they therefore have the same legal value. Protocols, in particular, often provide more technical information on certain features of the EU institutional framework, as is the case for the Protocols on National Parliaments, the Court of Justice of the European Union, the European Central Bank or the Eurogroup. Others spell out arrangements related to specific Member States and/or specific EU policies, as illustrated by the Protocols on Schengen, Denmark and the UK.

1.4.2 A Legal Order Shaped by the Court of Justice of the European Union

Although the proposal for a Treaty establishing a 'Constitution' for Europe was rejected in the early 2000s, the current EU Treaties perform some of the functions of a constitutional norm in the EU legal system: they provide the framework of reference for the understanding of the main institutional features and dynamics of the substantive law of the EU. They also rank at the top of the hierarchy of EU norms. Since 1986, pursuant to a case known as *Les Verts*, the Court of Justice has itself been referring to the Treaties as 'the basic constitutional charter'.[297] The Court of Justice has been further breathing life into the Treaties, building on their unique ambition to assert the particularly sophisticated nature of the EU legal order.

1.4.2.1 Primacy

The EU Treaties, and the law deriving therefrom, is integrated with the law of the Member States in a uniquely powerful way; hence its importance in the academic curriculum of law faculties, or advanced programmes on European affairs. In an early and famous case, *Costa* v. *ENEL* (1964), to which we will return later,[298] the Court of Justice noted that:

[293] See Chapter 1, note 287.

[294] Although with remaining specificities illustrating the intergovernmental origins of the policy, such as a particularly strong leading role of the European Council (Art. 68 TFEU); the possibility for a quarter of the Member States to initiate legislation for administrative cooperation in the field of justice and police cooperation on criminal matters (Art. 76(b) TFEU); the enhanced power of scrutiny of national parliaments in these fields (Art. 69 TFEU); as well as the word of caution by which the Treaty provisions on the AFSJ shall not affect the exercise of the responsibilities incumbent upon Member States with regard to the maintenance of law and order and the safeguarding of internal security (Art. 72 TFEU).

[295] See Chapter 1, Section 1.3.1.2. [296] Art. 51 TEU. [297] Case 294/83, *Les Verts*, EU:C:1986:166.

[298] See Chapter 4, Section 4.1.1.1, Origins and Definition.

> By contrast with ordinary international treaties, the EEC Treaty [now, 'the set of EU Treaties'] has created its own legal system which, on the entry into force of the Treaty, became an integral part of the legal systems of the Member States and which their courts are bound to apply.

The Court also held therein:

> The integration into the laws of each Member State of provisions which derive from the Community [now, 'Union'], and more generally the terms and the spirit of the Treaty [now, 'EU Treaties'], make it impossible for the States, as a corollary, to accord precedence to a unilateral and subsequent measure over a legal system accepted by them on a basis of reciprocity.[299]

This characteristic is commonly referred to as the primacy of EU law and is inherent in the EU legal system. Domestic authorities, in particular the courts, are bound to give precedence to acts of EU law over national acts from the date of the entry into force of an accession agreement between a State and the EU. This holds true irrespective of whether the Member State in question is monist or dualist;[300] thus without it being possible to make EU obligations conditional upon the adoption of measures authorising the emergence of, or reproducing, EU obligations in domestic legal systems.

1.4.2.2 Direct Effect

As a corollary, in *Van Gend en Loos* (1963), the Court of Justice also asserted that EU law confers rights and creates obligations not only for States, but crucially also for individuals:

> the Community [now, 'Union'] constitutes a new legal order of international law for the benefit of which the states have limited their sovereign rights, albeit within limited fields, and the subjects of which comprise not only Member States but also their nationals. Independently of the legislation of Member States, Community [now, 'Union'] law therefore not only imposes obligations on individuals but is also intended to confer upon them rights which become part of their legal heritage.[301]

This second feature is referred to as the ability of EU law to produce direct effect in domestic legal orders. Provisions of EU law fulfilling a number of characteristics related to the ability of domestic authorities to infer from them specific rights and obligations in individual situations, can be relied upon directly before domestic authorities, and before courts in particular. Read in conjunction, the primacy and the direct effect of EU law may result in setting aside contravening domestic rules. By way of example, we could imagine a trading company, importing goods from Poland to Germany that would be asked by

[299] Case 6/64, *Costa* v. *ENEL*, EU:C:1964:66.

[300] These notions are used to describe the way national constitutional systems organise their own relationship with international law. International law may either be treated as integrated in the domestic legal order, and rank above national law (monism), or as a distinct set of instruments (dualism). In the latter case, for international law to produce legal effects in the domestic legal order, it must be 'incorporated' in national legal systems through a provision of national law.

[301] Case 26/62, *Van Gend en Loos*, EU:C:1963:1.

German customs authorities to pay a tariff on import as requested by (a fictitious[302]) German rule. The company could directly rely on Article 30 TFEU, according to which 'Customs duties on imports [. . .] shall be prohibited between Member States', against the German customs authorities, with a view to refusing payment.

1.4.2.3 Autonomy

The specific nature of the legal system created by the treaties, as acknowledged by the Court of Justice in these early cases, results in EU law being autonomous. In Opinion 2/13 (2014), the Court elaborated on the concept as follows:

> the Member States have, by reason of their membership of the EU, accepted that relations between them as regards the matters covered by the transfer of powers from the Member States to the EU are governed by EU law to the exclusion, if EU law so requires, of any other law.[303]

The concept of autonomy relates to the position that the EU occupies between national and international law. Internally, the EU has its own institutional machinery enabling it to adopt legally binding norms, to ensure their implementation and compliance therewith. This system, which will be further elaborated upon in this book, allows the primacy of EU law to be ensured over national law, and its unity and effectiveness to be protected.[304] The Court of Justice of the European Union is the guardian of the uniform interpretation of the EU Treaties, and the law deriving therefrom.[305]

This institutional machinery of the EU also allows it to interact with States and international organisations on its own terms. As a result, the Court of Justice has stated that the EU could not become a party to an international agreement that would require it to interpret EU law in a way that could affect the primacy, unity and effectiveness of EU law,[306] or, that could affect the delicate balance established by EU law between Member States, such as in relation to mutual trust between them on matters of fundamental rights compliance, as discussed in the said Opinion 2/13.

EU law is thus autonomous from both national and international law. This is commonly illustrated by the Court's case law developing its own definition of key notions of EU law and granting them an 'autonomous meaning'.[307] Yet it shall be recalled that the EU legal order cannot exist without the support of its constituent members, as expressed in the primary legal framework set out in the EU Treaties; it only operates within the parameters defined therein. Furthermore, international law often resonates very strongly within the EU legal system.[308]

[302] Most rules of that sort have now been eliminated within the EU, but the example is modelled on the facts of the *Van Gend en Loos* case (1963).

[303] Opinion 2/13, Accession of the European Union to the European Convention for the Protection of Human Rights and Fundamental Freedoms, EU:C:2014:2454, para. 193.

[304] C-399/11, *Melloni*, EU:C:2013:107, para. 60. [305] Art. 19(1), para. 1 TEU.

[306] Opinion 2/13, Accession of the European Union to the European Convention for the Protection of Human Rights and Fundamental Freedoms, EU:C:2014:2454, para. 189.

[307] A concept that has been subject to attention in recent years is that of 'detention' in the context of EU law on international protection. The Court of Justice developed its own definition: see Joined Cases C-924/19 PPU and C-925/19 PPU, *Országos*, EU:C:2020:3673, para. 223, and related debates in the Opinion of Advocate General Pikamäe, C-808/18, *Commission* v. *Hungary (Reception of Applicants for International Protection)*, EU:C:2020:493, paras. 128–142.

[308] See Chapter 3, Section 3.5.1.2.

1.4.3 Differentiated Integration within the EU Treaties

Despite, or perhaps because of, its powerful legal infrastructure as just outlined, the European Union is host to a great diversity of legal arrangements. While some are primarily enshrined in the EU Treaties and related protocols, others may derive from EU rules adopted thereupon.[309] This introductory book will focus on the most general features of the EU legal system, on what brings 'unity' to the European Union legal order.[310] Yet before doing so, and as this may be of major political and legal importance, some examples of differentiated integration will be outlined briefly.[311]

These atypical mechanisms are often the translation of different paces of integration, for different Member States or groups of Member States. This differentiation may be referred to as 'multi-speed Europe'. Sometimes though, and although this is less common, as for the UK in relation to the Schengen Area, differentiation simply illustrates the desire not to adhere to a specific policy or objective of the EU. Other expressions, such as variable geometry or Europe à la carte, are therefore in use, each with strengths and weaknesses.

Reference will be made here to the fairly neutral notion of differentiated integration, with a focus on modes of operation that have developed between the Member States of the EU.[312] The two most well-known forms of differentiated integration in the EU are the Schengen Area and the euro area. Both have developed between a number of Member States of the EU. They illustrate cross-fertilisation of intergovernmental cooperation between the Member States and EU law. These forms of differentiated integration coexist with specific arrangements for new Member States after enlargements and the more standardised forms of enhanced cooperation.

It shall be noted that when not all Member States participate in decision-making, specific rules on the calculation of the voting thresholds at the Council will apply. The rules on decision-making within the Commission and the Parliament, however, remain unchanged; so does the jurisdiction of the Court of Justice of the European Union.

1.4.3.1 The Schengen Area

The Schengen Area is commonly associated with the idea of an area without internal border controls, and with common monitoring of external borders.[313] It was established by the Schengen Agreement, signed in 1985 by five Member States of the EU, although this was in their independent capacity and in the form of a traditional international agreement.[314]

[309] It shall be noted that EU rules adopted on the basis of mainstream EU law, dealt with in the remainder of this book, may well formally and intentionally have different impacts on different Member States or parts of Member States. For instance: 'In order to tackle the under-representation of one of the major religious communities in the police service of Northern Ireland, differences in treatment regarding recruitment into that service [. . .] shall not constitute discrimination insofar as', Art. 15(1) of 'Council Directive 2000/78/EC of 27 November 2000 Establishing a General Framework for Equal Treatment in Employment and Occupation', OJ L 303, 2.12.2000, p. 16; T. Duttle, 'Opting Out from European Union Legislation: The Differentiation of Secondary Law', *Journal of European Public Policy*, 24 (2017), pp. 406–428.

[310] Borrowing from C-399/11, *Melloni*, EU:C:2013:107, para. 60.

[311] See further B. De Witte, 'An Undivided Union? Differentiated Integration in Post-Brexit Times', *Common Market Law Review*, 55 (2018), pp. 227–250.

[312] For differences in the relationship with third States, see Section 1.2.2.

[313] Art. 77 TFEU.

[314] 'Agreement between the Governments of the States of the Benelux Economic Union, the Federal Republic of Germany and the French Republic on the Gradual Abolition of Checks at their Common Borders', OJ L 239, 22.9.2000, p. 13.

It was complemented by a Convention on its implementation in 1990;[315] it grew in geographical scope and led to the first abolition of internal border controls between seven participating States (the Schengen area) in 1995.

Since 1999,[316] the law derived from the initial Schengen Agreement, the Schengen acquis, has been incorporated into EU law by means of what is today Protocol 19, attached

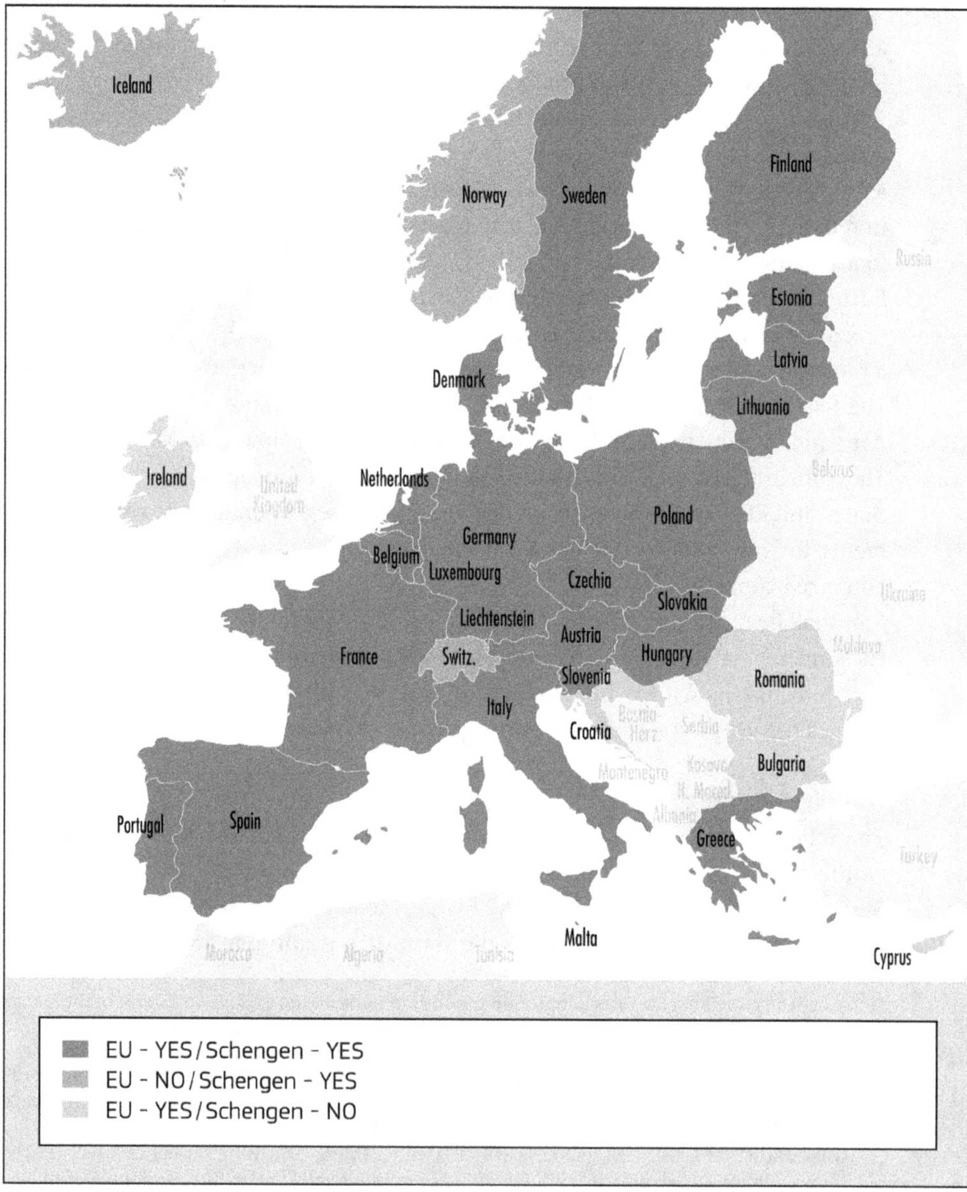

Map 1.2 Membership of the EU and/or of the Schengen Area[317]

[315] 'Convention Implementing the Schengen Agreement', OJ L 239, 22.9.2000, p. 19.

[316] This corresponds to the entry into force of the Treaty of Amsterdam.

[317] This map draws on that available freely at schengenvisainfo.com.

to the TEU and TFEU. The growth and success of the Schengen area was not welcomed by all Member States of the EU. Denmark, Ireland and the UK each negotiated different derogatory statuses, also enshrined in protocols attached to the TEU and TFEU.[318] In essence, they do not take part in the related EU policy unless they opt in, which they may do through procedures and with effects that differ from State to State. The UK has now left the EU altogether. Denmark is not bound by the rules on Schengen as a matter of EU law, but is bound by many of them as a matter of international law.[319] Ireland remains outside of the area without border controls. This is why one still has to go through border checks when travelling between France and Ireland, or between Belgium and Ireland, for example.

Conversely, a set of non-EU Member States have shown an interest in the Schengen area, as is the case of Norway and Switzerland; in principle there is no need to show an identity card if coming from an EU and Schengen Member State within these non-EU Member States belonging to the Schengen area.[320] As a consequence, and also bearing in mind that the latest waves of enlargements of the EU have not automatically resulted in enlargements of the Schengen area, as will be noted subsequently, the list of countries in the Schengen area does not include all EU Member States, but does include some non-EU States. This is illustrated in Map 1.2.

1.4.3.2 The Euro Area

The other well-known form of differentiated integration is the euro area. Since the creation of the EEC, that has now become the EU, the Member States intended to ensure a certain level of coordination of their economic policies, with a view to ensuring a global balance of payments, as well as trust in their currencies.[321] Building on earlier incentives and mechanisms, in 1992, the EU was tasked by its Member States to establish an EMU, which would proceed in three stages and culminate in the creation of a single currency and a single monetary policy.[322] As noted earlier, this made it possible for the euro, in the EU Member States participating in the common currency (also known as euro area), to be launched in 1999 as an accounting unit,[323] and for the relevant banknotes and coins to be introduced from the early 2000s. Furthermore, the euro area States have a number of specific institutional arrangements.[324]

Once again, though, at the time of the creation of the common currency, the Member States of the EU did not all share enthusiasm for the common monetary policy. Denmark and the UK both negotiated the possibility of remaining outside the third stage of the EMU, the creation of the single currency in the euro area.[325] Other States are expected to join, but may only do so once they meet a set of conditions established in the TFEU, as well as in a set of other complementary instruments.[326] As will be elaborated upon subsequently and as illustrated in Map 1.3, several of the new Member States of the EU are not yet part of the euro area. As for Sweden, it was working towards meeting these conditions, but in 2003 the

[318] See Protocols 19–22 annexed to the EU Treaties. [319] Protocol 22, Arts. 2 and 4.
[320] See Chapter 1, Section 1.2.2. [321] Art. 104 TEEC (1957).
[322] Arts. 2 and 3(a)(2) TEC (1992); see also Art. 119 TFEU.
[323] 'Council Decision of 3 May 1998 in Accordance with Article 109j(4) of the Treaty', OJ L 139, 11.5.1998, p. 30.
[324] See Chapter 2, Sections 2.3.3.6 and 2.3.4.7. [325] See Protocols 15 and 16 attached to the TEU and TFEU.
[326] These conditions relate to price stability, sound and sustainable public finances, exchange rate stability, long-term interest rates: see, inter alia, Art. 140 TFEU and Protocol 13 on the Convergence Criteria.

Map 1.3 Membership of the EU and of the euro area[327]

government's proposal to adopt the euro was rejected in a referendum. As a consequence, the map of EU Member States using the euro is also different from that of the EU, as well as being different from that of the Schengen area. A number of third States have also decided of their own will to use the euro as a currency, as for example, in the Vatican City State or in Kosovo.

[327] This map draws on that available freely at europa.eu.

The economic and financial crisis called into question the foundations of the euro area. In response, and adding to the complex picture outlined previously, a set of international agreements and other forms of collaboration outside the legal framework of the EU were adopted to support the EU framework. The most familiar expression of this phenomenon is the Treaty Establishing the European Stability Mechanism, a mechanism that also stood ready to support euro area States in response to the COVID-19 crisis.[328] Understanding the functioning of the euro area therefore requires not only looking at a selected number of EU States, but also at the joint actions of these States outside of the EU legal framework.[329]

1.4.3.3 Accession Processes

Differentiated integration may also be related to the accession process by new States to the EU. In recent enlargements, it has become common to allow a third State to join the EU, but to remain under a transitory regime for a period of time in relation to specific areas of EU law. This was the case for the rules on the free movement of workers that did not automatically and fully apply to the new Member States after the 2004 enlargement.[330]

Furthermore, a Member State must fulfil a number of specific conditions before it can actually be given access to either the Schengen area or the euro area. New States have therefore been allowed to become members of the EU,[331] even if they do not yet fulfil these conditions, and are expected to work towards fulfilling them.[332] As a consequence, countries such as Romania and Bulgaria, who acceded to the EU in 2007, are still in the process of seeking accession to the Schengen area.[333] Similarly, like many other new Member States, they are still working towards meeting the criteria to access the euro area. One would have to go through border control and change currency if travelling to either of these countries from a Schengen area and euro area State, such as Germany or France.

1.4.3.4 Enhanced Cooperation

As the reader will undoubtedly have noticed, the coexistence of parallel legal regimes, of which different States are members and with sets of rules that are often outside the EU legal system, creates an impression of high complexity. With a view to addressing this concern, since the late 1990s,[334] the EU Treaties provide for a sort of template for differentiated integration, known today as enhanced cooperation.

[328] See Chapter 1, note 273. E.g. European Stability Mechanism, 'ESM Board of Governors Backs Pandemic Crisis Support', press release, 15.5.2020. The other key example is the Treaty on Stability, Coordination and Governance in the Economic and Monetary Union (Fiscal Stability Treaty), 2.3.2012.

[329] See further A. De Gregorio Merino, 'Legal Developments in the Economic and Monetary Union during the Debt Crisis: The Mechanisms of Financial Assistance', *Common Market Law Review*, 49 (2012), pp. 1613–1646.

[330] Treaty between the Member States of the European Union and the Czech Republic, the Republic of Estonia, the Republic of Cyprus, the Republic of Latvia, the Republic of Lithuania, the Republic of Hungary, the Republic of Malta, the Republic of Slovenia, the Slovak Republic, Concerning Accession to the European Union, OJ L 236, 23.9.2003, pp. 17–930, Art. 24.

[331] The accession procedure will be discussed further in Chapter 2, Section 2.1.2.

[332] In particular, by virtue of the principle of sincere cooperation.

[333] See Chapter 1, Section 1.4.3.1. A specific instrument was furthermore created to monitor progress in these two Member States in the fields of judicial reform and the fight against corruption (and organised crime); see further Chapter 4, Section 4.3.2.

[334] Treaty of Amsterdam, Art. K.12.

The central idea is encapsulated in Article 20 TEU: a group of at least nine EU States may exercise EU competences[335] and make use of EU institutions in order to further the objectives of the EU, protect its interests and reinforce its integration process.[336] The cooperation shall be open at any time to all other EU Member States. Because this option allows this to occur without all EU States being involved, it can only be used as a last resort when the objectives cannot be attained within a reasonable period by the EU as a whole, which is for the Council to assess.[337] The procedure is designed with the aim of carefully balancing the interests of participating States with those of non-participating States, as well as those of the EU as a whole. For instance, it can only be initiated with the approval of a qualified majority of the Member States gathered in the Council and consent from the Parliament. Furthermore, the law resulting from enhanced cooperation will not be part of the EU acquis that candidate States for accession to the EU ought to accept.[338]

The mechanism has been fairly successful.[339] It led, for instance, to the creation of unitary patent protection currently including all EU Member States, except for Spain and Croatia. Another example is the authorisation for enhanced cooperation concerning financial transaction tax, which was the subject matter of a legal challenge. The challenge failed and the enhanced cooperation has so far not been put into practice, but it may be back on the agenda.[340] It shall be noted that these developments have not prevented the emergence of differentiated integration outside the context of EU law, in particular in response to the economic and financial crisis, as illustrated by the creation of the European Stability Mechanism.[341] There are also more specific forms of advanced or enhanced cooperation within EU law in particularly sensitive areas, such as the area of defence and criminal law.[342]

[335] These must be competences that do not exclusively belong to the EU. CJEU Joined Cases C-274/11 and C-295/11, *Spain and Italy* v. *Council*, EU:C:2013:240, para. 17.

[336] This is subject to the limits and must be in accordance with the detailed arrangements laid down in Art. 20 TEU and Arts. 326–334 TFEU. In particular, the enhanced cooperation shall not undermine the internal market. See further Joined Cases C-274/11 and C-295/11, *Spain and Italy* v. *Council*, EU:C:2013:240, paras. 68, 75–78.

[337] Joined Cases C-274/11 and C-295/11, *Spain and Italy* v. *Council*, EU:C:2013:240, para. 53.

[338] Art. 20(4) TEU.

[339] See further I. Kiendl Krišto and C. Isaksson, *Implementation of the Treaty Provisions Concerning Enhanced Cooperation* (European Parliamentary Research Service, 2018); D. Thym, 'Enhanced Cooperation within the Union', in R. Schütze and T. Tridimas (eds.), *Oxford Principles of European Union Law* (Oxford University Press, 2018), ch. 26.

[340] 'Council Decision of 22 January 2013 Authorising Enhanced Cooperation in the Area of Financial Transaction Tax', OJ L 22, 25.1.2013, pp. 11–12; C-209/13, *United Kingdom* v. *Council*, EU:C:2014:283; European Council Conclusions, Brussels, 21.7.2020, paras. A29, 149.

[341] Further discussing the link between that instrument, enhanced cooperation and the possibility for the mechanism to be part of EU law: C-370/12, *Pringle*, EU:C:2012:756, paras. 167–168; Commission, 'Proposal for a Council Regulation on the Establishment of the European Monetary Fund', COM(2017) 827 final, 6.12.2017, pp. 11–12. See also further attempts to incorporate the Fiscal Stability Treaty (Chapter 1, Section 1.4.3.2, note 328) in EU law: Commission, 'Proposal for a Council Directive Laying Down Provisions for Strengthening Fiscal Responsibility and the Medium-Term Budgetary Orientation in the Member States', COM(2017) 824 final, 6.12.2017.

[342] Recent examples include a permanent structured cooperation in the area of defence (Art. 42(6) TEU; see Chapter 1, Section 1.3.2.1) or for the creation of a European Public Prosecutor's office (Art. 86(1) TFEU; see Chapter 2, Section 2.3.8.3).

1.4.4 A Legal Order Subject to Change

One cannot but notice how dynamic the legal framework on which the EU legal order relies has been since its early days. Despite its unique characteristics, tainted with strong supranational features, when it comes to the reform of its own design, the EU legal order remains subject to procedures anchored in international law logic. As it stands today, there are several ways to reform the EU Treaties. Most are set out in one of the final provisions of the Treaty on European Union itself, in its Article 48.

1.4.4.1 The Ordinary Treaty Revision Procedure

We start with what the TEU itself identifies as the 'ordinary revision procedure' set out in Article 48(2–5) TEU.[343] This procedure may be used, in particular, to either increase or limit the competences conferred on the EU. The proposal comes from a Member State, the Parliament or the Commission and is submitted to the Council, which will then submit it to the European Council and notify national parliaments.

The European Council will decide (by simple majority), after consulting the Parliament and the Commission,[344] whether to examine the proposed amendments. If they decide to do so, the President of the European Council will in principle convene a Convention. Relying on earlier practice,[345] such a Convention will bring together representatives of the European as well as national parliaments, of the Member States and of the Commission. The Convention is expected to make a recommendation (by consensus) to a conference of representatives of the governments of the Member States (IGC). If the extent of the amendments considered does not justify calling for a Convention, as assessed by the European Council (by simple majority) with the consent of the Parliament, the European Council will set the terms of reference for the IGC itself.

In any case, an IGC will subsequently be convened by the President of the Council for the purpose of determining by common accord the amendments – and any such amendments would have to be ratified by all the Member States in accordance with their constitutional requirements. The latter usually require parliamentary ratification, and sometimes a referendum. They also create possibilities for legal challenges before national constitutional courts.[346] In the event that, after two years from signature of the treaty deciding on amendments, four-fifths of the Member States have ratified it, but one or more have encountered difficulties, the matter shall be referred to the European Council. This procedure largely codifies the approach followed after the negative referenda on the Treaty establishing a Constitution for Europe.[347]

The ordinary revision procedure thus illustrates a fairly traditional back and forth between the Council and the European Council, requires the common accord of the Member States, formalises the recourse to a Convention for extensive amendments of the EU Treaties, as well as the recourse to a back-up reflection period in case of difficulties with

[343] Please note that procedures for the adoption of legislation (such as the ordinary legislative procedure; see Chapter 3, Section 3.6.1.1) are not to be confused with the procedures for the reform of the EU Treaties.

[344] And possibly the Central Bank, in the case of institutional changes in the monetary area.

[345] On the drafting of the Charter and Treaty establishing a Constitution for Europe, see Chapter 1, Section 1.3.2.3.

[346] See, for instance, Chapter 1, Section 1.3.2.2, note 171.

[347] See Chapter 1, Section 1.3.2.3.

the ratification process. Yet, importantly, all Member States must support *and* ratify any final amendments. There have been several attempts to use the procedure that have resulted in a few changes without calling for a Convention; one of them has allowed the adoption and entry into force of a Protocol on the concerns that the Irish people had expressed in a negative referendum on the Treaty of Lisbon itself.[348]

1.4.4.2 The Simplified Treaty Revision Procedures

Amendments to Part III TFEU

The first simplified revision procedure, provided for in Article 48(6) TEU, may be used to revise 'all or part' of Part III TFEU on the internal policies and actions of the EU, but not to increase EU competences. The proposal also comes from a Member State, the Parliament or the Commission and is submitted directly to the European Council. The latter decides, after consulting the Parliament and the Commission,[349] on possible treaty amendments. A decision on such amendments may only enter into force after approval by the Member States in accordance with their respective constitutional requirements.

There is therefore no convening of a Convention, nor even an IGC. Yet both unanimity at the European Council level and support from each Member State domestically will be necessary for treaty change. An example of reliance on such a procedure came with the insertion, in the midst of the economic and financial crisis, of a new paragraph in Article 136 TFEU, to the effect that euro area Member States 'may establish a stability mechanism to be activated if indispensable to safeguard the stability of the euro area as a whole'.[350] The Member State indeed created a European Stability Mechanism.[351] In the context of litigation regarding that mechanism, the Court of Justice was called upon to check that the conditions set out in Article 48 TEU had been duly respected for the related treaty amendment. In the *Pringle* case, the Court concluded in the affirmative.[352]

The General Passerelle Clause

The second simplified revision procedure, to be found in Article 48(7) TEU, has an even more specific nature. It can only be used where the TFEU provides for the Council to act by unanimity, or for the use of a special legislative procedure; and for the purpose of changing these procedures in favour of qualified majority voting at the Council, or use of the ordinary legislative procedure, respectively.[353]

In other words, Article 48(7) TEU allows for a simplified treaty revision procedure to make law-making in the EU more supranational. The said changes will indeed result in individual

348 'Protocol on the Concerns of the Irish People on the Treaty of Lisbon', OJ L 60, 2.3.2013, p. 131.

349 As well as the Central Bank in the case of institutional changes in the monetary area.

350 '2011/199/EU: European Council Decision of 25 March 2011 Amending Article 136 of the Treaty on the Functioning of the European Union with Regard to a Stability Mechanism for Member States whose Currency is the Euro', OJ L 91, 6.4.2011, p. 1.

351 See Chapter 1, Section 1.4.3.2. 352 C-370/12, *Pringle*, EU:C:2012:756, paras. 36, 76.

353 By virtue of Art. 353 TFEU, Art. 48(7) TEU may not be used to modify some of the rules on decision-making on the EU system of own resources (Art. 311, paras. 3–4 TFEU; see Chapter 3, Section 3.6.3.1), the multi-financial framework (Art. 312(2), subpara. 1 TFEU; see Chapter 3, Section 3.6.3.2), the flexibility clause (Art. 352 TFEU; see Chapter 3, Section 3.2.3.3) and the voting arrangements for the implementation of the rule of law mechanism enshrined in Art. 7 TEU (Art. 354 TFEU; see Chapter 4, Section 4.3.2.1). All four exceptions have highly sensitive implications.

Member States having less blocking power within the Council, and the Parliament being more involved. The proposal to bridge towards (hence the informal name, passerelle clause) more supranational law-making is formally in the hands of the European Council, although other actors may invite that institution to act. The latter ought to notify national parliaments, which are given six months to make known their possible opposition. Each national parliament therefore has the possibility to interrupt the procedure. In the absence of opposition though, the European Council, with the consent of the Parliament, may adopt the decision.

Here again, there is no convening of a Convention, nor an IGC. Neither is there any reference to the requirement of ratification by all or acceptance by the Member States in accordance with their respective constitutional requirements. Yet there must be unanimity at the European Council level, the consent of the Parliament (with the high threshold of a majority of its component members), and each national parliament, in practice, has a veto power.

1.4.4.3 Treaty Change: Article 48 TEU and Beyond

As will have become clear from previous observations, the procedures provided for in Article 48(6–7) TFEU may at first sight appear to be more simple than the ordinary treaty revision procedure, but in any case, they require strong support from Member States and their domestic institutions.

Importantly, the list of treaty revision procedures provided for in Article 48 TEU is not exhaustive. Across the EU Treaties, there are several examples of other treaty revision procedures. Examples that have been discussed in recent years relate to amendments to the Statute of the Court of Justice of the European Union, which is enshrined in a Protocol,[354] extension of the powers of the European Public Prosecutor mentioned in the TFEU,[355] or the special passerelle clause allowing for the extension of the use of qualified majority voting in the Council in relation to certain areas of the CFSP.[356]

Furthermore, along with the procedures discussed so far, the reader shall keep in mind that the Member States remain entitled to conclude agreements among themselves outside the scope of EU law: as long as these agreements do not encroach on EU law, they may borrow the institutions of the EU and contribute to furthering common objectives.[357]

[354] Art. 281 TFEU; e.g. 'Regulation (EU, Euratom) 2015/2422 of the European Parliament and of the Council of 16 December 2015 Amending Protocol No. 3 on the Statute of the Court of Justice of the European Union', OJ L 341, 24.12.2015, p. 14.

[355] Art. 86 TFEU. See Commission, Communication, 'A Europe that Protects: An Initiative to Extend the Competences of the European Public Prosecutor's Office to Cross-border Terrorist Crimes', COM(2018) 641 final, 12.9.2018.

[356] Art. 31(3) TEU. See Commission, Communication, 'A Stronger Global Actor: A More Efficient Decision-Making for EU Common Foreign and Security Policy', COM(2018) 647 final, 12.9.2018; see also R. Böttner, 'The Treaty Amendment Procedures and the Relationship between Article 31(3) TEU and the General Bridging Clause of Article 48(7) TEU', *European Constitutional Law Review*, 12 (2016), pp. 499–519.

[357] The matter was discussed at length, *inter alia*, in a case related to the Treaty Establishing the European Stability Mechanism signed and ratified by Member States of the EU whose currency is the euro, C-370/12, *Pringle*, EU:C:2012:756, paras. 77–182.

Several proposals have been made by the Juncker Commission, inviting the European Council to make use of passerelle clauses in recent years.[358] To date, however, none has been followed up. At the time of writing, a Conference on the Future of Europe has also been launched and is expected to result in reports and recommendations before the summer of 2022.[359] How this reflection on the future of Europe, which is co-governed by representatives of the Parliament, the Council and the Commission and relies heavily on citizens' participation, may impact the prospect of treaty reform remains unclear at the time of writing.

[358] E.g. Commission, Communication, 'Towards a More Efficient and Democratic Decision-Making in EU Tax Policy', COM(2019) 8 final, 15.1.2019; Commission, Communication, 'A More Efficient and Democratic Decision-Making in EU Energy and Climate Policy', COM(2019) 177 final, 9.4.2019; Commission, Communication, 'More Efficient Decision-Making in Social Policy: Identification of Areas for an Enhanced Move to Qualified Majority Voting', COM(2019) 186 final, 16.4.2019.

[359] Conference on the Future of Europe, 'Rules of Procedure'; follow up its work at futureu.europa.eu.

2

The Actors of the EU Integration Process

The dynamics of the EU legal order result from interactions between a great diversity of actors. The main characteristics of key actors explain the specific role attributed to each of them in the functioning of the EU, as will be further set out in subsequent chapters. The Member States, to start with, play a prominent and decisive role in shaping the nature and boundaries of the EU legal order (Section 2.1). Alongside this, nationals of the Member States are today an important part of the system of checks and balances, and are referred to as EU citizens (Section 2.2). Yet it is to the specific and sophisticated set of institutions (Section 2.3) and complementary organs (Section 2.4) that breathe life into the EU legal order that much of our attention in this chapter will be devoted.

2.1 MEMBER STATES

The EU is first and foremost shaped by the high contracting parties to the EU Treaties: the Member States.[1] Their central function in the process of European integration is the reason why processes of accession by States to, and withdrawal from, the EU Treaties are particularly sensitive and structured by advanced legal mechanisms.

2.1.1 The Member States and the EU

As noted in Chapter 1, the Member States are the primary holders of the power to decide on the shape and content of the EU Treaties. The agreement of each of them is needed for a new State to accede to the EU.[2] Furthermore, the Member States retain a number of key functions in their capacity as sovereign States even within the EU legal system, such as for the appointment of judges to the Court of Justice of the European Union.[3]

Within the EU legal order, the Member States are prominently represented within the European Council (at the level of Heads of States or Governments) or the Council (at ministerial level).[4] Member States are furthermore bound by the duty of sincere cooperation: as well as a commitment to contribute through positive action to facilitating the

[1] Art. 1 TEU. [2] Art. 49, para. 2 TEU.

[3] This is by 'common accord of the governments of the Member States', Art. 19(2), subpara. 3 TEU. Such acts are not subject to judicial review by the Court of Justice of the European Union in the context of annulment actions within the meaning of Art. 263 TFEU. E.g. C-685/20 P, *Eleanor Sharpston* v. *Council*, EU:C:2021:485, paras. 46–51. Other similar types of acts include decisions on the seat of EU institutions, Art. 341 TFEU and Protocol 6.

[4] Art. 10(2), subpara. 2 TEU; see also Chapter 2, Sections 2.3.3 and 2.3.4.

achievement of the EU's tasks, they have a very broad negative duty to 'refrain from any measure which could jeopardise the attainment of the Union's objectives'.[5]

It is among representatives of the Member States at the highest level, either as part of an EU institution (the European Council) or in their sovereign capacity that key political choices at European level are often made.[6] This occasionally results in confusion as to whether the Member States are acting collectively as part of an EU institution, or collectively in their sovereign capacity. An example of such confusion is the statement issued jointly with the Republic of Turkey to set out a joint action plan designed to strengthen cooperation in response to the migration influx resulting from the humanitarian crisis in Syria in 2015. There is much controversy as to whether the statement was issued by the EU with Turkey, or by the States (of the European Union) with Turkey.[7]

2.1.2 Accession

While created by and composed of six Member States in 1957, the EU as we know it today is composed of twenty-seven States.[8] This process of considerable expansion, resulting from successive 'enlargements' (and one withdrawal) as illustrated in Map 2.1, results from a combination of key political decisions on the orientation of the process of European integration and procedural requirements.

The interactions of the EU with a number of other partners at European level are illustrative of evolving geopolitics.[9] For instance, several members of EFTA have wished to accede to the EU, which means leaving the former to join the latter.[10] In that context, the coexistence of the two projects – EFTA primarily concerned with free trade and economic integration, and the EU progressively engaging in a deeper integration process – has resulted in changes in memberships between the two structures. Another example of a geopolitical shift affecting membership to the EU has been the end of the Cold War. After the fall of the Berlin Wall in 1989, it soon became clear that several members of the former Soviet Union would seek accession to the EU, as indeed occurred from 2004 onwards.[11] The impact of the Russian military aggression on Ukraine on accession processes in the region remains unknown as this book goes to press.

Naturally, decisions on enlargements do not only relate to developments on the world stage. They are also intimately linked with internal politics in candidate countries, as well as in existing Member States. Several European States, such as Norway, contemplated accession before withdrawing interest in order to respond to domestic voters; another State, the

[5] Art. 4(3), subpara. 3 TEU. See further T. Roes, 'Limits to Loyalty: The Relevance of Article 4(3) TEU', *Cahiers de Droit Européen*, 1 (2016), pp. 253–283; see also Chapter 1, Section 1.1.2.

[6] See Chapter 1, Section 1.2.3.

[7] The General Court of the Court of Justice of the European Union has ruled that the statement was issued by the Heads of State or Government (of the European Union), by opposition to the European Council as an EU institution, in Case T-192/16, *NF* v. *European Council*, EU:T:2017:128, paras. 69–71. The case has been subject to an appeal that was dismissed as being manifestly inadmissible; Joined Cases C-208/17 P to C-210/17 P, *NF and Others* v. *European Council*, EU:C:2018:705.

[8] See Chapter 1, Section 1.3.

[9] See Chapter 1, Section 1.2.2.

[10] The former EFTA States that have joined the EU are: in 1973, Denmark and the UK (the latter's membership now having been withdrawn); in 1986, Portugal; in 1995, Austria, Finland and Sweden.

[11] European Council, Conclusions of the Presidency, Copenhagen, 21–22.6.1993, para. 7(A)(iii).

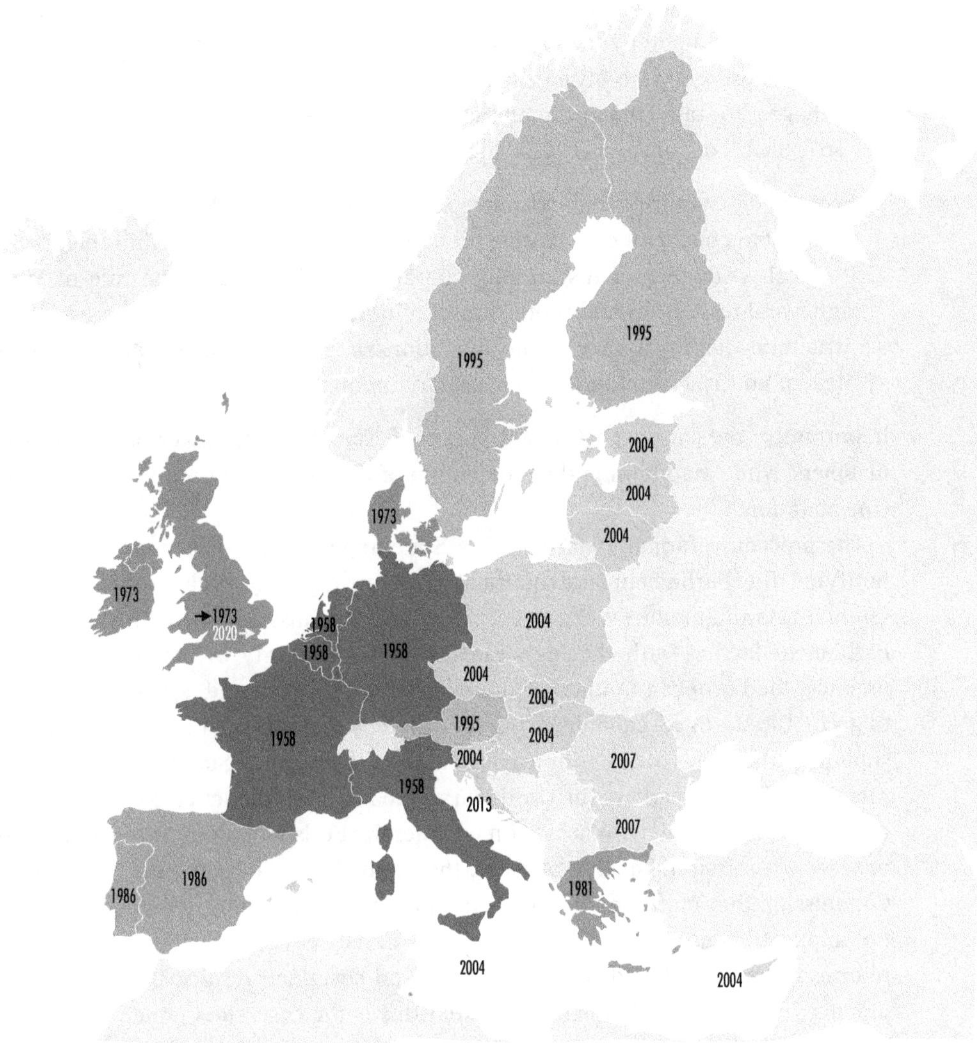

Map 2.1 EU membership per years of accession and withdrawal

United Kingdom, acceded and subsequently withdrew.[12] Others have applied for membership, but the process has stalled. This is best illustrated by reference to the relationship between the EU and Turkey, as made particularly explicit by the Council after the coup from 15 July 2016 and as a reaction to 'continuing and deeply worrying backsliding on the rule of law and on fundamental rights including the freedom of expression'.[13]

The procedure to follow for a State to accede to the EU is set out in Article 49 TEU. This article is addressed to '[a]ny European State'. What constitutes a 'European' State is not defined by the EU Treaties, and thus is subject to unanimous agreement by the existing Member States, as we shall see. That European State ought to respect the values referred to

[12] Elaborating on the close ties between the EU and these States, see Chapter 1, Section 1.2.2.
[13] Council, Conclusions on Enlargement and Stabilisation and Association Process, 26.6.2018, paras. 31–35.

in Article 2 TEU, and be committed to promoting them.[14] Furthermore, the conditions of eligibility agreed upon by the European Council must be considered.

These conditions were primarily set out by the European Council meeting in 1993 in Copenhagen, to frame the future relationship with the former States of the Soviet Union.[15] The so-called 'Copenhagen criteria' are threefold:

1. Economic – requiring the existence of a functioning market economy as well as the capacity to cope with competitive pressure and market forces within the EU;
2. Political – stability of institutions guaranteeing democracy, the rule of law, human rights and respect for and protection of minorities;
3. Structural – ability to take on the obligations of membership, including adherence to the aims of political, economic and monetary union.

Importantly, the European Council specified that the 'Union's capacity to absorb new members, while maintaining the momentum of European integration, is also an important consideration.'[16]

The procedure formally starts with a State applying for accession to the Council and notifying the Parliament and national parliaments. According to Article 49 TEU, the Council acts unanimously after consulting the Commission and with the consent of the Parliament (acting with the high threshold of a majority of component members). In practice, the European Council also makes its voice heard and 'agrees [with the Council] to grant' the status of 'candidate country', thereby kickstarting the process with the visible support of the Heads of States or Governments of the Member States gathered therein.[17] The role of the Council is then, further down the road (and, in practice, as further endorsed by the European Council[18]), to decide on whether the EU is willing to start actual negotiations in view of accession. For that purpose, the Council relies in particular on the work of the Commission that monitors the situation in the candidate country and advises on whether the applicant State has sufficiently demonstrated its determination to advance the EU reform agenda and has delivered tangible and sustained results. If the Council (and, in practice, the European Council), finds that this is the case, the Council sets a negotiation mandate on the basis of a proposal from the Commission, and the country officially becomes a candidate country.

The negotiations take place in the framework of an IGC, in the context of which they are carried out on behalf of the EU by the Commission reporting to other institutions. The actual negotiations, as well as the preliminary screening before the decision to open them, are structured per chapter, which allows both sides to review the progress made by the candidate country sector by sector: the progress of the candidate country is checked against

[14] See Chapter 1, Section 1.1.3.

[15] In the context of possible enlargement to the Western Balkans, emphasis is also placed on good neighbourly relations and regional cooperation, which are so sensitive in the region.

[16] European Council, Conclusions of the Presidency, Copenhagen, 21–22.6.1993, para. 7(A)(iii).

[17] E.g. European Council, Conclusions, 1–2.3.2012, para. 39: 'The European Council endorses the Council conclusions of 28 February 2012 on Enlargement and the Stabilisation and Association Process, and agrees to grant Serbia the status of candidate country.'

[18] E.g. European Council, Conclusions, 26.3.2020, endorsing the Council Conclusions from the day before (25.3.2020, paras. 6, 10), in which it was decided to open accession negotiations with North Macedonia and Albania.

the set of rules of EU law that are in place pre-enlargement (the EU acquis), which that country ought in principle be ready to comply with by the time of accession.[19]

The final accession agreement is concluded, after a positive decision on the request of accession by the Council (acting by unanimity) and, in practice, with endorsement from the European Council, between all Member States in addition to the State concerned. The agreement is submitted to ratification in accordance with the respective constitutional requirements in each of these States.[20] It modifies primary law and has the same legal value as the EU Treaties. It adds a Member State to the text of the EU Treaties and incorporates all adjustments deemed necessary to make this possible – for instance, updating the rules on the composition of EU institutions. This may include transition periods when certain provisions of EU law do not apply, financial arrangements, and/or specific monitoring mechanisms.[21]

There is no specific time frame, or promise of a positive outcome, for any of the stages described previously. In February 2022, five countries have been granted the status of 'candidate country'. The negotiations have now actually started, and are ongoing, with four countries from the Western Balkans: Montenegro, Serbia, Albania and North Macedonia.[22] As noted already, negotiations with Turkey did start, but have stalled. Two more countries have been given the prospect of membership and are thus 'potential candidates': Bosnia and Herzegovina applied for accession in 2016 and has been supported by the EU in its process through a Stabilisation and Association Agreement since 2015; such an agreement has also been in place with Kosovo since 2016, although it is without prejudice to positions on the status on Kosovo's declaration of independence. Stabilisation and Association Agreements, together with financial support, are one of the many tools that the EU deploys to grant pre-accession assistance.[23]

EU institutions adopted a new political approach to the accession process in 2020.[24] In relation to potential future enlargement to the Western Balkans, emphasis will be placed, among other things, on better dealing with structural weaknesses in candidate countries, in particular in relation to the rule of law,[25] as well as to tackling malign third country influence.[26] The EU has signalled that negotiations could be put on hold (in certain areas), chapters could be reopened or reset if issues need to be reassessed; EU support through funding could be adjusted downward, with the exception of support to civil society; benefits of closer integration (e.g. unilateral concessions for market access) could

[19] There are thirty-five chapters to be covered, ranging from free movement of goods to financial, budgetary and institutional questions.

[20] Art. 49, para. 2 TEU. [21] See Chapter 1, Section 1.4.3 and Chapter 4, Section 4.3.2.1.

[22] Albania (applied for accession in 2009, and the decision to open negotiations was made in March 2020), North Macedonia (applied 2005, decision to open negotiations 2020), Montenegro (applied 2008, decision to open negotiations 2012), Serbia (applied 2009, decision to open negotiations 2014).

[23] See also 'Regulation (EU) 2021/1529 of the European Parliament and of the Council of 15 September 2021 Establishing the Instrument for Pre-accession Assistance (IPA III)', OJ L 330, 20.9.2021, pp. 1–26.

[24] Commission, Communication, 'Enhancing the Accession Process: A Credible EU Perspective for the Western Balkans', COM(2020) 57 final, 5.2.2020. This has been endorsed by the Council (Conclusions, 25.3.2020, para. 3) and by the European Council (Conclusions, 26.3.2020).

[25] This is related to concerns with the rule of law in Member States joining later; see Chapter 4, Section 4.3.2.

[26] Commission, Communication, 'Enhancing the Accession Process: A Credible EU Perspective for the Western Balkans', COM(2020) 57 final, 5.2.2020, pp. 1–2.

be paused or withdrawn.[27] Predictability and credibility, which are very important for applicant States where the prospect of accession to the EU may have considerable political importance, will also receive attention.

2.1.3 Withdrawal

As is apparent from Article 49 TEU on accession, the EU is composed of States which have freely and voluntarily committed themselves. As a counterpart, Article 50 TEU ensures the possibility for a Member State to withdraw its membership voluntarily and unilaterally.[28] Until the Treaty of Lisbon, there was no formal possibility set out in the EU Treaties for a Member State to do so. Today, the process of withdrawal is organised by Article 50 TEU. The UK, which had acceded in 1973, is the only State to date that has made use of such a procedure and indeed exited the EU on 31 January 2020 (Brexit).[29] This followed a referendum in which 51.9 per cent of UK voters (with a turnout of 72.2 per cent of the population) voted in favour of leaving the EU.[30]

In accordance with Article 50 TEU, any Member State may decide to withdraw in accordance with its own constitutional requirements.[31] It shall notify the European Council of its intention – as was done by Theresa May, then UK Prime Minister, on 29 March 2017. In response, the European Council, meeting in the absence of the representative of the State having decided to withdraw (so-called Article 50 format),[32] issues negotiation guidelines with a view to concluding an agreement on the arrangements for withdrawal.[33] The agreement shall be negotiated in accordance with the ordinary procedure for the negotiation of international agreements between the EU and third States.[34] Indeed, the Council asked the Commission to conduct the negotiations with the UK.[35] The Commission nominated the French politician Michel Barnier as Chief Negotiator.[36] This allowed the EU to present a united front in the negotiations.

[27] Ibid., p. 6. [28] C-621/18, *Wightman*, EU:C:2018:999, paras. 63, 58.

[29] Note that part of a Member State, Greenland, withdrew in 1985 due to a change in its internal status in Denmark, and after a related referendum. See Treaty Amending, with Regard to Greenland, the Treaties establishing the European Communities, OJ L 29, 1.2.1985, pp. 1–7; and today, Protocol 34 annexed to the EU Treaties on Special Arrangements for Greenland. Special arrangements were indeed found on fisheries. Greenland has the status of 'Overseas Country and Territory' under EU law and benefits from financial aid to support 'close and lasting links' with the EU as foreseen in the Treaty on Greenland.

[30] The referendum took place on 25 June 2016. The results showed stark differences between rural (trend in favour of 'leave') and urban (trend in favour of 'remain') areas, as well as between devolved entities: with results overall in favour of remaining particularly in Scotland and Northern Ireland.

[31] Similarly, the Member State that has notified its intention to withdraw can revoke that notification unilaterally, for as long as a withdrawal agreement between that Member State and the EU has not entered into force or, if no such agreement has been concluded, for as long as the two-year period laid down in Art. 50(3) TEU, possibly extended in accordance with that paragraph, has not expired. See C-621/18, *Wightman*, EU:C:2018:999, para. 69.

[32] Art. 50(4) TEU.

[33] E.g. European Council, Art. 50, Guidelines Following the United Kingdom's notification under Article 50 TEU, 29.4.2017.

[34] As set out in Art. 218(3) TFEU; see further Chapter 3, Section 3.6.2.1.

[35] Council, Directives for the negotiation of an agreement with the United Kingdom of Great Britain and Northern Ireland setting out the arrangements for its withdrawal from the European Union, 22.5.2017.

[36] The Commission decision was welcomed by the Heads of State or Government of twenty-seven Member States, as well as the Presidents of the European Council and the Commission, Brussels, 15.12.2016.

Such a 'withdrawal agreement' is concluded between the EU and the departing State by the Council (acting by qualified majority),[37] after obtaining the consent of the Parliament.[38] It is furthermore subject to ratification in accordance with national constitutional requirements on the side of the departing State. Importantly, the negotiations on withdrawal shall 'tak[e] account of the framework for its future relationship with the Union'.[39] The intention is indeed to ensure an orderly withdrawal, as well as to lay the ground for a sound future relationship; yet each of the two steps are addressed separately, one after the other. The terms of the withdrawal thus have to be agreed upon without yet knowing the details of the formal new relationship. For that reason, the Withdrawal Agreement concluded with the UK was accompanied by a *political* declaration setting out the framework for the future relationship.[40] In political terms, the European Council also required agreement on a number of key important points concerning the Withdrawal Agreement[41] *before* the EU would agree to discuss the framework of the future relationship with the UK.[42] In practice, the Withdrawal Agreement, as well as the political declaration, with the UK were ultimately endorsed and approved by the European Council, thus signalling support at the highest political level on the texts.[43]

The EU Treaties shall cease to apply to the State in question from the date of entry into force of the withdrawal agreement. However, it is foreseen that the negotiations on the withdrawal agreement, or its process of ratification, may stall. If that is the case, the EU Treaties shall cease to apply to the departing State two years after the notification to the European Council of its intention to withdraw (so-called 'no deal' scenario).[44] This deadline for negotiating the withdrawal agreement is softened by the possibility for the European Council to unanimously decide to extend the two-year period, which occurred three times during the Brexit process.[45]

[37] As the European Council, the Council gathers here in the absence of the representative of the State having decided to withdraw (Art. 50(4) TEU). The method to calculate the qualified majority is adjusted accordingly; see Art. 238(3)(b) TFEU; see also Chapter 2, Section 2.3.4.4, Qualified Majority Voting.

[38] The Parliament was thus kept informed, closely followed, and shared its views during the negotiation process through its Brexit Steering Group, coordinated and chaired by Guy Verhofstadt.

[39] Art. 50(2) TEU.

[40] 'Political Declaration Setting Out the Framework for the Future Relationship between the European Union and the United Kingdom 2020/C 34/01', OJ C 34, 31.1.2020, pp. 1–16.

[41] The priorities on the EU side were: (1) to guarantee the rights of citizens affected by withdrawal; (2) to ensure that each side respects the financial obligations resulting from the whole period of the UK membership in the Union; and (3) to find a solution to avoid a hard border on the island of Ireland (between Northern Ireland which is UK territory, and the State of Ireland which remains in the EU), while respecting the integrity of the EU legal order.

[42] European Council, Art. 50, Guidelines Following the United Kingdom's notification under Article 50 TEU, 29.4.2017, paras. 4–6.

[43] European Council. Art. 50, Conclusions, 25.11.2018.

[44] In the context of Brexit, the Commission consistently stressed that 'a withdrawal without an agreement will cause significant disruption both in the United Kingdom and in the EU27' and thus put forward contingency measures. Commission, Communication, 'Finalising Preparations for the Withdrawal of the United Kingdom from the European Union on 1 November 2019', COM(2019) 394 final, 4.9.2019, p. 1.

[45] Art. 50(3) TEU. Extensions were granted by European Council, Art. 50, Conclusions, 21.3.2019, 10.4.2019 and 29.10.2019. The UK requested extensions after the House of Commons repeatedly refused to give its support to the draft agreement on withdrawal. The Supreme Court of the UK had indeed ruled in *R (Miller)* v. *Secretary of State for Exiting the EU*, 24.1.2017, [2017] UKSC 5, that withdrawal from the EU was impermissible without prior Parliamentary approval domestically. In contrast, the devolved legislatures were said not to have a veto on the UK's decision to withdraw from the EU.

The withdrawal agreement allows the departing State to be disentangled from the EU legal system, but it may also include the maintenance of selected legal mechanisms.[46] As for accession agreements (although in the other direction), disentanglement has institutional and financial implications, and may include – as was indeed the case for the UK[47] – a transition period. The withdrawal agreement may also seek to protect certain interests and rights post-withdrawal, as the EU–UK Withdrawal Agreement does for affected EU and UK citizens, and the unique situation of the territory of Northern Ireland.[48] Once the State concerned has withdrawn, it becomes a third State with which the EU may conclude external agreements, as indeed is already the case with the UK.[49] Should that State wish to rejoin the EU, it shall make use of the standard procedure for accession set out in Article 49 TEU.[50]

2.2 EU CITIZENS

EU citizens feature prominently in EU law: they give purpose to the process of European integration which is intended to promote the well-being of its peoples, and grants them directly enforceable rights.[51] They also serve as a source of institutional legitimacy.[52] The status of 'citizen of the Union' is granted to every national of a Member State; it is thus additional to, but does not replace, national citizenship.[53] While this area of EU law is often examined primarily through the lens of the substantive rights attached to the status of EU citizens, the main focus here is on the link between national and EU citizenship, and the institutional design of the EU.

2.2.1 Institutional Role of Citizens and National Parliaments

EU citizens, as nationals of the Member States, may support changes to the EU Treaties,[54] as well as other major developments at the EU level through the attention the Treaties pay to

[46] For instance, the Withdrawal Agreement with the UK provides for the continuation of a certain role for the Court of Justice of the European Union (preliminary questions from UK courts on Part Two of the Agreement on Citizens' Rights) in the first eight years after the end of the transition period: 'Agreement on the Withdrawal of the United Kingdom of Great Britain and Northern Ireland from the European Union and the European Atomic Energy Community', OJ L 29, 31.1.2020, Art. 158.

[47] The transition ran from 31.1.2020, i.e. from the date of withdrawal, up to 31.12.2020 (the possibility of extension for up to two years was not used). During that time, EU law continued to apply to the UK (with some exceptions) and the UK continued to be bound under the jurisdiction of the Court of Justice of the European Union. Yet the UK had no institutional representation and no role in decision-making.

[48] See further M. Kellerbauer, E. Dumitriu-Segnana and T. Liefländer, *The UK–EU Withdrawal Agreement: A Commentary* (Oxford University Press, 2021).

[49] See Chapter 1, Section 1.2.2. [50] Art. 50(5) TEU. [51] See Chapter 4, Section 4.1.

[52] Art. 3(1) TEU; Art. 10(2), subpara. 2 TEU.

[53] Art. 9 TEU and Art. 20(1) TFEU, inserted into the EU Treaties by the Maastricht Treaty. Before that, reference was made to the citizens of the Member States. It is 'for each Member State, having due regard to [EU] law, to lay down the conditions for the acquisition and loss of nationality' (C-369/90, *Micheletti*, EU:C:1992:295, para. 10). See however, on loss – or renunciation – of nationality of a Member State and link with EU citizenship, C-135/08, *Rottmann*, EU:C:2010:104, paras. 42, 48; C-221/17, *Tjebbes*, paras. 41, 45; C-118/20, *Wiener Landesregierung (revocation of an assurance of naturalisation)*, EU:C:2022:34, paras. 43, 58.

[54] See Art. 48 (on Treaty revision procedures), Art. 49, para. 2 TEU (on accession/enlargement), Art. 50(1) TEU (on withdrawal).

such changes being carried out in line with respective constitutional requirements.[55] The latter may indeed include a referendum, or various degrees of national parliamentary scrutiny. To that effect, national parliaments must be informed in case important Treaty reform, or accession by a new State, is foreseen.[56]

EU citizens are also represented in the functioning of EU institutions, as emphasised by a specific title of the TEU on 'Provisions on Democratic Principles'. The functioning of the EU is founded on 'representative democracy'.[57] The latter principle is given effect in the design of EU institutions in two complementary ways. Firstly, citizens are represented directly in the European Parliament.[58] Second, citizens are given a voice by the representatives of their States either at the highest level (Heads of States or Governments) in the European Council or at ministerial level in the Council. In the Member States, these State representatives are indeed accountable either to their national parliaments or directly to their citizens.[59]

National parliaments, which represent nationals of the Member State and thus EU citizens, also contribute to the democratic legitimacy of the daily work of EU institutions. National parliaments are expected to contribute actively to the proper functioning of the EU.[60] They are kept informed of the work of EU institutions. National parliaments ought to receive all Commission consultation documents, as well as the annual legislative programme and any other instrument of legislative planning or policy.[61] This enables an ongoing political dialogue with the Commission, whereby national parliaments may share views on the documents it issues.[62] In particular, they receive all draft legislative acts. This allows them to control compliance with the principle of subsidiarity, which they have at least eight weeks to do by examining draft legislative acts from the moment they receive them.[63]

National parliaments also receive a broader range of related documents, such as the minutes of meetings of the Council deliberating on draft legislative acts, allowing them to follow the work of governmental representatives of their State deliberating on the said acts.[64] In practice though, much of the work of the Council does not relate to such legislative acts, and/or the preparatory work of the Council is conducted behind closed doors. These limits to transparency are the subject matter of continuous criticisms in so far as they hinder the ability of national parliaments to perform their monitoring functions.[65] Furthermore, national parliaments have an enhanced role in monitoring the implementation of EU

[55] Examples include the EU's accession to the ECHR (Art. 218(8), subpara. 2 TFEU) and the adoption of the decision on the EU's own resources (Art. 311, para. 3).

[56] Arts. 48(2), subpara. 1, 49, para. 1 TEU. [57] Art. 10(1) TEU. [58] Art. 10(2), subpara. 1 TEU.

[59] Art. 10(2), subpara. 2 TEU.

[60] Art. 12 TEU; see further Protocol 1 on the role of national parliaments in the European Union.

[61] Protocol 1, Art. 1.

[62] One may observe the functioning of the political dialogue on the European Commission website: 'National Parliament opinions and Commission replies', https://ec.europa.eu/dgs/secretariat_general/relations/relations_other/npo/index_en.htm. See also Commission, 'Annual Report 2020 on the Application of the Principles of Subsidiarity and Proportionality and on Relations with National Parliaments', COM(2021) 417 final, 23.7.2021.

[63] See Chapter 3, Section 3.4.1.

[64] Protocol 1, Art. 5. See further E. Griglio, 'Divided Accountability of the Council and the European Council: The Challenge of Collective Parliamentary Oversight', in D. Fromage and A. Herranz-Surrallés, *Executive-Legislative (Im)balance in the European Union* (Hart, 2020), pp. 51–66.

[65] See Chapter 2, Section 2.3.4.4, Meetings, Votes and Transparency.

policies related to the AFSJ, which relates to migration, asylum, judicial cooperation in civil and criminal matters and police cooperation.[66]

It is expected that national parliaments, as well as the European Parliament, engage in 'effective and regular' interparliamentary cooperation.[67] This is done in a variety of instances,[68] such as committees discussing sectoral developments in relation to the CFSP and the Common Security and Defense Policy,[69] or stability, economic coordination and governance.[70] The Conference of Parliamentary Committees for Union Affairs (COSAC) has a more horizontal and yet more formal mandate.[71] The agenda of COSAC is adjusted to follow the working programme of the Council, the Parliament and the Commission, to which it may submit non-binding contributions. Furthermore, the Conference of Speakers, made up of the Speakers of the national parliaments and the President of the European Parliament, oversees the coordination of interparliamentary EU activities.[72]

2.2.2 Political and Administrative Rights

As noted already, the functioning of the EU is founded on 'representative democracy'.[73] For the various components of the democratic process to function properly, and for citizens and their representatives to be able to actively engage with EU organs, decisions must be taken as openly as possible to citizens.[74] This requires giving citizens, as well as representative associations and civil society, the opportunity to communicate with EU institutions. The Commission, in particular, ought to broadly consult the public to ensure coherence and transparency in the actions of the EU.[75]

EU citizens have a number of specific political rights, enabling them to contribute to the democratic process at EU level. First and foremost, the EU shall observe the principle of equality of its citizens, who shall receive equal attention from EU institutions, bodies, offices and agencies of the EU (EU organs).[76] EU citizens may vote and stand both in elections to the European Parliament and in municipal elections in the Member State of residence.[77] They have a right of petition to the European Parliament. This enables them to

66 Arts. 70 (on all policies in the field), 85 (on Eurojust) and 88 (on Europol) TFEU. See, for instance, the specialised Joint Parliamentary Scrutiny Group created to scrutinise Europol's activities ('Regulation (EU) 2016/794 of the European Parliament and of the Council of 11 May 2016 on the European Union Agency for Law Enforcement Cooperation Europol', OJ L 135, 24.5.2016, p. 53, Art. 51).

67 Art. 12(f) TEU and Protocol 1, Art. 9; see also Protocol 1, Art. 10.

68 Conference of the Speakers of the European Union Parliaments, Guidelines for Inter-Parliamentary Cooperation in the European Union, Stockholm, 15.5.2010. The various activities can be followed on the specifically dedicated open-access online platform for EU Interparliamentary Exchange: ipex.eu.

69 The committee has its own rules of procedures, Rome, 5–7.11.2014.

70 Also with its own rules of procedures, Luxembourg, 10.11.2015.

71 Protocol 1 annexed to the EU Treaties, Art. 10; 'Rules of Procedure of the Conference of Parliamentary Committees for Union Affairs of Parliaments of the European Union', OJ C 229, 4.8.2011, p. 1.

72 Conference of the Speakers of the European Union Parliaments, Guidelines for the Conference of Speakers of EU Parliaments, Stockholm, 15.5.2010.

73 Art. 10(1) TEU. 74 Art. 10(3) TEU. 75 Art. 11 TEU. 76 Art. 9 TEU; Art. 20 CFEU.

77 Art. 20(2)(b) TFEU; Arts. 39–40 CFEU. See further Chapter 2, Section 2.3.2.2, on elections to the Parliament. For municipal elections, see Art. 22 TFEU; 'Council Directive 94/80/EC of 19 December 1994 Laying Down Detailed Arrangements for the Exercise of the Right to Vote and to Stand as a Candidate in Municipal Elections by Citizens of the Union Residing in a Member State of which they Are not Nationals', last consolidated version: OJ L 368, 31.12.1994, p. 38; Commission, 'Proposal for a Directive Laying Down Detailed Arrangements for the Exercise of the Right to Vote and to Stand as a Candidate in Municipal

put forward a request, a complaint or an observation concerning EU law.[78] They also have a right to apply to the European Ombudsman, thereby raising a complaint about the more specific issue of maladministration by an EU organ.[79] EU citizens furthermore enjoy the protection of the diplomatic and consular authorities of any Member State if theirs is not represented in a third country.[80]

Importantly, EU citizens are entitled to address, and to receive an answer from, EU institutions and advisory bodies in any official language of the EU.[81] The EU Treaties shall be translated into all official languages of the EU, and may be translated into any other languages determined by a Member State to enjoy official status.[82] These languages are also the working languages of the institutions of the EU.[83] There are twenty-four official languages.[84] While certain languages, such as French, Dutch or German, are common to several countries, others are only official languages in a single Member State, and certain Member States make use of several official EU languages – for instance, English and Irish in Ireland. Documents of general application are drafted in each of these official languages and published in the Official Journal of the EU (available freely online).[85] This allows all of us to easily check all key legal instruments in one of those twenty-four languages.

On a related note, EU citizens have a right of access to documents of EU organs, regardless of their form.[86] This right is not unlimited, as it may be restricted to administrative tasks in certain EU institutions, such as the Court of Justice of the European Union, as well as on grounds of public or private interest. Nevertheless, each EU organ must set out rules of procedure on access to documents to enhance transparency.[87] EU citizens also have a right to good administration.[88] EU organs are to handle the affairs of an EU citizen impartially, fairly and within a reasonable time. The right to good administration includes, in relation to individual measures, a right to be heard, to have access to his or her file and to be given reasons for a decision. It also includes the right to have the EU make good any

Elections by Union Citizens Residing in a Member State of which They Are Not Nationals' (recast), COM (2021)733 final, 25.11.2021.

78 Arts. 20(2)(d), 227 TFEU; Art. 44 CFEU. 79 Art. 20(2)(d) TFEU; Art. 43 CFEU.

80 Art. 20(2)(c) TFEU; Art. 46 CFEU. See further Art. 23 TFEU; 'Council Directive (EU) 2015/637 of 20 April 2015 on the Coordination and Cooperation Measures to Facilitate Consular Protection for Unrepresented Citizens of the Union in Third Countries', OJ L 106, 24.4.2015, p. 1.

81 Art. 20(2)(d) TFEU; Art. 41(4) CFEU. 82 Art. 55 TEU; Art. 358 TFEU.

83 'Regulation No. 1/58 Determining the Languages to Be Used by the European Economic Community', OJ 17, 6.10.1958, p. 385 (last amended 2013), Art. 1.

84 All are equally authentic: Bulgarian, Croatian, Czech, Danish, Dutch, English, Estonian, Finnish, French, German, Greek, Hungarian, Irish, Italian, Latvian, Lithuanian, Maltese, Polish, Portuguese, Romanian, Slovak, Slovenian, Spanish and Swedish.

85 'Regulation No. 1/58 Determining the Languages to Be Used by the European Economic Community', OJ 17, 6.10.1958 (last amended 2013), Arts. 3–4. See eur-lex.europa.eu.

86 Art. 15(3) TFEU; Art. 42 CFEU. See further 'Regulation (EC) No 1049/2001 of the European Parliament and of the Council of 30 May 2001 Regarding Public Access to European Parliament, Council and Commission Documents', OJ L 145, 31.5.2001, p. 43. For a synthetic overview see M. Klamert, 'Commentary on Art. 41 CFEU', in M. Kellerbauer, M. Klamert and J. Tomkin (eds.), *The EU Treaties and the Charter of Fundamental Rights: A Commentary* (Oxford University Press, 2019), pp. 397–404.

87 See, for instance, Chapter 2, Section 2.3.4.4, Meetings, Votes and Transparency.

88 Art. 41 CFEU; see further 'Explanations Relating to the Charter of Fundamental Rights', OJ C 303, 14.12.2007, p. 17, on the right to good administration; and European Ombudsman, *The European Code of Good Administrative Behaviour*, 1.3.2002. For a synthetic overview, see T. Lock, 'Commentary on Art. 41 CFEU', in Kellerbauer et al. (eds.), *The EU Treaties and the Charter of Fundamental Rights*, pp. 2204–2207.

damage it caused.[89] Some of the rights of EU citizens, such as the right to access EU documents and the right to good administration, can also benefit persons based in the EU who are not EU citizens.[90] The rights that bring individuals closer to active political participation in EU democratic processes, however, are specific to EU citizens.

Such an example results from the Treaty of Lisbon and relates to the possibility, enshrined in Article 11(4) TEU,[91] for a group of EU citizens to invite the Commission to propose the adoption of a legal act. This 'European citizens' initiative' must fulfil certain conditions in order to be registered. Firstly, the initiative must relate to something that the Commission is legally able to follow up on. For that purpose, the initiative must not be 'manifestly': (a) outside the framework of the Commission's powers to submit a proposal for a legal act of the EU for the purpose of implementing the Treaties;[92] (b) abusive, frivolous or vexatious; or (c) contrary to the values set out in Article 2 TEU and the rights enshrined in the CFEU.[93] Second, it must be supported by no less than one million EU citizens, coming from at least a quarter of the Member States (currently seven), and in each of them the number of signatories must be significant.[94]

If the initiative fulfils the first set of conditions – which is not always obvious – it can be registered and open to collection of statements of support. If it attracts enough support, in line with the second set of conditions, it can actually be submitted.[95] The group of organisers will then be invited to explain the initiatives to the Commission, as well as to present it at a public hearing before the Parliament.[96] The addressee of the initiative is the Commission, which is 'invited' to act, and thus not bound to follow up in any specific way. This nuance is intended to protect the power of initiative of the Commission, at the risk of disappointing citizens. Yet the Commission will communicate its conclusions on the initiative, the action it intends to take, if any, and its reasons for taking or not taking action.[97]

In practice, while the European citizen's initiative may prove useful to mobilise a group of citizens around a given topic and with a pan-European dynamic, it has so far proven

[89] See also Art. 340 TFEU; and Chapter 4, Sections 4.1.3.3 and 4.3.1.4.

[90] Also, the right to refer a case to the European Ombudsman or the right to petition the Parliament are broadly formulated (Arts. 43–44 CFEU).

[91] See also Art. 24 TFEU; 'Regulation (EU) 2019/788 of the European Parliament and of the Council of 17 April 2019 on the European Citizens' Initiative', OJ L 130, 17.5.2019 (last consolidated 2020), p. 55.

[92] This may include a proposal for the Commission to recommend that the Council cancel the negotiating mandate for the Transatlantic Trade and Investment Partnership and not conclude the Comprehensive Economic and Trade Agreement, as the latter seeks to modify the EU legal order: T-754/14, *Efler and others* v. *Commission*, EU:T:2017:323, paras. 37, 41.

[93] Art. 11(4), subpara. 1 TEU; 'Regulation (EU) 2019/788 of the European Parliament and of the Council of 17 April 2019 on the European Citizens' Initiative', OJ L 130, 17.5.2019 (last consolidated 2020), Art. 6(3)(c)–(d).

[94] 'Regulation (EU) 2019/788 of the European Parliament and of the Council of 17 April 2019 on the European Citizens' Initiative', OJ L 130, 17.5.2019 (last consolidated 2020), Art. 3. Minimum thresholds of signatories per Member State are set out in Annex I. These numbers correspond to the number of the Members of the European Parliament elected in each Member State, multiplied by the total number of Members of the European Parliament at the time of registration of the initiative.

[95] Ibid., Arts. 12–13. [96] Ibid., Arts. 14–15.

[97] Art. 11(4), subpara. 1 TEU; 'Regulation (EU) 2019/788 of the European Parliament and of the Council of 17 April 2019 on the European Citizens' Initiative', OJ L 130, 17.5.2019 (last consolidated 2020), Art. 15(2). See further C-418/18 P, *Puppinck and others* v. *Commission*, EU:C:2019:1113, paras. 57–71; A. Karatzia, 'The European Citizens' Initiative and the EU Institutional Balance: On Realism and the Possibilities of Affecting EU Law-Making', *Common Market Law Review*, 54 (2017), pp. 177–208.

difficult to make use of it for the purpose of triggering legal change. Six initiatives have reached the requisite number of signatures and have been submitted to the Commission.[98]

The Commission has responded, for instance by proposing amendments to the Directive on the quality of water intended for human consumption.[99] Nevertheless these results remain very modest. Difficulties have been manifold: lack of public awareness of the mechanism, administrative and technical challenges with collecting signatures, challenges against the Commission's assessment – often deemed too rigid – of whether initiatives are actually legally feasible in accordance with the first condition set out previously. Recent case law of the Court of Justice of the European Union stressing the link between the mechanism and the democratic life of the EU, in conjunction with reforms of the procedure, have aimed at tackling these weaknesses.[100] The Commission must state sufficient reasons to explain any decision to refuse to register a proposed initiative. The Commission will further guide those interested: online tools and contact points are being developed; there is now a possibility for those initiating the process to introduce certain amendments, and/or for the Commission to only accept the part for which it has powers to follow up.

2.2.3 Right to Non-discrimination and Free Movement

The notion of EU citizenship introduced by the Treaty of Maastricht, thus going beyond the coexistence of various nationalities, can be seen as a step towards better connecting the European integration process to citizens. Entire sections of the TFEU, as well as of the CFEU, are devoted to EU citizenship.[101] These go beyond granting the political and administrative rights already mentioned: central to the rights of EU citizens are the prohibition of discrimination on grounds of nationality,[102] and the right to move and reside freely within the territory of the Member States.[103] While a detailed study of these rights would go beyond the scope of this book, the main characteristics of this legal framework ought to be outlined briefly. EU citizenship and the related rights are often perceived to epitomise the advanced stage of the process of European integration.

EU legislation asserts that EU citizenship 'should be the fundamental status of nationals of the Member States when they exercise their right of free movement and residence'.[104] In the view of the Court of Justice, EU citizenship is 'destined to be the fundamental status of

[98] These initiatives are: Right2Water (on water as a public good), One of Us (on protecting human embryos), Stop Vivisection, Ban Glyphosate, Minority SafePack (for diversity in Europe) and End the Cage Age (on the welfare of farm animals).

[99] 'Directive (EU) 2020/2184 of the European Parliament and of the Council of 16 December 2020 on the Quality of Water Intended for Human Consumption' (recast), OJ L 435, 23.12.2020, p. 1; see, for instance, Preamble (4).

[100] See, in particular, C-589/15 P, *Anagnostakis*, EU:C:2017:663, paras. 24, 28. The latest version of 'Regulation (EU) 2019/788 of the European Parliament and of the Council of 17 April 2019 on the European Citizens' Initiative', OJ L 130, 17.5.2019 (last consolidated 2020) on the European citizens' initiative is mentioned in Chapter 2, note 91. See further N. Athanasiadou, 'The European Citizens' Initiative in Times of Brexit', *European Papers*, 3(2018), pp. 1379–1390.

[101] Part II TFEU; Title V CFEU. [102] Art. 18, para. 1 TFEU; Art. 21(2) CFEU.

[103] Arts. 20(2)(a), 21(1) TFEU; Art. 45 CFEU.

[104] 'Directive 2004/38 of the European Parliament and of the Council of 29 April 2004 on the Right of Citizens of the Union and their Family Members to Move and Reside Freely within the Territory of the Member States Amending Regulation 1612/68 and repealing Directives 64/221, 68/360, 72/194, 73/148, 75/34, 75/35, 90/364, 90/365 and 93/96', OJ L 158, 30.4.2004 (last amended 2011), Preamble (3).

nationals of the Member States, enabling those who find themselves in the same situation to enjoy the same treatment in law irrespective of their nationality'. The extent to which this is actually materialising as far as some would hope for, however, remains subject to debate.[105]

The rights to equal treatment, free movement and residence are important to the shape of the EU legal order, but they are not unlimited. They apply within the scope of application of the Treaties and are subject to the limitations and conditions set out in that primary law, as well as the measures adopted to give it effect.[106] Today, this legal regime is primarily set out in Article 18 TFEU and in the Citizenship Directive that is devoted to the rights of citizens of the EU and their family members.[107] The Directive provides a common framework, complemented by more specific instruments[108] and related case law, to simplify and strengthen the right of free movement and residence of all EU citizens, thus benefiting workers and self-employed persons, as well as students and other economically inactive persons. Importantly, these rights to move and reside freely, including the right to enter Member States, extend to the family of EU citizens[109] – they also cover the right of an EU citizen to return to their State of origin with their family.[110]

Along with the general right to equal treatment enshrined in Article 18 TFEU, the Citizenship Directive sets out a legal regime related to the right for EU citizens and their family members to exit, enter and reside in the territories of Member States. The legal regime starts by providing for an (initial) period of up to three months of unconditional residence in other Member States. After five years of legal residence in one Member State (and where compliance with various conditions has been demonstrated), EU citizens and

[105] C-184/99, *Grzelczyk*, EU:C:2001:458, para. 31. See further Jo Shaw, 'EU Citizenship: Still a Fundamental Status?', in R. Bauböck (ed.), *Debating European Citizenship* (Springer Open, 2018), pp. 1–20.

[106] E.g. Arts. 18, para. 1, and 21(1) TFEU.

[107] 'Directive 2004/38 of the European Parliament and of the Council of 29 April 2004 on the Right of Citizens of the Union and their Family Members to Move and Reside Freely within the Territory of the Member States Amending Regulation 1612/68 and repealing Directives 64/221, 68/360, 72/194, 73/148, 75/34, 75/35, 90/364, 90/365 and 93/96', OJ L 158, 30.4.2004 (last consolidated 2011). See further E. Guild, S. Peers and J. Tomkin, *The EU Citizenship Directive: A Commentary*, 2nd ed. (Oxford University Press, 2019); C. Barnard, *The Substantive Law of the EU: The Four Freedoms*, 6th ed. (Oxford University Press, 2019).

[108] See Part III, Title IV, Chapters 1–3 TFEU on the free movement of persons (workers or those exercising the freedom of establishment or free movement of services); and specific legislative instruments such as 'Regulation (EU) No. 492/2011 of the European Parliament and of the Council of 5 April 2011 on Freedom of Movement for Workers within the Union', OJ L 141, 27.5.2011, p. 1, and 'Regulation (EC) No. 883/2004 of the European Parliament and of the Council of 29 April 2004 on the Coordination of Social Security Systems', OJ L 166, 30.4.2004, p. 1 (both last amended 2019).

[109] As defined in 'Directive 2004/38 of the European Parliament and of the Council of 29 April 2004 on the Right of Citizens of the Union and their Family Members to Move and Reside Freely within the Territory of the Member States Amending Regulation 1612/68 and repealing Directives 64/221, 68/360, 72/194, 73/148, 75/34, 75/35, 90/364, 90/365 and 93/96', OJ L 158, 30.4.2004 (last amended 2011), Art. 2(2). See, for instance, C-673/16, *Coman and Others*, EU:C:2018:385, paras. 28–51. The case relates to an EU citizen who has made use of his freedom of movement to a Member State (host State) other than the Member State of which he is a national (State of origin), and, while there, has created or strengthened a family life with a third-country national of the same sex to whom he is joined by a marriage lawfully concluded in the host State. The Court of Justice ruled that Art. 21(1) TFEU precludes the competent authorities of the State of origin from refusing to grant that third-country national a right of residence in the territory of the State of origin on the ground that the law of the State of origin does not recognise marriage between persons of the same sex. To the extent that the recognition of this marriage is for the *sole* purpose of granting a derived right of residence, the duty under EU law to recognise it does not undermine the institution of marriage in the State of origin, which is defined by national law. See further C-490/20, *Stolichna obshtina, rayon 'Pancharevo'*, EU:C:2021:1008.

[110] C-370/90, *Surinder Singh*, EU:C:1992:296, para. 21.

their family members enjoy an almost unconditional right of permanent residence with full equal treatment rights. In between these two categories, economically active citizens and their family members enjoy an unconditional right of residence and equal treatment. In contrast, for those who are economically inactive and are not family members of an EU citizen from whom they may derive rights, the right of residence is conditional upon having 'sufficient resources for themselves and their family members not to become a burden on the social assistance system of the host Member State', as well as having comprehensive sickness insurance.[111] Students must also have comprehensive sickness insurance and assure the relevant national authority that they have sufficient resources.[112] Restrictions on the right of entry and the right of residence may be justified on grounds of public policy, public security or public health. Such restrictions, however, must be proportionate, as is now hotly debated in relation to restrictions on free movement due to the COVID-19 pandemic.[113]

2.3 INSTITUTIONS

There are currently seven EU institutions which are all identified in Article 13 TEU: Parliament, European Council, Council, Commission, Court of Justice of the European Union, European Central Bank (Central Bank) and Court of Auditors. Before discussing each of them in turn, it is worth outlining the way they are primarily intended to interact, as well as the principles on which the system of checks and balances between them is set up.

2.3.1 A Balanced Institutional Framework

2.3.1.1 Institutional Framework

Painted in very broad strokes, most of the general work of the EU is in the hands of the first 'big five' institutions. The Commission 'shall promote the general interest of the Union and take appropriate initiatives to that end',[114] while the Parliament and the Council jointly

[111] 'Directive 2004/38 of the European Parliament and of the Council of 29 April 2004 on the Right of Citizens of the Union and their Family Members to Move and Reside Freely within the Territory of the Member States Amending Regulation 1612/68 and repealing Directives 64/221, 68/360, 72/194, 73/148, 75/34, 75/35, 90/364, 90/365 and 93/96', OJ L 158, 30.4.2004 (last amended 2011), Art. 7(1)(b). See further C-333/13, *Dano*, para. 78, in which the Court of Justice noted that a Member State must 'have the possibility [. . .] of refusing to grant social benefits to economically inactive Union citizens who exercise their right to freedom of movement solely in order to obtain another Member State's social assistance although they do not have sufficient resources to claim a right of residence'. This can be contrasted with the situation of a mobile EU citizen who, before he became unemployed in the host Member State, had worked there and had sent his children to school there: he and the children have the right of residence based on 'Regulation (EU) No. 492/2011 of the European Parliament and of the Council of 5 April 2011 on Freedom of Movement for Workers within the Union', OJ L 141, 27.5.2011, Art. 10 (see Chapter 2, note 108) and related equal treatment rights. See C-181/19, *Krefeld*, EU:C:2020:794, para. 65 *et seq.*

[112] 'Directive 2004/38 of the European Parliament and of the Council of 29 April 2004 on the Right of Citizens of the Union and Their Family Members to Move and Reside Freely within the Territory of the Member States Amending Regulation 1612/68 and repealing Directives 64/221, 68/360, 72/194, 73/148, 75/34, 75/35, 90/364, 90/365 and 93/96', OJ L 158, 30.4.2004 (last amended 2011), Art. 7(1)(c).

[113] E.g. 'Council Recommendation (EU) 2020/1475 of 13 October 2020 on a Coordinated Approach to the Restriction of Free Movement in Response to the COVID-19 Pandemic', OJ L 337, 14.10.2020, p. 3 (amended multiple times since).

[114] Art. 17(1) TEU.

'exercise legislative and budgetary functions' on the basis of proposals from the Commission.[115] Each of these first three institutions is assisted by advisory organs composed of, on the one hand, representatives of employers, employees and civil society gathered in the Economic and Social Committee, and on the other hand, representatives of the regional and local bodies gathered in the Committee of Regions.[116] A fourth institution, the European Council, provides 'the necessary impetus', defining 'general political directions and priorities'.[117] As for the Court of Justice of the European Union, it ensures that 'in the interpretation and application of the Treaties the law is observed'.[118] The work of the big five is complemented by that of the Central Bank, which applies a sectoral focus on monetary policy,[119] and the Court of Auditors, which audits all revenue and expenditure of EU organs.[120]

The institutions are introduced and elaborated upon in a different order in the EU Treaties, an order that we will follow in this chapter, as it is that chosen by the Member States at the time of drafting the current version of the Treaties. As will be explained subsequently, this order reflects a nuanced and complex quest for a careful balance between diverse sources of legitimacy and functions of the various institutions. This overall institutional framework 'shall aim to promote [the] values [of the EU], advance its objectives, serve its interests, those of its citizens and those of the Member States, and ensure the consistency, effectiveness and continuity of its policies and actions'.[121]

2.3.1.2 Guiding Principles

Article 13 TEU sets out the institutional framework, but also asserts two foundational principles, each of which may be subject to judicial review, as illustrated subsequently. Firstly, each institution shall act within the limits of the powers conferred on it in the Treaties. This is a specific expression of the principle of conferral, to which we will return.[122] Because the EU may only act if it has been given the competence to do so by the EU Treaties, its institutions may only act within the limits of the powers conferred on them. Such limits result, in particular, from specific procedures, conditions for action and objectives further set out in the provisions of the EU Treaties granting competence to the EU, and thus its institutions, to act.

In order to have a complete overview of the respective function of each institution, it is thus necessary, in principle, to be familiar with the details of each provision of the EU Treaties enabling them to act. These provisions specify the existence of an EU competence and the procedure for the exercise of that competence;[123] these may be further informed by complementary legal acts,[124] practices or judicial interpretation. This creates a complex and nuanced prism through which the relationship between the various institutions is understood in terms of the balance of powers between institutions[125] – or institutional balance – with variations in the equilibrium depending on the field of EU action. For instance, in the

[115] Arts. 14(1) and 16(1) TEU. [116] Art. 13(4) TEU; Art. 300 TFEU. [117] Art. 15(1) TEU.
[118] Art. 19(1), subpara. 1 TEU. [119] Art. 282(1) TFEU. [120] Art. 285, para. 1 TFEU. [121] Art. 13(1) TEU.
[122] Art. 4(1) TEU; see also Chapter 3, Section 3.2.1. [123] See Chapter 3, Sections 3.2–3.4.
[124] For instance, the Parliament, the Council and the Commission may conclude between them interinstitutional agreements to 'make arrangements for their cooperation', Art. 295 TFEU.
[125] Case 9/56, *Meroni*, EU:C:1958:7, p. 152.

context of the CFSP of the EU, the balance is in the European Council and the Council's favour; in contrast, the Commission and the Parliament are strongly present alongside the Council in relation to law-making for the functioning of the internal market. The Court of Justice of the European Union is committed to ensuring that legal remedies are available so that the 'fundamental interest in the maintenance and observance of the institutional balance laid down in the Treaties' prevails,[126] and its jurisdiction is limited in relation to the CFSP.[127]

Second, and on a related note, institutions are under a duty to 'practice mutual sincere cooperation'. Even when the respective role of each institution is not specifically set out in applicable provisions of EU law, EU institutions have a duty of good faith towards each other, as well as the EU in general, and the Member States.[128] By way of example, in the field of external relations, the principle requires the Commission – usually acting in negotiations of international agreements on behalf of the EU on a mandate of the Council – to consult the Council beforehand if it intends to express positions on the EU's behalf before an international court.[129]

It may be further noted that EU organs, and EU institutions in particular, are subject to a set of general rules of EU administrative law. These cover a broad range of matters, such as staff regulations, financial management, protection of personal data, access to documents and transparency.[130] We will come back to some of these provisions when discussing the specifics of each EU institution.

2.3.2 The Parliament

2.3.2.1 A Brief Description

The Parliament is an institution that has evolved considerably since its inception. As its change of name, from Assembly in the Treaty establishing the European Coal and Steel Community (1951) to Parliament in the Single European Act (1986), illustrates, it has mutated from an advisory organ composed of national parliamentarians into a fully-fledged institution of the EU. Since the first European elections in 1979 it has been composed of members who directly represent EU citizens.[131] It has gained a set of important

[126] C-70/88, *Parliament* v. *Council (Chernobyl)*, EU:C:1990:217, para. 26. [127] See Chapter 4, Section 4.4.1.
[128] Art. 13(2) and (1), subpara. 1 TEU.
[129] C-73/14, *Council* v. *Commission (International Tribunal for the Law of the Sea)*, EU:C:2015:663, para. 86.
[130] See further Arts. 298 (administrative support) and 335 (legal capacity and administrative autonomy) TFEU; 'Regulation 31/62 Laying Down the Staff Regulations of Officials and the Conditions of Employment of Other Servants of the European Economic Community and the European Atomic Energy Community', OJ P 45, 14.6.1962, p. 1385 (last amended 2014); 'Regulation (EU, Euratom) 2018/1046 of the European Parliament and of the Council of 18 July 2018 on the Financial Rules Applicable to the General Budget of the Union', OJ L 193, 30.7.2018, p. 1 (last amended 2021); 'Regulation (EU) 2018/1725 of the European Parliament and of the Council of 23 October 2018 on the Protection of Natural Persons with Regard to the Processing of Personal Data by the Union Institutions, Bodies, Offices and Agencies and on the Free Movement of such Data', OJ L 295, 21.11.2018, p. 39; 'Regulation (EC) No 1049/2001 of the European Parliament and of the Council of 30 May 2001 Regarding Public Access to European Parliament, Council and Commission Documents', OJ L 145, 31.5.2001, p. 43; 'Interinstitutional Agreement of 20 May 2021 between the European Parliament, the Council of the European Union and the European Commission on a Mandatory Transparency Register', OJ L 207, 11.6.2021, p. 1.
[131] Art. 10(2), subpara. 1 TEU.

decision-making powers – in particular in the exercise of legislative and budgetary functions, together with the Council.

In the latest European elections, in spring 2019, voter turnout for the entire EU was at 50.66 per cent, ranging from a very high participation rate in countries such as Belgium (where voting is mandatory) to very low ones in countries such as Slovakia (22.74 per cent). In past elections, the overall turnout was even lower (42.61 per cent in 2014). Although the rate of participation in the European elections thus remains disappointing, it may be hoped that it is rising as result of greater political attention, and thus natural and healthy political controversies on the directions to be chosen for European integration. The key challenge in such campaigns is for candidates to bridge the gap between national politics and European affairs on sensitive matters such as the stability of the euro, European migration and asylum policy, the need to take joint responsibility for the environment or the rule of law in the Member States. The ability, or inability, to bridge the gap is important not only for the quality and legitimacy of the upcoming legislative output, but also for the appointment of a number of high-level figures in European affairs and other key decisions, as we shall see.

The key features of the Parliament are set out in the Treaty on European Union, more specifically in Article 14 TEU, quoted in Box 2.1 to remind readers of the importance of reading directly from the EU Treaties. That provision is complemented by several others in the TFEU.[132]

Box 2.1 **Rough guide to the Parliament**

Article 14 TEU

1. The European Parliament shall, jointly with the Council, exercise legislative and budgetary functions. It shall exercise functions of political control and consultation as laid down in the Treaties. It shall elect the President of the Commission.

2. The European Parliament shall be composed of representatives of the Union's citizens. They shall not exceed seven hundred and fifty in number, plus the President. Representation of citizens shall be degressively proportional, with a minimum threshold of six members per Member State. No Member State shall be allocated more than ninety-six seats.

The European Council shall adopt by unanimity, on the initiative of the European Parliament and with its consent, a decision establishing the composition of the European Parliament, respecting the principles referred to in the first subparagraph.

3. The members of the European Parliament shall be elected for a term of five years by direct universal suffrage in a free and secret ballot.

4. The European Parliament shall elect its President and its officers from among its members.

[132] Arts. 223–234 TFEU.

2.3.2.2 Elections

Elections to the Parliament take place every five years by direct universal suffrage in a free and secret ballot.[133] EU citizens have the right to vote and stand in these elections in their Member State of residence.[134] The electoral procedure is governed by national law; these elections are thus organised in and by each Member State.[135] Nevertheless, this must be in accordance, at EU level, with the Act concerning the election of the representatives of the Assembly by direct universal suffrage from 1976 as last amended (the Electoral Act).[136] Elections shall be held on the dates and times set by each State, but within the same electoral period, starting on a Thursday morning and ending on the following Sunday.[137] Furthermore, results may not be made public until the close of polling where electors are the last to vote.

The Electoral Act has been amended several times to increase the consistency of the electoral procedure across the EU. It asserts that the diversity of national approaches to the electoral procedure shall not affect the essentially proportional nature of the voting system.[138] Nevertheless the Member States retain an important degree of discretion on a number of points.[139] For instance, Member States may use a list system or the single transferable vote, and they may also authorise voting based on a preferential list system. Each Member State may establish constituencies for elections or subdivide its electoral area in a different manner. States may also set a minimum threshold for the allocation of seats, which, at national level, may not exceed 5 per cent of votes cast.[140] States may also set a ceiling for candidates' campaign expenses.

Updates to the Electoral Law may result from proposals for change by the Parliament itself, if approved by the Council (acting unanimously) and after consulting the Parliament (acting by a majority of its component members).[141] For such a change to enter into force, it has to be approved by the Member States in accordance with their respective constitutional requirements. This is a very loaded legislative procedure with requirements that bring it close to a revision of the EU Treaties. This may explain why the possibility of creating a

[133] Art. 14(3) TEU. Secrecy ought to be ensured even in case of advance voting, postal voting, and electronic and internet voting (Electoral Act, Art. 4(a)).

[134] Art. 20(2)(b) TFEU. Citizens may only vote once; Member States may take the measures necessary to allow those of their citizens residing in third countries to vote in elections to the Parliament, Electoral Act, Arts. 9, 9a. See further 'Council Directive 93/109/EC of 6 December 1993 Laying Down Detailed Arrangements for the Exercise of the Right to Vote and Stand as a Candidate in Elections to the European Parliament for Citizens of the Union Residing in a Member State of which They Are Not Nationals', OJ L 329, 30.12.1993, pp. 34–38; Commission, 'Proposal for a Council Directive Laying Down Detailed Arrangements for the Exercise of the Right to Vote and Stand as a Candidate in Elections to the European Parliament for Union Citizens Residing in a Member State of which They Are Not Nationals' (recast), COM(2021) 732, 25.11.2021.

[135] Election results are those declared by each Member State, C-502/19, *Junqueras*, EU:C:2019:1115, para. 70.

[136] OJ L 278, 8.10.1976, pp. 5–11 (last amended 2018, although the amendment has not yet entered into force, pending approval by the Member States in accordance with their respective constitutional requirements; references to the act herein do not take these amendments into account unless specified; the first elections took place in 1979). The latest amendments were adopted on the basis of Art. 223(1) TFEU.

[137] The electoral period is defined by the Council (voting by unanimity) after consulting the Parliament. See Electoral Act, Arts. 10(1) and 11.

[138] Ibid., Art. 8. [139] Ibid., Arts. 1–4.

[140] As from the entry into force of the 2018 amendment to the Electoral Act, States in which the list system is used *shall* set a minimum threshold (2–5 per cent) for the allocation of seats for constituencies which comprise more than thirty-five seats (Electoral Act, new version of Art. 3(2)).

[141] Art. 223(1) TFEU.

uniform electoral procedure, brushing away the possibilities for divergent approaches identified previously, has so far not been used. Despite these challenges, when taking up the position as President of the Commission, Ursula von der Leyen indicated that 'new rules should be in place well in time for the European elections of 2024'.[142]

2.3.2.3 Composition

The number of persons thereby elected in each Member State to act as Members of the European Parliament (MEPs) is said to be 'degressively proportional'.[143] This is a version of proportional representation (the larger the population of a State, the more representatives it has) that is adjusted to reflect the varying sizes in population of the Member States. As a result of this correction, MEPs from more populous States each represent more citizens than MEPs from less populous States. The number of MEPs per States thus grows more slowly than it should under a strictly proportional system; hence its 'degressive' nature. If instead the system were strictly proportional, the number of MEPs for large States would almost prevent citizens from small States from being represented. For instance, if all seats in the Parliament were to be distributed in accordance with a strict proportionality system, Germany would have close to 140 MEPs, while Malta would hardly have one, out of a total of 751 seats – instead of ninety-six and six, respectively, as things stand currently, as indicated in Figure 2.1.[144]

The basic parameters of degressive proportionality enshrined in Article 14(2) TEU further require a minimum of six MEPs per State (thus in the favour of citizens from small States) and a maximum of ninety-six seats (to the detriment of citizens from large States). The European Council (deciding by unanimity) is to put these principles into practice by adopting, on a proposal by the Parliament and with its consent, a decision on the more specific allocation of seats per State.[145] In practice, such decisions are adopted before each election. As a result, the current allocation of seats of MEPs per Member State is set out in Figure 2.1.

The Treaty demands that the total number of MEPs shall not exceed 750, plus the Parliament's President.[146] In recent years, the allocation of seats has changed to reflect the accession of Croatia (2013)[147] and the withdrawal of the UK from the EU (2020). The total number of MEPs is currently 705. As a result of Brexit, the UK lost its seventy-three

[142] Commission President, Political Guidelines for the Next European Commission 2019–2024, p. 21. One item on the agenda relates to transnational lists that would overcome, at least in part, the division of the European electorate along national constituencies. The concept has supporters, who believe that this could help to create a genuinely European political debate, and also detractors, who fear that Members of the European Parliament thereby elected would be disconnected from the electorate and are concerned about how to reconcile this new approach with the requirement of degressive proportionality.

[143] Art. 14(2) TEU.

[144] These figures are calculated with reference to the size of the population of each of these Member States and the total population of the EU (with twenty-seven States, thus without the UK), as reported by Eurostat as of 1 January 2019.

[145] Art. 14(2), subpara. 2 TEU.

[146] Art. 14(2) TEU. Note that specific transitions had been foreseen until the end of the 2009–2014 parliamentary term, which had started before the entry into force of the Treaty of Lisbon: Declaration of the European Council, Brussels, 11–12.12.2008; Protocol 36 annexed to the EU Treaties, Art. 2.

[147] 'Act Concerning the Conditions of Accession of the Republic of Croatia and the Adjustments to the Treaty on European Union, the Treaty on the Functioning of the European Union and to the Treaty establishing the European Atomic Energy Community', OJ L 112, 24.4.2012, pp. 21–34, Art. 19.

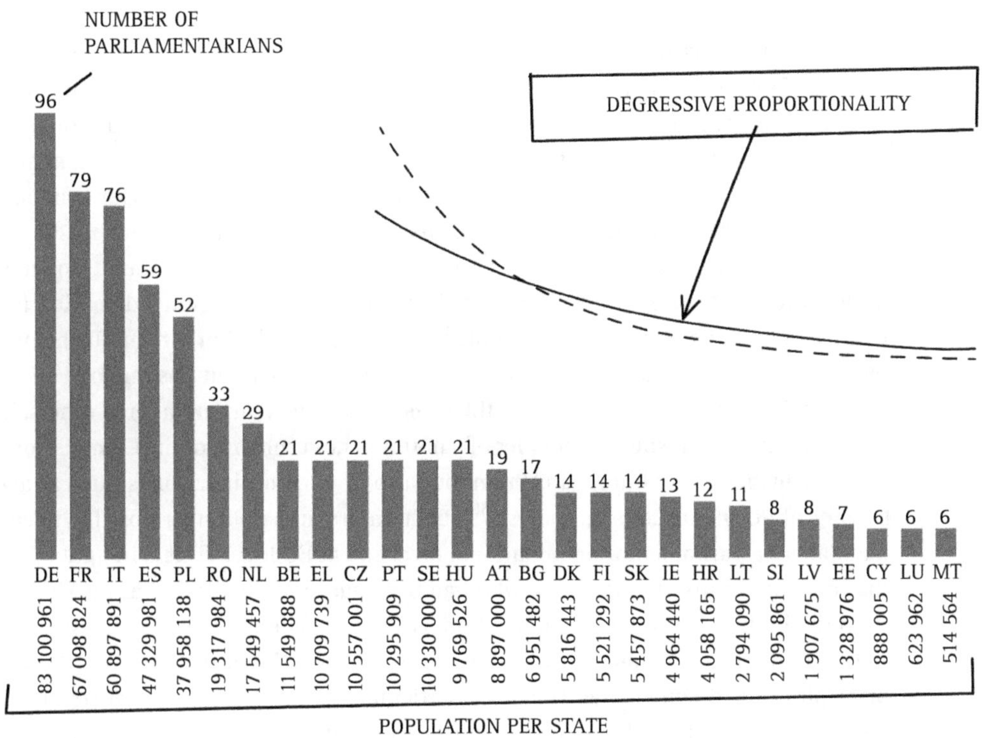

Figure 2.1 Distribution of parliamentary seats per Member State after Brexit[148]

seats in the Parliament: twenty-seven were redistributed to other countries in order to reflect, as closely as possible, the sizes of the respective populations of the Member States (for instance, France and Spain each received 5 extra seats); the remaining 46 seats have been kept in reserve for further enlargement.[149]

2.3.2.4 Members

MEPs vote on an 'individual and personal basis'. They shall not be bound by any instructions,[150] shall not receive a binding mandate[151] and are protected by a set of privileges, in particular to facilitate their free movement to attend professional meetings, and immunities.[152] This set of rights is meant to ensure the full independence of parliamentarians, in the interest of the good functioning of democracy.[153]

Certain immunities are very strongly protected by EU law, such as through protection against inquiry, detention or legal proceedings for opinions expressed in the performance

[148] Based on data from 1.2.2020.

[149] 'European Council Decision (EU) 2018/937 Establishing the Composition of the European Parliament', OJ L 165 I, 2.7.2018, p. 1.

[150] These rules are without prejudice to political discipline within a specific party to ensure coherence in political bargaining games.

[151] Statute of Members, Arts. 2 and 3.

[152] Electoral Law, Art. 6; Art. 343 TFEU; Protocol 7 on the Privileges and Immunities of the European Union, Arts. 7–9.

[153] C-502/19, *Oriol Junqueras Vies*, EU:C:2019:1115, paras. 63, 83.

of parliamentarian duties.[154] Others are less protected. In their own State, MEPs receive the same immunity as members of their national parliament. In the territory of any other Member State than their own, MEPs enjoy immunity from any detention measure and from legal proceedings. Nevertheless, such immunity cannot be claimed if one is found in the act of committing an offence; it may also be waived by the Parliament itself. In interpreting these provisions, the focus will be on protecting the proper functioning and independence of the Parliament.[155] This matter came to the fore after the 2019 elections when the Spanish authorities swiftly requested a waiver of the immunity of the Catalan leader Oriol Junqueras Vies before their placing of him in provisional detention for his role in the Catalan independence movement.[156] In early 2021, the Parliament further waived the immunity of the well-known Catalan leader Carles Puigdemont Casamajó.[157]

On a related note, the function of MEP is incompatible with a number of others, including high-level functions such as member of a national government, of the Commission or of the Court of Justice of the European Union; but also of more ordinary ones, such as active civil servant of EU institutions or bodies.[158] Furthermore, it is no longer possible to cumulate a mandate as a parliamentarian at national level and at EU level.[159] It is in light of these rules that in 2019, Frans Timmermans, who had been successfully elected as an MEP, withdrew from the Parliament to take up a position as Vice-President of the Commission.

The work of MEPs shall be guided by 'mutual respect' and be 'based on the values and principles laid down in the Treaties', particularly in the CFEU. Members shall 'respect Parliament's dignity and shall not harm its reputation'.[160] This is accompanied by a number of instructions on proper behaviour.[161] MEPs are under additional obligations to contribute to the transparency of their financial interests. They shall submit a declaration of financial interests;[162] and they 'should' adopt the systematic practice of only meeting interested representatives (lobbyists) that have registered in the Transparency Register,[163] and publishing online all scheduled meetings with such representatives.[164]

The general conditions concerning the performance of duties of MEPs are specified in accordance with an atypical procedure that emphasises the strong autonomous power of the Parliament in this internal context: the Parliament acts of its own initiative after seeking an opinion from the Commission and consent from the Council.[165] The current version of

[154] Protocol 7 annexed to the EU Treaties, Art. 8. The link with duties must be 'direct and obvious', C-163/10, *Patriciello*, EU:C:2011:543, paras. 33, 35.

[155] C-502/19, *Oriol Junqueras Vies*, EU:C:2019:1115, para. 85. [156] Ibid., para. 91.

[157] European Parliament decision of 9 March 2021 on the request for waiver of the immunity of Carles Puigdemont Casamajó, 2020/2024(IMM). Several related legal proceedings were brought to the attention of the Court of Justice; see, in particular, C-158/21, *Ministerio Fiscal, Abogacía del Estado, Partido político VOX* v. *Carles Puigdemont Casamajó (et al.)*, OJ C 217, 7.6.2021, p. 21 (pending at time of writing).

[158] Electoral Law, Art. 7(1).

[159] Ibid., Art. 7(2). Each Member State may also extend national rules to incompatibility in the context of European elections.

[160] Parliament, 'Rules of Procedure', Rule 10.

[161] E.g. On what may be 'offensive' language in breach of these rules, ibid., Rule 10(4).

[162] Ibid., Annex I: Code of Conduct, Art. 4.

[163] 'Interinstitutional Agreement of 20 May 2021 between the European Parliament, the Council of the European Union and the European Commission on a Mandatory Transparency Register', OJ L 207, 11.6.2021, p. 1.

[164] Parliament, 'Rules of Procedure', Rule 11.

[165] Art. 223(2) TFEU; rules or conditions relating to taxation would require unanimity voting at the Council (instead of qualified majority voting for other aspects).

the Parliament's decision (Statute of Members)[166] makes it clear that Members shall be entitled to an 'appropriate salary to safeguard their independence'.[167] Since the 2009 elections, the amount of that salary is the same for all MEPs.[168] Before that, MEPs were remunerated in accordance with the law of their countries of origin, which created significant discrepancies among members of the same Union institution (e.g. EUR 11,000 for an Italian MEP, EUR 800 for an MEP from Lithuania[169]).

Members are also entitled to reimbursement of expenses incurred in the exercise of their mandate, as well as to paid assistance from personal staff (whom they may freely choose) and use of office facilities, telecommunications equipment and official vehicles under specific conditions.[170] Certain financial benefits may be reduced in case of excessive absence during sessions in which votes take place.[171] OLAF, the Parliament itself and the Court of Justice of the European Union ensure that appropriate use is made of these public resources, as illustrated by the request made by the Parliament to former French MEP Marine Le Pen to recover amounts unduly spent.[172] Parliament's documents shall be translated and speeches shall be interpreted simultaneously into all the official languages.[173]

2.3.2.5 Functioning and Organisation

Political Groups and Non-attached Members

Although MEPs are elected at national level, they organise themselves at European level by political affiliation. Members are encouraged to form themselves into political groups,[174] and in practice most do so due to the importance of these groups in the functioning of the institution, as will be explained subsequently (Section 2.3.2.5, Governing Structure). As can be seen in Figure 2.2, the two main political groups are the Christian Democrats (European People's Party), and the Socialists and Democrats. In the 2019 election, groups of the centre (Renew Europe and the Greens) became more important.

To form a political group, MEPs ought to fulfil certain conditions: there must be MEPs from at least one-quarter of the Member States, a minimum of twenty-three MEPs and a common 'political affinity'.[175] MEPs who do not fulfil the conditions to form a group, or do not want to join or form a group, are known as 'non-attached' Members (*non-inscrits*, as they are commonly known in French). Informal (intergroup) gatherings complement the formal functions of groups to enhance contact between MEPs as well as with civil society.[176]

166 '2005/684/EC, Euratom: Decision of the European Parliament of 28 September 2005 Adopting the Statute for Members of the European Parliament', OJ L 262, 7.10.2005, pp. 1–10.

167 Statute of Members, Art. 9(1).

168 It amounts to 38.5 per cent of the basic salary of a judge at the Court of Justice of the European Union (Statute of Members, Art. 10).

169 J. P. Jacqué, *Droit Institutionnel de l'Union Européenne*, 4th ed. (Dalloz, 2006), p. 257.

170 Statute of Members, Arts. 20–22.

171 'Decision of the Bureau of 19 May and 9 July 2008 Concerning Implementing Measures for the Statute for Members of the European Parliament', OJ C 159, 13.7.2009, p. 1 (last amended 2020), Art. 31.

172 T-161/, *M. Le Pen* v. *Parliament*, EU:T:2018:848, para. 56; Appeal rejected by C-38/19 P, *M. Le Pen* v. *Parliament*, EU:C:2019:952.

173 Parliament, 'Rules of Procedure', Rule 167; Statute of Members, Art. 7.

174 Statute of Members, Art. 8.

175 In forming a group together, 'the Members concerned accept by definition that they have political affinity. Only when this is denied by the Members concerned is it necessary for Parliament to evaluate whether the group has been constituted in accordance with the Rules' (Parliament, 'Rules of Procedure', Rule 33).

176 Ibid., Rule 35.

The political groups largely reflect the internal political dynamics of the institution. Yet votes occasionally align differently, at times illustrating national sensitivities and possibly announcing the split from the group by a national delegation. It has been observed, for instance, that the MEPs from the Hungarian political party Fidesz who were part of the European People's Party until 2021 were increasingly departing from the group's position on votes relating to migration and gender before their departure from that group.[177] Political groups within the Parliament have their own administrative support.[178] They are often flanked externally by political parties at European level. These parties are expected to 'contribute to forming European political awareness' and to structuring the expression of the will of citizens; they receive funding for that purpose.[179]

Each political family has its own internal rules. In the late 2010s and early 2020s, there has been much debate within the European People's Party about adherence to its Statutes by one set of its members from the Hungarian political party Fidesz – the ruling party in that State – which faced serious accusations of being responsible for 'rule of law backsliding'.[180] The adoption, by a majority vote, of the new rules of procedure within the political family ultimately came with a threat to exclude Fidesz.[181] The MEPs from Fidesz anticipated the decision, and notified their intention to leave the group in early 2021. As this example illustrates, membership of political groups is subject to movement. The most useful overall picture from recent years is perhaps that given after the 2019 elections, taking into account the changes that occurred after Brexit, as illustrated in Figure 2.2.

Governing Structure

Membership of a political group allows MEPs to collectively exert more influence in the internal work of the Parliament. This is particularly clear from the Rules of Procedure that the Parliament adopts for its internal organisation.[182] The leader of each political group is represented in the Conference of Presidents, together with the President of the Parliament (Roberta Metsola at time of writing). In contrast, only one non-attached Member may attend the meetings and has no voting rights.[183] The nuance is important, as the Conference of Presidents has key political functions.[184] These include taking decisions on the organisation of the Parliament's work and on matters of legislative planning, being responsible for relations between the Parliament and other organs, as well as with non-member countries, and for structured consultation with civil society. The Conference also makes proposals for the composition and competence of committees in which the daily work of the Parliament takes place, as we shall see subsequently.

[177] See graph, 'Evolution of National Parties: Degree of Alignment with EPP Group' (2015–2020), in VoteWatch, *European Parliament: Current and Future Dynamics*, 21.1.2021.

[178] Parliament, 'Rules of Procedure', Rule 24.

[179] Art. 10(4) TEU; Art. 224 TFEU; see further 'Regulation (EU, Euratom) No. 1141/2014 of the European Parliament and of the Council of 22 October 2014 on the Statute and Funding of European Political Parties and European Political Foundations', OJ L 317, 4.11.2014, p. 1 (last amended 2019). Note the proposal for reform: Commission, 'Proposal for a Regulation on the Statute and Funding of European Political Parties and European Political Foundations' (recast), COM(2021) 734 final, 25.11.2021.

[180] See Chapter 4, Section 4.3.2.1. [181] European People's Party, Statement on Fidesz, 3.3.2021.

[182] Acting by majority of its members, Art. 232 TFEU. [183] Parliament, 'Rules of Procedure', Rule 26.

[184] Ibid., Rule 27.

Political groups, unlike non-attached Members,[185] are also responsible for making proposals to the Bureau[186] that is in charge of the practical internal organisation of the institution.[187] This includes the appointment of a Secretary-General, supported by the General Secretariat to coordinate, organise and support Members in the exercise of their mandates.

The Conference of Presidents and the Bureau are thus the governing bodies of the institution. They act under the direction of the President of the Parliament, elected from among its members for two and a half years (a renewable period) by absolute majority of the votes cast by the MEPs by a secret ballot. The President directs the activities of these bodies as well as of the institution more generally.[188] In particular, the President presides over proceedings and ensures that they are well conducted, including through the control of the admissibility of amendments and decisions on putting matters to the vote. The President also represents the institution, for instance in relations with other organs and on ceremonial occasions; in particular, the President may be heard by the European Council.[189] The President benefits from the support of fourteen Vice-Presidents, who should also be elected while taking account 'of the need to ensure an overall fair representation of political views, as well as gender and geographical balance'.[190] A legal service advises the various entities of the Parliament on legal questions and represents it in legal cases.

Work Allocation: Committees and Plenary

In practice, the work of the Parliament is shared between the various MEPs whose tasks are structured in committee(s) to which they are appointed. It would indeed be unthinkable to have hundreds of MEPs discussing each proposal in detail.

In terms of their composition, these committees can be understood as 'mini versions' of the Parliament. At the beginning of each parliamentary term, the Conference of Presidents agrees procedures 'for reflecting the political diversity of Parliament in the committees'.[191] On the basis of a proposal from the Conference, the Parliament further sets up standing committees.[192] There are thus more than twenty standing committees of varying size,[193] covering a wide range of topics, such as Foreign Affairs (AFET), Economic and Monetary Affairs (ECON) and Civil Liberties, Justice and Home Affairs (LIBE).[194] Additional special or inquiry committees may be added,[195] such as the Special Committee on Beating Cancer. Political groups and non-attached members then appoint their MEPs to each committee. The composition of the committees 'shall, as far as possible, reflect the composition of Parliament'.[196]

The committees are antechambers to the Plenary within the Parliament. Their role is to examine questions referred to them by Parliament at a preliminary stage, and thus before discussion by the Plenary. For work on proposals for legally binding acts, committees are

[185] Proposals to the Bureau may also come from the Secretary-General, appointed by the Bureau and heading the secretariat.

[186] The Bureau consists of the President and the fourteen Vice-Presidents of Parliament (Parliament, 'Rules of Procedure', Rule 24).

[187] Covering matters such as finances, organizational matters, administration, conduct of sittings. See Parliament, 'Rules of Procedure', Rules 25, 234.

[188] Art. 14(4) TEU; Parliament, 'Rules of Procedure', Rules 15, 16, 19, 22. [189] Art. 235(2) TFEU.

[190] Parliament, 'Rules of Procedure', Rule 15(2); see also Rule 17. [191] Ibid., Rule 34(2). [192] Ibid., Rule 206.

[193] Ranging from around twenty-five to eighty members.

[194] Parliament, 'Rules of Procedure', Annex IV: Powers and Responsibilities of Standing Committees. The work of standing committees may be complemented by that of subcommittees (Rule 212). A Conference of Committee Chairs may make recommendations to the Conference of Presidents about the work of committees (Rule 29).

[195] Parliament, 'Rules of Procedure', Rules 207–208. [196] Ibid., Rule 209(2).

expected to agree on a report (including possible amendments to the act proposed, usually by the Commission) to be put forward to the Plenary, together with an explanatory statement.[197]

Within the committee, the political groups may designate one of their members to be a coordinator, to ensure consistency of the position of the said political group within the *policy* area covered by the committee. Coordinators of political groups within committees are influential in negotiations and vote, under the presidency of the committee chair, on the appointment of the 'rapporteur' in charge of reporting to the Plenary on a *specific file* and behalf of the committee – hence the importance of the fact that non-attached Members may *not* designate coordinators.[198] Political groups may also designate 'shadow rapporteurs' to follow progress on behalf of their group on the specific file, and to find compromises within the committee on the said file on behalf of the political group.[199]

The voting arrangements within the committee are the same as in the Plenary.[200] Despite this, it is not uncommon to have different outcomes when a vote is taken in the Plenary, in comparison to a vote in the committee. The position of the Parliament may only result from a final vote in the Plenary, as illustrated in Figure 2.2. Overall, the Parliament shall ensure

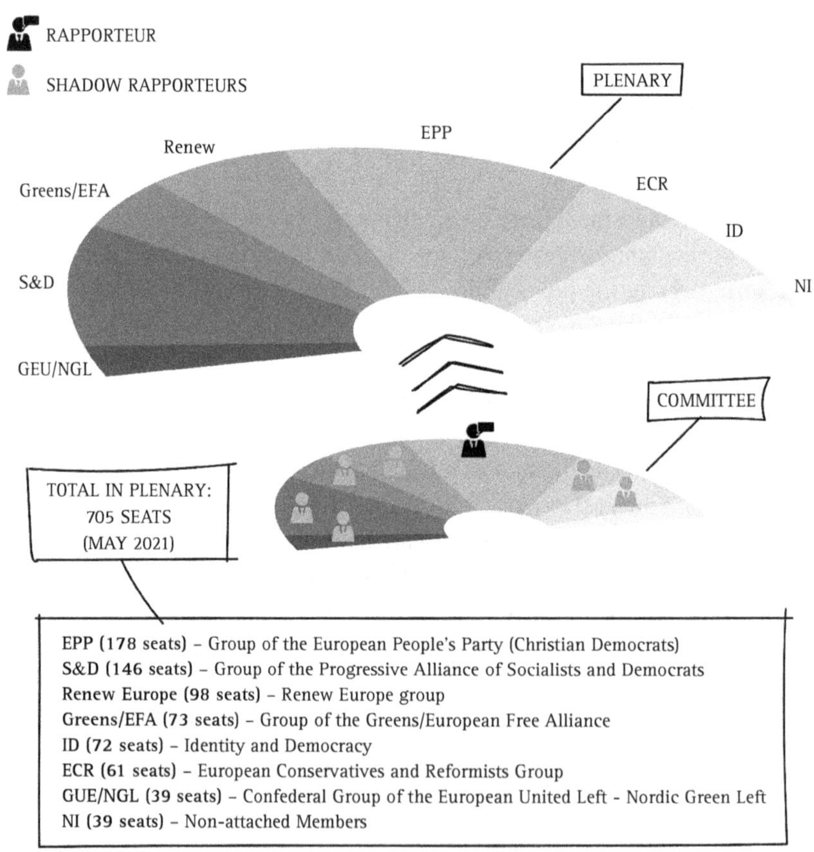

Figure 2.2 Workflow within the Parliament

[197] Ibid., Rules 51, 55. [198] Ibid., Rules 210, 214. [199] Ibid., Rule 215. [200] Ibid., Rule 219.

that its activities are conducted with the utmost transparency.[201] Debates in the Plenary have to be public, and committees also normally have to be convened in public.

Certain MEPs, due to their function within a committee and the quality of their work, may play a prominent role in the final adoption of a text. The Dutch MEP Judith Sargentini, from the political group the Greens, for instance, is well-known for her work as rapporteur for the LIBE committee: the Parliament (voting with a particularly high majority[202]) adopted a Resolution calling on the Council to determine the existence of a clear risk of a serious breach by Hungary of the values on which the EU is founded.[203]

The allocation of leadership positions within the Parliament is thus particularly important for the outcome of the political process, leading to the adoption of new acts of EU law. In order to ensure that the work in committees reflects the composition of the Parliament as a whole, as well as providing a fair representation of political views, gender and geographical balance,[204] in practice the allocation of key functions is made by relying on a mathematical formula known as the d'Hondt formula, or variations thereof.[205] This method takes into account the size of a political group, but also allows for a degree of rotation among all political families.

Voting Arrangements

In principle, and thus in the absence of specific mention on the voting arrangement, the Parliament acts by a majority of the votes cast.[206] In practice, it often occurs that MEPs do not vote, or decide to abstain. This voting arrangement thus looks at the actual votes; for the vote to be valid there must be at least one-third of the component Members of the Parliament present in the Chamber (at time of writing the quorum is 235).[207] As a general rule, Parliament shall vote by show of hands.[208] In certain cases, as was the case for the Parliament's decision to waive the immunity of the Catalan leader Carles Puigdemont Casamajó, the vote may be by secret ballot.[209] Such an option exists for appointments within the Parliament, for instance, and may also be requested by a group of Members.

By way of exception, and where specifically requested on the relevant legal basis enabling the Parliament to act, the latter may have to vote with higher thresholds,

[201] Art. 1, para. 2 TEU; Art. 15 TFEU; Art. 42 CFEU; Parliament, 'Rules of Procedure', Art. 121.

[202] A two-thirds majority of the votes cast, representing a majority of the component members is required for such a vote, Art. 354, para. 4 TFEU.

[203] 'European Parliament Resolution of 12 September 2018 on a Proposal Calling on the Council to Determine, Pursuant to Article 7(1) of the Treaty on European Union, the Existence of a Clear Risk of a Serious Breach by Hungary of the Values on which the Union Is Founded', OJ C 433, 23.12.2019, pp. 66–85. See Chapter 4, Section 4.3.2.1.

[204] Parliament, 'Rules of Procedure', Rule 213(3), referring back to Rule 15(2) already mentioned in relation to the election of President and Vice-Presidents of the Parliament.

[205] See further S. Kotanidis, 'Understanding the d'Hondt Method: Allocation of Parliamentary Seats and Leadership Positions', Briefing, 28.6.2019, European Parliamentary Research Service.

[206] Art. 231, para. 1 TFEU. [207] Parliament, 'Rules of Procedure', Rule 178.

[208] Alternatives, which may be decided upon by the President, include an electronic voting system, or even sitting and standing. There may be a single vote or a roll call (name by name). See ibid., Rules 187–188, 190.

[209] Ibid., Rule 191.

reflecting the increased importance of the subject matter of the vote. The most common of them is the requirement to vote by a majority of its component members (353 out of a total of 705 MEPs at time of writing), such as when its consent is requested in view of accession by a third State to the EU.[210] In rare cases, illustrating particularly high-level political tensions, such as for a motion of censure against the Commission or consent to the finding of the existence of a serious and persistent breach by a Member State of the values on which the EU is founded,[211] the Parliament votes by 'a two-thirds majority of the votes cast, representing a majority of the component members'.[212]

2.3.2.6 Functions and Powers

The Parliament's powers have increased considerably since the early days of the EU's legal order. While the specific role of the Parliament in each of these settings will be further elaborated on subsequently,[213] an overview of the key functions and powers that define the importance of the Parliament in today's institutional framework of the EU is provided here.

First and foremost, the Parliament is a co-legislator in the context of the 'ordinary' legislative procedure. Several revisions of the EU Treaties have sought to put the Parliament on an equal footing with the Council. The intention of the reform introduced by the Treaty of Lisbon was to make it common for the adoption of legislative acts.[214] The Commission proposal for a legislative act thus goes back and forth between the Council and the Parliament until an agreement can be reached for their joint adoption of the act.[215] The well-known General Data Protection Regulation (GDPR), for instance, was adopted jointly by the Parliament and Council.[216] The Parliament may have a weaker role in the legislative process, however. Most 'special' legislative procedures indeed consist of the adoption of the act by the Council, with the consent, or after mere consultation, of the Parliament. Whenever another institution, mostly the Commission, exercises powers delegated to it by a legislative act, the Parliament exercises a degree of control.[217]

[210] Art. 49, para. 1 TEU. [211] Art. 234, para. 2 TFEU; Art. 7 TEU read in conjunction with Art. 354, para. 4 TFEU.

[212] In such a case, abstentions are taken into account in order to ascertain, as required by Art. 354, para. 4 TFEU, that the votes in favour represent the majority of the component Members of Parliament (C-650/18, *Hungary* v. *Parliament*, EU:C:2021:426, para. 87).

[213] See Chapter 3, Section 3.6.

[214] Art. 289(1) TFEU. In practice, there are fewer legislative acts adopted through the ordinary legislative procedure (OLP) than through special legislative procedures (e.g. twenty-nine basic acts adopted through the OLP versus 259 basic acts adopted through special legislative procedures in 2018, which was the last full year of normal legislative activity before the 2019 elections according to statistics available on eur-lex.europa.eu). This quantitative observation shall not detract attention from the growing role of the OLP in the EU Treaties, nor from the importance of the policy areas for which it is used.

[215] See Chapter 3, Section 3.6.1.1, Legislative Procedures.

[216] 'Regulation (EU) 2016/679 of the European Parliament and of the Council of 27 April 2016 on the Protection of Natural Persons with Regard to the Processing of Personal Data and on the Free Movement of such Data', OJ L 119, 4.5.2016, p. 1.

[217] Art. 290(2) TFEU; see also Chapter 3, Section 3.6.1.2, Delegated Acts within the Meaning of Art. 290 TFEU.

Mirroring the growing role of the Parliament for the adoption of internal acts, the position of the institution has also been strengthened considerably in the external action of the EU. Since the Treaty of Lisbon, its consent is now necessary in a vast majority of procedures concerning the conclusion of international agreements negotiated on behalf of the EU with third States or international organisations.[218] The absence of parliamentary support can thus have a strong impact. For instance, the Parliament prevented the conclusion of a trade agreement between the EU and several third States on anti-counterfeiting.[219] The MEP who had been the rapporteur and had recommended rejection had expressed concerns that the treaty was too vague, open to misinterpretation and could therefore jeopardise citizens' liberties. To avoid such blockages, the Parliament must be kept informed in the negotiation process,[220] and it shares its views through resolutions, as illustrated in the context of negotiations on Brexit.[221]

Key to the positioning of the Parliament in the institutional framework of the EU are its budgetary powers. This was one of the first battlegrounds for the Parliament to strengthen its position.[222] In many ways, the efforts of the Parliament can be said to have succeeded, as today that institution co-decides on the annual budget of the EU with the Council,[223] and its consent is necessary for the adoption of the multiannual financial framework for the EU which is decided every seven years. The increasing complexity and fragmentation of decision-making over budgetary affairs, however, invites a nuanced view of this success. The powerful role of the European Council in the latest negotiations on the multiannual financial framework, as particularly visible in the context of the response to the COVID-19 crisis which added to the political stakes, also narrows the margin of manoeuvre of the Parliament in practice.[224]

The Parliament is closely involved in appointments to most high-level positions. This includes the election of the President of the Commission, as well as consent for the appointment of the College of Commissioners.[225] Other appointments in which the Parliament is involved include the President, Vice-President and other members of the Executive Board of the Central Bank, as well as the members of the Court of Auditors.[226]

[218] Art. 218(6) TFEU.

[219] 'European Parliament Legislative Resolution of 4 July 2012 on the Draft Council Decision on the Conclusion of the Anti-Counterfeiting Trade Agreement between the European Union and Its Member States, Australia, Canada, Japan, the Republic of Korea, the United Mexican States, the Kingdom of Morocco, New Zealand, the Republic of Singapore, the Swiss Confederation and the United States of America', OJ C 349E, 29.11.2013, pp. 552–552.

[220] Art. 218(10) TFEU; see also C-658/11, *Parliament* v. *Council (Mauritius Agreement)*, EU:C:2014:2025, para. 86.

[221] See also the commitment by the Commission President to engage with the Parliament for that purpose: European Commission, Directorate-General for Communication, U. von der Leyen, *Political Guidelines for the Next European Commission 2019–2024*, Opening Statement in the European Parliament Plenary session, 16 July 2019 (Publications Office, 2020), p. 20.

[222] See Chapter 3, Section 3.6.3. [223] Art. 314 TFEU.

[224] E.g. European Council, Conclusions on the recovery plan and multiannual financial framework for 2021–2027, 17–21.7.2021; European Council, Conclusions on the MFF and Next Generation EU, COVID-19, climate change, security and external relations, 10–11.12.2021. See further R. Crowe, 'The European Budgetary Galaxy', *European Constitutional Law Review*, 13(3), pp. 428–452.

[225] Art. 17(7) TEU; see further Chapter 2, Section 2.3.5.3.

[226] The Parliament is consulted. See respectively Arts. 283(2), subpara. 2, and 286(2), subpara. 1 TFEU.

These powers of appointment are part of a broader set of mechanisms by which the Parliament exercises its function of 'political control'[227] over other EU organs. In particular, the Parliament may vote, or – as has proven enough so far[228] – threaten to vote, on a motion of censure against the Commission. Such a motion specifically calls into question the activities of the Commission; and if the motion receives a two-thirds majority of the votes cast, representing a majority of the component members of the Parliament, the Commission 'shall resign as a body'.[229] The Parliament also, on a yearly basis, discusses the Commission's general report[230] and is invited to approve and comment on the way the Commission has been implementing the EU's annual budget (approval is known as 'granting budgetary discharge').[231] Lack of approval shows distrust in the Commission and possibly announces a political crisis.[232] The relationship between the Parliament and the Commission is further articulated in a special inter-institutional agreement.[233]

The Parliament may also make non-binding requests for the Commission to take (legislative) action.[234] It may pose questions to the Commission, and hear other institutions, such as the Council or European Council.[235] The President of the European Council, in particular, reports on each of the meetings of the European Council.[236] One way for the Parliament to exercise review over other institutions is by commencing legal action before the Court of Justice – for instance, in annulment actions against EU acts for the adoption of acts in which its position was marginalised.[237] It may also seek a judicial opinion in case of doubt on the compatibility of draft international agreements negotiated by other institutions with EU fundamental rights, as was successfully done in relation to the Agreement with Canada on the transfer of data from passengers of commercial airlines.[238] The Parliament can also create committees of inquiry to investigate possible contraventions or maladministration by public organs in the implementation of EU law.[239]

[227] Art. 14(1) TEU. [228] See Chapter 1, Section 1.3.2.3.

[229] Art. 17(8) TEU; Art. 234, para. 2 TFEU. Note that the High Representative of the Union for Foreign Affairs and Security Policy has a specific status in this context, as will be discussed subsequently, in Chapter 2, Section 2.3.6.3.

[230] Art. 233 TFEU. [231] Art. 319 TFEU. The Parliament acts on a recommendation from the Council.

[232] As illustrated in the late 1990s; see Chapter 1, Section 1.3.2.3. In practice, the Parliament grants separate discharge to all institutions, offices, bodies and agencies, thereby exercising political pressure on various actors. For further discussion of this practice, see M.-L. Sánchez-Barrueco, 'At the Crossroads of a Frozen Conflict: Political Oversight of the Council's Administrative Budget by the European Parliament', *Common Market Law Review*, 58 (2021), pp. 333–360.

[233] 'Framework Agreement on Relations between the European Parliament and the European Commission', OJ L 304, 20.11.2010, p. 47 (last amended 2018).

[234] Art. 225 TFEU; 'Interinstitutional Agreement between the European Parliament, the Council of the European Union and the European Commission on Better Law-Making', OJ L 123, 12.5.2016, p. 1, para. 10. During her mandate as President of the Commission, Ursula von der Leyen made a political commitment to follow up on such recommendations when they relate to a request to propose legislation by 'responding with a legislative act in full respect of the proportionality, subsidiarity, and better law-making principles' (von der Leyen, *Political Guidelines for the Next European Commission 2019–2024*).

[235] Art. 230 TFEU; 'European Council Decision of 1 December 2009 Adopting its Rules of Procedure', OJ L 315, 2.12.2009, Art. 5 (hereafter, European Council, 'Rules of Procedure'); see further Art. 36 TEU.

[236] Art. 15(6)(d) TEU.

[237] See, for instance, sensitivities related to the choice of legal basis: Chapter 3, Sections 3.2.2.1 and 3.2.4.

[238] On the finding of incompatibility, see Opinion 1/15, Transfer of Passenger Name Record data from the European Union to Canada, EU:C:2017:592.

[239] Art. 226 TFEU; Parliament, 'Rules of Procedure', Rule 208.

The Parliament elects an independent European Ombudsman who investigates complaints about maladministration in EU institutions and bodies.[240] Such complaints may come from citizens, any natural or legal persons from a Member State, or through MEPs. The Ombudsman may also act on its own initiative. If investigations lead to a finding of maladministration, the matter is referred to the organ responsible for it to share its views before a final report is sent to the said organ, as well as to the Parliament. The work of the Ombudsman has attracted significant attention in recent years, putting pressure on EU organs to reflect on their own rules and practices. For instance, the Ombudsman opened an own-initiative inquiry to look into how the European Border and Coast Guard Agency (Frontex) complies with its fundamental rights and obligations and ensures accountability in matters as sensitive as in relation to 'returns' of migrants.[241]

This non-exhaustive list of tools demonstrates that the Parliament is the institution that is best equipped to provide a forum for public debate at European level. For instance, it is before Parliament that the President of the Commission gives their yearly 'State of the Union Address'.[242] It is also there that the Head of State or Government chairing the rotating Presidency of the Council presents the country's priorities.[243] It is therefore no surprise that prominent public figures, such as the Pope, also use the platform to address a public audience at European level.[244] A number of other initiatives, such as the Sakharov Prize for Freedom of Thought, first awarded by the Parliament in 1988 to Nelson Mandela and Anatoli Marchenko, illustrate the broad range of instruments used by the Parliament to enrich public political debate at European level. The Parliament may further wish to make statements by means of own-initiative reports.[245]

Finally, the Parliament may be called on to contribute to shaping primary law or impacting on the fundamental structure of the EU. It may initiate, and contribute to, the reform of the EU Treaties,[246] as well as decisions against a Member State if it is threatening the values on which the EU is founded.[247] The consent of the Parliament is necessary for a new State to accede to the EU,[248] and for the conclusion of a withdrawal agreement with a State leaving membership of the EU.[249] Such consent is also necessary to authorise a group of Member States to develop enhanced cooperation.[250]

2.3.2.7 Sessions, Seat and Places of Work

The Parliament holds an annual session.[251] It is based in Strasbourg for monthly Plenary sessions, which include a budgetary session. Additional periods of Plenary sessions, as well as committee meetings, are held in Brussels. The General Secretariat is based in

240 The term of office is the same as for the Parliament; Art. 228 TFEU.

241 Ombudsman, Case OI/4/2021/MHZ, opened 4.3.2021.

242 'Framework Agreement on Relations between the European Parliament and the European Commission', OJ L 304 20.11.2010, p. 47 (as amended 2018), point 4, Annex IV, point 5.

243 E.g. Parliament, 'MEPs Debated the French Presidency's Priorities with Emmanuel Macron', press release, 19.1.2022.

244 Parliament, 'Pope Francis Delivers a Message "to all the citizens of Europe"', press release, 16.11.2014.

245 Parliament, 'Rules of Procedure', Rule 54. 246 Art. 48 TEU. 247 Art. 7 TEU. 248 Art. 49 TEU.

249 Art. 50 TEU. 250 Art. 329(1), subpara. 1 TFEU; see also Chapter 1, Section 1.4.3.4.

251 Art. 229, para. 1 TFEU.

Luxembourg. The complex organisation of this is set out in a Protocol.[252] These arrangements are the outcome of a compromise, within which France has explained a strong attachment to hosting one of the key EU institutions in a location symbolically bridging it with Germany (Strasbourg), while the daily work of most other institutions is actually done in Belgium (Brussels). The back and forth of parliamentarians between Brussels and Strasbourg occasionally gives rise to political disputes, as well as litigation before the Court of Justice.[253] In the context of the COVID-19 crisis, then President of the Parliament, David Sassoli, felt it necessary to recall that despite several special arrangements due to the sanitary crisis, 'Strasbourg is our capital'.[254]

2.3.3 The European Council

2.3.3.1 A Brief Description

The European Council emerged from a trend of the Heads of State or Government of the Member States to meet and discuss important matters on a regular and informal basis, in a setting distinct from gatherings by government representatives at ministerial level in the Council.[255] That practice developed in a way that was progressively recognised by various Treaty revisions, and the Treaty of Lisbon ultimately asserted that the European Council is now an 'institution' in which the Member States are represented at the highest political level.[256] This recognition came with a clearer set of powers and accountability mechanisms, as we will see subsequently.[257] The European Council is primarily, but not only, composed of the said European leaders who thereby contribute to democratic representation of citizens of the Member States in EU institutions.

European Council meetings, also known as 'summits', have come to attract much attention, in particular in times of crisis when political guidance at European level is needed. In July 2020 for instance, Charles Michel, President of the European Council, observed that the 'socio-economic fallout from the COVID-19 crisis requires a joint and innovative effort [. . .] in order to support the recovery and resilience of the member states' economies'. He further emerged from a much-awaited summit proudly stating, 'We did it: Europe is strong, Europe is robust, and above all, Europe is united.' The European Council had agreed to a comprehensive package of over EUR 1,824 billion. Although in practice, several other EU institutions and many sets of procedures would have to be set in motion to achieve this objective, the common 'necessary impetus'[258] for these developments was thereby communicated to the public.

The main task of the European Council is to provide political guidance for the EU. Unlike the Council, from which it must be distinguished, as will be further explained

[252] Protocol 6 annexed to the EU Treaties on the Location of the Seats of the Institutions and of Certain Bodies, Offices, Agencies and Departments of the European Union, which crystallises an agreement among the Member States (Art. 341 TFEU).

[253] For instance, France lost the following case: the Court of Justice allowed the Parliament to adopt a pragmatic approach to the planning of sessions involving discussion of the budget, in light of the unpredictability of the budgetary procedure, thereby allowing certain related meetings to take place in Brussels instead of Strasbourg, C-92/18, *France* v. *Parliament*, EU:C:2020:506.

[254] President of the Parliament, Speech at the opening of the December Plenary session, 14.12.2020.

[255] See Chapter 1, Section 1.3.2.2. [256] Art. 10(2), subpara. 2 TEU. [257] Art. 13(1) TEU.

[258] Art. 15(1) TEU.

subsequently,[259] the European Council does *not* exercise legislative functions. Its main features are set out in Article 15 TEU (Box 2.2), which is complemented by several provisions of the TFEU.[260]

Box 2.2 **Rough guide to the European Council**

Article 15 TEU

1. The European Council shall provide the Union with the necessary impetus for its development and shall define the general political directions and priorities thereof. It shall not exercise legislative functions.

2. The European Council shall consist of the Heads of State or Government of the Member States, together with its President and the President of the Commission. The High Representative of the Union for Foreign Affairs and Security Policy shall take part in its work.

3. The European Council shall meet twice every six months, convened by its President. When the agenda so requires, the members of the European Council may decide each to be assisted by a minister and, in the case of the President of the Commission, by a member of the Commission. When the situation so requires, the President shall convene a special meeting of the European Council.

4. Except where the Treaties provide otherwise, decisions of the European Council shall be taken by consensus.

5. The European Council shall elect its President, by a qualified majority, for a term of two and a half years, renewable once. [. . .]

2.3.3.2 Composition

At time of writing the European Council has twenty-nine members, twenty-seven of which are the Heads of State or Government of the Member States (European leaders). This explains the political salience of the activities of that institution. The democratic representation of these persons may be direct and/or indirect, depending on the conditions under which they have been appointed, and the related democratic accountability mechanisms are defined by each national constitutional tradition.[261] It is the responsibility of the Member States to adopt national measures, including constitutional measures, making it possible to determine whether they should be represented by one or other figure. National law may furthermore identify grounds which may lead to one of them being prevented from representing the State. In contrast, no EU institution – neither the European Council itself,

[259] The European Council must also not be confused with the Council of Europe; see Chapter 1, Section 1.3.2.1, note 68.

[260] Arts. 235, 236 TFEU.

[261] Art. 10(2), subpara. 2 TEU. See further W. Wessels and O. Rozenberg (Principal Investigators), *Democratic Control in the Member States of the European Council and the Euro zone summits* (Study commissioned by the European Parliament, 2013).

nor for that matter the Court of Justice of the European Union – will review the merits of allegations that a specific leader is ill-suited to represent the State, for instance because that leader finds themself in a situation of conflict of interest.[262]

The European Council also includes the President of the Commission and the President of the European Council.[263] This is one of the factors that distinguishes action by the European Council from action by the European leaders in their sovereign capacity.[264] The presence of the President of the Commission is important as it bridges the political impetus-power that European leaders have with the machinery of the Commission (which has a quasi-monopoly to initiate legislation as well as to initiate proceedings for the enforcement of EU law).[265] This bridge enhances the chances of political alignment between the two institutions. Yet this may also attract criticism if it threatens the independence of the Commission and risks sidelining other institutions, such as the Parliament.

The potential for alignment between the European Council and the Commission may indeed isolate the Parliament.[266] This was illustrated well in the conclusions following another summit in response to the COVID-19 pandemic. In December 2020, the European Council reached a deal in relation to a draft regulation intended to make access to EU funding conditional upon compliance with the rule of law. Certain Member States made the adoption – or at least the postponement of the enforcement – of that instrument a precondition for their approval of a package of measures to ensure financing of the response to the COVID-19 crisis at European level. By way of compromise, the European Council stated: 'the Commission intends to develop and adopt guidelines on the way it will apply the Regulation [. . .]. The Commission President will fully inform the European Council. Until such guidelines are finalised, the Commission will not propose measures under the Regulation.'[267] This arrangement allowed the file to be unlocked politically, and paved the way for the actual adoption of the said Regulation,[268] as well as other instruments important for the finances of the EU. In the meantime, though, this approach sidelined the Parliament. The latter reacted by expressing its strong regrets, actually challenging the institutional underpinnings of the approach.[269]

[262] T-715/19, *Wagenknecht* v. *European Council*, EU:T:2020:340, paras. 35–36. The action, motivated by allegations held against the Prime Minister of the Czech Republic, was dismissed as inadmissible.

[263] Art. 15(2) TEU. Note, however, that these two players have a lesser role when votes are taken within the European Council; see Chapter 2, Section 2.3.3.4.

[264] See Chapter 2, Section 2.1.1. [265] Art. 17(2) TEU; Art. 258, para. 1 TFEU.

[266] There is also a natural political alignment between the European Council and the Council, the latter being composed of representatives of the same Member States at ministerial level. For an overview of the interplay between the European Council and other institutions, see W. Wessels, 'The European Council', in Schütze and Tridimas (eds.), *Oxford Principles of European Union Law*, pp. 408–512.

[267] European Council, Conclusions on the MFF and Next Generation EU, COVID-19, climate change, security and external relations, 10–11.12.2021, point I.2.c.

[268] 'Regulation (EU, Euratom) 2020/2092 of the European Parliament and of the Council of 16 December 2020 on a General Regime of Conditionality for the Protection of the Union Budget', OJ L 433I, 22.12.2020.

[269] The Parliament noted that the content of the European Council conclusions on the Regulation is 'superfluous'. 'European Parliament Resolution on the Multiannual Financial Framework 2021–2027, the Interinstitutional Agreement, the EU Recovery Instrument and the Rule of Law Regulation', 2020/2923 (RSP), 17.12.2020, para. 4. The Parliament further initiated an action against the Commission for failure to ensure the full and immediate application of the regulation, C-657/21, *Parliament* v. *Commission*, OJ C 11, 10.1.2022, pp. 18–19 (pending at time of writing).

The other important person, besides European leaders acting within the context of the European Council, is its President.[270] While that position used to be occupied by one of the European leaders on a rotating basis,[271] since the Treaty of Lisbon, it has been occupied by a specifically appointed person for a mandate of two and a half years, renewable once. So far, the mandates of all such Presidents have been renewed, so that their mandate of five years has matched those of the newly elected Parliament and newly appointed Commission. The appointment of a person with a specific function to preside over the European Council was intended to help build consensus and to give stability as well as visibility to an institution that is otherwise a chameleon, as European leaders naturally depend on national politics. Indeed, while certain Heads of State or Government have been in power for many years, such as Angela Merkel from Germany, others tend to be in government for much less longer – for example, in Italy, due to many national political changes. The President is elected by the European Council itself, which votes by qualified majority voting.[272] Although that is not a formal requirement, all Presidents to date have been chosen from among acting leaders at the time of the election. An elected President must resign from their national position so that they can focus on being the President of the European Council.[273]

The European leaders, the President of the Commission and the President of the European Council may also be accompanied by the High Representative of the Union for Foreign Affairs and Security Policy. This latter figure is not a member of the European Council but shall 'take part in its work'.[274] This allows the consistency of EU representation on the external stage to be enhanced. In the field of foreign affairs and security policy, the High Representative indeed operates as an agent of both the Council and the Commission.[275] The members of the European Council may also each be assisted by one minister, or for the President of the Commission, by one Commissioner.[276] In contrast, the Parliament has no formal role in the European Council – although the President of the Parliament is regularly invited to be heard at the start of the meetings (and then invited to leave).[277] Meetings with other personalities, such as the President of the Central Bank, other States or international organisations, may also take place on the margins of the European Council.[278]

2.3.3.3 Functioning and Organisation

The European Council meets at least twice every six months, on invitation by its President, who may also convene additional 'special meetings', as occurred after the notification by the United Kingdom of its intention to withdraw from the EU.[279] In practice, the European

[270] Art. 15(2) and (5) TEU.

[271] The system was modelled on that currently applying for the Presidency of the Council, as will be discussed subsequently.

[272] It may be recalled that the President and Commission President themselves do not take part in the vote: Art. 15(5) TEU; Art. 235(1), subpara. 2 TFEU. In the event of an impediment or serious misconduct, the European Council can end the President's term of office in accordance with the same procedure.

[273] Art. 15(6), final subpara. TEU.

[274] Art. 15(2) TEU.

[275] This complex setting may also create confusion, as will be explained subsequently.

[276] Art. 15(3) TEU. The total number of accompanying personnel is limited; European Council, 'Rules of Procedure', Art. 4(4), subpara. 3.

[277] Art. 235(2) TFEU; European Council, 'Rules of Procedure', Art. 4(2), subpara. 1.

[278] European Council, 'Rules of Procedure', Art. 4(2), subpara. 2.

[279] Art. 15(3) TEU; European Council President, Invitation to the Members of the European Council (Art. 50), 28 April 2017.

Council formally meets around eight times per year and these summits often attract considerable attention. It meets in Brussels, unless otherwise decided in exceptional circumstances.[280] The meetings normally do not exceed two days.[281] A notable exception, when the summit spread over no fewer than five days, resulted in the July 2020 conclusions on the response to the COVID-19 crisis, set out previously.

The meetings themselves 'shall not be public',[282] and the deliberations are covered by the obligation of professional secrecy.[283] This is understood as facilitating compromises and consensus-building within an institution that deals with most sensitive matters, striving to identify a joint way forward. Nevertheless, the European Council makes its conclusions public after each formal meeting, and its decisions are published, as we shall see subsequently. The European Council may also decide to make public the results of certain votes, as well as specific statements or explanations;[284] furthermore the provisions concerning public access to documents are the same as for the Council.[285] Decisions of the European Council on urgent matters may be adopted by a written vote.[286]

The President of the European Council plays an important role in structuring the work of the institution, as well as making it visible. Its functions are set out in Article 15(6) TEU. They require the President to: (1) chair and drive forward the work as illustrated by the issuing of a 'Leaders' agenda', setting out the work programme of the President for the institution; (2) prepare and ensure continuity of work;[287] (3) facilitate cohesion and consensus – for instance, by informally approaching European leaders and/or pre-drafting key documents ahead of summits,[288] allowing the advisors of the leaders (sherpas) to prepare the meeting; (4) report to the Parliament after each of the meetings of the European Council; and (5) ensure at this level the external representation of the EU on issues concerning its CFSP. The latter function is without prejudice to the powers of the High Representative of the Union for Foreign Affairs and Security Policy.

The European Council has exercised its power of self-organisation by adopting its own Rules of Procedure.[289] These articulate, in particular, the role of the General Secretariat of the Council to support the work of the European Council.[290]

2.3.3.4 Decision-Making

Reflecting the high-level diplomacy that characterises the institution, the principle is that the European Council shall act by consensus. It is thus the rule that applies in the absence of reference to other specific requirements.[291] A number of provisions of the EU Treaties refer to other arrangements though. Some, such as Article 7 TEU for determining that there exists a serious and persistent breach by a Member State of the values in Article 2 TEU,[292] refer to 'unanimity'. Unlike consensus, Members of the European Council are for that purpose

[280] European Council, 'Rules of Procedure', Art. 1(2), subpara. 2. [281] Ibid., Art. 4(1), subpara. 1.
[282] Ibid., Art. 4(1), subpara. 2. [283] Ibid., Art. 11. [284] Ibid., Art. 10(1). [285] Ibid., Art. 10(2).
[286] Ibid., Art. 7.
[287] This is done in cooperation with the President of the Commission and on the basis of the work of the General Affairs Council, as further elaborated upon in the 'Rules of Procedure' of the European Council.
[288] European Council, 'Rules of Procedure', Art. 3(1), subpara. 3.
[289] Art. 235(3) TFEU (voting by simple majority): European Council, 'Rules of Procedure', pp. 52–55.
[290] Art. 235(4) TFEU; European Council, 'Rules of Procedure', Art. 13. [291] Art. 15(4) TEU.
[292] Art. 7(2) TEU.

invited to make their position explicit in the context of a vote. Others require qualified majority voting, in which case the voting arrangements are the same as within the Council.[293] Such a requirement of qualified majority voting applies, for instance, for decisions setting the configurations and rotating presidencies of the Council.[294] The European Council may also decide by simple majority, such as on procedural questions,[295] or to open up the ordinary procedure for revision of the EU Treaties.[296] It shall be noted that an abstention does not prevent the adoption of the act, even when unanimity is required.[297]

The vote will take place on the initiative of the President, and only if at least two-thirds of the members of the European Council are present. Importantly, the President of the European Council and the President of the Commission are not included in this quorum. Furthermore, when a vote is taken, the said Presidents do not take part in the vote.[298] The Presidents of the European Council and of the Commission are thus formal members of the institution, but have a lesser role when Members are asked to take a formal stand.

The dynamics within the European Council may not be oversimplified; they result from a combination of factors.[299] Equality among Member States is important for the model on which the European Union is based,[300] and each European leader naturally seeks to defend the interests of their own country. Yet the European Council is an institution where these leaders come together to look for a joint way forward. There is thus also the reality of different sizes in population, geographical locations, economics, culture, language and a broader range of political dynamics, such as military power, that play an important role in the search for compromises, depending on the nature of the matter under discussion.[301] Finally, the main European political forces represented in the Parliament seek to coordinate ahead of European Council summits.[302]

2.3.3.5 Functions and Powers

The main function of the European Council is to provide the EU with the 'necessary impetus'.[303] This impetus may respond to different needs. Firstly, the European Council defines general political directions and priorities.[304] It can set the tone and often does so across a broad range of policy areas, depending on the priorities of the European leaders, by making the conclusions of its meetings public, as shown in Box 2.3. In certain fields, this role of the European Council is more formalised, such as in relation to external action, economic and employment policies, and within the AFSJ.[305]

[293] Art. 235(1), subpara. 2 TFEU; see also Chapter 2, Section 2.3.4.4, Qualified Majority Voting.

[294] Art. 236 TFEU; another example relates to the appointment of the High Representative for Foreign Affairs and Security Policy, Art. 17(7), subpara. 3 TEU.

[295] Art. 235(3) TFEU. [296] Art. 48(3) TEU.

[297] Art. 235(1), subpara. 3 TFEU. A member of the European Council may act on behalf of not more than one other member, Art. 235 TFEU.

[298] Art. 235(1), subpara. 2 TFEU; European Council, 'Rules of Procedure', Art. 6(3–4).

[299] See further Wessels, 'The European Council', pp. 406–507.

[300] Art. 4(2) TEU; see also Chapter 1, Section 1.1.2.

[301] van Middelaar, *Alarums and Excursions*, pp. 151–171.

[302] See further S. Van Hecke and K. M. Johansson, 'Summitry of Political Parties at European Level', in E. Stetter, K. Duffek and A. Skrzypek (eds.), *In the Name of Political Union: Europarties on the Rise* (Next Left Book Series, 2013), pp. 62–76.

[303] Art. 15(1) TEU. [304] Ibid.

[305] Respectively, Art. 22(1) TEU; Arts. 121(2), subpara. 2, and 148(1-1) TFEU; Art. 68 TFEU.

Box 2.3 **Excerpt from European Council Conclusions**

European Council, Conclusions (Brussels, 18 October 2018)

II. Internal Security

9. The European Council [. . .] calls for measures to [. . .] strengthen the capacity to prevent and respond effectively to radicalisation and terrorism, in full respect of fundamental rights. The Commission proposal on preventing the dissemination of terrorist content online should be examined as a matter of priority. Solutions should be found to ensure swift and efficient cross-border access to e-evidence in order to effectively fight terrorism and other serious and organised crime, both within the EU and at international level; the Commission proposals on e-evidence and access to financial information, as well as to better combat money laundering, should be agreed on by the end of the legislature. The Commission should also urgently submit negotiating mandates for the international negotiations on e-evidence. The Commission initiative to extend the competences of the European Public Prosecutor's Office to cross-border terrorist crimes should be examined;

This function of the European Council as an agenda setter excludes the exercise of legislative functions.[306] Legislative functions are left to the Commission, the Parliament and the Council. Although this distinction remains fundamental, the line between defining general political directions and priorities for the EU, which the European Council is empowered to do, and initiating legislation or shaping it on particularly controversial points is sometimes blurred in practice. When such confusion exists, as explained previously, the Parliament is the main institution that is sidelined.

The second function of the European Council is to provide a forum to look for solutions to political blockages within the Council. This role may be taken up by the European Council to address a broad range of political impasses. This naturally derives from the fact that the institution is primarily composed of the European leaders of the same governments that are represented at a lower political and institutional level in the Council.[307] The role of the European Council as an impasse breaker is specifically formalised in relation to procedures for the adoption of rules that are anticipated to be particularly sensitive for the Member States. In such settings the mechanism is often referred to as the 'emergency brake' and indeed allows a specific discussion to be lifted from the Council to the European Council level, to search for a solution. This is the case in the field of CFSP and judicial cooperation in criminal matters, for instance.[308] The European Council will be engaged when a Member State considers that 'vital and stated reasons of national policy' or 'fundamental aspects of its criminal justice system'[309] may be affected by EU decision-making.

[306] Art. 15(1) TEU.

[307] Although this shall not be used to bypass the requirement for qualified majority voting within the Council; this would risk upsetting the institutional balance. See also Chapter 2, Section 2.3.1.2.

[308] See also in the area of social security, Art. 48 TFEU, police cooperation, Art. 87 TFEU, and for the creation of a public prosecutor, Art. 86 TFEU.

[309] E.g. Art. 31(2), final subpara. TEU; Arts. 82(3)–83(3) TFEU.

As a third function, the European Council strongly influences the organisation and composition of several other institutions. This includes proposing a candidate to the Parliament for election of the President of the Commission, as well as the final appointment of the College of Commissioners and of the High Representative for Foreign Affairs and Security Policy.[310] Other high-level appointments in which the European Council has a decisive role include those of the President, Vice-President and other members of the Executive Board of the Central Bank.[311] Similarly, the European Council decides on the configurations and order of rotating presidencies of the Council,[312] as well as on the composition of the Parliament.[313]

In a fourth function, the European Council plays a prominent role in shaping primary law or in decisions impacting on the fundamental structure of the EU. In particular, it plays a crucial role in most procedures for the reform of the EU Treaties,[314] as well as in decisions against a Member State for a serious and persistent breach of the values on which the EU is founded,[315] in the context of accession by a new State to the EU,[316] and for an orderly withdrawal by a State from the EU.[317] The European Council, which plays a prominent role in the CFSP, may also unanimously decide to create a common Union defence policy.[318]

Last but not least, in practice, the European Council is the natural forum for European leaders to seek joint responses to crises or major challenges of all sorts. The President may indeed convene a meeting whenever the situation so requires.[319] In situations of crises, the 'club' is thereby 'called upon to tame the storm'.[320] Summits were called in the context of the COVID-19 crisis, for instance, as illustrated previously, or in response to the migration influx resulting from the humanitarian crisis in Syria in 2015. Here, it is expected that leaders discuss and provide joint political impetus, sometimes blurring the legal boundaries between action by the European Council as an EU institution and by State representatives acting in their sovereign capacity.[321]

The functions above translate into the European Council exercising its powers in two main ways. Firstly, it may adopt decisions as provided for in several provisions of the EU Treaties. Decisions are legal acts because they are binding in their entirety,[322] and have to be published in the Official Journal of the European Union.[323] Since the Treaty of Lisbon, it is also clear that European Council decisions may be the subject matter of an action for annulment before the Court of Justice of the European Union.[324] European Council decisions may also be brought to the attention of the Court through other channels. In the *Pringle* case for instance, the Court of Justice was asked, in the context of a preliminary question raised by a national court, to review the validity of the decision by which the European Council amended Article 136 TFEU; the new Treaty provision explicitly allows the Member States whose currency is the euro to create among themselves a stability

[310] Art. 17(7) TEU; see further Chapter 2, Section 2.3.5.3. [311] Art. 283(2), subpara. 2 TFEU.
[312] Art. 236 TFEU; see also Chapter 2, Section 2.3.4.3, Rotating Presidency. [313] Art. 14(2) TEU.
[314] Art. 48 TEU; see also Chapter 1, Section 1.4.4. [315] Art. 7(2) TEU; see also Chapter 4, Section 4.3.2.1.
[316] Art. 49 TEU. [317] Art. 50 TEU. [318] Arts. 31(1), 42(2) TEU. [319] Art. 15(3) TEU.
[320] van Middelaar, *Alarums and Excursions*, p. 179. [321] See Chapter 2, Section 2.1.1. [322] Art. 288 TFEU.
[323] European Council, 'Rules of Procedure', Art. 12(1). [324] Art. 263(1), para. 1 TFEU.

mechanism to be activated, if indispensable to safeguard the stability of the euro area as a whole.[325]

Second, although the EU Treaties do not foresee other types of legal instruments for action by the European Council, the latter has developed a practice of acting through 'conclusions' to express consensus among its members on a given set of issues. European Council conclusions are particularly high-profile instruments, which are communicated to the public through the website of the European Council, in particular after each summit. The European Council may also decide to make public other types of statements or declarations. In principle, these instruments are not legally binding; nevertheless, in case of litigation, the Court of Justice of the European Union would look beyond the form of the act to check whether it may produce legal effects in the situation at hand.[326] The matter is particularly important when the content of European Council conclusions impacts on the relationships between EU institutions or has very specific implications for individuals. In such cases, third parties (including other institutions) may argue that their interests have been affected.

2.3.3.6 Relationship to Euro Summits

In addition to European Council meetings, the leaders of the Member States whose currency is the euro (thus within the euro area),[327] together with the President of the Commission, meet informally in the context of Euro Summits at least twice a year.[328] These meetings have been an important part of the political response to threats to the euro area since 2008, in the midst of the financial crisis.[329] These meetings allow discussions to take place relating to the specific responsibilities which euro area members share with regard to the single currency, as well as other issues concerning the governance of the euro area and strategic orientation for the conduct of economic policies to increase convergence in the euro area.[330]

The leaders of other Member States[331] also participate in Euro Summit meetings (which are then said to be in 'inclusive format') when these may be of general interest to them – for instance, because they relate to competitiveness, the global architecture of the euro area or its fundamental rules. These other European leaders shall also be kept informed of the work of Euro Summits[332] to avoid them being sidelined by this new informal organ. A President of the Euro Summit is appointed by its members (by simple majority) at the same time as the European Council elects its President, and for the same term of office. In practice so far, the President of the European Council has also presided over Euro Summits, even if they are from a non-euro area Member State, as was the case for Donald Tusk, who is from Poland. The role of the President of the Euro Summit is to prepare meetings in cooperation with the President of the Commission. The President of the Parliament may be invited to be heard, and the President of the Euro Summit shall report to the Parliament after each Summit meeting.[333]

[325] The Court of Justice accepted the admissibility of this preliminary question within the meaning of Art. 267 TFEU, and rejected the arguments on which the claim for a declaration of invalidity was founded: C-370/12, *Pringle*, EU:C:2012:756, paras. 38–44.

[326] See, in particular, Chapter 4, Section 4.3.1.1, Reviewable Acts.

[327] See Chapter 1, Section 1.4.3.2.

[328] Fiscal Stability Treaty, Art. 12(1). The first meeting took place on 12.10.2008, at the initiative of the French President Nicolas Sarkozy.

[329] van Middelaar, *Alarums and Excursions*, pp. 199–201.

[330] Fiscal Stability Treaty, Art. 12(2).

[331] Ibid., Art. 12(3) refers to the Leaders of 'the Contracting Parties other than those whose currency is the euro, which have ratified this Treaty'; these are now all the Member States of the EU.

[332] Ibid., Art. 12(6).

[333] Ibid., Art. 12(5).

As will become clear subsequently, these Euro Summits between leaders of the euro area closely interact with the work of ministers of finances of the same States meeting in the Eurogroup. Like the latter, and despite their political salience, the Euro Summit meetings are informal in nature and thus are not equated to the work of an EU institution or any other formal entity.

2.3.4 The Council

2.3.4.1 A Brief Description

The Council – the Council of the European Union or Council of Ministers – is composed of representatives of the Member States,[334] who, unlike the European Council, represent their governments at ministerial level. With key decision-making powers, in particular on policy coordination, as well as legislative and budgetary matters, the Council is central to the process of European integration, even if it is at times highly influenced by the European Council and increasingly shares some of its functions with the Parliament. The main features of the Council are set out in Article 16 TEU (see Box 2.4), which is complemented by several provisions of the TFEU.[335]

Box 2.4 Rough guide to the Council

Article 16 TEU

1. The Council shall, jointly with the European Parliament, exercise legislative and budgetary functions. It shall carry out policy-making and coordinating functions as laid down in the Treaties.

2. The Council shall consist of a representative of each Member State at ministerial level, who may commit the government of the Member State in question and cast its vote.

3. The Council shall act by a qualified majority except where the Treaties provide otherwise.

[...]

6. The Council shall meet in different configurations, the list of which shall be adopted in accordance with Article 236 of the Treaty on the Functioning of the European Union.

[...]

9. The Presidency of Council configurations, other than that of Foreign Affairs, shall be held by Member State representatives in the Council on the basis of equal rotation, in accordance with the conditions established in accordance with Article 236 of the Treaty on the Functioning of the European Union.

One of the main challenges in the institutional design of the Council has been to define the ways for it to make decisions. Unlike the European Council, which primarily sets political directions (by consensus), the Council is primarily expected to adopt legally

[334] Art. 10(2), subpara. 2 TEU. [335] Arts. 237–243 TFEU.

binding acts. The difficulty is thus to find a fair balance between allowing the expression and defence of national interests of the Member States represented therein and ensuring the ability of the EU to jointly move forward through actual decision-making. As we shall see, the related dilemma has crystallised in debates and changes on the method to calculate majorities in view of adoption of an act within the institution.

On other aspects, the Council has been fairly stable as an institution, despite the fact that its detailed composition evolves constantly. This is inherent in its design, which ought to reflect changes in the composition of governments at national level. Government representatives are indeed accountable to their national parliaments depending on national constitutional traditions, hence the recurrent claim for greater transparency to allow national parliamentarians to hold their ministers accountable for their work at EU level.[336]

2.3.4.2 Composition

The Council is composed of one representative per State at ministerial level. That requirement is formulated broadly to allow each Member State to decide in accordance with its own legal system which person is best placed to 'commit' the government in question and to 'cast its vote'.[337] In federal States, and depending on the policy area concerned, the matter may be complex. For instance, Belgium may be represented either by a representative of the federal government or by a representative of one of the communities or regions.[338] Much then depends on the policy area concerned and the level at which the competence is placed within the national system.

Importantly, the Commission shall be invited to take part in the meetings of the Council, as well as those of its preparatory organs, as will be described subsequently. Although Commission representatives are not part of the institution, their presence in the Council is important to ensure the good functioning of EU decision-making procedures that are indeed often initiated by the Commission.[339] The same applies to the Central Bank in cases where the Council discusses matters related to its competences.[340] However, the Council retains the possibility to decide to deliberate without these other institutions.[341]

2.3.4.3 Internal Organisation

Council Configurations

The representatives of the governments of the Member States meet in different configurations 'according to the subject matter dealt with'.[342] For instance, the twenty-seven government representatives in charge of the portfolio for agriculture at national level will come together to discuss the reform of the Common Agricultural Policy. The current list of configurations is set out in Box 2.5.[343]

[336] Art. 10(2), subpara. 2 TEU; see also Chapter 2, Section 2.2.1. [337] Art. 16(2) TEU.

[338] Special law on the reform of institutions of 8.8.1980, Art. 81, §6, read in conjunction with the cooperation agreement between the federal State, the communities and the regions from 8.3.1994.

[339] The importance of the presence of the Commission is confirmed by the duty to send the agenda ahead of each meeting, not only to the members of the Council, but also to the Commission; Council, 'Decision Adopting the Council's Rules of Procedure', OJ L 325, 11.12.2009, pp. 35–61 (last amended 2021), Art. 3(1) (hereafter, Council, 'Rules of Procedure').

[340] Art. 284(2) TFEU. [341] Council, 'Rules of Procedure', Art. 5(2). [342] Ibid., Art. 2(1).

[343] 'Decision of the Council (General Affairs) of 1 December 2009 Establishing the List of Council Configurations in Addition to those Referred to in the Second and Third Subparagraphs of Article 16(6) of the Treaty on European Union', OJ L 315, 2.12.2009, p. 46 (last amended 2010).

Box 2.5 List of Council configurations

Council Configurations

- General Affairs
- Foreign Affairs
- Economic and Financial Affairs (ECOFIN)[344]
- Justice and Home Affairs[345]
- Employment, Social Policy, Health and Consumer Affairs (EPSCO)
- Competitiveness (Internal Market, Industry, Research and Space)[346]
- Transport, Telecommunications and Energy
- Agriculture and Fisheries
- Environment
- Education, Youth, Culture and Sport.[347]

It is for each Member State to decide which of their representatives at ministerial level is best-placed to attend. As there is no hierarchy between the various configurations, divergent views between them tend to be addressed in the General Affairs formation, which ensures consistency in the works of the different Council configurations,[348] or, in practice and if necessary, in the European Council. Irrespective of the configuration in which a specific matter is discussed, any act is taken on behalf of the Council as a single institution. Any of the configurations can adopt an act that falls under the remit of another configuration, and no mention is made of the configuration in which the matter was discussed when the act is adopted. In practice, each configuration meets on average once a month, even if some meet more often than others. Although the list of configurations is established and updated by the European Council, the first two configurations listed previously are provided for by Article 16(6) TEU itself.[349]

These two configurations have pre-defined mandates. The General Affairs Council ensures the overall consistency of the work of the various configurations and deals with horizontal dossiers which affect several of the EU's policies, such as the negotiations on the multiannual financial framework.[350] It also prepares and follows up on meetings of the European Council, in liaison with the Presidents of the European Council and the Commission. As for the Foreign Affairs Council, its task is to elaborate the EU's external action on the basis of strategic guidelines laid down by the European Council, and to ensure the consistency of the EU's external action.[351] Depending on the political priorities of the day, each of the various configurations may be called upon to play a prominent role. By way

[344] Including budget. [345] Including civil protection. [346] Including tourism.
[347] Including audiovisual affairs. [348] Art. 16(6), subpara. 2 TEU. [349] Art. 236(a) TFEU.
[350] Such horizontal files also include enlargement, as well as operating rules for the EMU on request by the European Council; Council, 'Rules of Procedure', Art. 2(2).
[351] This refers to the whole of the EU's external action: the CFSP, CSDP, common commercial policy, development cooperation and humanitarian aid; Council, 'Rules of Procedure', Art. 2(5).

of example, in response to the economic and financial crisis, from early 2010, all eyes turned to the work of the Economic and Financial Affairs Council.

Rotating Presidency

The Presidency of the various configurations of the Council is normally held by the representative of the government of each Member State on a rotating basis.[352] The European Council (in practice, delegating decisions on the details to the Council)[353] establishes the order in which representatives of each Member State would preside over the Council in turn, as in the example in Box 2.6.[354] When deciding on this order, account must be taken of a set of elements: the equality of the Member States, their diversity and the geographical balance within the EU.[355]

In order to ensure a fair balance between these different considerations, the State in charge of the Presidency changes every six months and coordinates with another two States, which will also be in charge for six months each. A pre-established group of three Member States (or trio; see shading in Box 2.6) therefore prepares a joint draft programme of Council activities for every period of eighteen months, in close cooperation with the Commission and the President of the European Council, after appropriate consultations.[356] This system of a rotating Presidency, in principle, holds for preparatory organs within the Council.[357] The deputy permanent representative of the Member State that holds the six-month Presidency, for instance, will chair meetings of Coreper 1, as will be further explained subsequently.

Box 2.6 Balancing equality, diversity and geography: Rotating presidencies of the Council

Spain	July–December	2023
Belgium	January–June	2024
Hungary	July–December	2024
Poland	January–June	2025
Denmark	July–December	2025
Cyprus	January–June	2026

[352] Art. 16(9) TEU; Art. 236(b) TFEU.

[353] 'European Council Decision of 1 December 2009 on the Exercise of the Presidency of the Council', OJ L 315, 2.12.2009, p. 50, Art. 4.

[354] The list was last updated after the notification by the UK of its intention to withdraw and is now available: 'Council Decision of 1 December 2009 Laying Down Measures for the Implementation of the European Council Decision on the Exercise of the Presidency of the Council, and on the Chairmanship of Preparatory Bodies of the Council', OJ L 322, 9.12.2009, p. 28 (amended 2021). In accordance with Art. 3 of that Decision, the Council shall, before 31 December 2029, decide the order in which the Member States will hold the Presidency of the Council as from 1 January 2031.

[355] Declaration 9 annexed to the Final Act of the Intergovernmental Conference which adopted the Treaty of Lisbon; 'European Council Decision of 1 December 2009 on the Exercise of the Presidency of the Council', OJ L 315, 2.12.2009, Art. 1; Council, 'Rules of Procedure', Art. 1(4).

[356] Decision on the exercise of the Presidency of the Council, Art. 2; Council, 'Rules of Procedure', Art. 2(6).

[357] 'European Council Decision of 1 December 2009 on the Exercise of the Presidency of the Council', OJ L 315, 2.12.2009, Art. 2; Council, 'Rules of Procedure', Art. 19(4). These provisions also further elaborate on adjusted rules that apply, in particular, to the preparatory work for the Foreign Affairs Council configuration.

The Presidency has several functions; as well as chairing meetings, these include: contributing to preparing a draft programme for Council activities; ensuring that discussions are conducted smoothly; and (unless the Council decides otherwise) setting the order in which items are discussed and determining time allocated for discussion on these items.[358] Along with these organisational, leadership and brokering functions, the Presidency also represents the Council externally, such as before the Parliament.[359] The General Secretariat of the Council is involved in organising, coordinating and ensuring the coherence of the Council's work and the implementation of the eighteen-month programme of each pre-established group of three Member States for the Presidency, under the guidance of the latter.[360] A legal service ensures the drafting quality of proposals.

Despite its instability related to the fast rotation, this system of alternating Presidencies is understood as giving each Member State, on a regular basis, the opportunity to shape the political priorities of the agenda of the Council. Although meetings of the Council normally take place in Brussels, the Member State holding the Presidency also hosts a set of peripheral meetings and events that give visibility to the said State on the European stage, as well as to European affairs within that State.

The main exception to the system of rotating presidencies relates to meetings of the Council in the configuration that is devoted to Foreign Affairs on matters other than common commercial policy.[361] Such meetings are presided over by the High Representative of the Union for Foreign Affairs and Security Policy, and specific arrangements are also made for the Presidency of related preparatory meetings.[362] This is meant to contribute to the consistency of the EU's action externally.

Preparatory Work

The work of the representatives of the government in the Council is supported by a Committee of Permanent Representatives, known as Coreper. Its members are high-level diplomats by career, representing the Member States on a permanent basis in Brussels. As illustrated in Figure 2.3, the Coreper contributes to preparing the work of the Council.[363] It 'shall endeavour to reach agreement at its level', to then submit the subject matter of the agreement for adoption to the Council.[364] The Coreper is structured in two sub-entities, sharing the work by policy field. Coreper II deals with files that are often the most sensitive and which are subsequently dealt with by the Council configurations on Economic and Financial Affairs, Justice and Home Affairs, Foreign

[358] Council, 'Rules of Procedure', Arts. 2(6), 20.
[359] Ibid., Art. 26, where it is also specified that alternative arrangements may be made.
[360] Art. 240(2) TFEU; 'European Council Decision of 1 December 2009 on the Exercise of the Presidency of the Council', OJ L 315, 2.12.2009, Art. 3; Council, 'Rules of Procedure', Art. 23.
[361] Council, 'Rules of Procedure', Art. 2(5), subpara. 2, footnote.
[362] Arts. 16(9), 18(3) TEU; 'Council Decision of 1 December 2009 Laying Down Measures for the Implementation of the European Council Decision on the Exercise of the Presidency of the Council, and on the Chairmanship of Preparatory Bodies of the Council', OJ L 322, 9.12.2009, pp. 28–34 (last amended 2021), Annex II.
[363] Art. 16(7) TEU; Art. 240(1) TFEU.
[364] Council, 'Rules of Procedure', Art. 19(2).

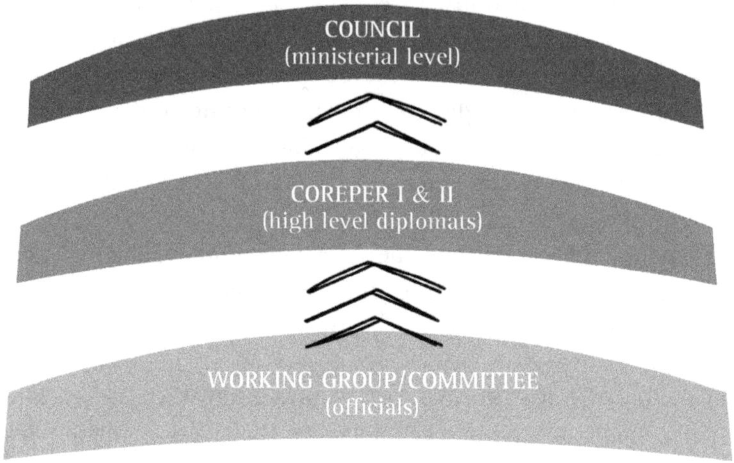

Figure 2.3 Ordinary workflow within the Council

Affairs and General Affairs. Coreper I prepares the work of the other Council configurations. Accordingly, the latter is composed of deputy permanent representatives, while the former is composed of the permanent representatives themselves.[365]

The work of these high-level diplomats is itself supported by that of national civil servants who are organised into committees or working parties. These (more than 150!) specialised preparatory bodies are where most of the technical and daily work is done. While some of them are already provided for in the EU Treaties,[366] others may be set up by or with the approval of Coreper.[367] The General Secretariat of the Council maintains a list of these preparatory bodies and further provides assistance in the preparatory work of the Council's activities.[368] There are, for instance, ad hoc Working Parties on the Cooperation and Verification Mechanism for Bulgaria and Romania (covering, in particular, areas of judicial reform and the fight against corruption since accession by these countries to the EU) and on Genetically Modified Organisms (examining legislation which allows Member States to restrict or prohibit the cultivation of GMOs). The Council occasionally receives direct support from these committees, which thereby bypass Coreper, as is the case for the Special Committee on Agriculture.[369]

[365] The preparatory work for Coreper I and II is in the hands of two informal groups of assistants of the high-level diplomats respectively known as the Mertens Group and the Antici Group.

[366] As is the case of the Trade Policy Committee, for instance; Art. 207(3) TFEU. See further J. Bauerschmidt, 'Council of the European Union: Internal Organisation', in S. Garben, L. Gormley, K. Purnhagen and M. Ruffert (eds.), *EU Encyclopedia* (Oxford University Press, 2021), online version.

[367] Council, 'Rules of Procedure', Art. 19(3).

[368] Art. 240(2) TFEU; see the latest list of Council preparatory bodies at consilium.europa.eu/en/council-eu/preparatory-bodies/.

[369] Décision des représentants des gouvernements des États membres de la Communauté économique européenne réunis au sein du Conseil, concernant l'accélération du rythme de réalisation des objets du traité, JO 58, 12.9.1960, 1217, Art. 5(4).

In preparation for meetings of the Council, a distinction is made between items for which it is expected that the members will grant approval without further discussion (A items), and others that require further discussion (B items). The Council decides on this final classification at the beginning of each meeting.[370] It is said that ministers only deliberate on about 40 per cent of what was pre-discussed before the matter was brought to their attention.[371] As imperfect and vulnerable to change as this figure may be, it illustrates how central Coreper is in the functioning of the Council; Coreper acts as a filter to enable the Council to focus on key issues. The Council, however, remains solely responsible for adopting final acts.[372]

2.3.4.4 Decision-Making

A vexed question in the institutional design of the Council has long related to its rules on decision-making. It is now established that, as a matter of principle, the Council acts by qualified majority voting. This is the rule that applies unless otherwise specified.[373] The very idea that a decision may be made without all Member States supporting it epitomises the autonomous law-making powers of the EU.

Qualified Majority Voting

The rules on qualified majority voting were for a long time based on a system of a different weighting of the vote of each State. With successive enlargements, the relative weight of the vote of each representative of the Member States in the Council had to be reconsidered. This was hotly debated because it formalised the respective importance given to each State in case of a vote, while also conditioning the ability of the institution to make decisions.

The Treaty of Lisbon considerably simplified the approach to qualified majority voting in the Council. Although the rules remained fairly complex during a transition period that expired in 2017, the rules are now those set out in Article 16(4) TEU.[374] These rules are formulated in abstract percentages so that, in principle, they can remain in place even in case of accession or withdrawal by a State. Several cumulative conditions must be fulfilled for an act to be deemed to be adopted when the Council acts by qualified majority voting. The vote of each member of the Council is counted in two ways, reflecting,

[370] Council, 'Rules of Procedure', Art. 3(6–8).

[371] O. Rozenberg, S. Novak, S. Bendjaballah and R. Dehousse, 'Avoiding Conflict? The EU Legislative Process in Times of Tension', *Les Cahiers Européens de Sciences Po*, 1 (2018), p. 12.

[372] This thus includes those pre-agreed at preparatory level; C-25/94, *Commission* v. *Council* (FAO), EU:C:1996:114, para. 27. This can be contrasted with situations in which Coreper acts in its own capacity rather than for the preparation and implementation of acts of the Council; C-626/15, *Commission* v. *Council (Antarctic MPAs)*, EU:C:2018:925, para. 61.

[373] Art. 16(3) TEU.

[374] See Protocol 36 on transitional provisions, Art. 2; Declaration 7 on Art. 16(4) TEU and Art. 238(2) TFEU; Protocol 9 on the Decision of the Council relating to the implementation of Article 16(4) TEU and Article 238(2) TFEU between 1.11.2014 and 31.3.2017 on the one hand, and as from 1.4.2017 on the other; 'Council Decision of 13 December 2007 Relating to the Implementation of Article 9C(4) of the Treaty on European Union [now Art. 16(4) TEU] and Article 205(2) of the Treaty on the Functioning of the European Union [now Art. 238(2) TFEU] between 1 November 2014 and 31 March 2017 on the one hand, and as from 1 April 2017 on the other' (2009/857/EC), OJ L 314, 1.12.2009, p. 73.

respectively, the principle of equality between States and the respective size of the population of each State.

By virtue of the first criterion, votes are counted on the basis of one vote per State, then at least 55 per cent of the members of the Council must vote in favour (fifteen out of twenty-seven).[375] This allows even small States, in terms of their population, to have a say. By virtue of the second criterion, the vote of each State is weighted to reflect the size of its population: the members of the Council representing at least 65 per cent of the population of the EU must vote in favour. Even if the votes from members of the Council in favour represent less than 65 per cent of the population, the qualified majority 'shall be deemed attained', if opposition comes from fewer than four Member States.[376] In other words (as illustrated in Figure 2.4), when making the calculation for the second criterion, attention should be paid to the fact that there must be at least four Member States to form a group that can prevent the adoption of the act – thus forming what is known as 'a blocking minority'. A blocking minority is indeed what is needed to prevent adoption.[377]

In practice, the requirement of at least four States to form a blocking minority means that any three of the most populous States cannot alone form an alliance to block the adoption

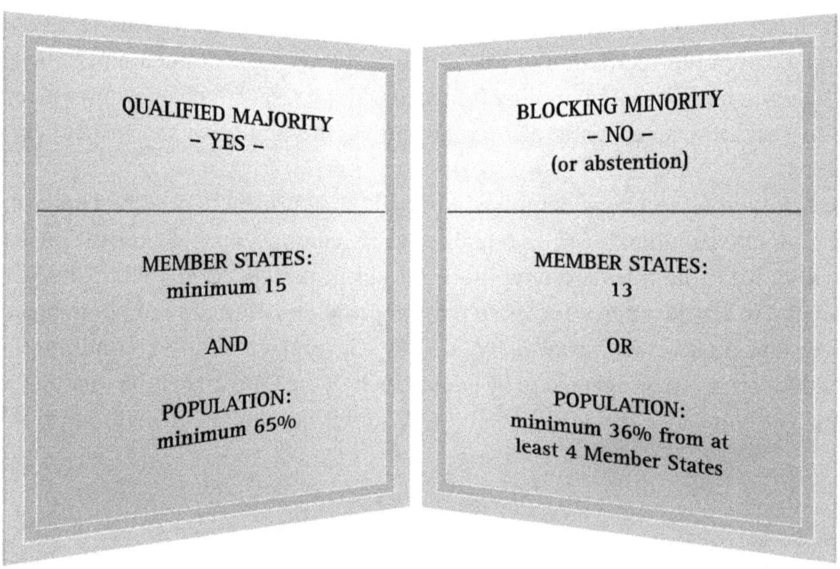

Figure 2.4 Qualified majority and blocking minority at the Council[378]

[375] Art. 16(3) TEU adds a requirement of at least fifteen Member States in favour. In a Union with twenty-seven Member States, as is the case at time of writing, this requirement is redundant.

[376] Art. 16(4), subpara. 2 TEU.

[377] In relation to the first criterion, a blocking minority exists if thirteen (or more) States out of twenty-seven vote against.

[378] The figures are based on a Union with twenty-seven Member States.

of an act within the Council.[379] In relation to the second criterion, this arrangement protects the interests of small States in terms of their population - the second criterion otherwise overall benefits populous States.[380] It may be recalled that Member States differ vastly in terms of the size of their population when compared to that of the EU as a whole. There is usually a distinction between large States such as Germany (18.54 per cent of the EU's population) and France (14.7 per cent), medium-sized States such as Spain (10.56 per cent) and Poland (8.47 per cent), and small States such as Slovenia (0.47 per cent) and Malta (0.11 per cent).[381] Medium-sized States were initially opposed to the calculation method for qualified majority voting set out in the Treaty of Lisbon, hence the initial transition period, which expired in 2017.

As will be explained further subsequently, instances of Member States being isolated and ostensibly placed in the minority are uncommon overall; a vast majority of acts of the Council are adopted without opposition.[382] Yet the efficiency of EU law-making does at times lead to tension due to interests that representatives of individual Member States feel they must absolutely protect. In the early years, the Luxembourg compromise[383] allowed Member States to be reassured that their important national interests would not be disregarded, even for the adoption of measures by qualified majority voting. It hindered decision-making within the Council, however, as it resulted in the possibility, at the very least, of significantly delaying the adoption of acts.

Although arrangements inspired by the Luxembourg compromise are hardly relied upon nowadays,[384] several mechanisms are available for Member States in the minority to

379 For instance, even if twenty-four Member States vote in favour, if the three States opposing the measure are Germany (with 18.54 per cent of the population of the EU), France (14.97 per cent) and Italy (13.58 per cent), the qualified majority will be deemed to be attained. Indeed, in so far as the second criterion is concerned, although the population of the twenty-four Member States in favour would only represent 52.91 per cent of the population of the EU (and thus an opposition representing the corresponding 47.09 per cent), the requirement of at least four Member States to form a blocking minority is *not* fulfilled. This simulation is based on figures available for 2021.

380 Note that even if the figures necessary to constitute a blocking minority are not met, if there is at least 55 per cent of the population, or 55 per cent of the number of Member States necessary to constitute a 'blocking minority', the Council shall in principle hold further discussions. The Council shall 'do all in its power to reach, within a reasonable time and without prejudicing obligatory time limits laid down by Union law, a satisfactory solution to address concerns raised by the members of the Council' concerned; 'Council Decision of 13 December 2007 Relating to the Implementation of Article 9C(4) of the Treaty on European Union [now Art. 16(4) TEU] and Article 205(2) of the Treaty on the Functioning of the European Union [now Art. 238(2) TFEU] between 1 November 2014 and 31 March 2017 on the one hand, and as from 1 April 2017 on the other' (2009/857/EC), OJ L 314, 1.12.2009, p. 73, Arts. 4–6. Nevertheless the Council's 'Rules of Procedure', Art. 11(1), remain applicable so that a simple majority of the Member States may decide to request a vote. This last point, as well as the culture of consensual decision-making in the shadow of the vote, explains why, in practice, Decision 2009/857 is hardly invoked. See J.-C. Piris, *The Lisbon Treaty: A Legal and Political Analysis* (Cambridge University Press, 2010), p. 223; P. Dann, 'The Council', in Schütze and Tridimas (eds.), *Oxford Principles of European Union Law*, p. 542. Note that Decision 2009/857 and the related Declaration 7 have to be read in light of Protocol 9 annexed to the EU Treaties.

381 Where the Council votes are calculated by reference to the population of the participating Member States, reference is made to figures set out in Annex III of the Council's 'Rules of Procedure', which are updated every year on the basis of data from the Statistical Office of the European Union; Council, 'Rules of Procedure', Art. 11(5–6). The statistics herein are those available for 2021. See the very useful voting simulator at www.consilium.europa.eu/en/council-eu/voting-system/voting-calculator/.

382 See Chapter 2, Section 2.3.4.4, Meetings, Votes and Transparency. 383 See Chapter 1, Section 1.3.2.2.

384 See Chapter 2, note 380.

channel their discontent over the (perspective of) adoption of an act by qualified majority voting. In certain areas of EU law, formal procedures allow a brake to be applied to the decision-making process and to refer the matter to the European Council. Such an emergency brake was used, for instance, in response to the proposal to create a European Public Prosecutor's office.[385] In other areas of EU law, where such a formal brake is not available, the political game occasionally enables isolated Member States to put pressure on the decision-making process. For instance, in 2020, Poland and Hungary made the adoption of important decisions on the future of EU finances, for which unanimity was necessary,[386] conditional upon the finding of compromises for the adoption of a new regime on (rule of law) conditionality for the protection of the EU budget for which qualified majority voting was requested, and to which they were strongly opposed.[387]

Furthermore, Member States may issue a statement or explanations on the vote to be made public, enabling the expression of their discontent without necessarily showing a no-vote.[388] Finally, States may (individually or in a coordinated fashion, and often unsuccessfully[389]) call into question the validity of the act that was adopted against their will before the Court of Justice of the European Union. A well-known example of an act adopted despite strong opposition by a Member State is the Working Time Directive.[390] The United Kingdom had been strongly opposed to it, but was in the minority. It initiated an action for annulment of the Directive after its adoption, which was largely dismissed.[391]

As well as the general rule on methods to calculate the qualified majority set out in Article 16(4) TEU, a number of arrangements are possible to address specific situations, such as where not all members of the Council participate in the vote.[392] This occurs, for instance, when a State is targeted by an act of the Council in the context of a possible breach of the values referred to in Article 2 TEU, or for excessive budgetary deficit as part of the economic policy of the EU.[393] The thresholds per members of the Council and size of the population remain unchanged, but the rules on the minimum number of States requested to form a blocking minority are adjusted.[394]

[385] In accordance with Art. 86(1), subpara. 2 TFEU, a group of seventeen Member States requested, by a letter of 14.2.2017, that the draft Regulation on the establishment of the EPPO be referred to the European Council. The EPPO was ultimately created in the form of enhanced cooperation: 'Council Regulation (EU) 2017/1939 of 12 October 2017 Implementing Enhanced Cooperation on the Establishment of the European Public Prosecutor's Office', OJ L 283, 31.10.2017, pp. 1–71 (last amended 2020).

[386] Arts. 311 (own resources), 312 (multiannual financial framework) TFEU.

[387] V. Hopkins, J. Shotter and S. Fleming, 'Hungary and Poland Harden Stance in EU Budget Stand-Off', *Financial Times*, 26.11.2020; European Council, Conclusions on the MFF and Next Generation EU, COVID-19, climate change, security and external relations, 10–11.12.2021, Point I.

[388] Council, 'Rules of Procedure', Arts. 7(4), 9.

[389] E.g. Joined Cases C-643/15 and C-647/15, *Slovak Republic and Hungary (supported by Poland)* v. *Council*, EU:C:2017:631. See further Joined Cases C-715/17, C-718/17 and C-719/17, *Commission* v. *Poland, Hungary and Czech Republic*, EU:C:2020:257.

[390] C-84/94, *UK* v. *Council (Working Time)*, EU:C:1996:431.

[391] The current version of the directive is 'Directive 2003/88/EC of the European Parliament and of the Council of 4 November 2003 Concerning Certain Aspects of the Organisation of Working Time', OJ L 299, 18.11.2003, p. 9.

[392] Art. 238(3) and (2) TFEU. [393] Art. 7 TEU; Arts. 354, 126(13) TFEU.

[394] This is subject to further adjustments if the proposal for adoption was not put forward by the Commission or the High Representative for Foreign Affairs and Security: there must be a higher number of votes representing the Member States; Art. 238(3)(b) TFEU. This latter set of arrangements is used, for instance, in the context of the withdrawal by a Member State from the EU; Art. 50(4) TEU.

Other Voting Procedures

Although qualified majority voting is the rule, provisions of EU law may specify that the Council shall act by other voting arrangements.[395] The Council may be requested to act by simple majority, in which case it shall act by a majority of its component members (fourteen out of twenty-seven).[396] This is how the Council decides on its own Rules of Procedure, for instance, to structure its work internally.[397] The Council may also be expected to decide by unanimity, as is the case in the context of the CFSP, as well as for procedures related to sensitive matters such as for accession by a State to the EU.[398] If unanimity voting is required, abstention shall not prevent adoption.[399]

Meetings, Votes and Transparency

The Council meets when convened by its President, either at the initiative of the President, or at the request of one of its members or of the Commission.[400] The Council further votes on the initiative of its President, who may also be required to open a voting procedure on an initiative of a member or of the Commission, supported by a majority of the members of the Council. The presence of a majority of the members of the Council is required to enable the Council to vote, and voting takes place in the order of the Member States laid down in the list of successive presidencies.[401] There is a possibility of having recourse to a written procedure in cases of urgency or special circumstances, and even a simplified written procedure in a set of predefined and less sensitive matters.[402] Unless otherwise specified, abstentions count as a vote against.[403]

As already noted, in principle, the Council decides by qualified majority voting. In this context, most procedures for which the adoption of an act requiring qualified majority voting are actually decided with all Member States voting in favour, with the effect that it is not common for the (preliminary) opposition by a State or a group of States to actually be visible.[404] This observation must not be misunderstood. It does not amount to transforming the requirement of qualified majority voting into unanimity or consensus. The representatives of the governments, and the Presidency in particular, constantly have in mind the thresholds necessary to pass a vote by qualified majority voting: they thus deliberate in the 'shadow of the vote'.[405] Nevertheless, such deliberations often lead to the adoption of a

[395] Art. 16(3) TEU. [396] Art. 238(1) TFEU. [397] Art. 240(3) TFEU. [398] Arts. 24(1), 49 TEU.

[399] Art. 238(4) TFEU. [400] Art. 237 TFEU; Council, 'Rules of Procedure', Art. 1(1).

[401] Council, 'Rules of Procedure', Art. 11(1–4). Any member of the Council may act on behalf of not more than one other member; Art. 239 TFEU. Although members of the Council who are prevented from attending may arrange to be represented, only representatives of each Member State at ministerial level may cast a vote; Art. 16(2) TEU; Council, 'Rules of Procedure', Art. 4.

[402] Council, 'Rules of Procedure', Art. 12. The related rules were made more flexible during the COVID-19 pandemic to allow the members of the Council to work remotely: 'Council Decision (EU) 2020/430 of 23 March 2020 on a Temporary Derogation from the Council's Rules of Procedure in View of the Travel Difficulties Caused by the COVID-19 Pandemic in the Union', OJ L 88I, 24.3.2020, pp. 1–2 (and this derogation has been extended several times).

[403] Art. 16(4) TEU (as regards qualified majority voting); Art. 238(1) TFEU (simple majority voting).

[404] It has been reported, for instance, that during the legislative period 2009–2014, an overall 70 per cent of legislative acts for which qualified majority voting was requested were adopted without opposition (understood as covering either votes against or abstentions); Rozenberg et al., 'Avoiding Conflict?', p. 14.

[405] J. Weiler, 'The Transformation of Europe', *Yale Law Journal*, 100 (1993), p. 2461: 'The possibility of breaking deadlocks by voting drives the negotiators to break the deadlock without actually resorting to the vote.'

decision that does not single out the reluctant State(s). This approach is understood to reflect the diplomatic culture of meetings of representatives of the government at ministerial level, and which is often deemed useful to encourage compromises and facilitate decision-making at EU level. It is that very culture that also attracts criticism for hindering transparency and democratic accountability, as most compromises are in fact made behind closed doors ahead of the final vote.

In an attempt to address these concerns, the Treaty of Lisbon made a distinction between deliberation and votes on legislative acts and non-legislative activities.[406] The distinction impacts on the publicity of the meeting and related minutes. Article 16(8) TEU establishes a duty on the Council to meet in public when it 'deliberates and votes on a draft legislative act'.[407] As a consequence, the results of votes and explanations of votes by members, as well as statements in the minutes, are made public, and meetings are accessible through audio-visual means and broadcasted.[408] By contrast, other parts (such as preparatory work, the importance of which has already been highlighted) or types (such as non-legislative procedures) of the decision-making process remain, in principle, not public. The Rules of Procedure of the Council, however, establish a set of circumstances in which deliberations, debates, votes and minutes may be made public, such as the first deliberation on important proposals for legally binding acts.[409] Furthermore, the standard legal regime on the right of public access to documents applies to Council documents.[410]

2.3.4.5 Functions and Powers

The primary role of the Council is to act as a legislator. In the context of the 'ordinary' legislative procedure, the Council is a co-legislator with the Parliament.[411] The latter has gained importance in that procedure with each Treaty revision, in particular since its members became elected by direct universal suffrage. In the context of 'special' legislative procedures, such as that for the adoption of legislation to combat discrimination,[412] or other procedures for the adoption of non-legislative acts on the basis of the EU Treaties, the Council is normally the main decision-maker, with a smaller role for the Parliament.[413] When the EU legislator confers delegated powers on the Commission, the Council has the same rights of control as the Parliament, namely to revoke the delegation or to object to a delegated act adopted by the Commission.[414]

[406] For a critical analysis, see D. M. Curtin and P. Leino, 'In Search of Transparency for EU Law-Making: Trilogues on the Cusp of Dawn', *Common Market Law Review*, 54 (2017), pp. 1673–1712. See further Chapter 3, Sections 3.5.3 and 3.6.

[407] See also Art. 15(2) TFEU.

[408] Council, 'Rules of Procedure', Art. 7(3–4). See, in particular, the database of the Council where votes on each instrument are made available: www.consilium.europa.eu/en/general-secretariat/corporate-policies/transparency/open-data/.

[409] Council, 'Rules of Procedure', Art. 8. Save otherwise specified, the deliberations of the Council shall be covered by the obligation of professional secrecy; Art. 6.

[410] Council, 'Rules of Procedure', Annex II; 'Regulation (EC) No 1049/2001 of the European Parliament and of the Council of 30 May 2001 Regarding Public Access to European Parliament, Council and Commission Documents', OJ L 145, 31.5.2001, p. 43. See further Bauerschmidt, 'Council of the European Union'.

[411] Art. 289(1) TFEU. [412] Art. 19(1) TFEU. [413] See Chapter 3, Section 3.6.1.1.

[414] For implementing powers conferred on the Commission, the Council does not have rights of control as such, but it may voice the view that the Commission exceeds its powers. On delegated and implementing acts, and related decision-making procedures, see Chapter 3, Sections 3.5.3.2, Tertiary Law, and 3.6.1.2.

The Council is the main decision-maker when it comes to the conclusion of international agreements in the context of the external action of the EU, although this is often subject to the consent of the Parliament.[415]

The Council has important budgetary powers.[416] It co-decides on the EU's annual budget with the Parliament.[417] It also decides, through an atypical legislative procedure, on the system of own resources of the EU, as well as, with the consent of the Parliament and, in practice, with strong guidance from the European Council, on the multiannual financial framework for the EU which is decided every seven years.[418]

The Council carries out general policy-making and coordinating functions, which are shared with the European Council (in charge of defining general political directions and priorities) and the Commission (which takes appropriate initiatives and has coordinating functions).[419] This function is largely carried out by each trio of Presidencies issuing their eighteen-month programme. In certain areas of EU law, the coordinating role of the Council is more formalised, as is the case in the context of economic and employment policy, where the impulse also comes from the European Council.[420]

The Council is also part of the system of checks and balances between EU institutions in several ways. It is involved in appointments to high-level positions. For instance, it is expected to put forward a list of names for members of the Commission in common accord with the President-elect of the Commission.[421] It makes recommendations for appointment to the President, Vice-President and other members of the Executive Board of the Central Bank, and makes the decision on who will become the members of the Court of Auditors.[422]

The Council further interacts with other institutions in several ways. It may make non-binding proposals for the Commission to take (legislative) action.[423] Its representatives may be heard by the Parliament.[424] The Council may commence legal action before the Court of Justice of the European Union against other institutions, although in practice the Council challenges the compatibility of EU acts with primary law less often than other institutions, given that it is usually the final authority adopting such acts.[425]

Finally, the Council may be called upon to contribute to shaping primary law or law impacting the fundamental structure of the EU. It contributes, for instance, to the enlargement and withdrawal processes, although this is, in practice, largely dependent on the European Council.[426] It also authorises, with the consent of the Parliament, a group of Member States to engage in and develop enhanced cooperation.[427]

[415] Art. 218(6) TFEU; see also Chapter 3, Section 3.6.2.
[416] For a more detailed and nuanced analysis of decision-making in this field, see Chapter 3, Section 3.6.3.
[417] Art. 314 TFEU. [418] Arts. 311, para. 3, 312(2) TFEU. [419] Arts. 15(1), 17(1) TEU.
[420] Arts. 121, 148 TFEU. [421] Art. 17(7) TEU.
[422] The Parliament is consulted. See, respectively, Arts. 283(2), subpara. 2, 286(2), subpara. 1 TFEU.
[423] Art. 241 TFEU; 'Interinstitutional Agreement between the European Parliament, the Council of the European Union and the European Commission on Better Law-Making', OJ L 123, 12.5.2016, p. 1, para. 10.
[424] Art. 230 TFEU. The Presidency, in particular, represents the Council before the Parliament; Council, 'Rules of Procedure', Art. 26. See further Art. 36 TEU.
[425] See Chapter 4, Section 4.3.1.1. [426] Arts. 49 and 50 TEU; see also Chapter 2, Sections 2.1.2 and 2.1.3.
[427] Art. 329(1), subpara. 1 TFEU; see also Chapter 1, Section 1.4.3.4.

2.3.4.6 Seat and Places of Work

The Council has its seat in Brussels. This is also where its General Secretariat, with more than 3,000 staff members, is based, and where Coreper, working groups and committees meet. During the months of April, June and October, the Council holds its meetings in Luxembourg.[428] Each of the rotating Presidencies of the Council hosts informal meetings in turn. Naturally, each Member State's representative is supported by its own support staff at national level, who may be based in Brussels as well as in the home country.

2.3.4.7 Relationship to the Eurogroup

Alongside meetings of the Council, and more specifically ahead of those of its configuration in charge of Economic and Financial Affairs, the ministers of the Member States whose currency is the euro meet regularly in the context of the Eurogroup. This practice of informal gatherings has developed since the late 1990s, in parallel with the advancement of the EMU.[429] It enables discussions on matters of 'key importance to fiscal, monetary and structural policies in the euro area', and a focus on themes of 'particular importance for the single currency, with a forward looking bias'.[430] Today, the existence of the Eurogroup is anchored in Article 137 TFEU and Protocol 14, and statements on the common positions resulting from its meetings are often eagerly awaited, in particular in times of economic hardship.

As well as the Member States whose currency is the euro (nineteen States at time of writing), the Commission shall take part in the meetings and the Central Bank shall be invited to join.[431] It is also common for the Eurogroup to invite fellow ministers from non-euro area countries to attend its meetings, or part thereof, which are then known as being in inclusive format. The meetings should be prepared by representatives of the ministers responsible for finances in Member States from the euro area, together with the Commission.[432] The Eurogroup elects its President from among its members for two and a half years, by a majority of its members.[433] The mandate is renewable.

The political salience of the activities of the Eurogroup has increased considerably in recent years, as aptly illustrated by its action in support of conditional financial assistance from the European Stability Mechanism to Member States in difficulties in the context of the economic and financial crisis. As a result, the ambiguity of its legal status has come to the fore. The existence of the Eurogroup is recognised by Article 137 TFEU, but Protocol 14 states that it 'shall meet *informally*' (emphasis added). The Court of Justice has clarified that the informal nature of the Eurogroup is a bar to its recognition as an EU institution (it cannot be equated to a configuration of the Council) or any body, office or agency for the purpose of triggering the liability of the EU in damages.[434] The activities of the Eurogroup are thus largely beyond the realm of judicial scrutiny by the Court of Justice of the European Union.[435] Instead, the

[428] Protocol 6 annexed to the EU Treaties on the location of the seats of the institutions and of certain bodies, offices, agencies and departments of the European Union, Art. 1(b).

[429] See Chapter 1, Section 1.3.2.3. [430] Eurogroup, Working Methods of the Eurogroup, 3.10.2008, point 1.

[431] Protocol 14 annexed to the EU Treaties, Art. 1. [432] Ibid., Art. 1.

[433] Ibid., Art. 2; Eurogroup, Working Methods of the Eurogroup, 3.10.2008, point 2.1.

[434] Joined Cases C-597/18 P, C-598/18 P, C-603/18 P and C-604/18 P, *Council* v. *K. Chrysostomides & Co. and others*, EU:C:2020:1028, paras. 80, 87, 88 thereby disagreeing on points of law with the General Court (see paras. 90, 97).

[435] The Eurogroup has been working on improving its transparency: Eurogroup, Transparency policy review and way forward, 20.9.2019.

work of the Eurogroup must be seen as preparatory to that of EU institutions, which may themselves be held accountable.[436]

2.3.5 The Commission

2.3.5.1 A Brief Description

The Commission's mandate, largely unchanged since its inception, is to promote the general interest of the EU. The Commission is understood to be the motor of European integration due to its powers to propose new policy developments and its right of legislative initiative. Importantly though, it could not play such a driving role in isolation: it needs the support of other institutions which contribute to political steering, several of which have the final say on decision-making. The Commission is also the guardian of the EU Treaties, shown through its important implementation and enforcement powers. The main features of the Commission are set out in Article 17 TEU (Box 2.7), which is complemented by several provisions of the TFEU.[437]

Box 2.7 **Rough guide to the Commission**

Article 17 TEU

1. The Commission shall promote the general interest of the Union and take appropriate initiatives to that end. It shall ensure the application of the Treaties, and of measures adopted by the institutions pursuant to them. It shall oversee the application of Union law under the control of the Court of Justice of the European Union. It shall execute the budget and manage programmes. It shall exercise coordinating, executive and management functions, as laid down in the Treaties. With the exception of the common foreign and security policy, and other cases provided for in the Treaties, it shall ensure the Union's external representation. It shall initiate the Union's annual and multiannual programming with a view to achieving interinstitutional agreements.

2. Union legislative acts may only be adopted on the basis of a Commission proposal, except where the Treaties provide otherwise. Other acts shall be adopted on the basis of a Commission proposal where the Treaties so provide.

3. The Commission's term of office shall be five years.
The members of the Commission shall be chosen on the ground of their general competence and European commitment from persons whose independence is beyond doubt.
In carrying out its responsibilities, the Commission shall be completely independent. [...]

4. The Commission [...] shall consist of one national of each Member State, including its President and the High Representative of the Union for Foreign Affairs and Security Policy who shall be one of its Vice-Presidents. [...]

[436] Joined Cases C-597/18 P, C-598/18 P, C-603/18 P and C-604/18 P, *Council* v. *K. Chrysostomides & Co. and others*, EU:C:2020:1028, para. 93. Furthermore, the Commission, which is present in Eurogroup meetings, ought to ensure that political agreements concluded therein are in conformity with EU law (para. 96).

[437] Arts. 244–250 TFEU.

To perform these functions, which are crucial to the process of European integration, evolutions of the institutional design of the Commission have taken place: a quest for independence from the Member States related, in particular, to the methods of appointment; a search for enhanced democratic legitimacy and accountability, in particular in relations with the Parliament and towards citizens; and never-ending concern for efficiency, which has translated into greater internal hierarchical structuring. We will return to these points subsequently.

The Commission is composed (at time of writing) of one Commissioner per Member State and seeks to balance two main trends. On the one hand, it is expected to provide expertise and technical support to the machinery of the EU legal order. On the other hand, due to its growing visibility (it is often mistakenly equated to the EU itself!), it is regularly called upon to play a greater political role.

2.3.5.2 Composition and Members

One National of Each Member State

The Commission is composed of twenty-seven members, including its President and the High Representative of the Union for Foreign Affairs and Security Policy, thus one member per Member State.[438] The EU Treaties make it possible to reduce the number of Commissioners to two-thirds of the number of Member States.[439] The transition to this new regime, which had initially been foreseen for 2014, had still not taken place at time of writing, despite occasional calls for it, such as from the French President Emmanuel Macron in 2017.[440]

Competence, European Commitment and Independence

The Commissioners, whose names are initially suggested by each Member State, shall be chosen 'on the ground of their general competence and European commitment from persons whose independence is beyond doubt'.[441] The candidates may – but do not have to – (have) run for the elections to the European Parliament; although if they are elected, they ought to resign from their function as an MEP to become a

438 They must be nationals of the Member States; Art. 17(4).

439 Note that, in the original system, large Member States had two commissioners, while smaller ones only had one.

440 See Art. 17(5), subpara. 1 TEU on the possibility for the European Council to depart from the initial plan, which was to reduce the number of Members; and also Declaration 10 annexed to the Treaty of Lisbon. That possibility became the subject matter of a compromise in the run-up to the ratification of the Treaty of Lisbon to appease concerns from the Irish people (European Council, Presidency Conclusions, 11–12.12.2008, point 2). See now '2013/272/EU: European Council Decision of 22 May 2013 Concerning the Number of Members of the European Commission', OJ L 165, 18.6.2013, p. 98. Note that Art. 244 TFEU foresees a system of rotation established unanimously by the European Council, with strictly equal rotation between nationals of the various Member States and reflecting the demographic and geographical range of all the Member States. Calling for change on that point, see, for instance, President Macron, Sorbonne speech, 26.9.2017.

441 Art. 17(3), subpara. 2 TEU. Commissioners may be reappointed.

Commissioner.[442] Members of the Commission may not engage in any other occupation.[443]

Key to the function of a member of the Commission is a notion of independence, which may be understood in two ways. Firstly, Commissioners shall be independent from the State that suggested their appointment. Member States are under a duty to respect the independence of the members of the Commission and shall not seek to influence them in the performance of their tasks.[444] Second, Commissioners shall be independent from the private sector and, especially, from commercial interests. For instance, members of the Commission may not during their term of office engage in any other occupation, whether gainful or not. They also commit to behave with integrity and discretion after their term of office.[445] In case of breach of these obligations, the Court of Justice may decide to compulsorily retire a Commissioner from their role, or to deprive a former Commissioner of their rights to a pension or other benefits.

The question of independence from the private sector has come to the fore in recent years, after former members of the Commission accepted high-level appointments with private undertakings, such as the Commission's former President Barroso's employment with Goldman Sachs Bank. In response, the institution reinforced its Code of Conduct for Commissioners.[446] For instance, the Code defines the notion of 'conflict of interest' so as to cover situations that may be reasonably perceived as a conflict of interest.[447] Furthermore, if former Commissioners intend to work in areas that are related to their former portfolios, they ought to consult an Independent Ethical Committee. Both the Commission's decisions and the Committee's opinions related to such decisions will be made public.[448]

2.3.5.3 Designation and End of Mandate

The methods for the designation and termination of mandates of members of the Commission have evolved significantly over time. Today, the procedure to designate the Commission is divided into two main stages, set out in Article 17(7) TEU. The President is designated before the other members. This allows the President-elect to be involved in the designation of these other members, and to have stronger influence than in the past on the

[442] 'Commission Decision of 31 January 2018 on a Code of Conduct for the Members of the European Commission', OJ C 65, 21.2.2018, p. 7, Art. 10(2); see further 'Framework Agreement on Relations between the European Parliament and the European Commission', OJ L 304 20.11.2010, p. 47 (as amended 2018), point 4. Note that members of the Commission may be chosen as lead candidates in the context of the informal system of Spitzenkandidaten for the position of Commission President; that system does not require the Spitzenkandidat to be running for the elections to the Parliament though. We return to the system of Spitzenkandidaten subsequently.

[443] Art. 245, para. 2 TFEU.

[444] Art. 17(3), subpara. 3 TEU; Art. 245, para. 1 TFEU.

[445] Art. 245, para. 2 TFEU.

[446] 'Commission Decision of 31 January 2018 on a Code of Conduct for the Members of the European Commission', OJ C 65, 21.2.2018, pp. 7–20.

[447] Ibid., Art. 2(6).

[448] Ibid., Art. 11(3) and (7). On the context in which the reform was adopted, and calling for yet further safeguards, see European Ombudsman, Recommendations in the joint inquiry into complaints 194/2017/EA, 334/2017/EA and 543/2017/EA on the European Commission's handling of post-mandate employment of former Commissioners, a former Commission President and the role of its 'Ethics Committee', 20.7.2018.

dynamics within the College of Commissioners. Furthermore, the Parliament has, over time, gained an increasing role in the designation of the Commission, as we shall see. Note that the specific case of the High Representative for Foreign Affairs and Security Policy, who is an atypical member of the Commission, is discussed separately in Section 2.3.6.

Election of President of the Commission

The procedure is triggered in the weeks that follow the elections to the Parliament. The European Council (acting by qualified majority), 'taking into account' these elections[449] and after appropriate consultations, proposes a candidate for the position of President of the Commission to the Parliament. The Parliament votes on this proposal to elect the President. For that purpose, the candidate is invited to present their political guidelines to Parliament, followed by a debate and a vote by secret ballot in which a majority of the component members of the Parliament must support the said candidate.[450] If that fails, the European Council must propose a new candidate within one month.

During the election campaign that preceded the 2014 elections to the Parliament, the main political forces in the outgoing Parliament interpreted Article 17(7), subparagraph 1 TEU in their favour. As the said article requires the European Council to take into account the outcome of the elections to the Parliament, the main political forces within the Parliament pre-emptively put forward names of chosen leading candidates from within their ranks. These candidates took the lead in representing the various political forces and giving them a face during the campaign, such as in the context of livestreamed debates intended to connect better with EU citizens. Political forces from within the Parliament thereby built on the threat not to elect, after the Parliament's elections, any other candidates for the position of President of the Commission than the ones they had identified before the elections.

This creative interpretation of Article 17(7), subparagraph 1 TEU is known as establishing a Spitzenkandidaten process.[451] It places parliamentarian forces in the driving seat for the choice of the President of the Commission. The technique was successful in 2014. Mr Jean-Claude Juncker had been the lead candidate identified by the European People's Party; the party won the elections and the Spitzenkandidat of this party was proposed by the European Council to become the future President of the Commission. Naturally, he was elected by the Parliament. In the subsequent elections from 2019, however, the European Council did not put forward the name of the Spitzenkandidat from the winning group in the Parliament – whose designation as lead candidate had been contested – but another name, that of Ms Ursula von der Leyen. As the name proposed was from the winning political group, the European Council was 'taking into account' the outcome of the Parliament's elections, as formally requested by Article 17(7) TEU, but the European Council but did not feel bound to opt for the candidate pre-identified within the Parliament before the elections. Ms von der Leyen was supported by a sufficient number of newly elected parliamentarians: she showed understandable relief when hearing the good news, and announced that more reflection on the Spitzenkandidaten system was needed.[452]

[449] Art. 17(7), subpara. 1 TEU; see also Declaration 11 annexed to the Treaty of Lisbon.

[450] Parliament, 'Rules of Procedure', Rule 124.

[451] In other words, a system based on the pre-designation of 'lead candidates'.

[452] Candidate for President of the European Commission, Opening Statement in the European Parliament Plenary session, 16.7.2019.

Appointment of the Commission as a Body

In the second stage of the procedure for the designation of the Commission, the Member States propose the names of their candidates to become members of the Commission. It is then up to the Council, 'by common accord' with the President-elect (Ms von der Leyen in the 2019 procedure), to adopt the list of the other persons proposed for appointments as members of the Commission. At this stage, not only are the candidates for each State being selected, but the portfolio that each future member will be responsible for within the Commission is also identified by the President-elect.

In that exercise, the Member States proposing candidates and represented within the Council (in practice, the matter is also discussed within the European Council) do not negotiate in a vacuum. They must do this, not only with the President-elect who is already shaping their future team, but also with the Parliament. Indeed, the list of the persons proposed for appointments as members of the Commission is put forward by the Council, together with the allocated portfolios in the form of 'mission letters' to the Parliament. The consent of the latter (acting by a majority of the votes cast) on the proposed full list of members of the Commission[453] is necessary before the European Council (acting by qualified majority) can ultimately appoint the Commission as a body.

Here again, the Parliament has developed a practice that strengthens its position in the process. Although it is formally only empowered to vote on the full list of proposed members of the Commission, it organises individual hearings with proposed commissioners ahead of the vote on the Commission as a body.[454] MEPs can therefore threaten not to consent to the appointment of the Commission as a body if controversial members remain part of the proposed team. After the 2004 elections, for instance, the Parliament applied pressure in order to replace the initial Commissioner-designate for the portfolio on justice, Mr Rocco Buttiglione: his stand on the role of women and on gay people was deemed unacceptable. The candidate was indeed replaced. In 2019, individual hearings of Commissioner-designates took a prominent position in European public debate, with pressure being successfully exercised by the Parliament against the designation of several of the candidates initially proposed.

Overall, the diversity of actors engaged in the designation of the Commission results in attention being paid to a multitude of factors, ranging from geopolitical representation to gender balance. Notably, the Commission appointed in 2019 included more women than ever before.[455] These factors are also often related to other political decisions on appointments in leading positions of other institutions.[456]

[453] This includes President and High Representative of the Union for Foreign Affairs and Security Policy, to which we will return in Section 2.3.6.

[454] Parliament, 'Rules of Procedure', Rule 125.

[455] There are thirteen female members out of a total of twenty-seven members, at time of writing.

[456] See, for instance, European Council, 'European Council Appoints New EU Leaders', press release, 2.7.2019, on the election of Charles Michel as President of the European Council, the proposal of Ursula von der Leyen to the European Parliament as candidate for President of the Commission, considering Josep Borrell Fontelles to be the appropriate candidate for High Representative of the Union for Foreign Affairs and Security Policy, as well as Christine Lagarde for President of the Central Bank.

End of Mandate

The Commission is normally appointed for a term of five years.[457] There are, however, several ways for individual Commissioners to leave the institution before the end of their mandate.[458] Firstly, individual Commissioners may naturally decide to resign, as occurred, for instance, when the Bulgarian Commissioner, Ms Kristalina Georgieva, left to become Chief Executive Officer at the World Bank in 2017. Second, it is now possible for the President of the Commission to request the individual resignation of one of its members.[459] This allows the President to be able to exercise authority over members and to address alleged misbehaviour from a member of the College on an individual basis, rather than risking a specific case affecting the overall stability of the Commission as a College.[460] Third, members of the Commission may be compulsorily retired by the Court of Justice.[461] This may happen if these persons no longer fulfil the conditions required for the performance of their duties, if they have been guilty of serious misconduct, or if they have acted in breach of their obligations under Article 245 TFEU, on independence in particular.[462] In such cases, the position will be filled by another national from the same Member State.[463]

In addition to these changes at individual level, it is also possible for the term of office of the Commission as a body to be terminated. This could result from the vote of a motion of censure by the Parliament. The latter, indeed, voting to reach the high threshold of 'a two-thirds majority of the votes cast, representing a majority of the component members', may force the resignation of the entire College of Commissioners. The vote on the motion of censure can only take place at least three days after it has been proposed, and by open vote.[464] Although the procedure has never reached its final stages, the threat of it being activated constitutes an important part of the mechanisms of accountability of the Commission towards the Parliament.[465] If a motion of censure is successfully voted upon, a new Commission would be appointed following the same procedure as for a first appointment, but only until expiry of the term of the initial Commission, to maintain alignment with the elections of the Parliament.[466]

[457] Art. 17(3), subpara. 1 TEU. [458] See further Art. 246 TFEU.

[459] Art. 17(6), final subpara. TEU. On the distinction between voluntary and forced resignation, see C-394/15 P, *Dalli* v. *Commission*, EU:C:2016:262 (former Commissioner Dalli was found to have resigned voluntarily). Note that even if forced resignation has hardly been used to date, the mere existence of the mechanism may nevertheless enhance the authority of the President.

[460] This is a lesson drawn from the crisis of the Santer Commission, which collectively resigned at a time when the President of the Commission had little power over individual Commissioners; see Chapter 1, Section 1.3.2.3.

[461] Art. 247 TFEU.

[462] The Court of Justice would be acting on application by the Council (simple majority) or the Commission.

[463] The procedure is set out in Art. 246 TFEU. It is fairly similar to that for the appointment of the Commission as a body, although downscaled to an individual appointment. Specific provisions are made for replacement of the President and the High Representative of the Union for Foreign Affairs and Security Policy.

[464] Art. 17(8) TEU; Art. 234 TFEU.

[465] It may be recalled that, under the Presidency of Jacques Santer back in 1999, the Commissioners resigned collectively, under a mounting threat of a vote on a motion of censure; see Chapter 1, Section 1.3.2.3.

[466] Art. 234, para. 2 TFEU. The same logic applies in case of collective resignation; Art. 246, para. 6 TFEU.

2.3.5.4 Decision-Making

The Commission is a 'collegiate body'.[467] The twenty-seven Commissioners are equal and act collectively – as a College – under the guidance of the President.[468] Commissioners decide on the basis of proposals from one or more members[469] and, in general, on a consensual basis, although a member may call for a vote, in which case a decision is taken by a majority of the members of the Commission.[470] The quorum corresponds to a majority of the number of Commissioners (fourteen out of twenty-seven at time of writing).[471]

The Commissioners meet at least once a week at the invitation of the President, usually on Wednesday mornings; they discuss and make decisions on the basis of the agenda adopted by the President.[472] The meetings are not public and discussions remain confidential,[473] which can be understood as protecting the collegiality of the decisions of the Commission and the independence of its members. It is possible, and in fact frequent for practical and efficiency reasons, for the Commission to decide through other and 'lighter' procedures than the oral one just mentioned – for instance, by written procedure on the basis of a written text drafted and circulated by one or more of its members.[474]

2.3.5.5 Functioning and Organisation

The internal organisation of the Commission is framed primarily by the provisions of the EU Treaties. These are further fleshed out in Rules of Procedure that the Commission adopts for itself, as empowered to do by the Treaties,[475] as well as by further administrative tools building upon them, which are frequently adjusted.

President and Other Members

Over time, the role of President has been given increasing weight in the functioning of the institution, due to several elements. Firstly, how the President is appointed, which now takes place *before* appointing the other members, enables the President to be part of the decision-making process on the choice of future members.

Second, the President decides on the internal organisation of the Commission, ensuring that it acts 'consistently, efficiently and as a collegiate body'.[476] Formally, the President does so, in particular, by allocating specific portfolios to each member and structuring the

[467] Art. 17(6)(b) TEU.

[468] Commission, 'Rules of Procedure of the Commission', OJ L 308 8.12.2000, p. 26 (last amended 2020), Art. 1 (hereafter, Commission, 'Rules of Procedure').

[469] Commission, 'Rules of Procedure', Art. 8(1).

[470] Art. 250, para. 1 TFEU; Commission, 'Rules of Procedure', Art. 8(2–3); President of the Commission, Working Methods of the European Commission, P(2019) 2, 1.12.2019, point I.2.

[471] Commission, 'Rules of Procedure', Art. 7. This includes members who participate through telecommunication systems in the context of exceptional procedures designed for that purpose.

[472] Ibid., Arts. 5, 6(1); President of the Commission, Working Methods of the European Commission, P(2019) 2, 1.12.2019, point I.3.

[473] Commission, 'Rules of Procedure', Art. 9. Meetings may be attended by a set of pre-identified persons (Art. 10), however.

[474] Ibid., Art. 12; see also Art. 13 (empowerment of one or more of the members) and Art. 14 (on delegation to Directors-General or Heads of Department). Responsibility for these acts remains collective. See further President of the Commission, Working Methods of the European Commission, P(2019) 2, 1.12.2019, point I.2; and for a more detailed analysis, Oliver and Martenczuk, 'The Commission', pp. 564–566.

[475] Art. 249(1) TFEU; Commission, 'Rules of Procedure'.

[476] Art. 17(6)(b) TEU; Art. 248 TFEU.

work of various members from the early stages of the Commission's formation. The President appoints Vice-Presidents from among the members of the Commission.[477] In practice, the allocation of portfolios and appointments to high-level functions within the Commission is closely entangled with the choice of the future Commissioners themselves. For instance, some of the top portfolios and responsibilities within the von der Leyen Commission were attributed to very high-level European politicians: the Dutch Mr Frans Timmermans and the Dane Ms Margrethe Vestager, now both Executive Vice-Presidents, had been Spitzenkandidaten for their political parties in the run-up to the Parliament's elections (respectively, Party of European Socialists and Alliance of Liberals and Democrats for Europe).

The President may reshuffle the allocation of responsibilities during the Commission's term of office.[478] For instance, after the resignation of the Irish Commissioner for Trade, who had been caught attending a large golf dinner in breach of COVID-19 guidelines, the President attributed the responsibility for trade to another Commissioner (the Latvian Executive Vice-President Mr Valdis Dombrovskis) and gave a different portfolio to the new Irish Commissioner Ms Mairead McGuiness. The members shall carry out the duties delegated to them by the President under the latter's authority, and shall resign if so requested. The President also structures the communication strategy of the institution and its members, to ensure quality and coherence.[479]

The powers of internal organisation of the President include a choice of the number of Vice-Presidents to be appointed, in addition to the High Representative of the Union for Foreign Affairs and Security Policy – which resulted in seven (Executive) Vice-Presidents being chosen in the 2019 Commission.[480] The President also decides on the order of precedence of members within the institution and the creation of other functions and structures.[481] President von der Leyen, for instance, created a position of Executive Vice-Presidents (the first of which – currently Mr Timmermans – may chair the College in the absence of the President[482]), along with ordinary Vice-Presidents. These (Executive) Vice-Presidents, in practice, chair – and thus often filter the work of – the groups of members of Commissioners created by the President, whose function is to coordinate and prepare the work of the College of Commissioners on specific themes.[483]

Third, the President's leadership role is given expression in the Political Guidelines which the President lays down and within which the Commission is to work.[484] Ms von der Leyen spelt out guidelines for her full mandate, stressing, in particular, her strong commitment to

[477] Art. 17(6)I TEU, other than the High Representative of the Union for Foreign Affairs and Security Policy.

[478] Art. 17(6), final subpara. TEU; Art. 248 TFEU. This does not apply to the specific case of the High Representative of the Union for Foreign Affairs and Security Policy, as will be discussed in Section 2.3.6.

[479] President of the Commission, The Working Methods of the European Commission, P(2019) 2, 1.12.2019, Annex 3.

[480] The High Representative of the Union for Foreign Affairs and Security Policy is automatically a Vice-President in the Commission and is appointed through a specific procedure, as will be explained in Chapter 2, Section 2.3.6; Art. 18(4) TEU.

[481] Commission, 'Rules of Procedure', Arts. 3, 22.

[482] President of the Commission, Working Methods of the European Commission, P(2019) 2, 1.12.2019, point II.1.

[483] Commission, 'Rules of Procedure', Art. 18; President of the Commission, Decision on the creation of Commissioners' Groups, P(2019) 4, 1.12.2019.

[484] Art. 17(6)(a) TEU.

working closely with the Parliament and her intention to focus on fighting climate change, harnessing digitalisation and building a social market economy for today's world.[485] On this basis, the College further agrees on a set of priorities that are implemented through a work programme communicated on a yearly basis.[486] The Commission's annual work programme is issued after the summer, shortly after the State of the Union address by which the President of the Commission broadly sketches their key priorities for the upcoming year before the Parliament (during its first Plenary session after summer). The said work programme is particularly interesting in that it announces future initiatives. As from 2020, for instance, stakeholders knew that the Commission would start reflecting on a proposal for legislation to improve the working conditions of people working through digital platforms in 2021.[487] This planning is crucial to enable preparation and dialogue with other actors in the process of law-making. Decisions are then made by the College on the basis of an agenda set by the President, yet closely related to the said work programme.

Finally, the President represents the institution, possibly with the assistance of other members, when interacting with other EU institutions or Member States.[488] It may be recalled that the President is also part of the European Council.[489]

Working Arrangements

The Commission has just over 32,000 staff members.[490] Each Commissioner is supported individually by a cabinet (approximately ten people, often – but not always – EU civil servants)[491] and has authority over larger groups of staff members organised in departments.[492] The latter are known as Directorates-General (DGs), and relate to the policy fields falling within the portfolio of the Commissioner in charge. The DGs are themselves subdivided into directorates, and directorates into units. For instance, at time of writing, the unit dealing with Wine, Spirits and Horticultural Products is part of the DG for Agriculture and Rural Development, under the authority of the Commissioner for Agriculture, Janusz Wojciechowski.

The current Commission President herself is, in addition to her own cabinet, assisted by a Secretary-General[493] and the administration attached to that person, the General Secretariat.[494]

485 von der Leyen, *Political Guidelines for the Next European Commission 2019–2024*.

486 The latest being: Commission, Communication, 'Commission Work Programme 2022: Making Europe Stronger Together', COM(2021) 645 final, 19.10.2021. This type of work programme may contain major legislative and non-legislative proposals for the following year, including repeals, recasts, simplifications and withdrawals.

487 This is a form of employment, often precarious, in which online platforms are used to access organisations or individuals to solve specific problems or to provide specific services in exchange for payment. This is common for food delivery, for instance.

488 Commission, 'Rules of Procedure', Art. 3(5); on the relationship between the Commission – including via its President – and the Parliament see 'Framework Agreement on Relations between the European Parliament and the European Commission', OJ L 304, 20.11.2010, p. 47 (last amended 2018).

489 Art. 15(2) TEU; see Chapter 2, Section 2.3.3.2.

490 Commission, HR Key Figures 2021.

491 President of the Commission, Rules governing the composition of the Cabinets of the Members of the Commission and of the Spokesperson's Service Brussels, P(2019) 3, 1.12.2019.

492 Commission, 'Rules of Procedure', Arts. 19, 21; see the overview in the annex to President of the Commission, Decision on the organisation of responsibilities of the Members of the Commission, P(2019) 1, 1.12.2019 (last amended 2020).

493 Commission, 'Rules of Procedure', Art. 20.

494 The General Secretariat is composed of around 600 staff members; Commission, HR Key Figures 2020.

Under the current Commission, the General Secretariat also assists the (Executive) Vice-Presidents. The task of the General Secretariat is to 'help to ensure political consistency', as well as the quality of documents, and consistency of Commission action with the principles of subsidiarity and proportionality, external obligations, interinstitutional considerations and the Commission's communication strategy.[495] As will be further explained in Section 2.3.6, one Commissioner, the High Representative of the Union for Foreign Affairs and Security Policy, has a specific infrastructure: they are assisted by 'a European External Action Service'.[496]

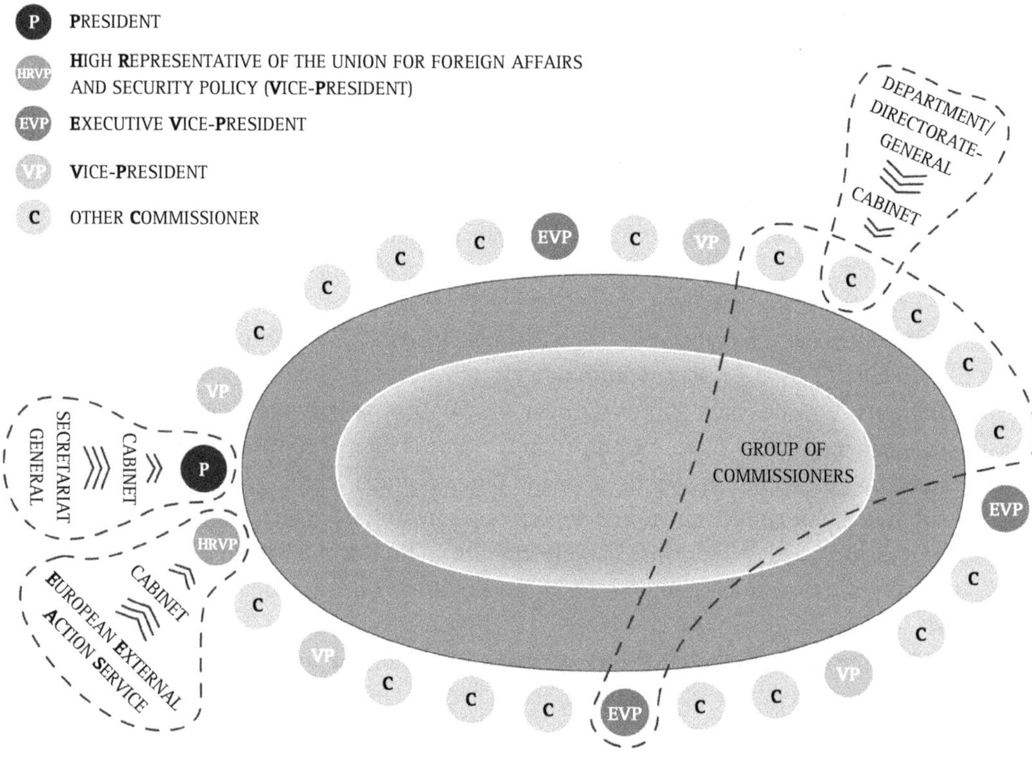

Figure 2.5 Internal organisation of the Commission

Any initiative that might be adopted by the Commission is first prepared at the level of the departments or DGs. The work is normally launched and steered by the department primarily responsible for preparing the initiative – for example, DG CLIMA for climate-related initiatives.[497] In the preparation process for each initiative, other thematically (relevant) departments and DGs need to be consulted, as well as two departments with a horizontal mandate: the Legal Service is consulted on all drafts or proposals for legal instruments and on all documents which may have legal implications; the General Secretariat is consulted on initiatives that stand out, for instance due to their political

[495] Commission, 'Rules of Procedure', Art. 20(2) *et seq.* [496] Art. 27(3) TEU.
[497] Commission, 'Rules of Procedure', Art. 23.

importance or because they are part of the Commission's annual work programme (in practice, for all initiatives to be adopted by the College). This process reflects the principle of collegiality guiding the work of the Commission. Once the initiative is prepared by the department or DG, it must then receive the support of the Commissioner as well as the (Executive) Vice-President in charge, before being discussed by the College of Commissioners, as illustrated in Figure 2.5. These discussions are additionally prepared by meetings of the Heads of Cabinet of the Commissioners (usually on Mondays), who work ahead of the College to ensure efficiency, and filter through key political issues.[498]

2.3.5.6 Functions and Powers

The Commission is first and foremost designed to 'promote the general interest of the Union'.[499] This primary function is performed pursuant to several sets of powers. Firstly, the Commission has an almost exclusive power of legislative initiative.[500] In other words, it is, in principle, the only institution that can put forward proposals for EU legislative acts to be negotiated between and within other EU institutions.[501] This power of initiative explains the practical importance of the political guidelines of the President of the Commission, and the related adoption by the College of Commissioners of a yearly work programme, which sets out most legislative initiatives foreseen. The Commission may also steer policy-making through non-legislative channels. It may, for instance, adopt recommendations[502] or a broader range of policy instruments, including white papers and communications that are the main channels for policy-making in any policy area.[503]

Taken together, these various forms of initiatives relate to the Commission acting as a 'motor' of European integration. For that purpose, the Commission interacts intensely with a broad range of stakeholders.[504] In particular, it initiates and seeks agreement with the Parliament and the Council on the annual and multiannual programming of the activities of the EU.[505] Importantly, the powers of initiative of the Commission extend to proposals for

498 President of the Commission, Working Methods of the European Commission, P(2019) 2, 1.12.2019, point I.3.

499 Art. 17(1) TEU.

500 Art. 17(2) TEU. The power of legislative initiative may be related to the influence of the Commission on the legislative process itself, in its early stages in particular; see further Chapter 3, Section 3.6.1.1.

501 Exceptions are specifically set out in the EU Treaties: Arts. 289(4), 294(15) TFEU. They relate, for instance, to the concurrent power of initiative of a quarter of the Member States for the adoption of legislation on judicial cooperation in criminal matters and police cooperation (Art. 76(b) TFEU); or to the power of initiative of the European Central Bank for certain amendments to the Statute of the European System of Central Banks and of the Central Bank in the context of the EU's monetary policy (Art. 129(3) TFEU). It may be recalled that the adoption of legislative acts is excluded in the context of the CFSP; Art. 24(1), subpara. 2 TEU.

502 Art. 292 TFEU. See, for instance, 'Commission Recommendation of 11 June 2013 on Common Principles for Injunctive and Compensatory Collective Redress Mechanisms in the Member States Concerning Violations of Rights Granted under Union Law', OJ L 201, 26.7.2013, p. 60; followed up a few years later by 'Directive (EU) 2020/1828 of the European Parliament and of the Council of 25 November 2020 on Representative Actions for the Protection of the Collective Interests of Consumers and Repealing Directive 2009/22/EC', OJ L 409, 4.12.2020, p. 1.

503 See Chapter 3, Section 3.5.2.3.

504 Art. 11(3) TEU; see Chapter 3, Section 3.6.1.1, Legislative Procedures.

505 Art. 17(1) TEU; 'Interinstitutional Agreement between the European Parliament, the Council of the European Union and the European Commission on Better Law-Making', OJ L 123, 12.5.2016, p. 1, Section II. E.g. 'Joint Declaration of the European Parliament, the Council of the European Union and the European Commission: EU Legislative Priorities for 2021' and 'Joint Conclusions of the European Parliament, the Council of the European Union and the European Commission on Policy Objectives and Priorities for 2020–2024', 17.12.2020.

the EU's multiannual financial framework and annual budget.[506] They further include the possibility of proposing and being part of the process of Treaty reform.[507]

Next, the Commission has executive functions. It is responsible for ensuring the application of EU law, a function that it carries out, in particular, through the adoption of implementing acts and (albeit to a lesser extent) delegated acts, as well as the execution of the EU budget and the management of its financial programmes.[508] In this context, the Commission also has coordinating functions which are particularly advanced in the context of certain policies, such as in relation to economic, employment and social policy or public health.[509]

Furthermore, the Commission oversees the application of EU law under the review of the Court of Justice of the European Union. As the guardian of EU law, it monitors, in particular, the transposition of directives in national law, and can receive complaints from Member States and citizens (possibly through petitions to the Parliament) on the lack of, or incorrect, application of EU law.[510] It also issues guidelines or other types of informative notes to shed light on the proper application of EU law, such as on the State aid rules and public service obligations applicable to the air transport sector during the COVID-19 outbreak. The Commission may trigger legal action against Member States which do not comply with their obligations, as well as against other EU organs.[511] In certain fields of EU law, such as competition policy, the Commission has advanced investigative and sanctioning powers.[512] It plays hardly any role in relation to the CFSP, however.

Finally, the Commission ensures the EU's external representation[513] towards third States, and international organisations in particular. On a mandate from the Council or the European Council, it negotiates international agreements, accession of third States and withdrawal of former Member States.[514] Once again, though, when it comes to the CFSP in particular, other organs – the Council (notably through the person of the High Representative for Foreign Affairs and Security Policy[515]) and the European Council[516] – play a prominent role in the external representation of the EU.

2.3.5.7 Seat

The seat of the Commission is in Brussels, with the headquarters in a building known as the Berlaymont, although certain departments are based in Luxembourg.[517]

506 Art. 17(2) TEU; Arts. 312(2), 314(2) TFEU. 507 See Chapter 1, Section 1.4.4.

508 Art. 17(1) TEU; see further Chapter 3, Sections 3.6.1.2, 3.6.3.3 and 3.6.3.4.

509 Art. 5 TFEU identifies the first set of policy areas as necessitating coordination; Art. 168(2) TFEU.

510 Directives, in particular, usually require that each Member State notifies to the Commission the measures adopted for the transposition of the obligations contained therein in national law.

511 The Commission may also trigger Art. 7 TEU on the protection of the values enshrined in Art. 2 TEU.

512 See further 'Council Regulation (EC) No. 1/2003 of 16 December 2002 on the Implementation of the Rules on Competition Laid Down in Articles 81 and 82 of the Treaty', OJ L 1, 4.1.2003, pp. 1–25 (last amended 2009). E.g. Commission, 'Antitrust: Commission Opens Investigations into Apple's App Store Rules', press release, 16.6.2020.

513 Art. 17(1) TEU. 514 Art. 218(3), TFEU; Arts. 49, 50(2) TEU. 515 Arts. 18(2), 27(2) TEU.

516 Art. 15(6) TEU.

517 Protocol 6 on the Location of the Seats of the Institutions and of Certain Bodies, Offices, Agencies and Departments of the European Union, Art. 1(c).

2.3.6 The High Representative of the Union for Foreign Affairs and Security Policy

2.3.6.1 A Brief Description

The position of High Representative of the Union for Foreign Affairs and Security Policy (High Representative), currently occupied by Mr Josep Borrell Fontelles, is an attempt at enhancing the coherence of the EU's visibility on the international stage. Originating in the Treaty of Amsterdam, the functions of the High Representative have expanded. Today, the High Representative is responsible for ensuring the consistency of the EU's external action to the extent that such action reflects traditional EU external policies, such as in the field of trade, as well as conducting the EU's CFSP, which has developed as a new EU policy since the Treaty of Maastricht and from which the Commission is largely excluded.[518] The key provision setting out the institutional characteristics of the High Representative is Article 18 TEU (see Box 2.8).

Box 2.8 **Rough guide to the position of High Representative**

Article 18 TEU

1. The European Council, acting by a qualified majority, with the agreement of the President of the Commission, shall appoint the High Representative of the Union for Foreign Affairs and Security Policy. The European Council may end his term of office by the same procedure.

2. The High Representative shall conduct the Union's common foreign and security policy. He shall contribute by his proposals to the development of that policy, which he shall carry out as mandated by the Council. The same shall apply to the common security and defence policy.

3. The High Representative shall preside over the Foreign Affairs Council.

4. The High Representative shall be one of the Vice-Presidents of the Commission. He shall ensure the consistency of the Union's external action. He shall be responsible within the Commission for responsibilities incumbent on it in external relations and for coordinating other aspects of the Union's external action. In exercising these responsibilities within the Commission, and only for these responsibilities, the High Representative shall be bound by Commission procedures to the extent that this is consistent with paragraphs 2 and 3.

2.3.6.2 A Twofold Institutional Anchorage

For the purpose of enhancing the coherence of the EU's visibility on the international stage, the High Representative is often said to wear two institutional hats, with important functions for the Council (and, although less directly, the European Council) and also being a member of the Commission.

[518] See Chapter 3, Section 3.6.2.1.

By way of exception to the system of rotating presidencies at the Council, the High Representative presides over the Foreign Affairs Council configuration[519] as well as all preparatory meetings, including those of the Political and Security Committee, which, among other things, prepares Council meetings in the field of CFSP.[520] On CFSP matters, including the common security and defense policy, the High Representative may make proposals for the development of policy.[521] They also put the policy into effect. Furthermore, the High Representative 'takes part in the work' of the European Council, without being a formal member.[522]

On the Commission's side, the High Representative is automatically a Vice-President of the Commission. In that role, they shall ensure the consistency of the EU's external action and that function may not be modified by the President of the Commission unilaterally, unlike for other members.[523] The High Representative is in charge of responsibilities incumbent on the Commission on the international stage and for coordinating other aspects of the external action of the EU.[524] In particular, the High Representative assists the President of the Commission in coordinating the external dimension of all Commissioners' work[525] and chairs the group of Commissioners working on 'a Stronger Europe in the World'.[526] This group contributes to the Commission being more geostrategic, by coordinating the external policies or those internal policies with an external dimension. In exercising these responsibilities within the Commission, the High Representative shall be bound by Commission procedures, as for other members of the College.[527]

This ambiguous institutional affiliation at times creates a high degree of complexity, which significantly limits the ability of the High Representative to enhance the coherence of the visibility of the EU on the international stage. For instance, the High Representative shall represent the EU on matters relating to the CFSP.[528] Yet, 'at his level and in that capacity', the President of the European Council shall also ensure the representation of the EU in this field, which they do, in particular, in reaction to international crises.[529] Furthermore, the Commission is responsible for representing the EU on matters that relate to its core external activities, such as trade policy.[530] It is thus not uncommon for another

[519] It may be recalled that the task of this Council configuration is to elaborate the EU's external action on the basis of strategic guidelines laid down by the European Council; and to ensure the consistency of the EU's external action. This refers to the whole of the European union's external action: the CFSP, CSDP, common commercial policy, development cooperation and humanitarian aid; Council, 'Rules of Procedure', Art. 2(5).

[520] Council, 'Rules of Procedure', Art. 19(4); Art. 38 TEU.

[521] Arts. 18(2), 27(1) TEU; Art. 218(3) TFEU. This right of initiative is often shared with others, such as individual Member States (Art. 42(4) TEU), the Commission (e.g. Art. 30(1) TEU) or even, to a certain extent, with the Council (Art. 22(1), subpara. 3 TEU). The High Representative and the Commission may also make joint proposals (e.g. Art. 22(2) TEU).

[522] Art. 15(2) TEU. [523] Art. 248 TFEU. [524] Art. 18(4) TEU.

[525] President of the Commission, Working Methods of the European Commission, P(2019) 2, 1.12.2019, point II.1.

[526] President of the Commission, Working Methods of the European Commission, P(2019) 2, 1.12.2019, point III.1; Ursula von der Leyen, Mission Letter to J. Borrell, 1.12.2019.

[527] Art. 18(4) TEU.

[528] Art. 27(2) TEU: the High Representative shall conduct political dialogue with third parties on the EU's behalf and shall express the EU's position in international organisations and at international conferences.

[529] Art. 15(6), penultimate para. TEU; see also Chapter 2, Section 2.3.3.2 and 2.3.3.3. [530] Art. 17(1) TEU.

member of the Commission to take the lead in exchanges with external entities on specific fields that are part of their portfolio. The Marrakesh Political Declaration on facilitating exchanges and cooperation between partner countries on the migration route in North, West and Central Africa and Europe, for instance, was endorsed by both the High Representative and the Commissioner for Migration, Home Affairs and Citizenship.[531]

2.3.6.3 Appointment and End of Term of Office

This institutional ambivalence is reflected in the procedure for the appointment of the High Representative, which is distinct both from any mechanism existing within the Council, and from that applicable to other members of the Commission. On the one hand, the High Representative is appointed by the European Council (acting by qualified majority), in agreement with the President-elect of the Commission.[532] On the other hand, it is subject to a vote of consent by the Parliament (by a majority of the votes cast), together with the other members of the Commission, before the Commission can be appointed by the European Council (acting by qualified majority).[533]

Similarly, the functions of the High Representative may be terminated by the European Council (acting by qualified majority), in agreement with the President-elect of the Commission.[534] The functions of the High Representative for the Commission may be brought to an end by a motion of censure against the Commission.[535] Were the President of the Commission to ask the High Representative to resign from their functions as part of the Commission, the agreement of the European Council (acting by qualified majority) would be necessary.[536]

2.3.6.4 The European External Action Service

Like other members of the Commission,[537] the High Representative receives support. They shall be assisted by a European External Action Service (EEAS; see Figure 2.5), which performs a function similar to the departments or DGs for other Commissioners, as well as a cabinet. The EEAS is based in Brussels.[538] Illustrating the multiplicity of EU organs involved in the field, the EEAS also has the task of assisting the President of the European Council, the President of the Commission and the Commission in the exercise of their respective functions in the area of external relations.[539]

The staff of the EEAS further reflects the twofold institutional anchorage of the High Representative: it comprises officials from relevant departments of the General Secretariat of the Council and of the Commission. Stressing the interdependence between the EU's external representation and that of the Member States, in particular

[531] Marrakesh Political Declaration, 2.5.2018. [532] Art. 18(1) TEU. [533] Art. 17(7), final para., TEU.
[534] Art. 18(1) TEU. [535] Art. 17(8) TEU; Art. 234(2) TFEU. [536] Arts. 17(6), final subpara., 18(1) TEU.
[537] President of the Commission, Rules governing the composition of the Cabinets of the Members of the Commission and of the Spokesperson's Service, P(2019) 3, 1.12.2019.
[538] Art. 27(3) TEU; '2010/427/EU: Council Decision of 26 July 2010 Establishing the Organisation and Functioning of the European External Action Service', OJ L 201, 3.8.2010, p. 30.
[539] '2010/427/EU: Council Decision of 26 July 2010 Establishing the Organisation and Functioning of the European External Action Service', OJ L 201, 3.8.2010, p. 30, Art. 2(2).

in the CFSP field, the EEAS also includes staff seconded from the national diplomatic services of the Member States. The High Representative is further responsible for the EU's delegations across the world,[540] as well as specially appointed representatives, such as the one for the Middle East Peace Process.[541]

2.3.7 The Court of Justice of the European Union

2.3.7.1 A Brief Description

The Court of Justice of the European Union is at the top of the EU's judicial architecture.[542] It is composed of prominent legal experts intended to represent the legal diversity of the Member States, and has had the responsibility since the early days of the EU's existence of ensuring that, in the interpretation and application of the EU Treaties, the law is observed.[543]

While this central function has remained unchanged, the EU legal order within which the function is exercised itself has undergone a profound evolution. The Court today rules on an ever greater number of cases and an ever broader range of issues, illustrating the salience of the activities of the institution. Themes covered now include the (lack of) independence of judges in the Member States threatening the functioning of the EU judicial system; the detention of migrants at the external borders of the EU; ambient air quality; and traditional themes related to economic integration.

Faced with an increasing workload, the Court of Justice of the European Union has been restructured several times, to the effect that today it is composed of two sub-entities: the General Court and the Court of Justice, the latter having the last word on the interpretation of EU law. Importantly, the Court of Justice of the European Union is at the top of the very vast EU judicial system, which is primarily composed of the judiciaries of the Member States.[544] The main features of the Court of Justice of the European Union are spelt out in Article 19 TEU (see Box 2.9), as complemented by several provisions of the TFEU,[545] and Protocol 3, specifically devoted to the Statute of the Court of Justice of the European Union (Statute).[546]

[540] Art. 35 TEU; 'Council Decision 2010/427/EU of 26 July 2010 Establishing the Organisation and Functioning of the European External Action Service', OJ L 201, 3.8.2010, p. 30, Art. 5.

[541] Art. 33 TEU; 'Council Decision (CFSP) 2021/710 of 29 April 2021 Appointing the European Union Special Representative for the Middle East Peace Process', OJ L 147, 30.4.2021, p. 12.

[542] For an in-depth overview of the institution and its work, see K. Lenaerts, I. Maselis and K. Gutman, ed. J. T. Nowak, *EU Procedural Law* (Oxford University Press, 2015).

[543] Art. 18(1) TEU. [544] Art. 19(1), subpara. 2 TEU. See further Chapter 4, Section 4.1.3.

[545] Arts. 251–281 TFEU.

[546] Note that, except for its Title I (on judges and advocates general) and Art. 64 (on language arrangements), Protocol 3 may be amended through a procedure that is less intensive than the usual ones for reform of the EU Treaties (Chapter 1, Section 1.4.4). Art. 281, para. 2 TFEU provides for use of an ordinary legislative procedure, triggered either by the Court of Justice with the consultation of the Commission, or by the Commission with the consultation of the Court of Justice. This procedure was last used in 2019; subsequent references are thus to the consolidated version of the Statute enshrined in the Protocol.

Box 2.9 **Rough guide to the Court of Justice of the European Union**

Article 19 TEU

1. The Court of Justice of the European Union shall include the Court of Justice, the General Court and specialised courts. It shall ensure that in the interpretation and application of the Treaties the law is observed.

Member States shall provide remedies sufficient to ensure effective legal protection in the fields covered by Union law.

2. The Court of Justice shall consist of one judge from each Member State. It shall be assisted by Advocates-General.

The General Court shall include at least one judge per Member State.

The Judges and the Advocates-General of the Court of Justice and the Judges of the General Court shall be chosen from persons whose independence is beyond doubt and who satisfy the conditions set out in Articles 253 and 254 of the Treaty on the Functioning of the European Union. They shall be appointed by common accord of the governments of the Member States for six years. Retiring Judges and Advocates-General may be reappointed.

3. The Court of Justice of the European Union shall, in accordance with the Treaties:

(a) rule on actions brought by a Member State, an institution or a natural or legal person;
(b) give preliminary rulings, at the request of courts or tribunals of the Member States, on the interpretation of Union law or the validity of acts adopted by the institutions;
(c) rule in other cases provided for in the Treaties.

2.3.7.2 Two Sub-courts: Court of Justice and General Court

Several reforms have reshaped the internal structure of the Court of Justice of the European Union. From the late 1980s, the institution has been divided into two main sub-courts.[547] As things stand currently, it is composed of the General Court and the Court of Justice. Most of the ordinary business of the Court of Justice of the European Union today is dealt with by the General Court (1,497 pending cases in 2020).[548] The Parliament and the Council also have the option to establish specialised courts that would be attached to the General Court. Although this possibility was exercised in the past, such courts do not exist today.[549]

As will be further explained subsequently, the Court of Justice (1,045 pending cases in 2020)[550] is not only competent to address appeals against rulings delivered by the General

[547] Alongside the Court of Justice, a second court was created: '88/591/ECSC, EEC, Euratom: Council Decision of 24 October 1988 Establishing a Court of First Instance of the European Communities', OJ L 319, 25.11.1988, p. 1. Initially called the Court of First Instance, it has been known as the General Court since the Treaty of Lisbon.

[548] Court of Justice of the European Union, 'Annual Report 2020: Judicial Activity', 2021, p. 347.

[549] Art. 257 TFEU provides for the use of an ordinary legislative procedure that may be initiated by the Court of Justice with the consultation of the Commission, or by the Commission with the consultation of the Court of Justice. A court specialised in dealing with disputes between the EU and its staff, the Civil Service Tribunal, existed between 2004 and 2016. Its tasks have now been transferred to the General Court: 'Regulation (EU, Euratom) 2016/1192 of the European Parliament and of the Council of 6 July 2016 on the Transfer to the General Court of Jurisdiction at First Instance in Disputes between the European Union and Its Servants', OJ L 200, 26.7.2016, p. 137.

[550] Court of Justice of the European Union, 'Annual Report 2020: Judicial Activity', 2021, p. 207.

Court (these constituted 17 per cent of the new cases before the Court of Justice in 2020).[551] It is also directly competent to deal with a significant number of cases without these going through the General Court in the first place. Such cases emerge from disputes that are institutionally more sensitive and potentially have greater legal implications, such as between Member States, between EU institutions, between EU institutions and Member States, or Member States and EU institutions on sensitive matters, and to support the dialogue between the Court of Justice of the European Union and national courts.

2.3.7.3 Members

Judges and Advocates General

The Court of Justice consists of one judge from each Member State (twenty-seven at time of writing) and the General Court is composed of two judges per Member State further to a reform rolled out in 2019, thus, in principle, numbering fifty-four.[552] Judges must be 'persons whose independence is beyond doubt'. For them to be appointed to the Court of Justice, they must hold 'qualifications required for appointment to the *highest* judicial offices in their respective countries or who are jurisconsults of recognised competence'.[553] For appointment to the General Court, they must show the 'ability required for appointment to *high* judicial office'.[554] In practice, the methods of appointment of judges and advocates general, which will be detailed subsequently, significantly contribute to ensuring the appointment of highly qualified lawyers to these positions.

At the Court of Justice, the work of judges is supported by that of advocates general, whose duty is to act in 'complete impartiality and independence' to make, in open court, 'reasoned submissions' on cases before they are decided upon.[555] The Court of Justice may decide, where it considers that the case raises no new point of law, to determine the case without seeking the Opinion of an advocate general.[556] Most often though, this Opinion of the advocate general in the case (as the advice is known) is eagerly awaited and attracts much attention. These Opinions are often very helpful to contextualise a specific case pending before the Court of Justice against the backdrop of broader developments of EU law. These Opinions are not binding on the judges deciding the case, and the responsible advocate general does not take part in the deliberations that result in the final ruling.[557]

[551] Ibid., p. 208.

[552] Art. 19(2), subpara. 2 TEU provides that the General Court shall include 'at least one judge per Member State'. It used to have one judge per Member State until recently, but this has now been doubled, as can be done by amending Protocol 3; Arts. 254, para. 1, 281 TFEU; see Statute, Art. 48(c); see Chapter 2, note 546.

[553] Art. 253, para. 1 TFEU. [554] Art. 254, para. 1 TFEU. [555] Art. 252 TFEU.

[556] Statute, Art. 20, final para.; see also Art. 23a (on expedited or accelerated procedures).

[557] Court of Justice, 'Rules of Procedure', OJ L 265, 29.9.2012, pp. 1–42 (last amended 2019; last consolidated 2020), Art. 32. Following up on rulings of the ECtHR assessing the compatibility of the function of Commissaire du Government of the French Conseil d'État with the fundamental right to a fair trial, and insisting on the possibility for parties to respond to the arguments put forward by the Commissaire, doubts emerged as to the compatibility of the function of the advocate general with the said fundamental right in the absence of such a right of response (e. g. ECtHR, *Kress* v. *France*, Application no. 39594/98, ECHR:2001:0607JUD003959498, paras. 72–76). The concerns have been dismissed by the Court of Justice itself, emphasis being placed on the specific nature of the function of the advocate general and on the possibility for the Court of Justice to reopen the oral part of the procedure if a case must be decided on the basis of an argument which has not yet been debated. See C-17/98, *Emesa Sugar (Free Zone)*, EU:C:2000:69, paras. 16, 18; Court of Justice, 'Rules of Procedure', Art. 83; and further, T. Tridimas, 'The Role of the Advocate General in the Development of Community Law: Some Reflections', *Common Market Law Review*, 34/6 (1997), pp. 1349–1387.

Although the EU Treaties state that there should be eight advocates general, the number can be increased: in fact, there are currently eleven advocates general at the Court of Justice.[558] Subject to the appointment procedure that will be introduced subsequently, France, Germany, Italy, Spain and Poland are each permanently entitled for one of their nationals to take up the role of an advocate general, and other Member States take turns to fill the other positions.[559] There are no predetermined advocates general at the General Court. A judge from the General Court, who may not then take part in the judgment of the case, may be called upon to perform that task – but this is extremely rare in practice.[560]

Judges, as well as advocates general, are assisted by a limited number of legal clerks – known as *référendaires* – and administrators.

Appointment and Term of Office

Judges and advocates general are appointed for a renewable term of six years through a system of partial replacement every three years, to ensure continuity and coherence in the work of the institution.[561] The procedure for such appointments is peculiar in two respects.

Firstly, each individual appointment results from a decision taken collectively by 'common accord of the governments of the Member States'.[562] In practice, and subject to the influence of the Article 255 panel that will be explained subsequently, nominations by the government of a Member State are hardly contested by others. In a dispute concerning the early termination of the mandate of a former advocate general in the context of Brexit and the appointment of her replacement, the Court of Justice clarified that such acts cannot form the subject matter of an action for annulment before the Court of Justice. The Member States are deemed not to be acting in their capacity as members of an EU institution, but as representatives of their government, thus retaining a decisive word on the process of appointment.[563]

Second, since the Treaty of Lisbon, and in the context of rapid enlargement of the EU with an increase in the number of new members joining the Court, the collective decision by the Member States is preceded by the consultation of a panel known as the Article 255 panel.[564] The panel, provided for in Article 255 TFEU, gives an opinion on the 'candidates' suitability' for the positions. Although EU law does not govern the procedure by which Member States decide on who to nominate for appointment, the panel insists on being informed on how candidates were selected. It stresses the importance of an open, transparent and rigorous national selection procedure led by an independent and impartial panel, suggesting an open call and evaluation based on professional merits.[565] The panel issues an opinion based on a written file as well as a hearing. It pays particular attention to legal capabilities, professional experience, ability to perform their duties with independence, impartiality, integrity and probity, knowledge of languages and aptitude for working in an international environment. The ability to acquire proficiency within a reasonable time in the working language of the European courts (which is French) constitutes an important assessment criterion.[566]

[558] Art. 252, para. 1 TFEU; 'Council Decision of 25 June 2013 Increasing the Number of Advocates-General of the Court of Justice of the European Union', OJ L 179, 29.6.2013, p. 92, Art. 1.

[559] Declaration 38 attached to the Treaty of Lisbon. [560] Statute, Art. 49.

[561] Arts. 253–254 TFEU. [562] Ibid.

[563] C-685/20 P, *Eleanor Sharpston* v. *Council*, EU:C:2021:485, paras. 46–51. [564] Arts. 253–254 TFEU.

[565] Sixth Activity Report of the panel provided for by Article 255 of the Treaty on the Functioning of the European Union, p. 11.

[566] Ibid., pp. 16, 18.

The panel comprises seven persons, appointed by the Council on the initiative of the President of the Court of Justice,[567] who are chosen from among former members of the Court of Justice and the General Court, members of national supreme courts and lawyers of recognised competence, one of whom is proposed by the Parliament. The opinions of the Article 255 panel are addressed to the representatives of the governments of the Member States and the panel does not disclose its full opinions to the public.[568] Although the opinion is not binding, so far all advice has been followed.[569] No unfavourable opinions have been delivered concerning candidates for renewal of a term of office, but 21 per cent of the opinions on candidates for a first term of office have been unfavourable.[570] These have resulted in the Member State concerned proposing new, and more convincing, candidates.

Status

Judges, as well as advocates general,[571] are expected to be impartial and conscientious, and to preserve the secrecy of deliberations.[572] They may not hold any political or administrative office and ought to be immune from legal proceedings, including after their term of office in respect of acts performed by them in their official capacity.[573] Apart from in exceptional circumstances, they may not engage in any occupation.[574] Their duties shall end at the expiry of their term or when they resign.[575] A judge or advocate general may be deprived of their office, or of the right to a pension or other benefits in its stead, if, in the unanimous opinion of the judges and advocates general of the Court of Justice, they no longer fulfil the requisite conditions or meet the obligations arising from their office.[576]

2.3.7.4 Internal Organisation

Each of the two sub-courts of the Court of Justice of the European Union has exercised its powers to adopt its own rules of procedure, subject to approval from the Council.[577] These put flesh on the bones of the EU Treaties, as well as on Protocol 3 of the Statute of the institution, to ensure its smooth functioning as follows.

Chambers

The Court of Justice and the General Court are each organised internally in chambers of three to five judges and a President to distribute the work between the members. Judges then sit in formations assigned for each case. There may be formations of a single judge at

[567] Operating rules of the panel are adopted through the same procedure.
[568] This approach is supported by the European Ombudsman: Decision in Case 1955/2017/THH on the Council of the European Union's refusal to grant public access to opinions evaluating the merits of candidates for appointment to the Court of Justice and the General Court of the European Union, paras. 22–25: it is feared, in particular, that full publicity would result in less frank and less thorough Panel opinions.
[569] Sixth Activity Report of the panel provided for by Article 255 of the Treaty on the Functioning of the European Union, p. 9.
[570] Ibid., p. 10.
[571] All provisions related to judges discussed herein equally apply to advocates general: Statute, Art. 8.
[572] Ibid., Art. 2. [573] Ibid., Arts. 3–4.
[574] See further Court of Justice of the European Union, 'Code of Conduct for Members and Former Members of the Court of Justice of the European Union', OJ C 397, 30.9.2021, pp. 1–8, and the list of external activities of the Members of the Court of Justice made public through the website of the institution on a yearly basis.
[575] Statute, Art. 5. Renewal is possible through the same procedure as above. [576] Ibid., Art. 6.
[577] Arts. 253, final para., 254, para. 5 TFEU; Court of Justice, 'Rules of Procedure'; General Court, 'Rules of Procedure', OJ L 105, 23.4.2015, pp. 1–66 (last amended 2018).

the General Court, three or five judges (in both Courts), a Grand Chamber (fifteen judges in both Courts, common at the Court of Justice, but rarely used at the General Court), or a full Court gathering all judges of the Court of Justice.[578] The formation depends primarily on the difficulty and importance of the case, or on particular circumstances of internal organisation. This means, for instance, that a full Court deals with cases that it considers to deserve the utmost attention. This includes Opinions of the Court of Justice on the compatibility of a draft international agreement between the EU and a third entity with EU primary law, for instance.[579] Similarly, it is useful for general EU lawyers to monitor rulings from the full Court and Grand Chamber of the Court of Justice to keep track of general trends of particular importance in the case law.

Judges and Advocates General Holding Special Office

The Court of Justice and the General Court each has a President and a Vice-President. These are elected and may be re-elected from among the judges of the Court concerned and by these judges, for a term of three years.[580] The function of each President (at time of writing, Mr Koen Lenaerts, Court of Justice, and Mr Marc van der Woude, General Court) is to represent the respective court, direct its judicial business and ensure the proper functioning of its services or administration.[581] The President presides, in particular, over the full Court (at the Court of Justice) and the Grand Chamber (at each Court). The Vice-President assists their President and replaces them when needed or so requested.[582] At the level of chambers with three to five judges, Presidents of each Chamber are elected from among the members of the Chamber.[583] Not only do they preside over the work of their chambers, but they also play an important role within the Grand Chamber, which must always include, along with the President and the Vice-President, a number of Presidents of Chambers.[584] Similarly, advocates general of the Court of Justice elect one of their members as First Advocate General.[585] One of the key functions of the latter is to assign the Court's cases among advocates general and to take steps if one of them is prevented from acting.[586]

Judicial Procedure

A case is brought to the Court of Justice or the General Court by written application to the respective Registrars.[587] In the case of preliminary questions from national courts or tribunals, the decision to refer the case to the Court of Justice ought to be notified to that

[578] Art. 251 TFEU; see also Statute, Arts. 16, 50; General Court, 'Rules of Procedure', Art. 15.

[579] Art. 218(11) TFEU; see, for instance, Opinion 2/13, Accession of the European Union to the European Convention for the Protection of Human Rights and Fundamental Freedom, EU:C:2014:2454. The full Court of Justice also has jurisdiction in a set of cases set out in Art. 16 of the Statute relating to the premature end of term of a number of high figures in EU institutions and organs. Furthermore, a Member State or an EU institution participating in the proceedings may request that the case be assigned to the Grand Chamber; Court of Justice, 'Rules of Procedure', Art. 60.

[580] Arts. 253, para. 3, 254, para. 3 TFEU; Statute, Arts. 9a, 47, para. 1. The vote is by secret ballot and the person elected is the one attracting the majority of the votes of the judges of the Court concerned; Court of Justice, 'Rules of Procedure', Art. 8; General Court, 'Rules of Procedure', Art. 9.

[581] Court of Justice, 'Rules of Procedure', Art. 9; General Court, 'Rules of Procedure', Art. 10.

[582] See further Court of Justice, 'Rules of Procedure', Art. 10; General Court, 'Rules of Procedure', Art. 11.

[583] Court of Justice, 'Rules of Procedure', Arts. 11–12; General Court, 'Rules of Procedure', Arts. 18–19.

[584] That composition differs between the Court of Justice and the General Court. See further Statute, Art. 16, para. 2; General Court, 'Composition of the Grand Chamber', OJ C 172, 20.5.2019, p. 2.

[585] Court of Justice, 'Rules of Procedure', Art. 14. [586] Ibid., Art. 16. [587] Statute, Arts. 21, 53.

Court.[588] The Registrar, appointed by the relevant Court,[589] is responsible, in particular, for the acceptance, transmission and custody of all documents. They have their own staff and act under the authority of the President.[590]

The judicial procedure then unfolds, in principle, in a written and, unless otherwise decided, an oral stage.[591] The written part consists of the communication, through the Registrar, of key documents – including the application, supporting documents and replies – to the parties in particular.[592] The oral part consists of a hearing before the Court at which the representatives of the parties, witnesses or experts present their submissions, and includes questions from the advocate general, if any.[593] Member States and EU institutions may at any point intervene in the proceedings before the Court, as can EU organs that have established an interest in the case.[594] Member States and EU institutions regularly use that opportunity, which is often a useful indicator of the sensitivity of a given case.

Within each of the Courts, and with some procedural nuances between them, the case is allocated by the respective President to a judge-rapporteur (*juge rapporteur*) in the early stages of the procedure.[595] The judge-rapporteur presents a preliminary report (*rapport préalable*), which shall contain, among other things, proposals as to whether particular measures of organisation of procedure or measures of enquiry should be undertaken. At the Court of Justice, the report also includes a proposal as to the formation to which the case should be assigned and proposals as to whether to dispense with an Opinion of the advocate general.[596] The Court decides on these procedural aspects before further analysis by the relevant Chamber. Two or more cases may be joined at any stage based on the connection between them.[597] Where a question referred for a preliminary ruling is identical to a question on which the Court has already ruled, where the reply to such a question may be clearly deduced from existing case law or where the answer to the question referred for a preliminary ruling does not raise any reasonable doubt, the Court may decide to rule by reasoned order.[598]

Several mechanisms enable the judicial procedure to be fast-tracked. In the context of actions brought by a Member State, an institution or a natural or legal person, the President may, where the nature of the case so requires and subject to procedural safeguards, decide that the Court shall deal with the case within a short period.[599] Such an 'expedited procedure' allows the reply and rejoinder elements of the procedure to be bypassed once

588 Ibid., Art. 23.

589 Arts. 253, para. 5, 254, para. 4 TFEU. The Registrar is appointed for a term of six years from outside the members of the Court, by all members of the Court concerned; Court of Justice, 'Rules of Procedure', Art. 18; General Court, 'Rules of Procedure', Art. 32.

590 Statute, Arts. 12, 52. 591 Ibid., Arts. 20, 53.

592 On the specificities of the preliminary ruling procedure, see Chapter 4, Section 4.2.3.

593 Hearings are, in principle, public; Statute, Art. 31.

594 Statute, Arts. 40, 53. In the context of preliminary rulings, Member States, EU institutions or organs may similarly submit statements (Art. 23).

595 Court of Justice, 'Rules of Procedure', Art. 15(1); General Court, 'Rules of Procedure', Arts. 26, 87.

596 Court of Justice, 'Rules of Procedure', Art. 59. Dispensing with a hearing is possible if the Court considers that it has enough information to give a ruling without one; Art. 76; see also General Court, 'Rules of Procedure', Art. 106(3). On the dispensing of an Opinion of the advocate general, see Chapter 2, Section 2.3.7.3, Judges and Advocates General.

597 Court of Justice, 'Rules of Procedure', Art. 54; General Court, 'Rules of Procedure', Art. 68(5).

598 Court of Justice, 'Rules of Procedure', Art. 99.

599 Court of Justice, 'Rules of Procedure', Art. 113 *et seq.*; General Court, 'Rules of Procedure', Art. 151 *et seq.*

the parties have already submitted their initial arguments. Specific mechanisms also apply in the context of the preliminary ruling procedure.[600]

Although actions brought before the Court of Justice of the European Union do not normally have suspensory effects, exceptions may be made to obtain suspension of the application of the contested act.[601] The Court of Justice of the European Union may also adopt interim measures in circumstances giving rise to 'urgency', in order to avoid serious and irreparable harm to the applicant's interests and if the pleas of fact and law establish a prima facie case.[602] These decisions are made, in principle, by the respective Presidents of the two Courts,[603] who must, where appropriate, also weigh up the interests involved.[604]

The language of a case may be any of the twenty-four official languages of the EU, in accordance with the relevant rule of procedure of the Court, and it shall, in principle, be used for the written and oral stages.[605] By custom, the common working language used within the institution, including for judges to deliberate, is French.

2.3.7.5 Decision-Making and Rulings

At the Court of Justice, as well as at the General Court, judges make decisions in the formation of the Court to which they are assigned, and on behalf of the Court they belong to. The judge-rapporteur is responsible for drafting the judgment on which the judges decide.[606] In practice, judges aim at consensus under the leadership of the President of the Chamber in charge; the judge-rapporteur often incorporates the suggestions of other judges in order to reach that consensus. Rulings shall state the reasons on which they are based and include the names of judges who took part in the deliberations: the latter, however, are, and remain, confidential.[607] As a result, and unlike in other judicial systems, such as that of the ECtHR, it is never possible to know the specific contribution or position of a specific judge in relation to the final ruling. On the one hand, this approach has the advantage of protecting the independence of judges and giving a sense of unity in a supranational context. On the other hand, rulings resulting therefrom are the outcome of a compromise between those involved, which sometimes results in rulings being unexpectedly concise or cryptic on sensitive aspects of the reasoning.

The references to a ruling provide a wealth of information on the procedural background of a case, as can be seen in Box 2.10, which is modelled on the referencing system used in this book – although the same information may validly be provided in a different order and format. The reference normally allows identification of: (1) the parties (here, Anagnostakis is challenging an act of the Commission); (2) whether the case was dealt with by the Court of Justice (case number starting with 'C') or the General Court (case number starting with 'T'); (3) whether the case is an appeal (case number followed by 'P') or a decision on interim measures (case number followed by 'R'); (4) the year the Court was seised (the two numbers

[600] See Chapter 4, Section 4.2.3.4. [601] Art. 278 TFEU.

[602] Art. 279 TFEU; Court of Justice, 'Rules of Procedure', Art. 160(3); General Court, 'Rules of Procedure', Art. 156(4). This may be applied against EU organs, as well as against Member States; see, for instance, C-441/17 R, *Commission* v. *Poland (for the Conservation of the Białowieża Forest)*, EU:C:2017:877.

[603] Statute, Art. 39; Court of Justice, 'Rules of Procedure', Art. 162; General Court, 'Rules of Procedure', Art. 157.

[604] C-404/04 P-R, *Technische Glaswerke Ilmenau GmbH* v. *Commission*, EU:C:2005:267, para. 10.

[605] Court of Justice, 'Rules of Procedure', Art. 36 *et seq.*; General Court, 'Rules of Procedure', Art. 44 *et seq.*

[606] The rules require majority decision-making: Court of Justice, 'Rules of Procedure', Art. 32; General Court, 'Rules of Procedure', Art. 21(4). Rules on quorum are set out in subsequent articles.

[607] Statute, Arts. 35–36.

Box 2.10 Understanding case numbers of a ruling of the Court of Justice or General Court

(2) (4)(3) (1) (2) (5)

C-589/15 P, *Anagnostakis v Commission* EU:C:2017:663

after the '/' indicate the last two decimals of the year); and (5) when the ruling was issued (this is indicated in four digits).

It should further be observed that the internal structure of a ruling of the Court of Justice or the General Court also provides useful information for a proper understanding of the ruling in question.[608] As illustrated in Box 2.11, this includes, among other things:

1. An indication as to whether the judgment is delivered by the Court of Justice or the General Court, as well as the formation of the Court.
2. The date of delivery.
3. A description of the parties or the interested persons referred to in Article 23 of the Statute who participated in the proceedings.
4. In the case of direct actions and appeals, a statement of the form of order sought by the parties.
5. A statement that the advocate general has been heard and, where applicable, the date of their Opinion.
6. A summary of the facts, if applicable (which is not the case in the example in Box 2.11, as it is an action for annulment – thus a challenge to the validity of an EU act independently from a concrete set of facts).
7. The grounds for the decision.
8. The operative part of the judgment, including, where appropriate, the Court's decision on costs.

Within the rulings by the Court of Justice and the General Court, legal analysis is supported by references to EU law, to a broad set of sources identified as having particular authority, as will be explained in Chapter 3, and to the Courts' own rulings. Both Courts are concerned with ensuring the 'primacy, unity and effectiveness of EU law',[609] to the effect that they seek to ensure consistency with earlier case law and, in principle, to explain nuances and divergences by distinguishing the cases. Express reversals are rare.[610] It is naturally the role of practitioners and academics to critically examine these developments further.

[608] Court of Justice, 'Rules of Procedure', Arts. 87, 94; General Court, 'Rules of Procedure', Art. 117.

[609] C-399/11, *Melloni*, EU:C:2013:107, para. 60. See further, K. Lenaerts and J. A. Gutiérrez-Fons, *Les méthodes d'interprétation de la Cour de justice de l'Union européenne* (Bruylant, 2020).

[610] E.g. Joined Cases C-267/91 and C-268/91, *Keck and Mithouard*, EU:C:1993:905, para. 16: It was decided that 'contrary to what has previously been decided, the application to products from other Member States of national provisions restricting or prohibiting certain selling arrangements is not such as to hinder directly or indirectly, actually or potentially, trade between Member States [. . .] so long as those provisions apply to all relevant traders operating within the national territory and so long as they affect in the same manner, in law and in fact, the marketing of domestic products and of those from other Member States'.

Box 2.11 **Rough guide to the structure of a ruling**

① JUDGMENT OF THE COURT (Grand Chamber)

② 8 December 2020*

(Action for annulment – Directive (EU) 2018/957 – Freedom to provide services – Posting of workers – Terms and conditions of employment – Remuneration – Duration of posting – Determination of the legal basis – Articles 53 and 62 TFEU – Amendment of an existing directive – Article 9 TFEU – Misuse of powers – Principle of non-discrimination – Necessity – Principle of proportionality – Extent of the principle of freedom to provide services – Road transport – Article 58 TFEU – Regulation (EC) No 593/2008 – Scope – Principles of legal certainty and legislative clarity)

In Case C-620/18,

ACTION for annulment under Article 263 TFEU, brought on 2 October 2018,

③ **Hungary**, represented by M. Z. Fehér, G. Tornyai, and M. M. Tátrai, acting as Agents,

applicant,

v

European Parliament, represented by M. Martínez Iglesias, L. Visaggio and A. Tamás, acting as Agents,

defendant,

supported by:

Federal Republic of Germany, represented by J. Möller and S. Eisenberg, acting as Agents,

French Republic, represented by E. de Moustier, A.-L. Desjonquères, C. Mosser and R. Coesme, acting as Agents,

Kingdom of the Netherlands, represented by M. K. Bulterman, C. Schillemans and J. Langer, acting as Agents,

Kingdom of Sweden, represented by C. Meyer-Seitz, H. Shev and H. Eklinder, acting as Agents,

European Commission, represented by L. Havas, M. Kellerbauer, B.-R. Killmann and A. Szmytkowska, acting as Agents,

interveners,

supported by:

Federal Republic of Germany, represented by J. Möller and S. Eisenberg, acting as Agents,

French Republic, represented by E. de Moustier, A.-L. Desjonquères, C. Mosser and R. Coesme, acting as Agents,

Kingdom of the Netherlands, represented by M. K. Bulterman, C. Schillemans and J. Langer, acting as Agents,

European Commission, represented by L. Havas, M. Kellerbauer, B.-R. Killmann and A. Szmytkowska, acting as Agents,

interveners,

Council of the European Union, represented initially by A. Norberg, M. Bencze and E. Ambrosini, then by A. Norberg, E. Ambrosini, A. Sikora-Kalėda and Zs. Bodnár, acting as Agents,

defendant,

THE COURT (Grand Chamber),

① composed of K. Lenaerts, President, R. Silva de Lapuerta, Vice-President, J.-C. Bonichot, M. Vilaras (Rapporteur), E. Regan, M. Ilešič and N. Wahl, Presidents of Chambers, E. Juhász, D. Šváby, S. Rodin, F. Biltgen, K. Jürimäe, C. Lycourgos, P. G. Xuereb and N. Jääskinen, Judges,

Advocate General: M. Campos Sánchez-Bordona,

Registrar: R. Şereş, Administrator,

having regard to the written procedure and further to the hearing on 3 March 2020,

⑤ after hearing the Opinion of the Advocate General at the sitting on 28 May 2020, gives the following

Judgment

1. By its application, Hungary asks the Court, principally, to annul Directive (EU) 2018/957 of the European Parliament and of the Council of 28 June 2018 amending Directive 96/71/EC concerning the posting of workers in the framework of the provision of services (OJ 2018 L 173, p. 16, and corrigendum, OJ 2019 L 91, p. 77) ('the contested directive') and, in the alternative, to annul a number of provisions of that directive.

Legal context

[...]

④ **Forms of order sought and procedure before the Court of Justice**

22. Hungary contends, that the Court should:
    - principally, annul the contested directive;
    - in the alternative:
        - annul the provision of Article l(2)(a) of the contested directive which establishes the wording of the new point (c) of the first subparagraph of Article 3(1), and the new third subparagraph of Article 3(1) of Directive 96/71;
        - annul Article l(2)(b) of the contested directive, which establishes the wording of Articles 3(la) of Directive 96/71;
        - annul Article l(2)(c) of the contested directive;
        - annul Article 3(3) of the contested directive; and
    - order the Parliament and the Council to pay the costs.

23. The Parliament and the Council contend that the Court should dismiss the action and order Hungary to pay the costs.

[...]

The action

27. In support of its action, Hungary relies on five pleas in law; respectively, the choice of an incorrect legal basis for the adoption of the contested directive; disregard of Article 153(5) TFEU and misuse of powers; an infringement of Article 56 TFEU; a further infringement of Article 56 TFEU in that the contested directive precludes the effective implementation of the freedom to provide services; and disregard of the 'Rome I' Regulation and the principles of legal certainty and legislative clarity.

The first plea in law: the choice of an incorrect legal basis for the adoption of the contested directive

Arguments of the parties

[...]

⑦ *Findings of the Court*

[...]

70. It follows from the foregoing that the first plea in law must be rejected.

The second plea in law: disregard of Article 153(5) TFEU and misuse of powers

Arguments of the parties

[. . .]

Findings of the Court

[. . .]

The third plea in law: infringement of Article 56 TFEU

Arguments of the parties

[. . .]

Findings of the Court

[. . .]

The fourth plea in law: infringement of Article 56 TFEU in that the contested directive precludes the effective implementation of the freedom to provide services

Arguments of the parties

[. . .]

Findings of the Court

[. . .]

The fifth plea in law; disregard of the 'Rome I' Regulation and of the principles of legal certainty and legislative clarity

Arguments of the parties

[. . .]

Findings of the Court

[. . .]

Costs

189. Under Article 138(1) of the Rules of Procedure of the Court of Justice, the unsuccessful party is to be ordered to pay the costs if they have been applied for in the successful party's pleadings. Since the Parliament and the Council have applied for costs to be awarded against Hungary, and the latter has been unsuccessful, it must be ordered to pay the costs.

190. In accordance with Article 140(1) of those rules, the Federal Republic of Germany, the French Republic, the Kingdom of the Netherlands, the Kingdom of Sweden and the European Commission shall bear their own costs as parties who intervened in the proceedings.

⑧ On those grounds, the Court (Grand Chamber) hereby:

1. **Dismisses the action;**
2. **Orders Hungary to bears its own costs and to pay the costs incurred by the European Parliament and the Council of the European Union;**
3. **Orders the Federal Republic of Germany, the French Republic, the Kingdom of the Netherlands, the Kingdom of Sweden and the European Commission to bear their own costs.**

[Signatures]

2.3.7.6 Jurisdiction

On a daily basis, EU law is primarily interpreted and applied by the courts and tribunals of the Member States, at the appropriate level. The Court of Justice of the European Union ensures the sound functioning of this judicial architecture. More specifically, as will be further explained in Chapter 4, the Court of Justice of the European Union: (1) deals with the review of the legality of EU acts; (2) ensures that the Member States comply with their EU law obligations; and (3) interprets EU law at the request of the national courts and tribunals. The Court thereby ensures that, in the interpretation and application of the EU Treaties, the law is observed.[611] For that purpose, the Court has exclusive jurisdiction; the Member States may *not* submit a related dispute to any other settlement mechanism – such as an external body that would be given the last word – than those provided for in the EU Treaties.[612]

The majority of cases are dealt with by the General Court, and are of an administrative nature with much discussion of factual issues.[613] This holds true for claims brought by private parties against EU organs, as well as for actions brought by the Member States against the Commission, or against the Council when the acts concerned are measures in respect of State aid, dumping and its implementing powers. The General Court also has jurisdiction in certain specialised claims (such as against the EU Intellectual Property Office and in disputes between the EU and its staff).[614]

The Court of Justice has jurisdiction to adjudicate on appeals against decisions of the General Court.[615] Appeals against rulings of the General Court must be lodged before the Court of Justice within two months of the official notification of the ruling that is being challenged.[616] Such appeals may only relate to points of law, on grounds of lack of competence of the General Court, breach of procedure that affects the interests of the appellant, or infringement of EU law.[617] If it disagrees with the General Court, the Court of Justice may either quash the decision and refer the case back to the General Court for final judgement in light of the guidance provided, or give final judgement itself if the proceedings so permit.[618] Such appeals occasionally expose divergences of approaches

[611] Art. 19(1), subpara. 1 TEU.

[612] Art. 344 TFEU. This may be related to the autonomy of the EU legal order, as introduced in Chapter 1, Section 1.4.2.3. See further T. Tridimas, 'The Court of Justice of the European Union', in Schütze and Tridimas (eds.), *Oxford Principles of European Union Law*, pp. 594–598. What the Member States may do, however, is to grant, under a special agreement, jurisdiction to the Court of Justice in disputes between them which relate to the subject matter of the EU Treaties (Art. 273 TFEU).

[613] Art. 256 TFEU; Statute, Art. 51.

[614] Art. 262 TFEU; 'Regulation (EU) 2017/1001 of the European Parliament and of the Council of 14 June 2017 on the European Union Trade Mark', OJ L 154, 16.6.2017, p. 1, Arts. 71–72; Statute, Art. 50a.

[615] Art. 256 TFEU; Statute, Art. 51. For instance, in 2020, 152 out of 204 were dismissed; Court of Justice of the European Union, 'Annual Report 2020: Judicial Activity', 2021, p. 171.

[616] Art. 256(1), subpara. 2 TFEU. For an appeal against the General Court concerning a decision of an independent board to be allowed to proceed, the Court of Justice will check that the appeal is 'significant with respect to the unity, consistency or development' of EU law; Court of Justice, 'Rules of Procedure', Art. 170a. This is intended to reduce the workload of the Court of Justice.

[617] Statute, Art. 58.

[618] The appeal must be brought within two months of the notification of the decision by the General Court; they may be brought not only by an unsuccessful party, but also, under specific conditions, by Member States and EU institutions; Statute, Arts. 56, 58, 61.

between the two Courts, as illustrated in the context of litigation on the criteria to be met for a natural or legal person to be able to bring an annulment action against an EU act (standing).[619]

The Court of Justice also has both first *and* ultimate jurisdiction in matters that are more likely to raise sensitive questions. As is the case in relation to questions from national courts and tribunals on the interpretation or the validity of EU law, procedures between Member States, between EU institutions, between institutions and Member States and between Member States and EU institutions (unless institutions act primarily as 'administrators', as noted previously in relation to the jurisdiction of the General Court). In this context, the Court of Justice may be asked, for instance, to give an Opinion on the compatibility of a draft international agreement between the EU and a third party with the EU Treaties.[620]

The jurisdiction of both Courts, as just described, calls for clarification and several caveats. What the Court of Justice of the European Union does *not* do is interpret national law and solve disputes at domestic level. Its role is to review the validity of EU acts, to interpret EU law and to provide guidance to national courts and tribunals when necessary on the matter before it. Furthermore, the Court of Justice of the European Union, in principle, does not have jurisdiction in relation to provisions of the TEU which are related to the CFSP.[621] This limitation is subject to two main exceptions.[622] One relates to adjudication on the relationship between the implementation of that policy, on the one hand, and the procedures and powers of the institutions laid down in the TFEU for the exercise of other EU competences, on the other hand. The other relates to reviewing the legality of decisions providing for restrictive measures against natural or legal persons adopted by the Council. As will be further explained subsequently, the limitations to the jurisdiction of the Court of Justice of the European Union have been interpreted restrictively, thereby enhancing the Court's jurisdiction in the field.[623] There are also, here and there, more specific restrictions to the jurisdiction of the Court of Justice of the European Union, notably in relation to economic governance.[624]

2.3.7.7 Seat

The Court of Justice of the European Union has its seat in Luxembourg.[625]

2.3.8 The Central Bank

2.3.8.1 The Central Bank in the Eurosystem

The European Central Bank is a peculiar institution in that it is primarily in charge of a specific policy of the EU – one of the most recent and dynamic ones: monetary policy.[626] To

[619] This is elaborated upon in detail in Chapter 4, Section 4.3.1.1, Non-privileged Applicants.
[620] Art. 218(11) TFEU; see Chapter 3, Section 3.5.3.1, Secondary Law in the Form of International Agreements.
[621] Art. 24(1), subpara. 2 TEU. It may be recalled that this policy corresponds to the former second pillar of the EU, as created by the Maastricht Treaty; see Chapter 1, Section 1.3.2.2.
[622] See further Art. 40 TEU; Art. 275, para. 2 TFEU. [623] See Chapter 4, Section 4.4.1.
[624] See Chapter 4, Section 4.4.1.
[625] Protocol 6 annexed to the EU Treaties on the location of the seats of the institutions and of certain bodies, offices, agencies and departments of the European Union, Art. 1(d).
[626] The first steps towards the creation of the Central Bank date back to the late 1980s; see Chapter 1, Section 1.3.2.3.

that effect, the European Central Bank is at the top of the so-called European System of Central Banks, which includes all central banks of the Member States of the EU.[627] Within this structure, the core work is actually done by the Central Bank (which has legal personality and is itself based in Frankfurt[628]), acting with the central banks of the Member States whose currency is the euro (Eurosystem): they conduct the monetary policy for the euro area.[629] The key provision setting out the Eurosystem and the central role of the Central Bank is Article 282 TFEU. It is to be read in conjunction with other provisions of the same Treaty,[630] as well as a specifically dedicated Protocol 4, which may be partly amended through facilitated procedures.[631]

While the primary objective of the Eurosystem – and of the Central Bank within it – is to 'maintain price stability', its subsidiary objective 'is to support the general economic policies' in the EU in order to 'contribute to the achievement' of the first objective, and with a view to supporting the overall objectives of the EU.[632] The relationship between both prongs of the mandate of the Central Bank has been at the core of heated debates in recent years. The Central Bank's proactive stand in response to the economic and financial crisis[633] has been praised by some and bitterly criticised by others. One of the key arguments put forward by opponents to the action of the Central Bank is that the Bank has exceeded its primary mandate focused on price stability, and unduly overstepped the boundaries of the area of economic policy, which is primarily a competence of the Member States and merely coordinated at the EU level.[634] The Court of Justice, however, has so far rejected these arguments and accepted the Central Bank's approach, which it deems to be compatible with the Bank's mandate under the EU Treaties.[635]

2.3.8.2 Internal Organisation and Independence

The European System of Central Banks is governed by the two main decision-making bodies of the European Central Bank.[636] Its Executive Board is made up of six members, including the President of the Bank (at time of writing, Ms Christine Lagarde) and a Vice-President, all appointed by the European Council, after consultation with, among others, the Parliament. Nominees are persons of recognised standing and professional experience

[627] Art. 282(1) TFEU. National central banks are thus an integral part of the system; Protocol 4, Art. 14.3.
[628] Art. 282(3) TFEU; Protocol 6 on the Location of the Seats of the Institutions and of Certain Bodies, Offices, Agencies and Departments of the European Union, Art. 1(i).
[629] Arts. 282(1), 139 TFEU; see Chapter 1, Section 1.4.3.2. [630] Arts. 127–133, 138, 283–284 TFEU.
[631] Protocol 4 annexed to the EU Treaties on the statute of the European System of Central Banks and of the European Central Bank (Protocol 4); procedures for amendments of parts of its provisions ought to be distinguished from the main avenues provided for in Art. 48 TEU to reform the EU Treaties (Art. 129(3) TFEU; Protocol 4, Arts. 40–41).
[632] Arts. 127(1), 282(2) TFEU.
[633] Such as through its decisions to buy financial assets from commercial banks and public sector securities in particular, under the Public Sector Purchase Programme, or PSPP, in question in *Weiss*; see note 635), to support economic growth across the euro area and help return to low inflation levels. See further Chapter 1, Section 1.3.3.1.
[634] See further Chapter 3, Section 3.3.1.
[635] C-62/14, *Gauweiler*, EU:C:2015:400, paras. 46–92; C-493/17, *Weiss*, EU:C:2018:1000, paras. 53–100.
[636] Arts. 129(1), 282(2) TFEU. Note that a third body, the General Council, is in existence as long as all Member States do not yet fulfil the conditions to be part of the euro area. The General Council gives these Member States and their national central banks, together with those of the euro area, a formal role during the transition, such as that of advising the Central Bank. See Protocol 4 annexed to the EU Treaties, Arts. 44, 46.

in monetary or banking matters for a non-renewable mandate of eight years.[637] The central function of the Executive Board is to implement monetary policy on the basis of instructions from the Governing Council.[638] The latter is indeed the main decision-making body. It ensures the performance of the tasks entrusted to the Eurosystem and formulates the monetary policy in particular.[639] It is composed of members of the Executive Board of the Bank, as well as the governors of the national central banks of the euro area. It is chaired by the President of the Bank, who also represents the institution externally.[640] The Governing Council acts by single majority of the members that have a voting right, which is based on a complex system.[641] The President of the Council and members of the Commission may participate in meetings of the Governing Council, but do not have a right to vote.[642]

One of the key characteristics of the Central Bank is its independence in exercising powers in carrying out its tasks and duties.[643] The institution and the members of its decision-making bodies take no instructions from EU organs, any government of the Member States or any other body. This principle is matched by a requirement of EU organs and governments not to seek to influence the Bank or its members. In this integrated system of governance, the same requirement of independence applies to the national central banks which form part of the Eurosystem.[644] Nevertheless, the Bank is accountable. It regularly addresses reports on the activities of the European System of Central Banks and on monetary policy to the Parliament, the Council, the Commission and the European Council.[645] The Parliament may hold general debates, and invites the President of the Central Bank to attend meetings of its committee in charge of economic and monetary affairs at least four times a year, to make a statement and answer questions; this is known as the 'monetary dialogue'.[646] The President and members of the Executive Board may be heard by the committees of the Parliament. The acts or omissions of the Bank shall be open to review or interpretation before the Court of Justice of the European Union.[647]

2.3.8.3 Functions and Powers

For Member States of the euro area, and with a view to achieving the objectives identified previously, the Central Bank together with the Eurosystem conduct the monetary policy of the EU.[648] The Central Bank alone may authorise the issue of euro banknotes, which are the only

637 Art. 283(2) TFEU. The European Council acts by qualified majority on a recommendation from the Council after consultation of the Parliament and of the Governing Council of the Central Bank. See further Protocol 4, Art. 11.

638 Protocol 4, Art. 12.1, subpara. 2. 639 Ibid., Art. 12.1, subpara. 1. 640 Ibid., Art. 13.

641 Ibid., Art. 10.2; the system takes into account the size of the economy and of the financial sectors of the Member State of origin of each of the governors of the national central bank.

642 Arts. 282(3), 284(1) TFEU. The President of the Council may submit motions for deliberations.

643 Arts. 130, 282(3) TFEU; Protocol 4, Art. 7.

644 See further Protocol 4 annexed to the EU Treaties, Art. 14. In particular, the Court of Justice has jurisdiction to review and annul a national act whereby the national anti-corruption office has temporarily prohibited the Governor of the Central Bank of the Member State concerned from performing his duties (see further Joined Cases C-202/18 and C-238/18, *Rimšēvičs*, EU:C:2019:139).

645 Art. 284(3) TFEU. See further Protocol 4, Art. 15. 646 Parliament, 'Rules of Procedure', Rule 135.

647 Protocol 4, Art. 35.

648 Those Member States whose currency is not the euro, as well as their central banks, retain their powers in monetary matters; Art. 282(4) TFEU.

notes to have legal tender and may be issued either by the Bank itself or by national central banks of the euro area.[649] The Bank also authorises the issue of euro coins by the Member States.[650] The Eurosystem conducts foreign exchange operations, holds and manages the official foreign reserves of the Member States and promotes the smooth operation of payment systems.[651] The Bank acts by way of regulations, decisions, recommendations and opinions; it can decide on whether or not to publish acts of the last three categories.[652] It may also adopt other types of acts internally, such as guidelines and instructions, to articulate its relations with national central banks. The Bank is entitled to impose fines or periodic penalty payments on undertakings for failure to comply with obligations it lays down,[653] and to trigger legal action against national central banks failing to comply with their obligations under the EU Treaties and Protocol 4.[654]

More generally, the Central Bank should be consulted on proposals for EU acts, as well as, under certain conditions, for national acts in its fields of competences (which include contributing to securing the euro's place in the international monetary system[655]). It may also submit opinions to EU and national organs in these fields.[656] It can, on rare occasions, submit proposals for the adoption of EU legislation.[657] The Bank further collects statistical information to enable the system to perform its tasks.[658]

In the context of the economic and financial crisis, which put much pressure on the euro area, the Central Bank has gained a prominent role in various notable ways. Firstly, it has made dynamic use of its powers, which it holds together with the national central banks, to operate on financial markets (buying or selling claims and marketable instruments) and to conduct credit operations. This is subject to the prohibition on EU organs or Member States to act as a lender of last resort, which has indeed been the subject of much discussion.[659] A recent illustration of reliance on this power is the Central Bank's Pandemic Emergency Purchase Programme, which was rolled out in March 2020 to counter serious risks to monetary policy and the outlook for the euro area posed by the COVID-19 outbreak.[660] Second, the Bank came to play an important role in the European Stability Mechanism created outside of the EU legal order to assist the Member States of the euro area experiencing or threatened by severe financing problems.[661] Third, this EU institution is increasingly involved in prudential supervision of credit institutions.[662] In particular, it now has exclusive competence to ensure that the system for the supervision of banks in the euro area (and other participating States) functions adequately, with a view to contributing to the

[649] Art. 128(1) TFEU. [650] Art. 128(2) TFEU. [651] Art. 127(2) TFEU. [652] Art. 132 TFEU.

[653] Art. 132(3) TFEU. [654] Art. 271(d) TFEU. [655] Art. 138 TFEU; see further Protocol 4, Art. 6.

[656] Arts. 127(4), 282(5) TFEU; Protocol 4, Art. 4(b).

[657] This relates to certain amendments to the statute of the European System of Central Banks and of the Central Bank in the context of the EU's monetary policy; Art. 129(3) TFEU.

[658] Protocol 4, Art. 5.

[659] Art. 123 TFEU; Protocol 4, Arts. 18, 21. Further examining the compatibility of measures adopted by the Central Bank with these provisions, and concluding in favour of the Central Bank, see C-62/14, *Gauweiler*, EU:C:2015:400, paras. 93–127; C-493/17, *Weiss*, EU:C:2018:1000, paras. 101–128.

[660] 'Decision (EU) 2020/440 of the European Central Bank of 24 March 2020 on a Temporary Pandemic Emergency Purchase Programme', OJ L 91, 25.3.2020, p. 1 (last amended 2021).

[661] Treaty Establishing the European Stability Mechanism, Brussels, 2.2.2012. Reliance by the European Stability Mechanism, created outside of EU law, on the Central Bank – an EU institution – is possible, as was discussed extensively in C-370/12, *Pringle*, EU:C:2012:756.

[662] Art. 127(5–6) TFEU.

safety and soundness of credit institutions and the stability of the financial system within the EU and each Member State.[663] The Central Bank directly supervises 'significant' banks, while 'less significant' banks continue to be supervised by the national competent authorities, in cooperation with the Bank.[664]

2.3.9 The Court of Auditors

2.3.9.1 The Guardian of the EU's Financial Resources

The Court of Auditors is the guardian of the EU's finances.[665] To avoid confusion that can be caused by its name, it does *not* perform a judicial function: it audits the EU's activities.[666] It is based in Luxembourg[667] and examines all the revenue and expenditure of EU organs, ranging from institutions to bodies, offices or agencies set up by the EU. It checks whether all 'revenue has been received and all expenditure incurred in a lawful and regular manner' and whether 'financial management has been sound'.[668] Its authority results from its ability to shed light on the way EU organs use the EU's financial resources and steer change by sharing its findings, in particular, in the form of reports.[669] The Court may also give opinions, for instance on proposals for EU legislation.[670]

The Court of Auditors is formed by members who are nationals of each Member State. These members are chosen from among persons 'who belong or have belonged in their respective States to external audit bodies or who are especially qualified for th[e] office'. They are appointed by the Council, after consultation of the Parliament, for a renewable term of six years.[671] The members are completely independent in the performance of their duties, and act in the EU's general interest.[672] The Court furthermore acts as a collegiate body, with reports or opinions adopted by a majority of its members agreeing, on behalf of the institution.[673]

[663] See 'Council Regulation (EU) 1024/2013 of 15 October 2013 Conferring Specific Tasks on the European Central Bank Concerning Policies Relating to the Prudential Supervision of Credit Institutions', OJ L 287, 29.10.2013, p. 63. Next to euro area Member States, Bulgaria and Croatia joined the system for European banking supervision through 'close cooperation' in October 2020.

[664] On the allocation of tasks between the Central Bank and national competent authorities for the supervision of national banks, see further C-450/17 P, *Landeskreditbank Baden-Württemberg – Förderbank* v. *European Central Bank*, EU:C:2019:372.

[665] The Court of Auditors originates in the Treaty amending certain financial provisions of the Treaties establishing the European Economic Communities and of the Treaty establishing a single Council and a single Commission of the European Communities, OJ L 359, 31.12.1977, p. 1.

[666] Art. 285, para. 1 TFEU. Distinguishing from judicial review: Case 294/83, *Parti écologiste 'Les Verts'* v. *Parliament*, EU:C:1986:166, para. 28; and Opinion of Advocate General Mancini in Case 204/86, *Greece* v. *Council*, EU:C:1988:259, para. 5.

[667] Protocol 6 annexed to the EU Treaties on the Location of the Seats of the Institutions and of Certain Bodies, Offices, Agencies and Departments of the European Union, Sole Art. (e).

[668] Art. 287(1–2) TFEU.

[669] The reports of the Court of Auditors 'are intended to give guidance to the budgetary authority required to discharge the accounts and, more generally, to all public bodies capable of contributing to the filling or correction of any lacunae or dysfunction observed by the Court of Auditors in those areas' (C-539/09, *Commission* v. *Germany*, EU:C:2011:733, para. 62).

[670] Art. 287(4), subpara. 2 TFEU; e.g. Art. 322(1) TFEU. [671] Art. 286(2) TFEU.

[672] Art. 285, para. 2 TFEU; Art. 286(1) and (3) TFEU.

[673] Art. 287(4), subpara. 3 TFEU; 'Rules of Procedure of the Court of Auditors of the European Union', OJ L 103, 23.4.2010, p. 1, Art. 1 (last amended 2020). Internally, the work is shared between Chambers of members; Arts. 10–11.

2.3.9.2 Investigating, Reporting and Recommending

With a view to performing its audits, the Court has access to records and any document or information necessary to carry out its task.[674] It may also carry investigations on the spot, on the premises of EU organs and in the Member States, including on the premises of any natural or legal person in receipt of payment from the EU budget. For that purpose, the Court acts in liaison with national competent authorities such as national audit bodies, with which it cooperates 'in a spirit of trust', each level maintaining its independence.[675]

The outcome of the work of the Court takes the form of several instruments building on different types of audits. Two of the main ones are highlighted here. Firstly, the Court issues annual reports on the extent to which the annual accounts are reliable, and income and spending transactions are in compliance with the applicable rules and regulations (thus based on compliance audits). The annual report includes a 'Statement of Assurance' addressed to the Parliament and the Council, reassuring them of the reliability of the accounts of EU organs as well as of the legality and regularity of the underlying transactions.[676] These reports are made public, together with the replies of other EU institutions to the observations made by the Court.[677] They are particularly important in that they form the basis of the Council and the Parliament's assessment of whether the Commission can be granted discharge for sound implementation of the EU budget, which is an element of political control.[678]

Second, the Court regularly issues special reports testing whether spending in a given prong of EU activities has been most economical, efficient and effective in the light of the intended objectives (thus based on performance audits).[679] For instance, in 2021, the Court of Auditors examined whether the Common Agricultural Policy supported practices able to reduce greenhouse gas emissions from agriculture and found that farm emissions were not decreasing. It made recommendations, including that the Commission take steps to reduce emissions from cultivated drained organic soils.[680] These reports may attract much attention, and other EU institutions and organs may be ill at ease with being lectured on how to manage a given policy.

2.3.9.3 Bridging with OLAF and EPPO to Protect the EU's Financial Interests

The Court of Auditors is furthermore under a duty to report on any cases of irregularity.[681] More specifically, the Court notifies any suspicion of fraud, corruption or other illegal activity affecting the EU's financial interests to OLAF, which is responsible for the EU's fight against fraud and protecting its financial interests.[682] Investigations by OLAF, which are,

[674] Art. 287(3), subparas. 1 and 2 TFEU. [675] Art. 287(3), subpara. 1 TFEU. [676] Art. 287(1), subpara. 2 TFEU.
[677] Art. 287(4), subpara. 1 TFEU.
[678] Arts. 287(4), subpara. 4, 319(1) TFEU; see further Chapter 2, Section 2.3.2.6.
[679] See further 'Regulation (EU, Euratom) 2018/1046 of the European Parliament and of the Council of 18 July 2018 on the Financial Rules Applicable to the General Budget of the Union', OJ L 193, 30.7.2018 (last amended 2021), Art. 33.
[680] Court of Auditors, Common Agricultural Policy and climate: Half of EU climate spending but farm emissions are not decreasing, Special Report 16/2021.
[681] Art. 287(2), subpara. 1 TFEU.
[682] 'Commission Decision 1999/352/EC, ECSC, Euratom of 28 April 1999 Establishing the European Anti-fraud Office (OLAF)', OJ L 136, 31.5.1999, p. 20 (last amended 2015). See further Decision 43/2017 on cooperation between the European Court of Auditors and OLAF concerning cases of suspected fraud identified by the European Court of Auditors during its audit work or provided to it as unsolicited denunciations from third parties, Luxembourg, 14.9.2017.

by nature, administrative, may be initiated by information reported by the Court, but are not limited to this. They can be triggered as soon as there is 'sufficient suspicion', which may be based on information provided by any third party or anonymously that there has been fraud, corruption or any other illegal activity affecting the financial interests of the EU.[683] Such investigations relate to fraud within EU organs, as well as by any external entity in the course of activities affecting the financial interest of the EU. After an investigation is concluded, the Office recommends the EU institutions and/or national governments concerned to take disciplinary, administrative, financial (including recovery of funds) or judicial action.[684] OLAF cannot carry out criminal investigations and prosecutions; only national authorities can do so and their powers largely stop at their national borders.

More recently, OLAF has been complemented by the European Public Prosecutor's Office (EPPO), in which twenty-two Member States take part.[685] Its task is not only to enable investigation, but also to prosecute and bring to judgment, in the competent courts of the Member States, crimes against the financial interests of the EU (such as large-scale VAT fraud or money laundering and corruption). It is also expected that the Court of Auditors, like any EU organ or competent national authority, will report, without undue delay, any criminal conduct to the EPPO.[686]

2.4 LOOKING BEYOND INSTITUTIONS

A multiplicity of entities gravitate around EU institutions and form a bridge between EU institutions, Member States and citizens. Some are provided for in the EU Treaties, while others are set out in EU acts adopted thereupon. It would be beyond the scope of this book, and actually impossible, to provide an exhaustive list. We ought to pinpoint the existence of a few key ones, however.

2.4.1 Advisory Bodies

EU institutions receive advice from several sources, due to consultations with a broad range of actors or to contributions from specific EU organs such as the Court of Auditors. Two EU bodies stand out, as they are identified in the EU Treaties as specifically designed to advise the Parliament, the Council and the Commission in decision-making.[687]

683 'Regulation (EU, Euratom) No. 883/2013 of the European Parliament and of the Council of 11 September 2013 Concerning Investigations Conducted by the European Anti-Fraud Office', OJ L 248, 18.9.2013 (last amended 2020), Art. 5(1).

684 Ibid., Art. 11(1).

685 Art. 86 TFEU; 'Council Regulation (EU) 2017/1939 of 12 October 2017 Implementing Enhanced Cooperation on the Establishment of the European Public Prosecutor's Office', OJ L 283, 31.10.2017. The EPPO started its operations in June 2021. Member States not taking part are: Denmark, Ireland, Hungary, Poland and Sweden.

686 'Council Regulation (EU) 2017/1939 of 12 October 2017 Implementing Enhanced Cooperation on the Establishment of the European Public Prosecutor's Office', OJ L 283, 31.10.2017, Art. 24(1).

687 Art. 13(4) TEU; Art. 300(1) TFEU. Details on these organs are provided in Arts. 300–307 TFEU.

2.4.1.1 The Economic and Social Committee

The Economic and Social Committee, to start with, consists of representatives of employers, employees and other parts of civil society (such as farmers, consumers and so on)[688] and is designed to give a voice to these socio-economic interests in EU decision-making processes. These members act completely independently, and in the EU's general interest.[689] The number of members differs for each Member State and shall not exceed 350. At time of writing it has 329 members.[690] They are appointed for a renewable mandate of five years by the Council, on the basis of proposals made by each Member State.[691] The Committee decides by a majority of the votes cast.[692]

This Committee issues opinions in three main types of settings.[693] Firstly, consultation by the Parliament, the Council or the Commission is mandatory when the EU Treaties so provide. This is naturally the case for the adoption of legislation in the social area, for instance, as illustrated by the recent opinion on the controversial legislative proposal submitted by the Commission for a directive on adequate minimum wages.[694] Second, consultation is optional in all cases in which the institutions consider it appropriate. Third, the Committee may issue opinions of its own initiative. It also takes other initiatives that focus on civil society and citizens' participation.

2.4.1.2 The Committee of the Regions

The Committee of the Regions is a more recent addition to the list of EU organs. It dates back to the Maastricht Treaty and illustrates the willingness to give a voice to sub-levels of governance in the EU. Indeed, as the ambition of the project of European integration grew, so did concerns for subsidiarity.[695] It has similar structural characteristics to the Economic and Social Committee. The Committee of the Regions consists of representatives elected or politically accountable at regional and local levels.[696] They are also independent, should not exceed 350 (there are 329 at time of writing)[697] and have a renewable five-year mandate.[698] They are appointed through a similar procedure and also decide by a majority of the votes cast.[699]

[688] Art. 300(2) TFEU. [689] Art. 300(4) TFEU.
[690] Art. 301 TFEU; 'Council Decision (EU) 2019/853 of 21 May 2019 Determining the Composition of the European Economic and Social Committee', OJ L 139, 27.5.2019, p. 15.
[691] Art. 302 TFEU.
[692] European Economic and Social Committee, 'Rules of Procedure' (last amended 2022), Rule 68. The quorum exists if more than half the members of the Committee are present or represented, Rule 59.
[693] Art. 304 TFEU.
[694] Art. 153(2) TFEU; European Economic and Social Committee, Opinion on 'Proposal for a Directive of the European Parliament and of the Council on Adequate Minimum Wages in the European Union', OJ C 220, 9.6.2021, p. 106.
[695] See Chapter 3, Section 3.4.1. See also Protocol 2 on the application of the principles of subsidiarity and proportionality, Art. 8, para. 2.
[696] Art. 300(3) TFEU.
[697] 'Council Decision (EU) 2019/852 of 21 May 2019 Determining the Composition of the Committee of the Regions', OJ L 139, 27.5.2019, p. 13.
[698] Arts. 300(4), 305 TFEU.
[699] Respectively, Art. 305, para. 3 TFEU; Committee of the Regions, 'Rules of Procedure' (last amended 2021), Rule 23. The quorum exists if more than half of the members of the Committee are present or represented (Rule 22).

We can also distinguish between the duty and the option for the Parliament, Council or Commission to consult the Committee.[700] Consultation is mandatory where provided for in the EU Treaties, such as in relation to environmental protection,[701] as well as where institutions consider it appropriate, such as for cross-border cooperation.[702] Consultation is optional in all other cases in which institutions consider it appropriate; and the Committee may issue opinions of its own initiative. In 2020, for instance, the Committee issued an own-initiative opinion setting out a roadmap for clean hydrogen, on the contribution of local and regional authorities to a climate-neutral Europe.[703]

2.4.2 EU Agencies

An increasing number of EU agencies operate in between EU institutions (mostly the Commission) and the Member States.[704] They are created on an ad hoc basis by a legal act of the EU institutions to meet specific needs. Agencies tend to attract much attention in times of crises, which call for coordinated responses at European level. For instance, we saw the establishment of agencies for the financial sector – such as the European Securities and Markets Authority[705] – in response to the economic and financial crisis of 2008. Similarly, the refugee crisis of 2015 resulted in the revamping of the European Border and Coast Guard Agency (known as Frontex), with the aim of equipping it with up to 10,000 standing corps (operational staff, such as border guards).[706]

Although each agency is different, the details depending on each legal act creating one of them (parent act), we outline here some of their general functions and characteristics.[707] These agencies are, in principle, bodies governed by EU public law, with their own legal personality and various degrees of administrative and financial autonomy. A first category of agencies are 'decentralised'. This means they are located across the EU and created by an EU legislative act to respond to specific needs: for expertise, information and cooperation, the provision of services, facilitation and support, as well as supervision, inspection and enforcement. It shall be noted that this list of tasks is not rigid, as agencies often perform cross-cutting functions. Examples of such agencies include: the European Food Safety Authority (Parma),[708] which provides scientific expertise to the Commission

[700] Art. 307 TFEU. [701] Art. 192 TFEU. [702] Art. 307 TFEU.

[703] Committee of Regions, Towards a Roadmap for Clean Hydrogen: the contribution of local and regional authorities to a climate-neutral Europe, 1.7.2020.

[704] On the principles governing the delegation of EU powers, see Chapter 3, Section 3.2.3.4.

[705] 'Regulation (EU, Euratom) No. 883/2013 of the European Parliament and of the Council of 11 September 2013 Concerning Investigations Conducted by the European Anti-Fraud Office', OJ L 248, 18.9.2013, p. 84 (last amended 2020).

[706] 'Regulation (EU) 2019/1896 of the European Parliament and of the Council of 13 November 2019 on the European Border and Coast Guard', OJ L 295, 14.11.2019, p. 1.

[707] See further E. Vos, *EU Agencies, Common Approach and Parliamentary Scrutiny* (Study commissioned for the Parliament, 2018), p. 33.

[708] 'Regulation (EC) 178/2002 of the European Parliament and of the Council of 28 January 2002 Laying Down the General Principles and Requirements of Food Law, Establishing the European Food Safety Authority and Laying Down Procedures in Matters of Food Safety', OJ L 31, 1.2.2002, p. 1 (last amended 2019), Art. 22 *et seq.*

for the latter to assess requests to authorise genetically modified organisms for the European market; the European Union Intellectual Property Office (Alicante), which provides exclusive rights for trademarks in the EU;[709] and the European Securities and Markets Authority (Paris), which sanctions credit rating agencies that have not respected EU financial law.[710]

A second category of agencies are said to be 'executive' in that they are created by the Commission to help that institution to implement the EU's financial programmes. They have managerial tasks and are set up for a fixed period. An example is the European Research Executive Agency, entrusted with the implementation of several EU programmes supporting advanced research through funding.[711]

The multiplication and influence of agencies has important implications for the system of institutional checks and balances between EU institutions, as well as between EU organs and Member States. While the structure of executive agencies is consistent overall and they are under the authority of the Commission,[712] the situation is more complex for decentralised agencies. Faced with a mushrooming of such decentralised agencies (more than thirty exist today), the Parliament, the Council and the Commission agreed on a 'Common Approach' in 2012. This is a non-binding instrument setting out common general features for the design of decentralised agencies. The structures of these agencies, modelled to various extents on the suggested common approach, illustrate the extent to which Agencies act as a bridge between EU institutions and Member States: a limited number of persons appointed by EU institutions are involved, often mostly from the Commission, and they coexist with a large number of persons appointed by the Member States.

This is well illustrated with reference to the European Medicines Agency (Amsterdam), which has played a crucial role in the EU's response to the COVID-19 crisis. It is responsible for 'coordinating the existing scientific resources put at its disposal by Member States for the evaluation, supervision and pharmacovigilance of medicinal products'.[713] It issued, for instance, a first recommendation to grant conditional marketing authorisation for the COVID-19 vaccine developed by AstraZeneca, which was followed by the Commission granting authorisation.[714] The internal structure of this agency can be summarised as follows:

[709] 'Regulation (EU) 2017/1001 of the European Parliament and of the Council of 14 June 2017 on the European Union Trade Mark', OJ L 154, 16.6.2017, Art. 142 *et seq.*

[710] See Chapter 2, note 705.

[711] 'Commission Implementing Decision (EU) 2021/173 of 12 February 2021 Establishing [. . .] the European Research Executive Agency [among others] and Repealing Implementing Decisions', OJ L 50, 15.2.2021, p. 9.

[712] See 'Council Regulation (EC) No. 58/2003 of 19 December 2002 Laying Down the Statute for Executive Agencies to Be Entrusted with Certain Tasks in the Management of Community Programmes', OJ L 11, 16.1.2003, p. 1.

[713] 'Regulation (EC) No. 726/2004 of the European Parliament and of the Council of 31 March 2004 Laying Down Community Procedures for the Authorisation and Supervision of Medicinal Products for Human and Veterinary Use and Establishing a European Medicines Agency', OJ L 136, 30.4.2004, p. 1 (last amended 2020), Art. 55.

[714] Implementing Decision granting a conditional marketing authorisation, C(2021) 698 final, Brussels 29.1.2021, see Preamble recital (5).

- An independent Management Board, which has a supervisory role and general responsibility for budgetary and planning matters. It is composed of high-level experts in the field, as follows: one representative of each Member State, two of the Commission, two of the Parliament, one of patients' organisations, one of doctors' organisations and one of veterinarians' organisations.[715]
- An Executive Director (appointed by the Management Board on a proposal from the Commission), who is the legal representative of the Agency and oversees the work of the staff that supports its work.[716]
- Scientific committees, working parties and related groups composed of European experts primarily designated by national competent authorities, such as for the Committee for Medicinal Products for Human Use.[717] The key task of the latter is to provide objective scientific opinions to the EU and to the Member States on the questions that are referred to it. For that purpose, members shall best endeavour to reach a scientific consensus. If such a consensus cannot be reached, the opinion shall consist of the position of the majority of members and divergent positions, with the grounds on which they are based.

Agencies are accountable to EU institutions. Their acts may be reviewed by the Court of Justice of the European Union.[718] Depending on the details of their parent act, decentralised agencies are, in principle, at least expected to report regularly to the Court of Auditors, the Parliament, the Council and the Commission.[719] Given the diverse and mixed nature of decentralised agencies standing in between Member States and EU institutions, however, there continues to be much debate as to who is ultimately in charge and who monitors whom.[720]

2.4.3 Other Entities

This overview of EU organs complementing the work of EU institutions is not intended to be – and, in any case, could not be – exhaustive. It suffices here to note that the EU Treaties refer to a number of other EU organs including the European Investment Bank,[721] which operates on a non-profit-making basis to grant loans, and give guarantees, facilitating the financing of projects in all sectors of the EU economy for the development of the EU's internal market; or the Ombudsman who investigates claims of maladministration by EU organs.[722]

Instruments adopted on the basis of the EU Treaties further add a mosaic of other entities. These range from (to name just a few and illustrate their diversity) the Partnership Council created under the Trade and Cooperation Agreement between the EU and the UK

[715] 'Regulation (EC) No. 726/2004 of the European Parliament and of the Council of 31 March 2004 Laying Down Community Procedures for the Authorisation and Supervision of Medicinal Products for Human and Veterinary Use and Establishing a European Medicines Agency', OJ L 136, 30.4.2004, Art. 65. The tasks are set out in Arts. 65–67.

[716] Ibid., Art. 64(1). [717] Ibid., Art. 61. [718] Art. 263, para. 1 TFEU. [719] Common Approach, para. 49.

[720] See further M. Chamon, *EU Agencies: Legal and Political Limits to the Transformation of the EU Administration* (Oxford University Press, 2016).

[721] Arts. 308–309 TFEU; Protocol 5 on the statute of the European Investment Bank.

[722] See Chapter 2, Section 2.3.2.6.

to 'oversee the attainment of the objectives' of the said Agreement,[723] to Equinet, which is the network bringing together equality bodies created under EU law to fight discrimination at the national level.[724] Importantly, and as will be further elaborated in Chapter 3, the EU does not operate in a vacuum. It interacts with a multiplicity of actors, who all, in one way or another, also contribute to shaping the EU legal order.[725]

[723] 'Trade and Cooperation Agreement between the European Union and the European Atomic Energy Community, of the One Part, and the United Kingdom of Great Britain and Northern Ireland, of the Other Part', OJ L 149, 30.4.2021, p. 10, Art. 7.

[724] See further 'Regulation (EU) 2021/692 of the European Parliament and of the Council of 28 April 2021 Establishing the Citizens, Equality, Rights and Values Programme', OJ L 156, 5.5.2021, p. 1, Art. 14(3).

[725] See Chapter 3, Section 3.5.1.2.

3 The EU System of Legal Norms

As outlined in Chapter 1, the EU Treaties[1] play a central role in the process of European integration. They set out the boundaries of the European Union legal order. Within these boundaries, it is not only the EU Treaties, but also a vast array of legal acts that may be adopted and that produce legal effects. The European Union thereby autonomously generates a structured set of instruments complementing the Treaty framework. With a view to shedding light on this system of legal norms, this chapter further elaborates on the primary legal framework of the EU legal order (Section 3.1), on the basis of which the system of allocation of competences between the EU and its Member States may then be set out. Indeed, the rules and principles governing the existence of an EU competence (Section 3.2), the various types of competences (Section 3.3) and the principles governing the exercise of these competences (Section 3.4) all derive therefrom. It is within this framework that further legal acts (Section 3.5) may be adopted by EU actors, in accordance with procedures established for that purpose (Section 3.6).

3.1 THE PRIMARY LEGAL FRAMEWORK

Elaborating on the importance of the EU Treaties, this section discusses the specific features of the EU Treaties, before turning to other instruments that have the same legal value as the EU Treaties and thus are also part of primary law. Within that category, we will insist on fundamental rights that have come to gain central importance in the EU legal order.

3.1.1 The EU Treaties

3.1.1.1 Functions of the EU Treaties

The EU Treaties constitute the EU's primary source of law. They constitute the core of EU primary law (we will return to other norms of primary law subsequently).[2] They can be said to perform three main functions in the EU legal system. They set out the rules for the functioning of the EU legal system, such as the institutional design and procedures for decision-making at EU level.[3] The EU Treaties also define fundamental values, objectives, principles and certain rules of EU substantive law, such as those ensuring the functioning of the internal market and the monetary union. Finally, they define the existence of, and the way to exercise, EU competences which allow the principles and rules set out therein to be complemented by and implemented through acts derived from the EU Treaties.

[1] By way of reminder: the Treaty on European Union and the Treaty on the Functioning of the European Union.

[2] Arts. 1 and 5(1–2) TEU; Art. 1 TFEU. As noted in Chapter 1, Section 1.4.1, protocols and annexes are deemed to constitute 'an integral part' of the Treaties. Amendments of the Treaties, including accession treaties, also form part of EU primary law: they amend the EU Treaties by extending their geographical scope and making the related necessary updates. Declarations attached to the EU Treaties are not legally binding, but they may be used as aids to interpret the context in which the provisions of the Treaties were drafted.

[3] See, particular, Chapter 2, Section 2.3 and Chapter 3, Section 3.6, respectively.

3.1.1.2 Actions and Restraints under the EU Treaties

The resulting web of EU norms and policies cover a broad set of subject matters, ranging from customs duties to consumer and environmental protection, economic and monetary union, asylum law or rights of the defendant in criminal proceedings. The diversity of areas in which the European Union is involved is well illustrated with reference to Part III TFEU (Box 3.1), along with the CFSP that is established in the TEU.

Box 3.1 Overview of areas of EU policies and internal action (Part III TFEU)

The related legal constraints vary greatly from field to field, and even from instrument to instrument within a given field. These constraints often result from a combination of legal techniques. To start with, provisions of the TFEU may *prohibit* a certain course of action. For instance, they ban unlawful obstacles to the functioning of the internal market – examples being the prohibition of discriminatory, unjustified or disproportionate obstacles to the free movement of goods.[4] This is often referred to as 'negative integration'. The process of negative integration is boosted when EU organs responsible for ensuring compliance with the EU Treaties, and the Court of Justice of the European Union in particular, engage in an extensive reading of the provisions preventing the Member States from acting in specific ways.

[4] Arts. 34, 35 TFEU.

Provisions of the EU Treaties also establish duties as well as possibilities for *actions*. It is common for provisions of the TFEU to empower EU institutions to set common standards to reduce regulatory divergence between the Member States. In this context, EU organs exercise competences conferred upon them by the EU Treaties to 'harmonise' national rules. It is often referred to as 'positive integration', as illustrated by the adoption of rules on the use of animals for scientific purposes in the internal market.[5] EU law may also operate in more complex and nuanced ways. By way of example, EU organs may be empowered to coordinate or steer Member States' actions by creating incentives and disincentives, possibly by threats of sanctions, as in the field of economic policy;[6] or using blame and shame techniques, as well as financial support, as in the field of employment;[7] or drawing general and strategic guidelines for the CFSP of the EU.[8] These possible actions result from the exercise of competences conferred by the EU Treaties on EU organs. They are thus examples of how the principle of allocated competences is put into practice, and will be discussed later in this chapter.

3.1.1.3 General Features of EU Law Applied to the EU Treaties

Different doctrines are used to articulate the forms of legal authority of EU law over national law. These doctrines are also relevant for sources of EU law other than the EU Treaties, including other sources of primary law, and are further developed in Chapter 4. Yet their specific application to the EU Treaties is briefly mentioned here in order to stress that, even in the absence of acts complementing them or exercising competences conferred on the EU (as will be further elaborated upon in this chapter), the EU Treaties deploy a vast array of legal effects in national legal orders.

Firstly, rules enshrined in the EU Treaties have a broad range of legal effects resulting from the primacy of EU law over national law. In particular, national authorities have a duty to interpret national law in conformity with EU primary law. These diverse legal effects may not be very obvious to see because the primacy of a provision of EU law does not always result in and of itself in the imposition of a specific course of action: such a course of action is often, instead, the outcome of a joint reading of several instruments of EU and national law in a specific factual context.

Second, certain provisions of the EU Treaties may be relied upon before national courts directly to create rights and obligations for individuals: either against the State or against other private actors.[9] For instance, a dispute against national authorities for breach of the

[5] 'Directive 2010/63/EU of the European Parliament and of the Council of 22 September 2010 on the Protection of Animals Used for Scientific Purposes', OJ L 276, 20.10.2010, pp. 33–79 (last amended 2019), adopted on the basis of Art. 114 TFEU.

[6] Arts. 121, 126 TFEU, and legislation adopted thereupon such as the Stability and Growth Pact: 'Council Regulation (EC) No. 1466/97 of 7 July 1997 on the Strengthening of the Surveillance of Budgetary Positions and the Surveillance and Coordination of Economic Policies', OJ L 209, 2.8.1997, p. 1 (last amended 2011); and 'Council Regulation (EC) No. 1467/97 on Speeding Up and Clarifying the Implementation of the Excessive Deficit Procedure', OJ L 209, 2.8.1997, p. 6 (last amended 2011).

[7] Arts. 148, 164 TFEU. [8] Arts. 25–26 TEU.

[9] The conditions to be met for a provision of EU law to produce direct effect are discussed in Chapter 4, Section 4.1.2.

Treaty rules on the prohibition of unlawful obstacles to the internal market may be relied upon before national courts.[10] This contributes to the process of negative integration introduced previously. Acknowledging the ability of provisions of the EU Treaties to produce such direct effects, even in the absence of any other EU acts addressing the matter, reveals the regulatory power of the relevant Treaty provisions.

Thirdly, the EU Treaties establish a far-reaching duty of sincere cooperation that is binding on EU organs and on the Member States.[11] In that context, the Member States are not only expected to ensure the fulfilment of their obligations under the Treaties or resulting from specific acts of EU institutions; they are also expected to 'facilitate the achievement of the Union's tasks', as well as to 'refrain from any measure which could jeopardise the attainment of the Union's objectives'.[12] This implies, for instance, a general duty to 'provide remedies sufficient to ensure effective legal protection in the fields covered by Union law',[13] in particular in the absence of further EU acts addressing the matter.[14]

The doctrines of primacy, direct effect and sincere cooperation, applied to and anchored in the EU Treaties thereby shape the interplay between the EU legal system and others in powerful ways. The system of EU norms is complemented by other norms of primary law, added to the EU Treaties over time to enhance individual protection, as we shall see subsequently. The EU Treaties also create a system of allocation of competences which enables the adoption of further instruments of EU law giving expression to, or implementing, the EU Treaties, as will be explained in Section 3.2 and subsequently.

3.1.2 Other Norms of Primary Law

The Court of Justice of the European Union has long acknowledged the existence of an unwritten source of law, referred to as 'general principles of EU law', in addition to the EU Treaties.[15] General principles may not extend the competences or powers of the EU as defined in the Treaties, but EU acts adopted on the basis of the Treaties must comply with, and be interpreted in light of, general principles of EU law. The latter thus have the same legal value as the EU Treaties and form part of EU primary law. There is no written version, and therefore no exhaustive list of these unwritten principles. Their unwritten nature is inherent in their 'gap filling function', similarly to unwritten constitutional principles in many national legal systems.[16]

In the ruling *Internationale Handelsgesellschaft*, the Court explained that the protection of rights enshrined in such general principles is inspired by 'the constitutional traditions common to the Member States' and 'must be ensured within the framework of the structure and objectives of the [Union]'.[17] In *Nold*, the Court added that international treaties 'on which the Member States have collaborated or of which they are signatories' can also

[10] E.g. relating to the direct effect of key provisions on eliminating obstacles to internal market: on the free movement of goods, Case 26/62, *Van Gend en Loos*, EU:C:1963:1 (Art. 30 TFEU); on the freedom of movement for workers, Case 167/73, *Commission* v. *France*, EU:C:1974:35 (Art. 45 TFEU).

[11] Art. 4(3) TEU. [12] Art. 4(3) TEU. [13] Art. 19(1), subpara. 2 TEU.

[14] Case 33/76, *Rewe*, EU:C:1976:188, para. 5; Case 45/76, *Comet*, EU:C:1976:191, paras. 12–13.

[15] Case 29/69, *Stauder*, EU:C:1969:57, para. 7.

[16] See further T. Tridimas, *The General Principles of EU Law*, 2nd ed. (Oxford University Press, 2006).

[17] Case 11/70, *Internationale Handelsgesellschaft*, EU:C:1970:114.

supply guidelines which should be followed within the framework of EU law.[18] Such general principles include fundamental rights (as will be discussed subsequently), as well as *other* types of principles of fundamental importance, such as legal certainty.[19]

Another source of EU primary law is the CFEU, which was drawn up in parallel to Treaty revisions.[20] In the aftermath of the failure to ratify the Treaty establishing a Constitution for Europe, it was decided that the CFEU would be published externally to the EU Treaties – not even as an annex, but literally *next to* the EU Treaties. Yet the legal authority of the CFEU is anchored in the EU Treaties, which grant it the same legal value as the Treaties.[21] The CFEU is thus also part of EU primary law. Like the general principles of EU law, the CFEU performs a different function to that of the EU Treaties: it shall not 'in any way' extend the competences of the EU as defined in the said Treaties. It does not establish any new power or tasks, or modify powers and tasks defined by the Treaties.[22] The CFEU may not, for instance, be the basis for the adoption of new acts of EU law. Yet EU acts adopted on the basis of the EU Treaties must comply, and be interpreted in light of, both the Treaties and the CFEU.

3.1.3 Focus on Fundamental Rights

3.1.3.1 Two Main Sources of Protection

The protection of fundamental rights has a very peculiar trajectory in EU law. Although the initial versions of the EU Treaties made no mention of fundamental rights, in *Stauder*, *Internationale Handelsgesellschaft* and *Nold*,[23] the Court of Justice made clear that these rights would be protected within the EU legal order by way of general principles of EU law. This is how EU law ensured the protection of fundamental rights until the Treaty of Lisbon. Since then, the EU has also had its own legally binding Charter.

Today, Article 6 TEU reflects this duality of the main sources for the protection of fundamental rights in the EU. Article 6(1) TEU refers to the legally binding nature of the CFEU, and Article 6(3) TEU recalls that fundamental rights – as they result, among other sources, from the constitutional traditions common to the Member States – 'shall constitute general principles of the Union's law'. Both sources thus coexist and the general principles continue to perform their gap-filling function.

[18] Case 4/73, *Nold*, EU:C:1974:51, para. 13.
[19] On the origins of the case law on general principles and fundamental rights protection in the EU, see Chapter 4, Section 4.1.1.1.
[20] See Chapter 1, Section 1.3.2.3. [21] Art. 6(1), subpara. 1 TEU.
[22] Art. 6(1), subpara. 2 TEU; see also Arts. 51(2), 52(2) CFEU. The tension between the perceived need for the EU to acquire its own legally binding list of fundamental rights, and concerns that this may unduly broaden the scope of intervention of the EU and encroach upon the preserve of national constitutional systems, is reflected in Protocol 30 attached to the EU Treaties on the position of the UK and Poland. The Protocol is often mistakenly referred to as an 'opt-out' for these countries. In fact, the concerns and reservations therein largely rephrase the provisions of the CFEU outlined already (C-411/10, *N.S.*, EU:C:2011:865, paras. 118–120). The only aspect of the protocol that might deserve further judicial interpretation is its Art. 1(2), asserting that nothing in the title on 'Solidarity' of the CFEU 'creates justiciable rights applicable to Poland or the United Kingdom except in so far as Poland or the United Kingdom has provided for such rights in its national law'.
[23] See Chapter 3, notes 15, 17, 18.

3.1.3.2 The New Star: The CFEU

The CFEU has gained a prominent role, as a source of protection, in contemporary EU law.[24] The final provisions of the CFEU invite us to distinguish between provisions containing 'principles', which need further implementation at national or EU level, and those containing 'rights'.[25] The first type of CFEU provisions 'shall be judicially cognizable only in the interpretation of [acts further implementing them] and in the ruling on their legality'. The CFEU does not identify which provisions contain 'rights' and which contain 'principles'. This is regrettable, as the latter have limited justiciability and are thus difficult to distinguish from rights which can more easily be relied upon before courts. The title on 'Solidarity', for instance, is often understood to mostly contain principles.[26]

There may be limitations on the exercise of rights and freedoms enshrined in the CFEU. These must be provided for by law and must respect the essence of those rights and freedoms. Limitations are also subject to the principle of proportionality. They may be made only if they are necessary and genuinely meet objectives of general interest recognised by the EU or the need to protect the rights and freedoms of others.[27] For instance, an interference with the fundamental right to property (Article 17(1) CFEU) in the form of bank deposits being restructured may be justified by the legitimate goal of protecting the stability of the banking system in the euro area as a whole, in the face of imminent risk of financial losses.[28] A provision of the CFEU also relates to the prohibition of abuse of rights.[29]

3.1.3.3 The Odd One Out: The ECHR

As well as the sources for the protection of fundamental rights listed previously, a few words ought to be devoted to the ECHR. The text dates back to the early 1950s[30] and was adopted in the context of the Council of Europe. Although the Council of Europe is distinct from the EU legal order, all EU Member States are also parties to the ECHR,[31] which also includes countries such as Turkey. The ECHR is therefore, inevitably, a powerful source of inspiration to shape fundamental rights within the EU legal order. This was confirmed by the Court of Justice in *Nold*, in which the ECHR was deemed to constitute an international treaty supplying guidelines to be followed within the EU legal system.[32] Today, as is clear

[24] E.g. Commission, Communication, 'Strategy for the Effective Implementation of the Charter of Fundamental Rights by the European Union', COM(2010) 573 final; see further M. Dawson, *The Governance of EU Fundamental Rights* (Cambridge University Press, 2017). A set of explanations was drawn up to provide guidance on the interpretation of CFEU provisions. These explanations 'shall be given due regard by the courts of the Union and of the Member States'; Art. 52(7) CFEU. See also the wording of Art. 6(2), subpara. 2 TEU.

[25] Art. 52(5) CFEU; see further Chapter 4, Section 4.1.2.3, Charter of Fundamental Rights of the EU.

[26] For an exception, see Joined Cases C-569/16 and C-570/16, *Bauer and Willmeroth*, EU:C:2018:871, para. 85.

[27] Art. 52(1) CFEU. [28] Joined Cases C-8/15 P to C-10/15 P, *Ledra Advertising*, EU:C:2016:701, paras. 73–74.

[29] Art. 54 CFEU. [30] See Chapter 1, Section 1.3.2.1.

[31] In 2005, in the *Bosphorus* case (Application 45036/98, CE:ECHR:2005:0630JUD004503698), the ECtHR recalled that the EU Member States are liable under the ECHR for 'all acts and omissions of its organs regardless of whether the act or omission in question was a consequence [. . .] of the necessity to comply with international legal [here EU] obligations' (para. 153). Furthermore, it also stated – this is now known as the Bosphorus presumption – that 'State action taken in compliance with such legal obligations is justified as long as the relevant organisation [here the EU] is considered to protect fundamental rights, as regards both the substantive guarantees offered and the mechanisms controlling their observance, in a manner which can be considered at least equivalent to that for which the Convention provides [. . .]. However, any such finding of equivalence could not be final and would be susceptible to review in the light of any relevant change in fundamental rights protection' (para. 155).

[32] Case 4/73, *Nold*, EU:C:1974:51, paras. 12–13.

from Article 6(3) TEU, the fundamental rights guaranteed by the ECHR 'shall' constitute general principles of EU law as introduced previously. There is thus no doubt that the ECHR 'has special significance' as a source of inspiration for the protection of fundamental rights in the EU legal order.[33]

The same reform that gave legal authority to the CFEU, the Treaty of Lisbon, also resulted in the insertion of a new competence, even a duty (it 'shall'), for the EU to accede to the ECHR, and such accession 'shall not affect the Union's competences'.[34] As a result of this change, a draft agreement providing for the accession of the European Union to the ECHR was prepared.[35] The Commission asked the Court of Justice whether the draft agreement was compatible with the Treaties and, in Opinion 2/13, the Court answered in the negative.[36] Since then, back in 2014, and in light of the challenges already faced by the EU in the context of the negotiations on Brexit,[37] work on the EU's accession to the ECHR has overall been minimal. The negotiations were relaunched in 2020.[38]

3.1.3.4 Interaction between the Various Sources

As will not have escaped the reader's attention, when it comes to identifying the sources for the protection of fundamental rights in the EU legal order, things get a little messy. It gets even worse if one recalls that specific fundamental rights are spelt out in the EU Treaties as such, and given expression in EU legislation – as is the case of the right to equal pay for men and women for work of equal value, for instance.[39] The EU may also be party to international agreements in the field, such as the United Nations Convention on the Rights of Persons with Disabilities.[40]

The relationship between these sources is complex. Several provisions of the CFEU, the latest and most comprehensive instrument of them all, seek to clarify the matter. The key idea, in Article 53 of the CFEU, is that the Charter itself may not restrict or adversely affect human rights and fundamental freedoms recognised by EU law, by international law, by international agreements to which the EU or all the Member States are party, or by the

[33] C-260/89, *Elliniki Radiophonia Tiléorassi (ERT)*, EU:C:1991:254, para. 41.

[34] Art. 6(2) TEU; see also Protocol No. 8.

[35] Council of Europe, Final report to the Steering Committee for Human Rights (CDDH), Strasbourg, 10.06. 2003.

[36] In the view of the Court, as it was drafted, the draft agreement would compromise the specific characteristics of EU law and its autonomy; was liable to affect Art. 344 TFEU (according to which Member States undertake not to submit a dispute concerning the interpretation or application of the Treaties to any method of settlement other than those provided for therein); and failed to have regard to the specific characteristics of EU law in CFSP matters: Opinion 2/13, Accession of the European Union to the European Convention for the Protection of Human Rights and Fundamental Freedoms, EU:C:2014:2454.

[37] Before the referendum on Brexit, David Cameron, then prime minister of the United Kingdom, had left open the possibility for the country to withdraw from the ECHR.

[38] Commission, 'The EU's Accession to the European Convention on Human Rights: Joint Statement on Behalf of the Council of Europe and the European Commission', press release, 29.9.2020. Follow up at coe.int, 'EU Accession to the ECHR'.

[39] Art. 157(1) TFEU; Art. 23 CFEU; 'Directive 2006/54/EC of the European Parliament and of the Council of 5 July 2006 on the Implementation of the Principle of Equal Opportunities and Equal Treatment of Men and Women in Matters of Employment and Occupation' (recast), OJ L 204, 26.7.2006, p. 23.

[40] 'Council Decision of 26 November 2009 Concerning the Conclusion, by the European Community, of the United Nations Convention on the Rights of Persons with Disabilities', OJ L 23, 27.1.2010, p. 35.

Member States' constitutions. The CFEU may, however, ensure higher levels of protection than these sources.[41]

A set of further provisions seeks to ensure a harmonious coexistence between CFEU rights and Treaty provisions,[42] CFEU rights and ECHR rights,[43] and CFEU rights and constitutional traditions common to the Member States.[44] Despite these efforts, the relationship between the various sources is occasionally a matter of controversy. This is the case, for instance, in relation to the prohibition of discrimination on grounds of religion, or in relation to asylum seekers. These debates illustrate that the EU is becoming an increasingly powerful actor when it comes to defining standards of fundamental rights protection in Europe.[45]

3.1.3.5 Scope of Application of EU Fundamental Rights

A mere allegation of breach of a fundamental right will not create an automatic obligation to protect the fundamental right in question under EU law. For EU fundamental rights law to apply, the situation must fall within the scope of EU law. In other words, it must be within the ambit of EU law by establishing a sufficient link with other provisions of EU law. With a view to establishing such a link, two main categories of actors can be distinguished.[46]

EU organs, normally acting as straightforward agents of the EU, ought to comply with EU fundamental rights law.[47] That is the case, for instance, when the Council designs a regulation on the financing of the common agricultural policy of the EU, thereby exercising an EU competence conferred on it by the EU Treaties. The Council may not impose an obligation to publish personal data relating to beneficiaries of European aid without paying attention to the fundamental right of the beneficiaries to the protection of personal data and respect for private life.[48]

It may be more difficult to determine whether action by national authorities falls within the scope of EU law. National authorities may be agents of the EU, in which case EU fundamental rights law applies; but they may also only be acting in the exercise of their national sovereignty, in which case EU fundamental rights law does not apply. National authorities are deemed to be agents of the EU in several settings: when they implement an obligation under EU law; when they legitimately restrict the functioning of the internal market; when they exercise their margin of discretion or use an authorisation granted by EU

[41] Note that, in practice, it is not always easy to identify what is a higher level of protection of a given fundamental right.

[42] Art. 52(2) CFEU. [43] Art. 52(3) CFEU. [44] Art. 52(4) CFEU.

[45] See further A. Torres Pérez, 'Melloni in Three Acts: From Dialogue to Monologue', *European Constitutional Law Review*, 10 (2014), pp. 308–331; S. O'Leary, 'A Tale of Two Cities: Fundamental Rights Protection in Strasbourg and Luxembourg', *Cambridge Yearbook of European Legal Studies*, 20 (2018), pp. 3–31; Prechal, 'Mutual Trust before the Court of Justice of the European Union'.

[46] Art. 6 TEU; Art. 51(1) CFEU. In exceptional circumstances, characterised by the existence of an EU Directive destined to regulate the situation of private parties and containing the same right as the one protected in the CFEU, the CFEU may be relied upon directly *against* a private actor (rather than a public authority, as discussed in this section): Joined Cases C-569/16 and C-570/16, *Bauer and Willmeroth*, EU:C:2018:871; see also Chapter 4, Section 4.1.2.3, Charter of Fundamental Rights of the EU.

[47] For a more advanced discussion of the duties of EU institutions acting beyond their mandate under EU law, as requested by an international agreement among states of the EU, to comply with the CFEU, see Joined Cases C-8/15 P to C-10/15 P, *Ledra Advertising*, EU:C:2016:701.

[48] See, by analogy, Joined Cases C-92/09 and C-93/09, *Volker und Markus Schecke*, EU:C:2010:662.

law to pursue further an objective defined by the EU; and when they design a system of procedural rules giving effect to EU law obligations.[49]

For instance, when national authorities use the possibility made available to them by EU law to derogate from the principles on the determination of the Member State responsible for an application for asylum under the Common European Asylum System, Member States ought to comply with the prohibition of inhuman and degrading treatment enshrined in EU fundamental rights law.[50] This is the case, for example, if Germany could take responsibility, instead of Greece, in the event of a sudden influx of migrants in Greece. Conversely, when deciding on whether to grant a third-country national the status of 'economic migrant' designed exclusively at national level, the protection of the fundamental rights of the person concerned is not a matter of EU law.

If no sufficient link to EU law can be shown,[51] the situation is said not to fall within the scope of EU law. The situation must then be analysed by turning to national law and other applicable sources within that legal system. As a result, the Commission and the Court of Justice of the European Union have no authority on such matters, even if the fundamental right invoked is clearly stated in the CFEU. Indeed, the latter does not extend the competences of the EU, as will be further explained subsequently.

3.2 THE EXISTENCE OF AN EU COMPETENCE

3.2.1 The Principle of Conferral

The principle of conferral has a central place in the functioning of the EU legal order.[52] It is defined by Article 5(2) TEU as follows:

> Under the principle of conferral, the Union shall act only within the limits of the competences conferred upon it by the Member States in the Treaties to attain the objectives set out therein. Competences not conferred upon the Union in the Treaties remain with the Member States.

Article 5(2) TEU positions the EU Treaties as the EU's primary source of EU competences – a source that sets out conditions and limits for the adoption of other, 'derived' acts of EU law. Member States are identified as being the original source of authority conferring competences on the EU, as well as the ultimate entity retaining authority over competences that have not been conferred on the EU. Competences not conferred on the EU by the Treaties may not be lawfully exercised by the EU.

[49] See Case 260/89, *ERT*, EU:C:1991:254, para. 43; Joined Cases C-609/17 and C-610/17, *TSN*, EU:C:2019:981, para. 50; C-617/10, *Åkerberg Fransson*, EU:C:2013:105, paras. 27–29. The scope of application of the CFEU has been interpreted broadly, to match the scope of application of general principles of EU law, despite the seemingly narrow wording of Art. 51 CFEU. See further 'Explanations Relating to the Charter of Fundamental Rights', OJ C 303/17, 14.12.2007, in relation to Art. 51.

[50] Joined Cases C-411/10 and C-493/10, *N. S. et al.*, EU:C:2011:865, para. 68.

[51] The mere fact that national measures come within an area in which the EU has powers cannot bring those measures within the scope of EU law, there must be a more concrete link: Joined Cases C-609/17 and C-610/17, *TSN*, EU:C:2019:981, para. 46.

[52] Art. 4 TEU.

The principle of conferral is no mere technicality. It lies at the heart of the most passionate disputes on the EU and its future. For instance, in the context of debates on the rule of law in certain Member States: to what extent can the EU react to Member States' decisions to amend the architecture of their judicial system threatening the independence of the judicial branch? The EU has limited competences in that field. And yet the sound functioning of the judicial system nationally is a precondition for accession to the EU, as well as for the continued existence of the judicial architecture of the EU itself and the proper functioning of the EU's policies.[53]

The principle of conferral must be read in light of the dynamic process of European integration. As noted in Article 5(2) TEU, the EU shall act, not only within the limits of its competences, but also to attain the objectives set out in the Treaties. The EU is a purposive organisation: its overall objective is to work towards 'an ever closer union among the peoples of Europe'.[54] This meta-objective is given specific expression through a subset of policy objectives set out in Article 3 TEU, themselves made operational through the broad range of provisions of the EU Treaties creating and organising specific EU competences.[55] The objectives of the policies for which the EU has competences are often referred to by EU institutions to shed light on the interpretation to be given to specific EU competences and the way they are to be exercised.[56]

The principle of conferral does not only articulate the relationship between the EU and its Member States; it also has implications for the system of checks and balances between EU organs. As well as having a duty of mutual sincere cooperation, when they exercise competences conferred on the EU competences, the institutions must act within the limits of the powers granted to them in the Treaties, and in conformity with the procedures, conditions and objectives set out therein.[57]

3.2.2 The Legal Basis

3.2.2.1 Important Functions

A corollary of the principle of conferral is the need for EU action to have a legal basis. A legal basis is a provision of EU law that enables EU organs to take action, and thereby ensures compliance with the principle of conferral. The legal basis may be found in EU primary law, or in another source of EU law itself derived from EU primary law. It is normally[58] formulated in enabling terms. For instance, Article 192(1) TFEU states as follows:

> The European Parliament and the Council, acting in accordance with the ordinary legislative procedure and after consulting the Economic and Social Committee and the Committee of the Regions, shall decide what action is to be taken by the Union in order to achieve the objectives referred to in Article 191 [TFEU, on Union policy on the environment].

[53] See Chapter 4, Section 4.3.2. [54] Art. 1 TEU. [55] Art. 3(6) TEU.
[56] See further, for instance, Chapter 3, Section 3.2.3.1. [57] Art. 13(2) TEU; see also Chapter 3, Section 3.6.
[58] See, however, 'implied powers' in Chapter 3, Section 3.2.3.2.

A legal basis performs several functions, as this example illustrates. Firstly, it identifies the existence of an EU competence. This definition of the EU competence, read in light of the underlying policy objectives, will have consequences for the relationship between EU and national competences, as will be explained later.[59] It shall be noted that some provisions of the EU Treaties also exclude certain types of EU intervention. For instance, Article 153 TFEU, which is the main legal basis for the adoption of EU social legislation, specifies that it 'shall not apply to pay, the right of association, the right to strike or the right to impose lock-outs'.[60]

Second, a legal basis defines the procedure to be used for the EU to exercise the said competence. It normally explains (or refers to another provision that does so) which EU institutions, and possibly other organs, may be involved and in which ways.[61]

A legal basis therefore articulates the allocation of competences both between the EU and the Member States, and between EU organs. The European Parliament (the Parliament), for instance, deems it useful to verify the legal basis of proposed legally binding acts.[62] Member States also attach great importance to the choice of legal basis since it directly affects their position in the EU legal system. This is well illustrated in the challenge by Poland against reliance on Article 192(1) TFEU for the adoption of an EU instrument on a market stability reserve for the EU greenhouse gas emission trading scheme. Poland argued instead in favour of reliance on Article 192(2) TFEU. The latter legal basis would have required unanimity voting within the Council (instead of qualified majority voting under the ordinary legislative procedure mentioned in Article 192(1) TFEU), allowing Poland to have a veto power, and to better protect its approach to energy supply – which relies heavily on coal.[63] Poland lost the case.

Third, it is not uncommon for a legal basis to specify the form that EU intervention should take when EU organs exercise their competence. By way of example, the general principles and limits governing the right of EU citizens to access the documents of EU institutions shall be determined by means of 'regulations'.[64]

The choice of legal basis is of such importance that EU organs are under a duty to expressly indicate the legal basis of any act intended to have legal effects therein.[65] This is an essential procedural requirement that ensures compliance with the principle of legal certainty, which is a general principle of EU law[66] and allows for judicial review. Furthermore, legal acts shall state the reasons on which they are based; thus the choice of legal basis ought to be duly justified.[67]

[59] See Chapter 3, Sections 3.2 and 3.3.

[60] This explains some of the controversies on Commission, 'Proposal for a Directive of the European Parliament and of the Council on Adequate Minimum Wages in the European Union', COM(2020) 682, 29.10.2020, proposed on the basis of Arts. 153(1)(b), 153(2) TFEU.

[61] Procedures are explained in Chapter 3, Section 3.6.

[62] Parliament, 'Rules of Procedure', Rule 40.

[63] C-5/16, *Poland* v. *Parliament and Council (Choice between energy sources)*, EU:C:2018:483, paras. 24, 29.

[64] Art. 15(3), subpara. 2 TFEU. 'Regulations' are defined at Chapter 3, Section 3.5.3.2.

[65] On the relevance of the concepts and principles discussed herein for non-legally binding acts, see L. Sanden, 'Soft-Law and Its Implications for Institutional Balance in the EC', *Utrecht Law Review*, 1 (2005), pp. 79–99.

[66] C-325/91, *France* v. *Commission*, EU:C:1993:245, paras. 26, 30. Note that there would be no infringement of essential procedural requirements if the legal basis for a measure might be determined from other parts of the measure; C-600/14, *Germany* v. *Council*, EU:C:2017:935, para. 84.

[67] Art. 296, para. 2 TFEU.

3.2.2.2 Challenges with Identification of the Legal Basis

The first step when reflecting on the existence of an EU competence for the purpose of enabling EU intervention[68] is to ask: What is the main goal or component of the intended legal act? Where does the centre of gravity of the measure lie? The Court of Justice held in the *Titanium dioxide* case that the response may not depend simply on an institution's conviction. It must be based on 'objective factors which are amenable to judicial review [. . .]. Those factors include in particular the aim and content of the measure'.[69] (Once an act is adopted, One would look at the preamble and key provisions of the proposed measure in order to identify its main goal).

Once the main objective or component of a projected action is identified, one ought to look for a legal basis on which the said initiative could be legally anchored. In practice, this often involves scanning through the table of contents of the treaties, identifying relevant policy areas of EU intervention, and checking within each of the relevant sections of the EU Treaties if any specific provision enables EU organs to act. The main objective or component pursued by the intended legal action ought to be matched by the rationale and definition of the EU competence to act. Now, the authors of the Treaties could not possibly have anticipated all subsequent initiatives for legal action at EU level. As a consequence, the way the main objective or component of the proposed action is expressed and the wording of the legal basis are not always easy to match. It is a point that sometimes feeds into concerns of 'competence creep', whereby EU organs are said to make an extensive, if not manipulative, use of the list of EU competences.[70] The traditional legal criteria for the choice of legal basis must be read in conjunction with the political nature of the negotiations between the relevant EU organs on what the main objective of a measure may be and its match with a given legal basis, as will be explained in the following sections.[71]

It is not uncommon to be able to identify several legal bases that seem relevant to support EU intervention. Where that is the case, decision-makers ought to opt for the most specific one to match the main objective of the act to be adopted.[72] The availability of several bases does not justify circumventing an express exclusion of harmonisation enshrined in the Treaties.[73] For instance, Article 149 TFEU enables EU institutions to 'adopt incentive measures designed to encourage cooperation between Member States and to support their action in the field of employment', but specifies that those measures 'shall not include harmonisation of the laws and regulations of the Member States'.[74] No other legal bases shall be used to achieve what is explicitly excluded by Article 149 TFEU: the underlying idea is to ensure compliance with the principle of conferral.

It is also not uncommon for intended EU action to pursue several objectives or to have several components. Decision-makers ought to identify the (most specific) legal basis matching the predominant objective of EU intervention. Such a predominant objective is often

[68] Note that the rules spelt out subsequently apply not only to the adoption of internal acts, but also to the conclusion of international agreements; C-658/11, *Parliament* v. *Council*, EU:C:2014:2025, paras. 56–58, 60.

[69] C-300/89, *Commission* v. *Council (Titanium dioxide)*, EU:C:1991:244, para. 10.

[70] S. Weatherill, 'Competence Creep and Competence Control', *Yearbook of European Law*, 23 (2004), pp. 1–55; see also Chapter 3, Section 3.2.4.

[71] See, in particular, Chapter 3, Section 3.2.4.

[72] C-338/01, *Commission* v. *Council*, EU:C:2004:253, para. 60.

[73] C-376/98, *Germany* v. *Parliament and Council*, EU:C:2000:544, paras. 78–79.

[74] On the distinction between harmonisation and incentive measures, see Chapter 3, Section 3.1.1.2.

identified by applying the 'centre of gravity' test.[75] The unfolding of the test is well illustrated by the *Danube River* case, concerning the approval by the Council of a Convention for the protection and sustainable use of the Danube River. The Court of Justice observed:

> according to its aim and its content, the *primary* purpose of the Convention is the protection and improvement of the quality of the waters of the catchment area of the river Danube, although it also refers, albeit *incidentally*, to the use of those waters and their management in its quantitative aspects.[76]

As a consequence, this type of EU action could validly have been adopted with reference to competences on the environment in its qualitative aspects (primary purpose), by opposition to competences on the management of water resources in its quantitative aspects (incidental purpose). It is thereby accepted, as seems almost inevitable, that an EU instrument may have incidental effects on areas of law that are not covered by the legal basis.

Yet multiple predominant objectives or components of a proposed action may have the same or comparable importance, and it is not always possible or desirable to prioritise one over the other(s). For EU action to be possible, each of the equally important predominant objectives or components ought then to have a legal basis. The adopted measure shall thus have multiple legal bases.[77] An example of a measure having multiple legal bases is the Citizenship Directive[78] on the right for EU citizens to move and reside freely within the territory of the Member States. It lays down the conditions under which several categories of EU citizens, including workers, service providers, self-employed persons and economically inactive EU citizens can exercise free movement rights. As the Directive was conceived as a horizontal instrument, replacing the previous sector-by-sector, piecemeal approach to the right of free movement and residence,[79] it has five legal bases.[80]

Things become difficult if multiple predominant objectives or components of the same importance require the use of several legal bases that, on the one hand, do create competences for the EU, but on the other hand, require the use of different procedures for the adoption of an EU act. One solution, to avoid tensions between different procedural requirements for the adoption of the act, is to split and revise the envisaged instrument into several instruments having separate objectives or components, thus requiring separate legal bases.

Yet it may be that the multiple predominant objectives or components of the legal act foreseen are inseparably linked. By way of example, the act contemplated may have as an objective, on the one hand, the reduction of pollution caused by waste from the titanium dioxide industry, and on the other, the improvement of the conditions of competition in that industry.[81] We know from the case law of the Court of Justice that it is not possible to

[75] See further, A. Engel, *The Choice of Legal Basis for Acts of the European Union: Competence Overlaps, Institutional Preferences, and Legal Basis Litigation* (Springer, 2018).

[76] C-36/98, *Spain* v. *Council*, EU:C:2001:64, para. 74 (emphasis added).

[77] C-165/87, *Commission* v. *Council*, EU:C:1988:458, para. 11.

[78] 'Directive 2004/38 of the European Parliament and of the Council of 29 April 2004 on the Right of Citizens of the Union and their Family Members to Move and Reside Freely within the Territory of the Member States Amending Regulation 1612/68 and repealing Directives 64/221, 68/360, 72/194, 73/148, 75/34, 75/35, 90/364, 90/365 and 93/96', OJ L 158, 30.4.2004, p. 77 (last amended 2011).

[79] Ibid., Recital 4.

[80] In their current numbering, these are Arts. 18, 21, 46, 50, 59 TFEU.

[81] By imposing obligations concerning the treatment of waste, the act is directed, at the same time, towards the protection of the environment and the establishment of greater uniformity of production conditions – therefore

jointly use legal bases requiring procedures of adoption that are not compatible, for instance because one requires mere consultation of the Parliament and unanimity at the Council, while the other requires the Parliament to be a full co-decision-maker, with qualified majority voting at the Council.[82] As a consequence, the form and scope of the legal action being contemplated ought to be rethought to ensure compliance with the principle of conferral both in its vertical (EU versus Member State) and horizontal (EU organ versus EU organ) components.

Which procedures are deemed to be compatible or not though, remains subject to complex – and possibly unclear – case law, in particular in the field of the external relations of the EU.[83] It shall be noted that, in such situations of incompatible procedural requirements, the Court of Justice has invited decision-makers to further investigate the relationship between the available legal bases: they may themselves provide indications of how they relate to one another, and one may give way to the other.[84] It is sometimes argued that decision-makers should, in cases of inseparably linked predominant objectives or components and legal bases requiring different procedures for the adoption of the act, opt for a solution ensuring the greatest involvement of the Parliament. There is limited evidence, however, to support the view that such involvement should affect the rules above on the choice of legal bases.[85] It should be recalled that, as a matter of principle, where there is no legal basis for EU action, the competence to act lies with the Member States.

3.2.3 The Dynamics of EU Competences

The rules on the choice of legal basis spelt out previously are those that apply as a matter of principle to regulate the allocation of competences to, and between organs of, the EU. In practice, they call for a number of observations related to the nature, or teleology, of certain provisions of the EU Treaties through which competences are conferred on the EU. The nature and teleology of provisions of EU law influence the actual power of EU organs to act, as well as the reflection on who may be empowered to act. In this section, we focus on selected provisions of EU law and jurisprudential developments to illustrate these dynamics.

towards the uniformity of conditions of competition. Both the objective of the protection of the environment and that of the elimination of disparities in conditions of competition are here indissociably linked. See C-300/89, *Commission v. Council*, EU:C:1991:244, paras. 10–13.

82 C-130/10, *Parliament* v. *Council*, EU:C:2012:472, paras. 45–46.

83 See, for instance, C-166/07, *Parliament* v. *Council*, EU:C:2009:499, para. 69 on the joint use of the ordinary legislative procedure (which normally requires qualified majority voting at the Council) required under Art. 175 TFEU, and unanimity voting at the Council, required by the flexibility clause. See further G. de Baere, 'From "Don't Mention the Titanium Dioxide Judgment" to "I Mentioned It Once, But I Think I Got Away with It All Right"', *Cambridge Yearbook of European Legal Studies*, 15 (2013), pp. 537–562.

84 In the *Titanium Dioxide* case, the Court of Justice reads into the relevant provisions that the protection of the environment shall be a component of other EU policies and that the approximation of the laws of the Member States on matters of environmental protection may contribute to the good functioning of the internal market. The Court concludes than an internal market legal basis was best suited for the adoption of an instrument on waste from the titanium dioxide industry; C-300/89, *Commission* v. *Council*, EU: C:1991:244, paras. 22–25.

85 Case C-155/07, *Parliament* v. *Council*, EU:C:2008:605, paras. 82–84; contrast with C-130/10, *Parliament* v. *Council*, EU:C:2012:472, paras. 79–82.

3.2.3.1 Article 114 TFEU: A Particularly Dynamic Legal Basis

The internal market is the area of EU law where we find one of the most famous legal bases for the adoption of EU legislative acts. Article 114(1) TFEU reads as follows:

> Save where otherwise provided in the Treaties, the following provisions shall apply for the achievement of the objectives set out in Article 26 [i.e. 'establishing or ensuring the functioning of the internal market']. The European Parliament and the Council shall, acting in accordance with the ordinary legislative procedure and after consulting the Economic and Social Committee, adopt the measures [i] *for the approximation of the provisions laid down by law, regulation or administrative action in Member States* which [ii] *have as their object the establishment and functioning of the internal market.* (Bracketed letters and emphasis added)

Article 114(1) TFEU is subject to a number of exceptions,[86] and it coexists with several more specific legal bases[87] – thus limiting its use – for the adoption of legislation on the internal market. It can best be described as a horizontal legal basis for the adoption of legislation in the field when no more specific provisions are applicable. It is common for legislation adopted on that basis to set common European standards – thus to 'harmonise' – for the protection of certain legitimate interests,[88] with a view to reducing divergences among the Member States and facilitating the functioning of the internal market.[89] For instance, a directive may be adopted on that basis to set standards for the accessibility of products and services for persons with disabilities, thereby facilitating the free movement of these products and services in the internal market, as was the case with the Accessibility Act.[90]

The establishment of the internal market has been the main driving force of the process of integration since its inception, and that legal basis has played a particularly important role. Its horizontal nature and frequent use are not only an obvious strength of this provision, they are also a source of controversy. Article 114(1) TFEU is formulated in such broad and purposive terms that it could be feared that virtually any proposed legislative action, based on a mere finding of disparities between national rules and of the abstract risk of obstacles to the functioning of the internal market could fall within its scope, and thus empower the EU to act.

It is precisely that concern which came to the fore in the context of litigation on the regulation by the EU of the rules on advertising for tobacco products. In 2000, the Court of Justice clarified its understanding of the limits of Article 114(1) TFEU:

> To construe that article as meaning that it vests in the [Union] legislature a general power to regulate the internal market would [...] be incompatible with the principle embodied in [Article 5 TEU] that the powers of the [Union] are limited to those specifically conferred on it.[91]

86 Art. 114(2) TFEU specifies that Recital 1 does not apply to fiscal provisions, the free movement of persons or the provisions relating to the rights and interests of employed persons.

87 Such as Arts. 46, 48 TFEU on the freedom of movement of workers, and Art. 113 TFEU on taxation.

88 Such as those listed in Art. 36 TFEU, including the protection of health by way of example.

89 See further V. Kosta, *Fundamental Rights in EU Internal Market Legislation* (Hart Publishing, 2015).

90 'Directive (EU) 2019/882 of the European Parliament and of the Council of 17 April 2019 on the Accessibility Requirements for Products and Services', OJ L 151, 7.6.2019, p. 70.

91 Case C-376/98, *Germany* v. *Parliament and Council* (*Tobacco advertising I*), EU:C:2000:544, para. 83, and see also para. 84.

As a consequence, a measure adopted on the basis of Article 114(1) TFEU must genuinely have as its object the improvement of the conditions for the establishment and functioning of the internal market (see [ii] in the quote from Article 114(1) TFEU previously). More specifically, in that case, the Court noted that the directive in question allowed Member States to adopt stricter requirements concerning the advertising or sponsorship of tobacco products to guarantee the health protection of individuals, and contained no provision ensuring the free movement of products which conform to its provisions. The legislator thus could not rely on the need to eliminate obstacles to the free movement rules within the meaning of Article 114(1) TFEU and the directive under scrutiny was annulled.[92]

Meanwhile, for the choice of 'measures for the approximation of the provisions laid down by law, regulation or administrative action in the Member States', the wording of the Treaty confers on the EU legislator 'discretion'[93] (see [i] in the quote from Article 114(1) TFEU previously). For instance, the legislator can decide to delegate to an EU body, office or agency powers for the implementation of the harmonisation sought. Furthermore, the formula encompasses the EU's power to lay down measures relating to a specific product or class of products, as well as, if necessary, individual measures concerning those products. For instance, the EU legislator, acting on the basis of Article 114(1) TFEU, could validly delegate to the European Securities and Markets Authority, in strictly circumscribed circumstances, the power to take decisions directed at specific natural or legal persons.[94] Article 114(1) TFEU thus remains a very generous legal basis, despite the ruling in *Tobacco Advertising I*.[95]

3.2.3.2 Implied Powers

While legal bases are often explicit as to the powers they grant to EU organs, this is not always the case. In the early 1970s, in the famous *ERTA* case, the Court of Justice asserted that the authority of EU institutions to adopt legal acts 'arises not only from an express conferment by the Treaty [. . .] but may equally flow from [the] provisions of the Treaty and from measures adopted, within the framework of those provisions'.[96] In other words, in certain circumstances, the existence of powers to act not expressly stated in the relevant provision of EU law may be 'implied' therefrom. These 'implied powers' perform a gap-filling function.

In the field of EU external relations, since the entry into force of the Treaty of Lisbon, the applicable formula is now enshrined in Article 216(1) TFEU:

> The Union may conclude an agreement with one or more third countries or international organisations [1] where the Treaties so provide or [2] where the conclusion of an agreement is necessary in order to achieve, within the framework of the Union's policies, one of the objectives referred to in the Treaties,

[92] C-376/98, *Germany* v. *Parliament and Council* (*Tobacco advertising I*), EU:C:2000:544, paras. 101–105.
[93] C-217/04, *UK* v. *European Parliament and Council*, EU:C:2006:279, paras. 43–45.
[94] C-270/12, *UK* v. *Parliament and Council (Short Selling)*, EU:C:2014:18, paras. 99–117.
[95] See further S. Weatherill, 'The Limits of Legislative Harmonization Ten Years after Tobacco Advertising: How the Court's Case Law has become a "Drafting Guide"', *German Law Journal*, 12 (2011), pp. 827–864.
[96] Case 22/70, *Commission* v. *Council (ERTA)*, EU:C:1971:32, paras. 15–16.

or [3] is provided for in a legally binding Union act or [4] is likely to affect common rules or alter their scope.[97] (Bracketed numbering added)

Article 216(1) TFEU identifies four settings. While some are provided in EU law (options 1 and 3), others are less obvious. In this latter context, the article refers to where a provision of EU law sets a clear objective, and defines a procedure to be used for the exercise of the related EU competence at internal level, but no provision of EU law is equally explicit for the EU to define its relationship with non-EU States in the related field (option 2). This asymmetry between internal and external powers in the wording of the EU Treaties creates the danger that the coherence of internal EU action may be negatively affected by Member States acting individually (or collectively) externally. Similarly, the powers of the EU to act externally may have to be implied if, in the absence of an express statement, the lack of a power for the EU to act could result in affecting common rules adopted on the basis of the EU Treaties or altering their scope (option 4).[98]

While Article 216(1) TFEU lists the situations in which the EU has the power to conclude an international agreement, including by formalising the possibility to rely upon the implied powers doctrine, it does not prescribe any formal or procedural requirements for doing so. The procedure to be followed for the exercise of an implied power must therefore be inferred from the provision of the Treaties from which the power is implied and where procedural guidance on internal action is provided. This provision will constitute the substantive legal basis for the act and will help in identifying the appropriate procedure to be followed for external action.[99]

It shall be noted that the doctrine of implied powers is sometimes also deemed to be relevant in a purely internal context.[100]

3.2.3.3 Article 352 TFEU: The 'Flexibility Clause'

In addition to the examples outlined previously, where a specific provision of the EU Treaties, or several of them jointly, act as an anchor on the EU's power to act, the said

[97] See also Art. 3(2) TFEU and C-600/14, *Germany* v. *Council*, EU:C:2017:935, paras. 46–48, on the distinct issue of the nature of the related EU competence; see also Chapter 3, Section 3.3.

[98] C-600/14, *Germany* v. *Council*, EU:C:2017:935, paras. 48–49.

[99] E.g. Art. 91 TFEU (substantive legal basis for EU internal action on transport and related implied external competence) and Art. 218(9) TFEU (specifying the procedure to be used for external action) may constitute joint provisions enabling the Council to establish, by way of a Decision, the EU position in negotiations on the Convention concerning International Carriage by Rail (COTIF) within the Intergovernmental Organisation for International Carriage by Rail (OTIF); C-600/14, *Germany* v. *Council*, EU:C:2017:935, paras. 85–92.

[100] For instance, where a provision of the EU Treaties gives EU institutions a specific and precise task, it is accepted that it implicitly confers on the institution 'the powers which are indispensable in order to carry out that task' (T-240/04, *France* v. *Commission*, EU:T:2007:290, paras. 36–37). In that context, there is no equivalent to Article 216(1) TFEU, and the Court of Justice only relies on its own case law. See, for instance, Joined Cases 281, 283, 284, 285 and 287/85, *Germany, France, Netherlands, Denmark and UK* v. *Commission*, EU:C:1987:351, paras. 28–31: the Court found in favour of the Commission's 'implied' competence to adopt legally binding acts to establish a communication and consultation procedure on migration policies in relation to non-member countries on the basis of Article 118 TEEC as it existed in the mid-1980s and related to social policy. (The Commission lost the case on other grounds.) In such cases, though, the reasoning of the Court is usually articulated around the concern to ensure the effectiveness of an existing EU provision, rather than acknowledging the existence of an implied power (Case 176/03, *Commission* v. *Council (Sanctions in the field of environmental protection)*, EU:C:2005:542, para. 48).

Treaties also provide a default legal basis, commonly referred to as the 'flexibility clause' for that very reason. The key part of Article 352(1) TFEU reads as follows:

> If action by the Union should prove necessary, within the framework of the policies defined in the Treaties, to attain one of the objectives set out in the Treaties, and the Treaties have not provided the necessary powers, the Council, acting unanimously on a proposal from the Commission and after obtaining the consent of the European Parliament, shall adopt the appropriate measures.

The flexibility clause also performs a gap-filling function; it can only be triggered if the anchorage of the power for the EU to act cannot be ensured by another Treaty provision, even impliedly.[101] It comes into play when the options examined previously are unavailable, yet with a view to attaining an objective set out in the Treaties; as is the case, for instance, of the regulation on measures concerning the implications of the withdrawal of the UK from the EU on the EU budget.[102]

In order to ensure compliance with the principle of conferral, reliance on the flexibility clause comes with a number of safeguards. The first one is of a procedural nature; this legal basis requires unanimity voting on the part of the Council, as well as the consent of the Parliament. It is thus a demanding procedure, requiring support from all the Member States and the Parliament. Second, the Commission shall draw the attention of national parliaments to enable them to monitor compliance with the principle of subsidiarity.[103] Third, the flexibility clause may not be used for harmonisation purposes where the Treaty has excluded such harmonisation.[104] Fourth, Article 352(1) TFEU cannot serve as a basis for attaining objectives pertaining to the CFSP, and any acts adopted pursuant to it shall respect the limits set out in Article 40, paragraph 2 TEU, articulating the relationship between the two Treaties.[105]

Although less frequently used than in the early years of the European integration project, due to the multiplication of prevailing specific legal bases with the various treaty reforms, the flexibility clause remains a salient feature of the architecture of the EU Treaties. It has been the legal basis of instruments of high relevance to contemporary EU law, such as the one creating the Fundamental Rights Agency.[106] Furthermore, it is often associated with fears of intrusion by the EU into national competences, as confirmed by Declaration 42 annexed to the Treaty of Lisbon, which states: Article 352 TFEU 'cannot be used as a basis for the adoption of provisions whose effect would, in substance, be to amend the Treaties without following the procedure which they provide for that purpose'. This explains

[101] Note that it might be used in conjunction with other legal bases to fill a specific gap not covered by the other legal basis and thereby allowing for the adoption of the instrument (e.g. C-166/07, *Parliament* v. *Council*, EU:C:2009:499, para. 69).

[102] 'Council Regulation (EU, Euratom) 2019/2234 of 19 December 2019 on Measures Concerning the Implementation and Financing of the General Budget of the Union in 2020 in Relation to the Withdrawal of the United Kingdom from the Union', OJ L 336, 30.12.2019, p. 1. Such measures were necessary in order to implement the EU's budget in this specific context, but the Treaties do not provide for the necessary powers to adopt such transitory measures.

[103] Art. 352(2) TFEU; see also Chapter 3, Section 3.4.1.

[104] Art. 352(3) TFEU.

[105] See also Declaration 41, annexed to the Treaty of Lisbon.

[106] 'Council Regulation (EC) No. 168/2007 of 15 February 2007 Establishing a European Union Agency for Fundamental Rights', OJ L 53/1, 22.2.2007, p. 1.

controversies on proposals such as the creation of a European Monetary Fund, incorporating the European Stability Mechanism[107] into EU law, on that legal basis.[108]

3.2.3.4 Delegation of Powers to Private or Public Organs

In recent years, and due to the increasing number of EU agencies, much attention is devoted to whether the power to exercise EU competences may be delegated in settings others than those explicitly provided for in the EU Treaties.[109]

In the foundational case of *Meroni* (back in 1958, and relating to the High Authority of the ECSC),[110] the Court of Justice made it clear that an EU authority may decide to delegate powers to a *private body* under specific conditions. These require that such powers do not differ from those that the delegating authority itself receives under the prevailing EU rule, and that such powers comply with the conditions to which they would have been subject if adopted directly by the delegating authority under these rules.[111] Furthermore, the delegation of powers is only legitimate if the delegating authority deems the said powers to be necessary for the performance of its task. Finally, a delegation of powers cannot be presumed and must be the subject matter of an express decision.[112]

On the extent of the delegation, the Court of Justice distinguishes as follows:

> the consequences resulting from a delegation of powers are very different depending on whether *it involves clearly defined executive powers* the exercise of which can, therefore, be subject to strict review in the light of objective criteria determined by the delegating authority, or whether *it involves a discretionary power*, implying a wide margin of discretion.[113] (Emphasis added)

While the first kind of delegation, related to clearly defined executive powers, is normally unproblematic, the delegation of the second kind, allowing replacement of the choices by the delegating authority with those of the delegated authority, calls into question the allocation of responsibilities under the EU Treaties.

In a case related to the delegation of powers to a *public EU body* this time – the European Securities and Markets Authority (which is an EU agency) – the Court further specified that powers delegated by EU legislation may involve a degree of decision-making power, as long as the delegation is 'precisely delineated and amenable to judicial review in the light of the objectives established by the delegating authority'.[114]

In *Romano*, the Court of Justice could have been understood to prohibit delegated authorities from being granted the power to adopt acts 'having the force of law'. In the

[107] See Chapter 1, Section 1.4.3.2.

[108] Commission, 'Proposal for a Council Regulation on the Establishment of the European Monetary Fund', COM(2017) 827 final, 6.12.2017.

[109] The question raised herein is distinct from the possibility for EU institutions to confer on another EU institution the power to adopt delegated or implementing acts, as specifically allowed for by Arts. 290–291 TFEU (Chapter 3, Sections 3.6.1.2, Delegated Acts within the Meaning of Art. 290 TFEU and Implementing Acts within the Meaning of Art. 291 TFEU). Although the EU Treaties are not fully explicit on the matter, practice and case law enable EU institutions to pass on their powers to other types of private or public organs, such as an EU agency, as exemplified in this section. See C-270/12, *UK* v. *Parliament and Council (Short Selling)*, EU:C:2014:18, paras. 77–86.

[110] Case 9/56, *Meroni*, EU:C:1958:7. [111] Ibid., p. 150. [112] Ibid., p. 151. [113] Ibid., p. 152.

[114] C-270/12, *UK* v. *Parliament and Council (Short Selling)*, EU:C:2014:18, paras. 44–55.

ruling, the Court concluded that a body set up under secondary law could not require the use of specific methods, or impose specific interpretations for the application of EU law.[115] Yet in the *European Securities and Markets Authority* case, the Court swiftly clarified that the ruling in *Romano* could not prevent a delegated authority – here, an EU agency – from being required 'in strictly circumscribed circumstances, to adopt measures of general application', including measures affecting any natural or legal person, as long as the *Meroni* conditions outlined previously have been complied with.[116] This approach has been subject to much controversy.[117]

3.2.4 The Politics of EU Competences

The rules spelt out in the previous sections, on the principle of conferral and the legal bases, provide a common framework for relevant actors to shape the exercise of EU competences.[118] In practice, these organs engage in vivid discussions and negotiations seeking to identify the main objective of a measure and to match it with its appropriate legal basis, moulding the draft instrument while seeking a compromise on how best to articulate it within an EU competence. Quite naturally, each actor – whether an institution, Member State, agency or other – seeks to promote its own interest in this process. Indeed, the directions, scope, modes of intervention and pace for legal action at EU level action are inherently political. The rules set out previously are thus best understood as setting the parameters within which actors will operate under the threat of judicial review (which can lead to annulment of the act for breach of the rules set out previously), while leaving significant leeway for political choices to be made therein.

3.3 THE TYPES OF EU COMPETENCES

Once it is established that the EU has competence to take action,[119] and in principle only then,[120] can one distinguish between different types of EU competences defined by their relationship to national competences. Since the entry into force of the Treaty of Lisbon, the early provisions of the TFEU have provided an overview of the main types of EU competences.

[115] Case 98/80, *Romano*, EU:C:1981:104, para. 20.

[116] C-270/12, *UK* v. *Parliament and Council (Short Selling)*, EU:C:2014:18, paras. 65–66.

[117] For an in-depth analysis, see J. Mendes, 'Bounded Discretion in EU Law: A Limited Judicial Paradigm in a Changing EU', *The Modern Law Review*, 80 (2017), pp. 443–472.

[118] The following is particularly helpfully explained in P. Leino, 'The Institutional Politics of Objective Choice: Competence as a Framework for Argumentation', in S. Garben and I. Govaere (eds.), *The Division of Competences between the EU and the Member States: Reflections on the Past, the Present and the Future* (Hart, 2017), pp. 210–232.

[119] Note that the EU Treaties may sometimes been seen as 'reserving' certain competences to the Member States, as is the case, for instance, of Art. 72 TFEU on the Member States' responsibilities for the maintenance of law, order and the safeguarding of internal security. Yet the Court of Justice has been reluctant to date to accept blanket protections from the requirement of EU law. See further K. Lenaerts, P. Van Nuffel and T. Corthaut, *EU Constitutional Law* (Oxford University Press, 2021), p. 108.

[120] Arts. 2–6 TFEU, discussed subsequently, do not establish the *existence* of EU competences. They only shed light on the *nature* of the EU competence.

3.3.1 Exclusive Competences

The first type of EU competence is said to be exclusive as it relates to areas for which 'only the Union may legislate and adopt legally binding acts'.[121] In these fields, the Member States may act only if empowered to do so by the EU, or for the implementation of EU acts. Article 3 TFEU specifies that the EU shall have exclusive competence in areas such as the customs union, common commercial policy or monetary policy for Member States whose currency is the euro.

The common features of these examples is that, in these areas of EU law, uniform action at European level is required: the competence of the EU would be deprived of its effectiveness if Member States were able to act independently without prior authorisation from the EU. The EU also has exclusive competence for the conclusion of an international agreement provided for in an EU legislative act or, if necessary, to enable the EU to exercise its internal competence, or in so far as the conclusion of the international agreement may affect common rules or alter their scope.[122]

The exclusive nature of EU competences has been particularly hotly debated in the context of controversies on whether specific actions of the Central Bank in response to the economic and financial crisis relate to monetary policy, and thus constitute an exclusive EU competence, or to economic policy, in which case it would have to be carefully articulated with national competences.[123]

As will be further explained subsequently, the exercise of competences shared between the EU and the Member States may result in EU law fully pre-empting a specific matter and thus, in practice, also preventing national authorities from acting.

3.3.2 Supporting, Coordinating or Supplementary Competences

At the other end of the spectrum are areas where the EU, under the conditions laid down in the Treaties, 'shall have competence to carry out actions to support, coordinate or supplement the actions of the Member States'.[124] In these areas, EU intervention does not supersede Member State's competences and any legally binding acts of the EU cannot lead to harmonisation.

Examples of such competences are provided in Article 6 TFEU and include, for instance, culture or education. An illustration of the exercise of such an EU competence is the Erasmus+ programme, supporting national actions and activities with a European added value and allowing young students to study abroad, without interfering in the Member States' ability to design their own educational programmes.[125]

[121] Art. 2(1) TFEU.

[122] Art. 3(2) TFEU. Elaborating further on the existence and nature of EU competences in the field of external relations, see A. Ott, 'EU External Competence', in R. Wessels and J. Larik (eds.), *EU External Relations Law* (Hart, 2020), ch. 3.

[123] See Chapter 3, Section 3.3.4; e.g. contrast the ruling by the Court of Justice in C-493/17, *Weiss*, Judgment of the Court (Grand Chamber), 11.12.2018, EU:C:2018:1000, paras. 46–70, with the Judgment of the BVerfG, 2 BvR 859/15, 5.5.2020 – 2 BvR 859/15, para. 120 *et seq.* On the economic and financial crisis, see Chapter 1, Section 1.3.3.1.

[124] Art. 2(5), subpara. 1 TFEU.

[125] 'Regulation (EU) 2021/817 of the European Parliament and of the Council of 20 May 2021 Establishing Erasmus+: The Union Programme for Education and Training, Youth and Sport', OJ L 189, 28.5.2021, p. 1, adopted on the basis of Arts. 165(4), 166(4) TFEU.

3.3.3 Shared Competences

Competences conferred on the EU that are not deemed to be either exclusive, or supporting/coordinating/supplementary competences, are shared competences. The latter can thus be understood as a 'default category'[126] in comparison to the former. These constitute the bulk of EU competences.

This type of EU competence allows for the two main categories of actors of governance in the EU to act: 'the Union and the Member States may legislate and adopt legally binding acts in that area'.[127] These competences are thus indeed 'shared' between the two. Examples of this open-ended category can be found in Article 4 TFEU and include the internal market as well as social policy, consumer protection, the environment, and the AFSJ – which are very active areas of EU law.

In principle, the sharing is constrained, in that the Member States may exercise their competence only to the extent that the EU has not exercised its own – or to the extent that the EU has decided to cease exercising its competence.[128] This is referred to as the principle of pre-emption. As a consequence, such EU and national competences can be said to actually compete with each other; with the EU being a powerful player, as its action prevents the Member States from further intervening.

There is great diversity in the degree of constraint on national authorities depending on the degree of intervention of the EU. There are numerous examples of minimum harmonisation: setting a common European standard, but allowing Member States to intervene beyond the minimum established by EU law. For instance, Member States shall ensure that each worker has an individual right to parental leave of *at least* four months that is to be taken before the child reaches a specified age, up to the age of eight.[129] A specific aspect of shared competence may also be fully pre-empted by EU action (such as in the case of maximum harmonisation), thus, in practice, preventing additional action from the Member States and thereby becoming exclusive. However, – unlike for competences that are exclusive by nature, as introduced previously and set out in Article 3 TFEU – the EU may here cease to exercise its competence, and then Member States regain the competence.[130]

Certain areas of shared competences operate without pre-emption[131] and thus exist in parallel to national competences rather than competing with the latter. An example is in the area of research or humanitarian aid, for which one can assume that the more each actor acts, the better.

[126] Art. 4(1) TFEU. [127] Art. 2(2) TFEU.

[128] Note that the scope of the exercise by the EU of its competence 'only covers those elements governed by the Union act in question and therefore does not cover the whole area' (Protocol 25, sole article). For an example of withdrawal of EU legislation, see the saga on the Data Retention Directive. See also Declaration 18, annexed to the Treaty of Lisbon, and T. Konstadinides, 'The Competences of the Union', in Schütze and Tridimas (eds.), *Oxford Principles of European Union Law*, pp. 200–201.

[129] 'Directive (EU) 2019/1158 of the European Parliament and of the Council of 20 June 2019 on Work-Life Balance for Parents and Carers and Repealing Council Directive 2010/18/EU', Art. 5(1), OJ L 188, 12.7.2019, p. 79.

[130] See further Konstadinides, 'The Competences of the Union', pp. 195–198. Another difference with exclusive competences by nature as set out in Art. 3 TFEU, is that the principle of subsidiarity (examined further subsequently) applies to the exercise of EU shared competences.

[131] These areas are listed in Art. 4(3–4) TFEU.

3.3.4 The Odd Ones Out

As well as the three main types of EU competences identified previously, two specific areas of EU law are singled out. In relation to economic and employment policies,[132] the TFEU states that the 'Member States shall coordinate [. . .] within arrangements as determined by this Treaty, which the Union shall have competence to provide'.[133] Further details are provided in Article 5 TFEU, including a reference to specific provisions to Member States' whose currency is the euro,[134] and to the coordination of social policies. An example of the exercise of such a peculiar EU competence whereby the Member States are primarily in charge, yet within a framework provided by the EU, is the European Semester. It is a multilateral surveillance mechanism for closer coordination of economic policies and sustained convergence of the economic performance of the Member States.[135] It is complemented by a number of tools, sometimes drawn from other areas of EU law, to support its effectiveness.[136]

As regards the CFSP, the competence of the EU to define the policy (including the progressive framing of a common defence policy) shall be 'in accordance with the provisions of the Treaty on European Union'.[137] The EU's competence in this field shall cover 'all areas of foreign policy and all questions relating to the EU's security'. It is subject to specific rules and procedures set out in the TEU, excluding the possibility of adopting legislative acts.[138] The relevant provisions are thus not fully clear and the whole field sits uneasily with the typology of EU competences outlined previously. This must be read in light of the very special trajectory and nature of this area of law in the process of European integration.[139] An example of the exercise by the EU of such competences is the launch of the military crisis management operation IRINI, to contribute to preventing arms trafficking in the context of the arms embargo on Libya and, among other things, to assist in the development of the capacities and in the training of the Libyan Coast Guard and Navy in law enforcement tasks at sea.[140]

3.4 THE EXERCISE OF AN EU COMPETENCE

Once the existence and the nature of EU competences have been identified, one turns to the principles that regulate the actual exercise of the said competence.[141] These, Article 5(1)

[132] Note that the terms are not clearly defined in EU law. This may create uncertainties with crucial implications – for instance, on the distinction between economic policy and monetary policy, the latter being an exclusive competence of the EU; see Chapter 3, Section 3.3.1 and note 125 therein.

[133] Art. 2(3) TFEU. [134] See Art. 136 TFEU *et seq.*

[135] 'Regulation (EU) No. 1175/2011 of the European Parliament and of the Council of 16 November 2011 Amending Council Regulation (EC) No. 1466/97 on the Strengthening of the Surveillance of Budgetary Positions and the Surveillance and Coordination of Economic Policies', OJ L 306, 23.11.2011, p. 12.

[136] See further P. Dermine, 'The New Economic Governance of the Eurozone: A Rule of Law Analysis', thesis defended at Maastricht University and KU Leuven, 2020; and, more recently, 'Regulation (EU) 2021/241 of the European Parliament and of the Council of 12 February 2021 Establishing the Recovery and Resilience Facility', OJ L 57, 18.2.2021, pp. 17–75, Arts. 10 *et seq.*

[137] Art. 2(4) TFEU.

[138] Art. 24(1) TEU; see also Declarations 13 and 14, annexed to the Treaty of Lisbon, on the CFSP.

[139] See Chapter 1, Section 1.3; G. de Baere, 'The CFSP in Contrast with EC External Relations', in de Baere, *Constitutional Principles of EU External Relations* (Oxford University Press, 2008), ch. 4.

[140] 'Council Decision (CFSP) 2020/472 of 31 March 2020 on a European Union Military Operation in the Mediterranean (EUNAVFOR MED IRINI)', OJ L 101, 1.4.2020, p. 4 (last amended 2021).

[141] This ordering of the concepts is necessary for a sound understanding of the legal construct on which the EU is based. In the practice of daily politics, and negotiations on a given draft EU act, it may naturally be that

TEU tells us, are the principles of subsidiarity and proportionality, and as we shall see, there is a set of complementary mainstreaming duties. Importantly, as will be further elaborated upon subsequently, before proposing legislation, the Commission ought to consult widely, taking into account the regional and local dimension of the action envisaged.[142] Furthermore, national parliaments ought to receive all draft legislative acts.[143] The latter must be justified with regard to the principles of subsidiarity and proportionality, along with a detailed statement making it possible to appraise compliance with these two principles.[144]

3.4.1 Subsidiarity

Subsidiarity is a principle that is used to define whether or not action must be taken at EU level.[145] It is thus only relevant for competences that do not fall within the exclusive competence of the EU set out in Article 3 TFEU,[146] and where both layers of governance may claim a degree of competence, as is the case for shared competences. It will also be subject to specific attention if the flexibility clause is in use.[147]

The principle is defined by Article 5(3) TEU. This article provides for a two-stage approach intended to compare the efficiency[148] of each level of governance to achieve the objective pursued. Firstly, the EU shall act 'only if and in so far as the objectives of the proposed action cannot be sufficiently achieved by the Member States'. For that purpose, and from the perspective of EU law, it is irrelevant that the Member States would be acting at central, regional or local level – the point of reference is any form of Member State action. Second, and in addition, it must be shown that the result 'can rather, by reason of the scale or effects of the proposed action, be better achieved at Union level'.

Review of compliance with the principle of subsidiarity as hereby defined is particularly delicate for the Court of Justice of the European Union to perform. It requires the use of criteria that are often difficult to grasp through purely legal reasoning, and involves instead political choices.[149] The Court of Justice's approach to the matter is well illustrated in its answer to a challenge by the United Kingdom against the Working Time Directive. The Court explained that it does not see its own function as allowing it 'to review the expediency of measures adopted by the legislature'. The Court specified that '[o]nce the Council has found that it is necessary to improve the existing level of protection [. . .] and to harmonize [. . .], achievement of that objective through the imposition of minimum requirements necessarily presupposes [Union]-wide action'.[150] The Court thus defers to the institution in charge.

the various actors use various concepts simultaneously or in a different order. Ultimately though, these actors must be able to demonstrate that the act adopted complies with the legal rules set out herein. See also Chapter 3, Section 3.2.4.

142 Protocol 2, Art. 2. 143 Protocol 1, Art. 2. 144 Protocol 2, Art. 5.

145 Tridimas, *The General Principles of EU Law*, p. 176.

146 In such a case, the question asked by the principle of subsidiarity is answered: the EU level is understood to be the appropriate level for action.

147 Art. 352(2) TFEU; see also Chapter 3, Section 3.2.3.3.

148 G. Davies, 'Subsidiarity: The Wrong Idea, in the Wrong Place, at the Wrong Time', *Common Market Law Review*, 43 (2006), pp. 63–84.

149 See further elements of definition: Protocol 2, Art. 5.

150 C-84/94, *UK* v. *Council*, EU:C:1996:431, paras. 23, 47.

Although compliance with subsidiarity is, in principle, justiciable,[151] it is difficult to actually find cases in which the Court struck down a measure for breach of the principle of subsidiarity. If anything, the Court of Justice of the European Union will insist on the procedural safeguards to ensure compliance with the principle, such as the duty to state reasons and the due operation of procedural safeguards that will now be spelt out.[152] Article 5(3) TEU indeed specifies that the review shall primarily take place upstream in the decision-making process, and identifies national parliaments[153] as the ones primarily in charge of exercising review of the EU institutions. As noted previously, national parliaments must receive all draft legislative acts.[154] This enables them, within eight weeks, to send to the EU organs in charge (which often includes, at the very least, the Commission) 'reasoned opinions', stating why they consider that a draft legislative act does not comply with the principle of subsidiarity.[155] Reasoned opinions on non-compliance by a single national parliamentary chamber in unicameral systems count for two; while in the case of a bicameral parliamentary system, each of the two chambers shall have the possibility of submitting one reasoned opinion, each counting for one.[156] This results in there always being two votes per State.

Since the Treaty of Lisbon, the reasoned opinions sent by national parliaments may have specific consequences. The author of the draft legislative act 'shall take account of the reasoned opinions'.[157] Two options are envisaged by Article 7 of Protocol 2 on the application of the principles of subsidiarity and proportionality. According to its second paragraph, where the number of reasoned opinions on a draft legislative act alleging non-compliance with the principle of subsidiarity represent at least one-third of all the votes allocated to the national parliaments (or a quarter in the case of acts adopted on the basis of Article 76 TFEU on specific aspects of the AFSJ[158]), the draft must be reviewed. The author of the draft may then decide to maintain, amend or withdraw the draft, and must explain that decision. This mechanism allows national parliaments to issue an early warning, but does not create an obligation for the author of the draft to suspend, terminate or modify the draft legislative act; it is often referred to as the 'yellow card procedure' by analogy to football.

According to the third paragraph of Article 7 of Protocol 2, and in the case of draft legislative acts in the more specific context of the ordinary legislative procedure,[159] if the total amount of votes reaches at least a simple majority of the votes, additional requirements are imposed on the author of the draft. If the Commission decides to maintain the

[151] See, for instance, Protocol 2, Art. 8.

[152] C-358/14, *Poland* v. *Parliament and Council*, EU:C:2016:323, para. 113.

[153] Where the national parliamentary system has more than one chamber, this refers to the component chambers; Protocol 1, Art. 8.

[154] Protocol 1, Arts. 1, 2.

[155] Ibid., Arts. 3, 4. Note that it is for each national Parliament, or each chamber, to consult, where appropriate, regional parliaments with legislative powers, in accordance with national constitutional requirements; Protocol 2, Art. 6, para. 1.

[156] Protocol 2, Art. 7(1), subpara. 2. [157] Ibid., 2, Art. 7(1), subpara. 1.

[158] This concerns, more specifically, legislation on judicial cooperation in criminal matters and police cooperation, as well as the related administrative cooperation, and thus illustrates the continued specificity of the former third pillar in today's EU Treaties; see Chapter 1, Sections 1.3.2.2 and 1.3.2.3.

[159] See Chapter 3, Section 3.6.1.1, Legislative Procedures.

proposal, it will have to justify why it considers that the proposal complies with the principle of subsidiarity and to ensure that the EU legislature receives the two sets of diverging views. Once the draft is then examined by the Parliament and the Council, acting as the co-legislators, these institutions shall consider, at an early stage, whether the proposal is compatible with the principle of subsidiarity taking these views into account. If by a majority of 55 per cent of the members of the Council, or a majority of the votes cast in the Parliament, one of these institutions is of the opinion that the proposal is not compatible with the principle of subsidiarity, the legislative proposal is not to be given further consideration. Greater opposition from national parliaments thus results in heavier burdens on the EU institutions concerned, but again, it does not result in an obligation to suspend, modify or withdraw the draft legislative act. This is often referred to as the 'orange card procedure' (to be distinguished from a red card that leads to exclusion in football).[160]

These two mechanisms only relate to draft legislative acts, which will be discussed later in this chapter.[161] The second is even more specifically focused on one particular type of legislative act – that resulting from an ordinary legislative procedure. Other types of EU acts[162] also have to comply with the principle of subsidiarity, but they are subject to a less formal type of scrutiny. Overall, national parliaments only make limited use of their power to issue reasoned opinions.[163] In recent years, most discussion on the principle of subsidiarity has taken place in the context of the yellow card procedure, as can be seen from the dedicated website.[164] While the threshold for the orange card has never been reached, the yellow card procedure has been triggered three times and, in this context, exchanges between national parliaments and the Commission – as the main institution proposing legislation at the EU level – have attracted much attention. The procedure has been understood by national parliaments as a channel to interact with EU institutions,[165] and to voice concerns that are, in practice, not always strictly related to subsidiarity within the meaning identified previously.[166] This is well illustrated by the yellow card issued against the proposal to amend the Directive on the posting of workers in the EU, which was actually maintained, as the Commission highlighted that the objections raised were not related to subsidiarity. Continued negotiations on the draft ultimately led to the adoption of a legislative act.[167] Discontent with the proposal resulted in two annulment actions brought after the adoption of the directive, but these challenges did not allege breaches of the principle of subsidiarity. Both challenges have failed.[168]

[160] In practice, due to the political interconnection between representatives of national governments and national parliaments, it may be difficult, in any case, for the Council to support the adoption of an act against which so many national parliaments have issued a reasoned opinion.

[161] See Chapter 3, Section 3.5.3.2, Secondary Law.

[162] See Chapter 3, Section 3.5.3.

[163] See further Commission, Communication, 'The Principles of Subsidiarity and Proportionality: Strengthening their Role in Policy Making', COM(2018) 703 final, 23.10.2018. See also T. Jaroszynski, 'National Parliaments' Scrutiny of the Principle of Subsidiarity: Reasoned Opinions 2014–19', 16/1 (2020), *European Constitutional Law Review*, p. 99.

[164] See secure.ipex.eu.

[165] It is not the only one. See also the 'political dialogue', Chapter 2, Section 2.2.1.

[166] Jaroszynski, 'National Parliaments' Scrutiny of the Principle of Subsidiarity', pp. 102–103.

[167] The process can be tracked at secure.ipex.eu. The instrument that was ultimately adopted is 'Directive (EU) 2018/957 of the European Parliament and of the Council of 28 June 2018 Amending Directive 96/71/EC Concerning the Posting of Workers in the Framework of the Provision of Services', OJ L 173, 9.7.2018, p. 16.

[168] C-626/18, *Poland* v. *Parliament and Council*, EU:C:2020:1000; C-620/18, *Hungary* v. *Parliament and Council*, EU:C:2020:1001.

3.4.2 Proportionality

The principle of proportionality is more rooted in traditional judicial reasoning. While the principle is frequently used to balance restrictions to fundamental rights and the pursuit of objectives of general interest, it is examined here as a principle that articulates the exercise of EU competences.[169] According to Article 5(4) TEU, the principle requires that 'the content and form of Union action shall not exceed what is necessary to achieve the objectives'.[170] For instance, EU institutions ought to choose the type of act that is the most proportionate.[171] Review of this principle comes after testing compliance with the principle of subsidiarity in situations where subsidiarity is applicable, as well as in any case when an EU competence (including if exclusive) is exercised, to decide if EU 'action is necessary and seeks to define its scope'.[172]

The Court of Justice traditionally distinguishes between two prongs of the test.[173] Firstly, the Court assesses the *appropriateness*, or suitability, of an act to achieve its objective.[174] Second, the measure must not go beyond what is *necessary* to achieve its objective. When there is a choice between several appropriate measures, this second prong of the test can be answered by opting for the least onerous option. This is often referred to as the least restrictive alternative test. The Court will allow the legislator broad discretion in areas that involve political, economic and social choices, and in which it is called on to undertake complex assessments. In such settings, it is only if there is a manifest error that the lawfulness of such a measure will be affected.[175] It is indeed not for the Court to substitute the legislator: its role is only to police the exercise of EU competences.

The Court's case law on the Working Time Directive illustrates the Court's traditional approach to the principle of proportionality usefully. In the context of a challenge against the Directive, the Court observed that the legislator had not committed a manifest error in considering that rest breaks after six hours of work, weekly rest periods of twenty-four hours, a maximum weekly working time of forty-eight hours, or the requirement of four weeks of annual paid leave contributed to health and safety (appropriateness test).[176] Similarly, the legislator could consider that the contested measures were necessary to achieve

[169] For an in-depth and updated overview distinguishing between the two functions of the principle, see A. Bailleux and H. Dumont, *Le pacte constitutionnel européen: Tome II* (Larcier, forthcoming).

[170] See further elements of definition: Protocol 2, Art. 5.

[171] Art. 296 TFEU. It is sometimes said that the choice for directives, over regulations, ensures better compliance with the principle of proportionality, as they leave leeway to the Member States on the choice of form and methods for implementation; Treaty of Amsterdam, Protocol on the application of the principles of subsidiarity and proportionality, point 6 (this formulation has disappeared in today's version of the protocol).

[172] Tridimas, *The General Principles of EU Law*, p. 176. Note that the yellow and orange card procedures described previously in relation to the principle of subsidiarity are not intended to cover concerns related to this principle.

[173] Among many examples, see C-210/03, *Swedish Match*, EU:C:2004:802, para. 47. The Court sometimes identifies a third prong of the test, often referred to as 'proportionality in the strict sense' (e.g. C-62/14, *Gauweiler*, EU:C:2015:400, para. 91). Here, the disadvantages of the measure are assessed, not just in light of the objective pursued, but in light of the various interests in play, including, for instance, the economic and social hardships associated with the measure. In practice though, the second and third prongs of the test are often merged. Tridimas, *The General Principles of EU Law*, p. 139.

[174] The question to answer here is: are the means employed reasonably likely to achieve the objectives pursued by the measure? Tridimas, *The General Principles of EU Law*, p. 139.

[175] C-84/94, *UK* v. *Council*, EU:C:1996:431, para. 58. [176] C-84/94, *UK* v. *Council*, EU:C:1996:431, para. 59.

the objective of protecting the health and safety of workers (necessity test).[177] The provisions hereby identified were deemed not to be in breach of the principle of proportionality, and they are still in force today.[178]

3.4.3 Mainstreaming Duties

In the exercise of their competences, the relevant organs ought to keep the broad range of EU objectives in mind when giving shape to EU legal instruments. The TFEU includes a set of provisions having general application, which can be understood as the oil allowing the principles explored so far to operate smoothly. According to Article 7 TFEU:[179] 'The Union shall ensure consistency between its policies and activities, taking all of its objectives into account and in accordance with the principle of conferral of powers.'

A specific set of interests is identified by the following Treaty provisions and ought to be taken into account. These include: combatting discrimination; equality between men and women; a high level of employment, adequate social protection, the fight against social exclusion, and a high level of education, training and protection of human health; environmental protection, with the promotion of sustainable development; consumer protection; animal welfare; attention for churches, religious associations or communities, as well as philosophical and non-confessional organisations.[180]

The general and fairly vague nature of the duty to mainstream this eclectic set of interests across EU action shall not lead to underestimating the importance of these provisions. Although they do not create new competences – as they are not legal bases – these provisions influence the interpretation of other provisions of EU law and the exercise of EU competences by all EU organs. For instance, they can be used to support a social reading of the types of overriding reasons in the public interest that are deemed legitimate to explain restrictions to the functioning of the internal market at national level.[181]

Three provisions from the title of the TFEU on 'Provisions having general application' are of a slightly different nature than those just described. They relate to the importance of services of general economic interest, good administration and data protection. These sit uneasily with the mainstreaming duties discussed so far. They go beyond the latter as they may produce yet more tangible legal effects. Article 15 TFEU, for instance, extended the scope of the principle of transparency in EU law

[177] C-84/94, *UK* v. *Council*, EU:C:1996:431, paras. 60–67. The Court further noted that by 'minimum requirements', the EU Treaties do not mean to limit action to the lowest common denominator; it simply means that Member States are free to provide a level of protection more stringent than that resulting from EU law, high as it may be (para. 56).

[178] 'Directive 2003/88/EC of the European Parliament and of the Council of 4 November 2003 Concerning Certain Aspects of the Organisation of Working Time', OJ L 299, 18.11.2003, p. 9. The question of whether to include Sunday in the weekly rest period was left entirely to the Member State: the relevant provision of the initial version of the Directive was annulled after analysis of the legal basis of the Directive; C-84/94, *UK* v. *Council*, EU:C:1996:431, para. 37.

[179] See also Chapter 1, Section 1.1.2. [180] Arts. 8–17 TFEU.

[181] E.g. C-201/15, *AGET Iraklis*, EU:C:2016:972, para. 78.

compared to the pre-Lisbon era.[182] These additional provisions may also enable the adoption of further legislation, as illustrated by the adoption of the well-known GDPR.[183]

The TEU adds a number of general guiding principles for the EU's external action, including for the EU's CFSP. These are 'democracy, the rule of law, the universality and indivisibility of human rights and fundamental freedoms, respect for human dignity, the principles of equality and solidarity, and respect for the principles of the United Nations Charter and international law'.[184]

3.5 SOURCES OF LAW DERIVED FROM THE EU TREATIES

3.5.1 The Starting Point

As already noted, the EU Treaties play a central role in the system of EU norms: they are the starting point for the allocation of competences to the EU, the definition of the nature of these competences and of the principles guiding their exercise.

3.5.1.1 EU Treaties, Norms of Equal Value and the Family Tree

There are probably as many classifications of EU acts adopted on the basis of the EU Treaties as there are authors of EU law textbooks.[185] Here, a distinction will be made between the EU Treaties and norms with equal value as *primary* law, sources adopted on the basis of the EU Treaties and thus constituting a *second* layer of norms, and sources adopted on the basis of this second layer to form a *third* one. Each source of EU law below EU primary law thus has a family tree: a legal basis exists in the EU Treaties, the first generation of children are to be found in EU secondary law, and certain branches of the family have extended to another generation of sources, having their immediate legal basis in secondary law and forming tertiary law. The latter two generations of acts thus originate directly or indirectly – through the medium of an act of secondary law, in the case of tertiary law – in the EU Treaties.

Quite naturally, the younger generations have to respect their parents. Although it is not established that all acts of tertiary law ought to comply with all acts of secondary law, the tertiary act unquestionably ought to be compatible with the parent act, and each instrument must be interpreted light of higher-ranking rules within the lineage, as well as in light of the whole of primary law. This system of norms is often represented in the form of a pyramid (see Figure 3.1).

[182] Art. 15(3) TFEU now provides for a right of access to documents of the institutions, bodies, offices and agencies of the EU, including the Court of Justice of the European Union, the Central Bank and the European Investment Bank, where they exercise administrative functions; C-213/15 P, *Commission* v. *Breyer*, EU: C:2017:563, paras. 50–51; see also Chapter 2, Section 2.2.2.

[183] 'Regulation (EU) 2016/679 of the European Parliament and of the Council of 27 April 2016 on the Protection of Natural Persons with Regard to the Processing of Personal Data and on the Free Movement of such Data', OJ L 119, 4.5.2016.

[184] Arts. 21(1), subpara. 1, and 23 TEU.

[185] For instance, the notion of tertiary law introduced in this Chapter is often absorbed under the notion of secondary law.

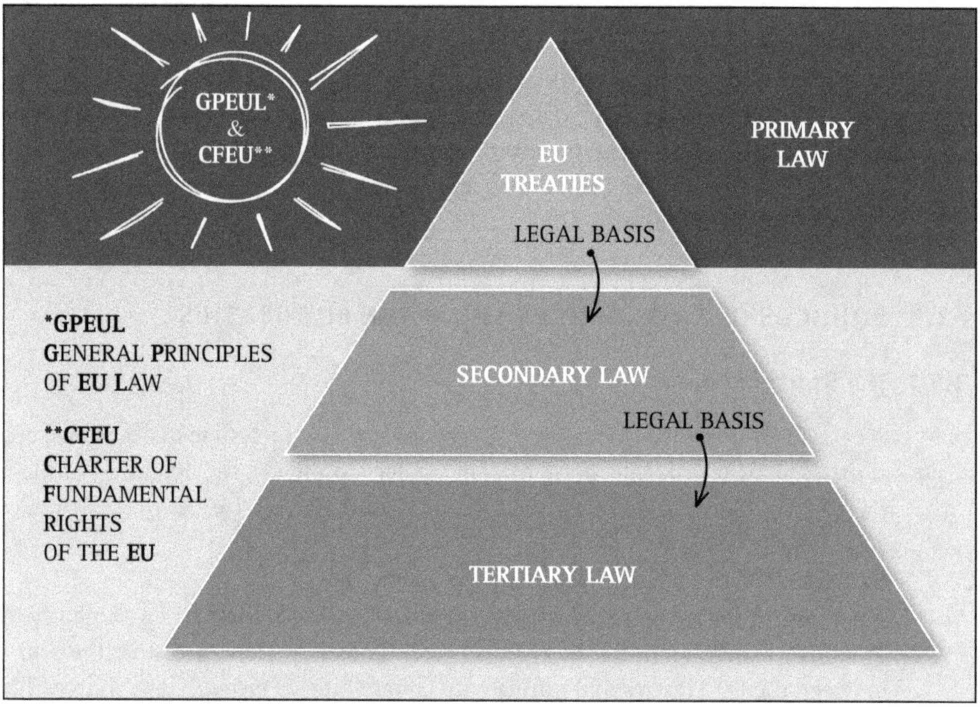

Figure 3.1 The various layers of EU norms within a lineage

3.5.1.2 The EU Legal Order Does Not Exist in a Vacuum

Before investigating instruments adopted on the basis of the EU Treaties, it must be recalled that the EU legal order does not exist in a vacuum. It closely intertwines with national and international legal orders.

There are multiple references to national law, and to national constitutional requirements in particular, across the EU Treaties. Here are a few examples of the importance of national law: the EU Treaties are international agreements that are signed and ratified by the Member States in accordance with their own laws. Similarly, a Member State's decision to withdraw from the EU depends on national constitutional requirements. Furthermore, as made clear in Article 6(3) TEU, constitutional traditions common to the Member States shall constitute general principles of EU law.

It shall be remembered that accession to the EU does not deprive the Member States of the possibility to conclude international agreements between themselves, sometimes referred to as *inter se* agreements. Unless otherwise provided for by EU law, these agreements are not part of EU law. They ought to comply with the EU Treaties, however, as well as the full body of EU norms, which take precedence over subsequent acts.[186] For instance, such *inter se* agreements may not be developed in areas of competences belonging exclusively to the EU. Conversely, they may entrust tasks to EU institutions, such as the task of managing financial assistance, provided that this does not alter the essential character of the powers

[186] See Chapter 4, Section 4.1.1.1, Scope and National Perspectives.

conferred on those institutions by the EU Treaties.[187] The Treaty establishing the European Stability Mechanism is such an example.

Finally, there is a vast array of rules of international law that have special significance in the EU legal order. It would be beyond the scope of this book to provide an exhaustive list, but it may be helpful to give a few examples. International agreements concluded by the Member States before accession shall not be affected by the EU Treaties.[188] International treaties 'on which the Member States have collaborated or of which they are signatories' can supply guidelines which should be followed within the framework of EU law; under the form of general principles of EU law.[189] Furthermore, the Vienna Convention on the Law of Treaties may be taken into account for the interpretation of the EU Treaties.[190] Finally, under Article 3(5) TEU, the European Union is to contribute to the strict observance and the development of international law. This includes international customary law.[191] The EU's action on the international scene shall be guided by, and seek to advance, 'respect for the principles of the United Nations Charter and international law'.[192] Another example lies in the development of a CSDP, which has to be compatible with the common security and defence policy established within the framework of NATO.[193]

Even if the EU is not formally a party to a specific international law instrument (this hypothesis will be discussed subsequently), it may be that the implementation of an agreement or ensuring compliance with it falls within its competences[194] and/or that EU law itself refers to specific international law arrangements. In the aftermath of the terrorist attacks of 11 September 2001 in the United States, for instance, the UN Security Council adopted resolutions on combatting international terrorism to be implemented by the States belonging to the United Nations, and requesting the freezing of the assets of certain organisations, entities and individuals. The Member States of the EU considered that the EU was an appropriate avenue to implement these UN Security Council Resolutions.[195]

A particularly interesting example of the interplay between international law and the EU legal order emerged in this context, illustrating a tension between the authority of international law in the EU legal order and the autonomy of EU law.[196] In its ruling in the *Kadi* case, the Court of Justice framed the tension as follows:

[187] C-370/12, *Pringle*, EU:C:2012:756, paras. 100–101, 158.

[188] Art. 351 TFEU. Possible incompatibilities shall be eliminated, as required by that article.

[189] Case 4/73, *Nold*, EU:C:1974:51, para. 13; see also Chapter 3, Section 3.1.3.3.

[190] C-621/18, *Wightman*, EU:C:2018:999, paras. 70–71.

[191] C-366/10, *Air Transport Association of America*, EU:C:2011:864, para. 101.

[192] Art. 21(1), para. 1 TEU.

[193] Art. 42(2), subpara. 2 TEU.

[194] For instance, the Court of Justice has ruled that, in so far as the EU has assumed the powers previously exercised by Member States in the area governed by the GATT, the provisions of that agreement have the effect of binding the EU. Joined Cases 21-24/72, *International Fruit Company*, EU:C:1972:115, para. 18; contrast with C-366/10, *Air Transport Association of America* (ATAA), EU:C:2011:864, paras. 62–71, where the necessary conditions for the transfer of powers from the Member States to the EU and for the latter to be bound by the Chicago Convention on International Civil Aviation were not fulfilled.

[195] E.g. 'Council Regulation (EC) No. 2580/2001 of 27 December 2001 on Specific Restrictive Measures Directed against Certain Persons and Entities with a View to Combating Terrorism', OJ L 344, 28.12.2001, p. 70 (last amended 2019).

[196] See Chapter 1, Section 1.4.2.3.

> European Union measures implementing restrictive measures decided at international level enjoy no immunity from jurisdiction [...]. [W]ithout the primacy of a Security Council resolution at the international level thereby being called into question, the requirement that the European Union institutions should pay due regard to the institutions of the United Nations must not result in there being no review of the lawfulness of such European Union measures, in the light of the fundamental rights which are an integral part of the general principles of European Union law.[197]

The Court thus focused its attention on the EU measure, rather than the underlying requirements established by the UN Security Council, and imposed on EU institutions a duty to comply with EU standards of protection when giving effect to international law obligations. In turn, the Member States of the EU must work on enhancing safeguards within UN Security Council decision-making to avoid a clash between measures implementing UN obligations in EU law, and the EU legal order.[198]

3.5.2 The Role of the Court of Justice of the European Union

A second remark, before investigating instruments adopted on the basis of the EU Treaties, relates to the role of the Court of Justice of the European Union, made up of the Court of Justice and General Court, which is to ensure that 'in the interpretation and application of the Treaties the law is observed'.[199] The rulings of the Courts have the legal authority of the act of EU law that they interpreted. The Courts may not call into question the validity of primary law, their task being to interpret these sources. Instead, the Courts may check, for instance, the validity of acts derived from the EU Treaties against the said Treaties, as well as other sources having the same legal value. In that sense, the Court of Justice of the European Union interprets various layers of EU norms and ensures consistency.

From the perspective of EU law, it is that institution which frames the relationship between EU law, the law of the Member States and rules of international law as exemplified in the *Kadi* case, as well as in discussion on the primacy of EU law over national constitutional law.[200] Other jurisdictions, such as national constitutional courts, may have different approaches – reflecting their different mandates, functions and legal culture – to the relationship between these various legal systems. Actual conflicts of hierarchy between these legal systems, although hotly debated when they occur, remain fairly rare, and the plurality of approaches just described is often understood as an incentive to search for reasoned and balanced solutions in situations of tensions.[201]

[197] Joined Cases C-584/10 P, C-593/10 P and C-595/10 P, *'Kadi II'*, EU:C:2013:518, para. 67. See also Joined Cases C-402/05 P and C-415/05 P, *'Kadi I'*, EU:C:2008:461, paras. 288, 326.

[198] M. Nettesheim, 'UN Sanctions against Individuals: A Challenge to the Architecture of European Union Governance', *CMLR*, 44/3 (2007), pp. 594–595.

[199] Art. 19(1) TEU. [200] See Chapter 4, Section 4.1.1.

[201] T. Tridimas, 'The ECJ and the National Courts: Dialogue, Cooperation and Instability', in A. Arnull and D. Chalmers (eds.), *The Oxford Handbook of EU Law* (Oxford University Press, 2015); see further M. Poiares Maduro, 'Interpreting European Law: Judicial Adjudication in a Context of Constitutional Pluralism', *European Journal of Legal Studies*, 1 (2018) 1, pp. 137–152.

3.5.3 Derived Law

Putting flesh on the family tree introduced previously, EU institutions may adopt a broad range of acts. The relationships between these derived sources ought to be distinguished, depending on whether they look inwards to the EU legal system or outwards. On the one hand, external action articulates the relationship between the EU and third States or international organisations. On the other hand, internal action articulates the relationship between the EU, its Member States and/or other entities or individuals within the jurisdiction of the Member States. To ensure consistency on the international stage, internal acts of the EU must be in line with the EU's external commitments.

3.5.3.1 External Action

Secondary Law in the Form of International Agreements

International agreements may be concluded on behalf of the EU[202] – which has (international) legal personality[203] – with third States or international organisations.[204] Examples are the EU's Economic Partnership Agreement with Japan[205] and the EU being a party to the World Trade Organization. EU institutions regularly adopt internal acts intended to enhance the legal effects of these instruments within the EU legal order, either implementing international obligations or furthering international commitments.[206]

The competence to conclude external agreements is sometimes partly exclusively that of the EU, and partly exclusively that of the Member States, or actually shared between the two.[207] The EU may thus have to conclude an international agreement with a third State or international organisation *jointly* with the Member States concerned. Such an international agreement is said to be 'mixed' because both the EU and the Member States are parties to it. The political salience of mixed international agreements is usefully illustrated in the context of the signature of ambitious external agreements with third States, such as the Comprehensive Economic and Trade Agreement with Canada (CETA). Such international agreements often take the shape of mixed agreements. As a consequence, they are signed and ratified by the EU, as well as by each Member State. This requires, along with support at EU level, the support of national actors, as the opposition by selected Belgian authorities to CETA has illustrated on the European stage.[208]

202 Art. 216(1) TFEU. 203 Art. 47 TEU.

204 These secondary sources of EU law must not be confused with international agreements to which the EU is *not* a party; see Chapter 2, Section 2.1.1 and Chapter 3, Section 3.5.1.2.

205 'Council Decision (EU) 2018/1907 of 20 December 2018 on the Conclusion of the Agreement between the European Union and Japan for an Economic Partnership', OJ L 330, 27.12.2018, p. 1.

206 In relation to the Århus Convention on access to information, public participation in decision-making and access to justice in environmental matters, see, for instance, 'Directive 2003/35/EC of the European Parliament and of the Council of 26 May 2003 Providing for Public Participation in Respect of the Drawing Up of Certain Plans and Programmes Relating to the Environment and Amending with Regard to Public Participation and Access to Justice Council Directives 85/337/EEC and 96/61/EC – Statement by the Commission', OJ L 156, 25.6.2003, p. 17 (last amended 2016).

207 See Chapter 3, Section 3.3. There is much discussion as to how to articulate EU and Member State competences when the international agreement relates to an area that falls within the shared competences of the EU; see further L. Prete, 'The Constitutional Limits to the Choice of Mixity after EUSFTA, COTIF I, MPA Antarctic and COTIF II: Towards a More Constructive Discourse?', *European Law Review*, 45 (2020), pp. 113–127.

208 J. Rankin, 'EU Trade Deal with Canada on Brink of Collapse after Belgian Disarray', *The Guardian*, 24.10.2016.

To the extent that an international agreement is concluded by the EU, the said international agreement produces legal effects as a matter of EU law, as illustrated in Figure 3.2 below.[209] The agreement itself ought to comply with EU primary law.[210] At the same time, EU organs and Member States ought to comply with the content of this agreement.[211] As a consequence, such international agreements rank below EU primary law, but above internal sources of secondary and tertiary law.

In order to limit the risk of tensions between international agreements and higher norms of EU law that would put the EU in difficulty on the international stage if discovered too late, Article 218(11) TFEU provides for an *ex ante* control mechanism, as shown in Figure 3.2.[212] Any Member State, the Parliament, the Council or the Commission may ask the Court of Justice for an opinion as to whether an agreement envisaged is compatible with higher-ranking norms in the EU legal system. Where the opinion is adverse, the agreement envisaged may not enter into force unless it is amended or EU primary law is revised to eliminate the tension. The procedure in Article 218(11) TFEU is commonly used. For instance, it allowed the Parliament to obtain a negative opinion on the envisaged agreement with Canada on the transfer and processing of passenger name record data. The Court considered that the provisions on the draft agreement on the transfer of sensitive data to Canada and on the processing and retention of that data were incompatible with fundamental rights protected in the EU.[213]

Tertiary Law Adopted on the Basis of International Agreements

International agreements to which the EU is a party may have their own dynamic and allow for the adoption of a third layer of norms in the external sphere (Figure 3.2),[214] possibly under the jurisdiction of newly created courts. The Court of Justice has made it clear that 'the measures adopted by institutions set up by such agreements become an integral part of the [EU] legal order when they enter into force'.[215] For instance, Article 2(1)(b) of Decision 2/76 and the third indent of Article 6(1) of Decision 1/80 of the Council of Association established by the Association Agreement between the EU and Turkey result in a legally enforceable right for a Turkish worker, after a number of years' legal employment in a Member State, to enjoy free access to any paid

[209] On the direct effect of provisions of external agreements, see Chapter 4, Section 4.1.2.3, International Agreements between the EU and Third States or International Organisations.

[210] See, for instance, Art. 218(11) TFEU.

[211] Art. 216(2) TFEU. This includes, for instance, a duty to interpret derived internal acts in conformity with international agreements to which the EU is a party.

[212] Note that the ordinary ex post mechanisms, allowing interpretation of the international agreement or a challenge to the validity of the decision by an EU institution to conclude an international agreement, are also available. The latter, however, may trigger specific difficulties: international agreements are binding on the EU; in the event of non-performance, the EU could incur liability at international level. See Vienna Convention on the Law of Treaties between States and International Organizations or between International Organizations; C-327/91, *France* v. *Commission*, EU:C:1994:305, paras. 15–17, 25; see also Chapter 4, Section 4.3.1.1.

[213] Opinion 1/15, PNR Agreement, EU:C:2017:592.

[214] See, for instance, Art. 218(7) TFEU on the possibility for the Council to authorise the negotiator to approve modifications to an international agreement where the latter provides for such modifications to be adopted by a body set up by the agreement. Also, see further A. Ott, 'The EU Commission's Administrative Agreements: "Delegated Treaty-Making" in between Delegated and Implementing Rule-Making', in E. Tauschinsky and W. Weiß (eds.), *The Legislative Choice between Delegated and Implementing Acts in EU Law: Walking a Labyrinth* (Edward Elgar, 2018), ch. 8.

[215] Opinion 1/91, EU:C:1991:490, para. 37.

employment of their choice.[216] When implementing an international agreement in such a way, the Council of Association places the adopted measure within the institutional framework of the said international agreement,[217] and thus above internal EU acts.[218]

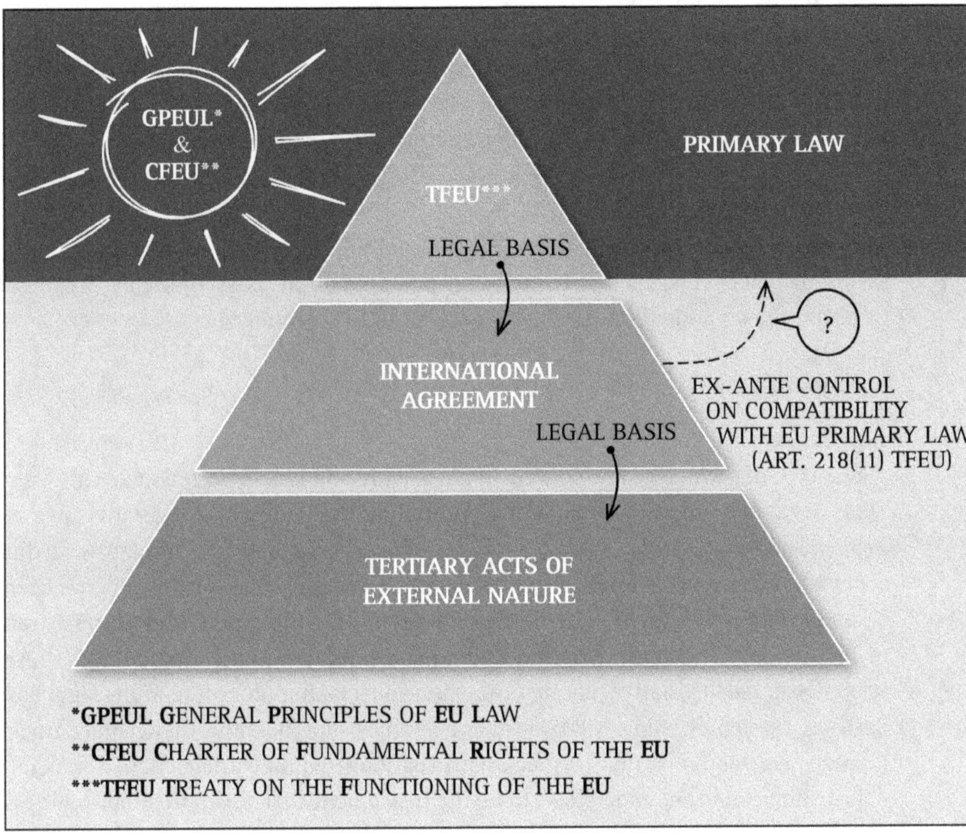

Figure 3.2 The layers of EU norms in (standard) external action

Specific Acts Adopted in the Context of the Common Foreign and Security Policy

In addition to international agreements to which the EU is a party and which may relate to the CFSP,[219] Article 25 TEU identifies a set of instruments specific to the CFSP. It is not possible to adopt legislative acts in that field.[220] Instead, the EU must conduct that policy by defining general guidelines, adopting decisions defining actions and positions to be taken by the EU, as well as arrangements for the implementation of the latter and the strengthening of systematic cooperation between Member States on the international stage. It flows from the logic of the Treaties that these sources ought to comply with EU primary law. Yet their precise legal authority and their relationship to other sources remain unclear; and the

[216] C-192/89, *Sevince*, EU:C:1990:322, para. 17.

[217] Case 204/83, *Greece* v. *Council (Special aid to Turkey)*, EU:C:1988:450, para. 20.

[218] See also, for instance, in relation to the Anti-Dumping Code, which was adopted for the purpose of implementing Art. VI of the GATT: C-69/89, *Nakajima* v. *Council*, EU:C:1991:186, para. 29.

[219] Art. 37 TEU. [220] Arts. 24(1), subpara. 2, and 31(1), subpara. 1 TEU.

jurisdiction of the Court of Justice of the European Union with respect to the provisions relating to the CFSP is limited.[221]

Before discussing internal acts, it shall be noted that acts adopted internally, without consent by a third party, may play an important role in the external relations of the EU and/or be directed to a third party. An example in the CFSP field is that a decision adopted in accordance with it may provide for the adoption of restrictive measures against natural or legal persons and groups or non-State entities related to one or more third countries within the EU. Such restrictive measures are ultimately adopted by the Council and are accompanied by legal safeguards and judicial scrutiny.[222]

3.5.3.2 Internal Action

Turning to legal acts that regulate EU internal action, and unfolding the family tree, we distinguish between acts of secondary law adopted on the basis of the EU Treaties, and acts of tertiary law adopted on the basis of an act of EU secondary law.

Secondary Law

Legislative Acts

A first type of secondary law acts are of a legislative nature. In accordance with Article 289(3) TFEU, legal acts 'adopted by legislative procedure shall constitute legislative acts'. In *Slovak Republic and Hungary* v. *Council*, the Court of Justice applied a fairly narrow reading of that statement, adding that a legal act can be classified as a legislative act only if it has been adopted (1) on the basis of a provision of the EU Treaties, *and* (2) if that provision expressly refers either to the ordinary legislative procedure or to the special legislative procedure.[223] An explicit reference to the 'legislative' nature of the decision-making procedure in the legal basis is thus decisive. These procedures will be further explained subsequently. They require, under various arrangements and to various degrees, participation from the Parliament and the Council.

Legislative acts are understood to be the instrument best suited to adopt rules essential to the subject matter and to make key policy choices, even though they may also be fairly technical and/or, under specific conditions, transfer powers to other institutions.[224] Their role in crystallising key choices is related to the legitimacy that they derive from the design of the institutions they emanate from, as well as from a number of procedural features specific to this type of act: draft legislative acts are subject to scrutiny for compliance with the principle of subsidiarity from national parliaments;[225] the Council ought to meet in public when it deliberates and votes on draft legislative acts;[226] and the conditions for access to judicial review of legislative acts are distinct from those of other types of acts discussed herein.[227]

[221] Arts. 24(1), subpara. 2, and 275, para. 1 TFEU. This is further elaborated upon in Chapter 4, Section 4.4.1.
[222] Arts. 215(3), 275, para. 2 TFEU.
[223] Joined Cases C-643/15 and C-647/15, *Slovakia and Hungary* v. *Council*, EU:C:2017:631, para. 62.
[224] E.g. Art. 290(1) TFEU; in the context of agriculture and fisheries, see Joined Cases C-103/12 and C-165/12, *Parliament and Commission* v. *Council*, EU:C:2014:2400, para. 50; as regards surveillance at the external borders of the EU with possible fundamental rights' implications, see C-355/10, *Parliament* v. *Council*, EU:C:2012:516, paras. 64–68, 76–79.
[225] See Chapter 3, Section 3.4.1.
[226] Art. 16(8) TEU and Art. 15(2) TFEU; see also Chapter 2, Section 2.3.4.4, Meetings, Votes and Transparency.
[227] Art. 263, para. 4, third limb TFEU; see also Chapter 4, Section 4.3.1.1, Categories of Applicants.

Non-legislative Acts of Secondary Law

In *Slovak Republic and Hungary* v. *Council*, the Court of Justice also specified that, in contrast, 'non-legislative acts are those that are adopted by a procedure other than a legislative procedure'.[228] This definition of non-legislative acts is open-ended; it is most often used to refer to acts of tertiary law adopted on the basis of an act of secondary law, as will be discussed subsequently. In some cases though, non-legislative acts are adopted on the basis of the EU Treaties themselves and thus constitute measures of secondary law.

For instance, Article 78(3) TFEU allows for the adoption of legal acts in response to an emergency situation characterised by a sudden inflow of nationals of third countries. This was used in 2015 to create schemes for the relocation to other EU countries of applicants for international protection in Italy and Greece. The procedure for adoption of the related decisions was similar to the one that characterises certain special legislative procedures, but there is no explicit mention of the use of a 'legislative' procedure. The resulting act is thus non-legislative.[229]

Tertiary Law

Acts of secondary law may themselves include legal bases for the adoption of a third layer of acts. In quantitative terms, the most common form of EU acts are indeed acts adopted on the basis of an act of EU secondary law. For instance, in 2021, EU institutions adopted 264 legislative acts (amendments included), whereas they adopted 82 delegated acts and 609 implementing acts, the latter two categories being examples of acts of tertiary law.[230]

Because these acts are not adopted on the basis of the EU Treaties, and without any reference to a 'legislative' procedure, these acts are by nature non-legislative acts. It is for the legislator to decide which type of non-legislative act to use, subject to the specific requirements in each of the relevant provisions discussed subsequently.[231] We may distinguish between three subcategories of acts of tertiary law.

[228] Joined Cases C-643/15 and C-647/15, *Slovakia and Hungary* v. *Council*, EU:C:2017:631, para. 58.

[229] Such a non-legislative act of secondary law may, in principle, under circumscribed circumstances, derogate from the provisions of a legislative act of secondary law; Joined Cases C-643/15 and C-647/15, *Slovakia and Hungary* v. *Council*, EU:C:2017:631, para. 78. Note that a non-legislative act of secondary law may implement EU law, even if it is not adopted in accordance with Art. 291(2) TFEU as introduced subsequently; Joined Cases C-124/13 and C-125/13, *Parliament and Commission* v. *Council*, EU:C:2015:790, para. 54; see also, for explanations, Joined Cases C-103/12 and C-165/12, *Parliament and Commission* v. *Council*, EU:C:2014:2400, para. 50).

[230] Data available at https://eur-lex.europa.eu/statistics/legislative-acts-statistics.html, 'Legal acts – statistics'.

[231] EU secondary law may not establish secondary legal bases for the adoption of tertiary law that would empower an institution to amend a decision-making procedure established by the Treaties; C-540/13, *Parliament* v. *Council*, EU:C:2015:224, paras. 32–34. Judicial review, in particular as to the distinction between implementing and delegated acts, as introduced by Arts. 290, 291 TFEU, is limited to manifest errors of assessment; C-427/12, *Commission* v. *Parliament and Council (Biocides)*, EU:C:2014:170, para. 40. Limited guidance is provided by the 'Interinstitutional Agreement between the European Parliament, the Council of the European Union and the European Commission on Better Law-Making', OJ L 123, 12.5.2016, p. 1, Section V, and its Annex on a 'Common Understanding between the European Parliament, the Council and the Commission on Delegated Acts', as well as the Interinstitutional Agreement on 'Non-binding Criteria for the Application of Articles 290 and 291 of the Treaty on the Functioning of the European Union', OJ C 223, 3.7.2019, p. 1.

Delegated Acts within the Meaning of Art. 290 TFEU

To start with, and in accordance with Article 290 TFEU and as illustrated in Figure 3.3, a legislative act may 'delegate' to the Commission the power to adopt acts that have four cumulative characteristics.[232] Firstly, the function of a delegated act is to 'supplement or amend'[233] the legislative act which forms its legal basis – hence its name, it is a *delegation* of legislative power. Second, and on a related note, such a delegated act ought to be of general application. In other words, it must apply to objectively determined situations and entails legal effects for categories of persons envisaged generally and in the abstract.[234] Third, the objectives, content, scope and duration of the delegation of powers must be explicitly defined in the legislative act.[235] Fourth, and crucially, the delegation of powers by EU legislative

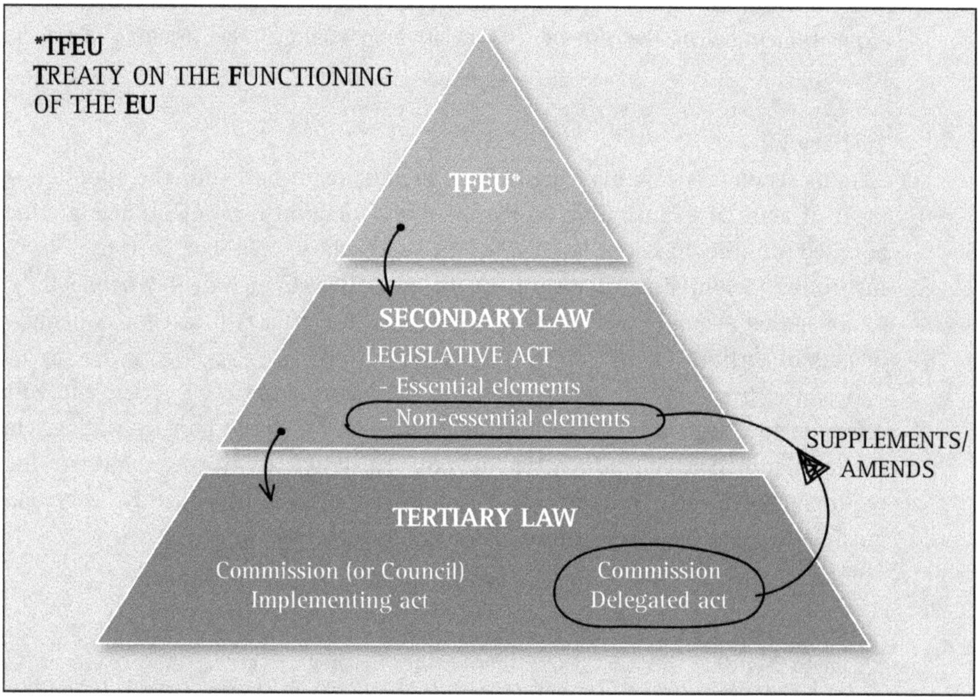

Figure 3.3 Delegated acts in the system of legal acts

[232] Note that certain acts of EU secondary law transfer powers to organs other than the Commission; in such cases the delegation of power is distinct from that provided for in Art. 290 TFEU. See also Chapter 3, Section 3.2.3.4.

[233] That requirement implies that the purpose of granting a delegated power is to achieve the adoption of rules coming within the regulatory framework as defined by the basic legislative act: C-427/12, *Commission* v. *Parliament and Council (Biocides)*, EU:C:2014:170, para. 38. On the distinction between amending and supplementing, see further C-286/14, *Parliament* v. *Commission (Connecting Europe Facility)*, EU: C:2016:183, paras. 41–42, 55–56.

[234] Interinstitutional Agreement on 'Non-binding Criteria for the Application of Articles 290 and 291 of the Treaty on the Functioning of the European Union', OJ C 223, 3.7.2019, p. 1.

[235] See further M. Chamon, 'Limits to Delegation under Article 290 TFEU: The Specificity and Essentiality Requirements Put to the Test', *Maastricht Journal of European and Comparative Law*, 25 (2018), pp. 231–245.

institutions to the Commission can only relate to 'certain non-essential elements of the legislative act'.[236] Indeed, the essential elements of an area shall be reserved for the legislative act.[237]

Since the Treaty of Lisbon, these types of acts adopted in accordance with Article 290 TFEU are recognisable by the fact that the adjective 'delegated' is inserted in the title of delegated acts. The procedure for their adoption will be discussed subsequently.[238] An example of a delegated act is when the Commission is requested to provide regular updates on diseases subject to specific rules for the prevention and control of transmissible animal diseases in an annex of a legislative instrument, with a view to incorporating latest scientific evidence.[239]

Implementing Acts within the Meaning of Art. 291 TFEU

Even more frequent are implementing acts adopted in accordance with Article 291 TFEU.[240] As a matter of principle, it is for the Member States to adopt measures for the implementation of legally binding union acts.[241] Nevertheless, an EU act may confer implementing powers on the Commission, or in certain cases the Council,[242] to adopt implementing acts at EU level, where 'uniform conditions for implementing legally binding Union acts are needed'. In this context, the Commission is called on to provide 'further detail in relation to the content of a legislative act, in order to ensure that it is implemented under uniform conditions in all Member States' (Figure 3.4).[243]

236 Art. 290(1) TFEU.

237 Ascertaining which elements of a matter must be categorised as 'essential' is for the assessment of the EU legislator, but it must be based on objective factors amenable to judicial review; C-696/15 P, *Czech Republic* v. *Commission*, EU:C:2017:595, para. 77.

238 See Chapter 3, Section 3.6.1.2, Delegated Acts within the Meaning of Art. 290 TFEU.

239 E.g. 'Commission Delegated Regulation (EU) 2018/1629 of 25 July 2018 Amending the List of Diseases Set out in Annex II to Regulation (EU) 2016/429 of the European Parliament and of the Council on Transmissible Animal Diseases and Amending and Repealing Certain Acts in the Area of Animal Health (Animal Health Law)', OJ L 272, 31.10.2018, p. 11.

240 It shall be noted that certain acts of EU secondary law implement the EU Treaties, even if they were not adopted in accordance with Art. 291(2) TFEU; see Chapter 3, note 229. Furthermore, certain acts adopted on the basis of EU secondary law may also be referred to as implementing acts, even though they are not adopted with reference to Art. 291(2) TFEU – for instance, because they are related to the implementation of EU acts, but do not lend themselves to implementation by the Member States (unlike those resulting from Art. 291(2) TFEU), instead relating to enforcement of EU law against a Member State (e.g. C-521/15, *Spain* v. *Council*, EU:C:2017:982, paras. 39–53, related to the powers conferred on the Council by 'Regulation (EU) No. 1173/2011 of the European Parliament and of the Council of 16 November 2011 on the Effective Enforcement of Budgetary Surveillance in the Euro Area', OJ L 306, 23.11.2011, p. 1, Art. 8(1): Sanctions Concerning the Manipulation of Statistics. In this section, we focus on implementing acts within the meaning of Art. 291(2) TFEU.

241 Art. 291(1) TFEU; see also Art. 4(3) TEU.

242 This takes place 'in duly justified specific cases' and in the cases provided for in Arts. 24, 26 TEU (on the CFSP); see also Chapter 3, Section 3.6.1.2, Implementing Acts within the Meaning of Art. 291 TFEU. The EU legislator must properly explain why exception is being made to the rule that it is the Commission that is responsible for exercising that power; C-440/14 P, *National Iranian Oil Company* v. *Council*, EU:C:2016:128, para. 60.

243 C-427/12, *Commission* v. *Parliament and Council (Biocides)*, EU:C:2014:170, para. 39.

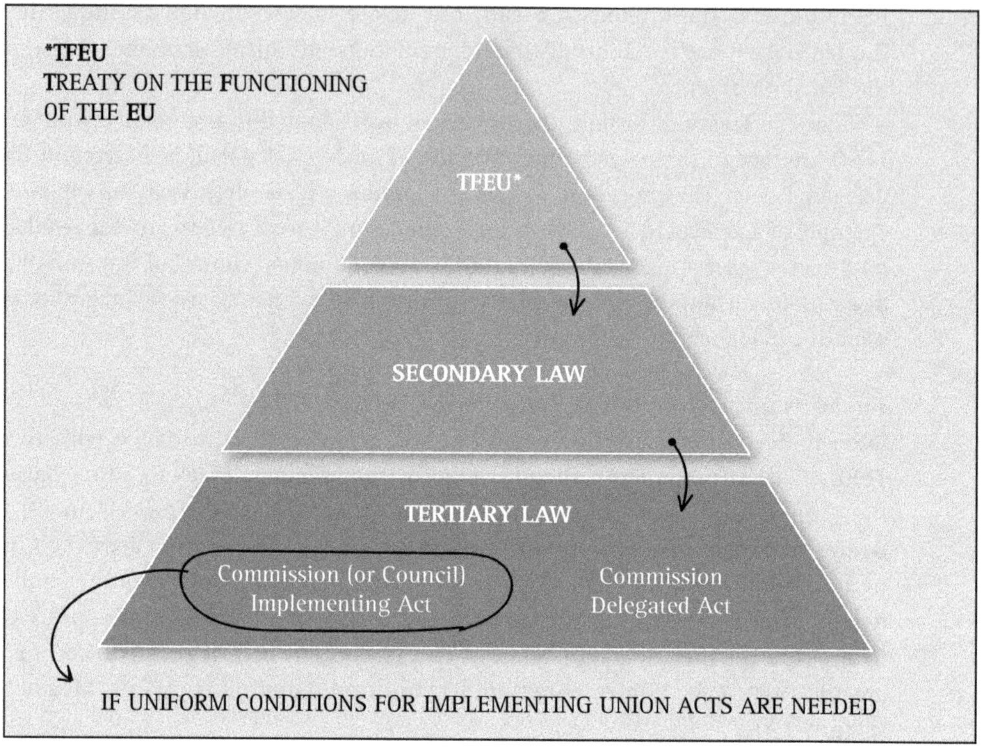

Figure 3.4 Implementing acts in the system of legal acts

Since the Treaty of Lisbon, these types of acts, adopted in accordance with Article 291 TFEU, are recognisable by the word 'implementing' that ought to be inserted in their title. The procedure for their adoption will also be discussed subsequently.[244] By way of example, such an instrument may be used to impose anti-dumping duties on imports of certain materials from third countries after review of the dumping causing an injury, as provided for in the legislative act.[245]

Other Acts of Tertiary Law

It would be beyond the scope of this book to seek to provide an exhaustive overview of acts of tertiary EU law. It suffices here to note that Articles 290 and 291 TFEU, introduced by the Treaty of Lisbon in an attempt to rationalise earlier experiences with similar types of acts, are not the only types of tertiary acts that may be adopted.[246] In particular, EU legislative acts may, under circumstances defined previously in this chapter, empower EU bodies,

[244] See Chapter 3, Section 3.6.1.2, Implementing Acts within the Meaning of Art. 291 TFEU.

[245] E.g. 'Commission Implementing Regulation (EU) 2020/2100 of 15 December 2020 Imposing a Definitive Anti-dumping Duty on Imports of Ammonium Nitrate Originating in Russia Following an Expiry Review Pursuant to Article 11(2) of the Regulation (EU) 2016/1036 of the European Parliament and of the Council', OJ L 425, 16.12.2020, p. 21.

[246] C-270/12, *UK* v. *Parliament and Council (Short Selling)*, EU:C:2014:18, paras. 78–86.

offices or agencies themselves to adopt acts.[247] These entities play a particularly powerful role in EU governance nowadays.

Nature of EU Internal Acts

In so far as EU internal action is concerned, acts of secondary law, as well as acts of tertiary law, usually take the form of legal acts defined in Article 288 TFEU. As will be explained below, other types of acts are also provided for on an ad hoc basis in the EU Treaties. The choice between the various instruments introduced subsequently is sometimes dictated by the legal basis itself.[248] Most often, though, the legal basis only identifies the existence of a competence and the procedure for the adoption of an EU act, and it is for the author of the act itself to choose the form of the instrument.[249]

The form of the act has important consequences on Member States' duties under EU law, as well as for the ability of individuals to rely on the said legal act before national courts.[250] While it is clear that certain types of legal acts create legal obligations, it may be less clear for others, as will be explained subsequently. In contrast, the form of the act does not provide information on whether the act ranks as secondary or tertiary law, which instead results from the legal basis of the act,[251] and may be seen in the title of the act for some of them.[252]

Legal Acts Defined in Art. 288 TFEU

Firstly, in the exercise of their competences, EU institutions may adopt a 'regulation'. A regulation has general application,[253] it is legally binding in its entirety and is directly applicable[254] in all Member States. The latter means that a regulation becomes part of the legal order of a Member State in the same way as any instrument of national law at the date specified for its entry into force. Unless otherwise specified by the regulation itself (as often happens), its application is thus independent of any measure of further national law.[255] This is the expression of its 'character of being EU law', meaning, for instance, that the regulation has primacy over conflicting national law.[256]

A second option is for EU institutions to adopt a 'directive'. A directive is legally binding 'as to the result to be achieved, upon each Member State to which it is addressed'.[257] Although a directive may sometimes also be very prescriptive, it is often understood as

[247] See further Chapter 3, Section 3.2.3.4 and notes 229, 240. See also M. Chamon, 'Institutional Balance and Community Method in the Implementation of EU Legislation Following the Lisbon Treaty', *Common Market Law Review*, 53 (2016), pp. 1501–1543.

[248] See Chapter 3, Section 3.2.2.1.

[249] With due respect for the principle of proportionality and stating the reasons on which it is based; Art. 296 (1–2) TFEU.

[250] See Chapter 4, Section 4.1.2.3. [251] See Chapter 3, Section 3.5.1.1.

[252] See Chapter 3, Section 3.5.3.2, Tertiary Law.

[253] It applies to objectively determined situations and entails legal effects for categories of persons envisaged generally and in the abstract.

[254] The 'direct applicability' of EU regulations is to be distinguished from the notion of 'direct effect' of EU law norms. The latter concept refers more specifically to the ability of individuals to invoke them before national courts. See Chapter 4, Section 4.1.2.

[255] C-34/73, *Variola* v. *Amministrazione italiana delle Finanze*, EU:C:1973:101, para. 10.

[256] B. De Witte and B. Smulders, 'Sources of European Union Law', in P. J. Kuijper, F. Amtenbrink, D. Curtin, A. McDonnell and S. Van den Bogaert (eds.), *The Law of the European Union*, 5th ed. (Wolters Kluwer, 2018), p. 206; see also Chapter 4, Section 4.1.1.2, Duty of Consistent Interpretation in Light of EU Law.

[257] Art. 288, para. 3 TFEU.

an instrument that allows the national authorities to choose their own form and methods to achieve the result identified therein. At the end of each directive (as illustrated in Box 3.2, in section 3.6.4 of this Chapter), there is a provision specifying the time given by the author of the EU act, *after* the entry into force of the instrument, for the Member States to transpose into national law the obligations contained in the directive.[258] It is only at the expiry of this so-called 'transposition period' that the directive will take full legal effect. If duly transposed though, the directive primarily takes effect through national transposition measures.[259]

A third option is for EU organs to adopt a 'decision'. Unlike a directive, a decision is legally binding in its entirety. A decision may specify to whom it is addressed, and if it does so, it is binding only on those addressees. It is an instrument that tends to be used for more specific forms of action. The Commission for instance used this instrument to declare the compatibility of the aid granted to some airports suffering from the negative financial consequences of the COVID-19 outbreak, under EU State aid rules.[260]

Article 288 TFEU furthermore refers to 'recommendations' and 'opinions'. These are legal acts, as they are provided for by the EU Treaties, but they do not, in principle, create legal obligations.[261] They are policy tools, close to other forms of legal acts not listed here, as will be explained subsequently. Recommendations are one of the key instruments used to coordinate Member States' economic policies at European level.[262]

Legal Acts Provided for Elsewhere in the EU Treaties

Although legal acts described in Article 288 TFEU are the most common, that article does not provide an exhaustive list of internal EU acts producing legal effects.[263] Examples of other instruments include interinstitutional agreements that allow the Parliament, the Council and the Commission to agree on arrangements for their cooperation. These agreements may produce legal effects, binding their parties.[264] They are of particular importance to ensure a smooth operation of the decision-making process at EU level, as shown by that on Better Law-Making.[265] Another example relates to the possibility for management and labour to conclude collective agreements at the EU level in the field of social policy.[266] It may also be recalled that, before the Treaty of Lisbon, certain instruments were specific to the second and third pillars of the EU. Some of the instruments

[258] This is often a period of two years, but may vary depending on the will of the institution adopting the act.

[259] See Chapter 4, Section 4.1.2.3, Directives.

[260] As provided for in Art. 108(3) TFEU; e.g. Decision, SA.57178, 'Romania – COVID-19 – Aid to Timişoara Airport', OJ 2020 C326, 2.10.2020, p. 1.

[261] The Court of Justice of the European Union, however, may look beyond the form of the act to investigate the legal effects that it may produce; see Chapter 4, Sections 4.2.3.2 and 4.3.1.1, Reviewable Acts.

[262] E.g. 'Council Recommendation of 9 July 2019 on the 2019 National Reform Programme of Italy and Delivering a Council Opinion on the 2019 Stability Programme of Italy', OJ C 301, 5.9.2019, p. 69.

[263] The approach by the Court of Justice on the reviewability of these acts is further discussed in Chapter 4, Sections 4.2.3.2 and 4.3.1.1, Reviewable Acts.

[264] Art. 295 TFEU; see also earlier case law on the legal effects of certain agreements: C-25/94, *Commission* v. *Council (FAO)*, EU:C:1996:114, para. 49.

[265] OJ L 123, 12.5.2016, p. 1; see also Chapter 3, Section 3.6.1.1, Legislative Procedures. Reflecting on the legal effects of the interinstitutional agreement on Better Law-Making, see Opinion of Advocate General Sharpston, C-482/17, *Czech Republic* v. *Parliament and Council*, EU:C:2019:321, para. 93 *et seq.*

[266] Art. 155(1) TFEU. In matters covered by EU social policy, social partners may further request the Commission to propose to the Council to implement the said collective agreement (Art. 155(2) TFEU); this has resulted in the adoption of several directives implementing EU-level collective agreements.

adopted in this context, such as the Framework Decision on the European Arrest Warrant, are still in force today; their legal effects will be preserved until they are repealed, annulled or amended.[267]

3.5.3.3 Other Modes of Action

Irrespective of when they act internally or externally, EU organs may make use of a broad range of instruments not expressly provided for in the EU Treaties, or which are provided for but not considered to be traditional legal instruments such as the ones identified previously. It is, for instance, very common for the Commission to adopt communications, white papers, green papers or even non-papers, and for the European Council to adopt conclusions.[268] These form a toolkit to stimulate or shape public debate and exchanges, depending on the function of the EU organ responsible for their adoption. In recent years, we have also seen an intense use of press releases containing legal information, as exemplified in the context of the response to the German Federal Constitutional Court's (BVerfG) ruling in the *Weiss* case.[269] The press releases of the Eurogroup and the Central Bank have also been subject to much attention.[270] The use of atypical instruments, as well as informal arrangements, also takes place in the external action of EU organs. This is particularly sensitive in the field of migration.[271]

In principle, and as for recommendations and opinions mentioned in Article 288 TFEU, such instruments are deemed not to be legally binding. The Court of Justice of the European Union, however, has indicated that it is willing to take a pragmatic approach to the definition of the legal effects of EU acts, thus looking beyond their mere form.[272] There is only a fine line between policy-making and the creation of legal constraints. The concern with the latter is that non-binding instruments and informal practices may be used to circumvent a broad range of fundamental legal principles – for instance, the principles of attribution of competences, institutional balance, transparency, accountability, judicial review and fundamental rights' protection.

3.6 PROCEDURES FOR THE ADOPTION OF EU ACTS

Now, how do EU acts actually come into being? How are they adopted? Although decision-making procedures may be perceived as very technical, this allows us to look at how the relationship between EU organs is structured to balance competing interests in crystallising political choices into law. The relevant procedures are indeed at the crossroads between the rules regulating the EU's actors and the main features of the system of EU norms,[273] because procedures organise the way the different EU organs interact through rules on the allocation and exercise of competences, and with a view to the adoption of new sources of EU law.

[267] Protocol 36, Art. 9; see also Chapter 4, Section 4.4.1.

[268] See Chapter 2, Section 2.3.3.5.

[269] See Chapter 3, note 125; Court of Justice of the European Union, 'Press release Following the Judgment of the German Constitutional Court of 5 May 2020', Press release 58/20 (BVerfG, 2 BvR 859/15 ff., 5.5.2020); Statement by President Von Der Leyen on the recent ruling of the BVerfG, 10.5.2020.

[270] See, respectively, C-597/18 P, *Chrysostomides*, EU:C:2020:1028 and C-62/14, *Gauweiler*, EU:C:2015:400.

[271] See, for instance, C. Molinari, 'The EU and Its Perilous Journey through the Migration Crisis: Informalisation of the EU Return Policy and Rule of Law Concern', *European Law Review*, 44 (2019), pp. 824–840.

[272] See Chapter 4, Section 4.3.1.1, Reviewable Acts.

[273] As discussed in Chapter 2, Section 2.3 and Chapter 3, Section 3.5, respectively.

The previous section discussed the EU's external action before its internal action, to help the reader to visualise the ranking of international agreements to which the EU is a party between EU primary law, on the one hand, and EU internal acts, on the other hand. In this section, however, we start with internal action: an important feature of the procedures for the adoption of international agreements is that they often mirror the dynamics of internal law-making. This is to ensure, in particular, that the Parliament is involved in the procedure leading to the conclusion of an international agreement, when the latter relates to a subject on which the Parliament is normally involved as a co-legislator for internal purposes. So let us look at internal action first.

3.6.1 Internal Action

The diversity of procedures for the adoption of EU internal acts reflects the diversity of institutional arrangements wished for by the authors of the EU Treaties, to accommodate various sensitivities across the different fields of EU internal action. It may be recalled that the choice of procedure is determined by the legal basis enabling EU organs to act. As well as the specifics of each procedure detailed subsequently, the legal basis may further require the consultation of given advisory bodies, or EU institutions acting in an advisory capacity. Furthermore, national parliaments are formally involved in the preliminary stages of the legislative process.[274]

Overall, the procedures structuring EU internal action have evolved to distinguish more clearly between the procedures for the adoption of legislative acts (which are part of secondary law) from the main procedures for the adoption of implementing acts (which are part of tertiary law). The first set of procedures is intended to give legal shape to most prominent political choices. Related procedures have evolved to mark an ever-greater involvement of the Parliament alongside the Council, as illustrated in what has been known since the Treaty of Lisbon as the ordinary legislative procedure. The second set of procedures normally deals with more traditional administrative matters.

3.6.1.1 Acts of Secondary Law

Legislative Procedures

Various legislative procedures are set out in the EU Treaties. Article 289 TFEU distinguishes between two different types of procedures, both resulting in the adoption of legislative acts, which are understood to be the instrument best suited to adopt rules essential to the subject matter and to make key policy choices.[275] The most common procedure for the adoption of legislative acts is the so-called ordinary legislative procedure. It is characterised by the joint adoption of the act by the Parliament and the Council acting as co-legislators. Conversely, the special legislative procedures, of which there are different sorts, give an asymmetrical weight to one institution over the other: the Council is often the final decision-maker.

[274] See Chapter 2, Section 2.2.1 and Chapter 3, Section 3.4.1.

[275] See Chapter 3, Section 3.5.3.2, Secondary Law.

Legislative Initiative and Legislative Cycle

In both settings, the power to propose a draft legislative act for adoption is in the hands of the Commission.[276] The power to initiate legislation is shared with others only in very limited settings,[277] and must be read in light of the fact that the Parliament, the Council and groups of EU citizens can invite the Commission to act,[278] as well as the fact that the European Council can give specific impetus and can define general political directions.[279] The Commission's quasi-monopoly of the power of legislative initiative is central to its function, which is to 'take appropriate initiatives' with a view to promoting the general interest of the EU.[280] Unless otherwise stated by the EU Treaties, this places the Commission in the driving seat to decide on whether or not, what (subject matter, objectives, content) and when to propose legislative acts which can turn key political choices into law at the European level.

A significant part of the work of the Commission is thus to prioritise and prepare legislative action.[281] For every mandate of five years, the President of the Commission announces their political priorities, which may be adjusted or refined on a yearly basis, as can be seen in the annual State of the Union address before the Parliament. The College of Commissioners furthermore adopts an annual work programme intended to put into practice the political priorities of the Commission. The implementation of this work programme, which does not exclude additional ad hoc initiatives, requires intense technical work, as well as consultations with the parties concerned.[282] Such programming is developed in a context of dialogue with the EU's co-legislators.[283]

Once the draft legislative act receives the support of the College of Commissioners, it is forwarded to the institutions and other entities which are described in its legal basis as being involved in the legislative procedure. For instance, the proposal for a Directive on minimum wages, envisaged for adoption on the basis of Article 153(2) and Article 153(1)(b) TFEU, was sent to the co-legislators – the Parliament and the Council – as well as to the Economic and Social Committee, the Committee of the Regions acting in an advisory capacity, and national parliaments.[284]

The power of initiative of the Commission results in this institution having a number of important powers even *after* the legislative procedure has been initiated. These powers enable the Commission to continue to drive the legislative process forward in the early stages of the legislative procedure. First, throughout the procedure, the Commission seeks to steer the proposal

276 Art. 17(2) TEU; Arts. 289(4), 294(2) TFEU.

277 The EU Treaties may allow the initiative to be taken by a group of Member States, the Parliament, upon a recommendation from the Central Bank or a request from the Court of Justice, or the European Investment Bank; Art. 289(4) TFEU. When that is the case, with the exception of initiatives from the Parliament, the specific role of the Commission during the ordinary legislative procedure is slightly adjusted; see Art. 294(15) TFEU.

278 The Commission may also be requested to act by the Parliament (Art. 225 TFEU) or the Council (Art. 241 TFEU), or invited to act by a European Citizens' Initiative (Art. 11(4) TEU). These invitations are not legally binding, but the Commission ought to state reasons if it does not follow up.

279 See Chapter 2, Section 2.3.3.2.

280 Art. 17(1) TEU.

281 See also Chapter 2, Section 2.3.5.7.

282 See also Art. 11(3) TEU; Protocol 2, Art. 2; 'Interinstitutional Agreement between the European Parliament, the Council of the European Union and the European Commission on Better Law-Making', OJ L 123, 12.5.2016, p. 1, point 9.

283 'Interinstitutional Agreement between the European Parliament, the Council of the European Union and the European Commission on Better Law-Making', OJ L 123, 12.5.2016, p. 1, points 4–11; see also Interinstitutional Agreements, 'Framework Agreement on Relations between the European Parliament and the European Commission', OJ L 304, 20.11.2010, p. 47 (as amended 2018).

284 Commission, 'Proposal for a Directive on Adequate Minimum Wages in the European Union', COM(2020) 682 final, 28.10.2020.

forward and facilitate compromises.[285] Second, the Commission may alter its proposal until the institutions acting as legislators have formally acted.[286] This includes a power to withdraw the proposal, for instance if the proposal is not relevant any more, or if it is clear that the institutions with the power to adopt the act show that they may amend the proposal in a way that would be contrary to the objectives the Commission initially had in mind.[287] Third, the Council may only amend the Commission's proposal if it is acting unanimously.[288] Similarly, in the specific context of the ordinary legislative procedure, if the proposal is considered by the Council a second time (second reading) and the Council acts in relation to amendments proposed by the Parliament on which the Commission issued a negative opinion, the Council must act unanimously.[289] The Council, in any case, ought to remain within the scope of the initial proposal.[290]

The power of initiative of the Commission ties into the idea of a 'legislative cycle'.[291] This refers to an iterative process where the focus is not only on the preparation of a draft legislative act and subsequent support through the legislative process, but also subsequent reflection on the need to reform existing legislation. In recent years, attention has been drawn to the need for simplicity, clarity and consistency in the EU's legislative output, as well as transparency of the legislative process. For that purpose, the three key institutional partners in the legislative procedure, the Commission, Parliament and Council, have agreed on a Better Law-Making Agenda.

This Agenda takes the form of an interinstitutional agreement which formalises some of the key commitments of each institution to improve the legislative process and output of the EU.[292] Ahead of the proposal for a legislative act, much emphasis is placed on impact assessments to shed light on the potential economic, environmental and social aspects of *envisaged* (legislative) action, using both qualitative and quantitative analyses.[293] These assessments may touch upon compliance with principles such as subsidiarity, proportionality or fundamental rights, depending on the policy area. Attention is also paid to evaluating legislative acts *after* their adoption.[294] More specifically, the Commission has established a regulatory fitness and performance programme (REFIT), which is intended to result in simplifying legislation, avoid overregulation and reduce administrative burdens. The extent to which the objectives of the Better Law-Making Agenda are achieved or not may be open to debate,[295] but the Agenda illustrates the concern of the institutions to reflect on how to improve law-making at EU level.

[285] E.g. Art. 294(11) TFEU.

[286] Both the Parliament and the Council at first reading in the context of the ordinary legislative procedure, and the Council in most special legislative procedures; Art. 293(2) TFEU.

[287] The decision to withdraw is amenable to judicial review. The Commission's withdrawal is subject to compliance with the principles of conferral and institutional balance, thus requiring the Commission to motivate its choice, and to the principle of sincere cooperation relating, in particular, to the timing of the withdrawal; C-409/13, *Council* v. *Commission (Macro-financial assistance)*, paras. 74–78, 97–104.

[288] Unless the procedure has gone beyond a second reading in the ordinary legislative procedure or if the procedure relates to certain aspects of EU financial law; Art. 293(1) TFEU.

[289] Art. 294(9) TFEU. [290] E.g. C-408/95, *Eurotunnel and others* v. *Seafrance*, EU:C:1997:532, paras. 38–39.

[291] See the particularly helpful schematic overview of the cycle from within the Commission: President of the Commission, Working Methods of the European Commission, P(2019) 2, 1.12.2019, p. 10.

[292] 'Interinstitutional Agreement between the European Parliament, the Council of the European Union and the European Commission on Better Law-Making', OJ L 123, 12.5.2016, p. 1.

[293] Ibid., points 12–18. [294] Ibid., points 20–24.

[295] For a critical assessment of the added value of these processes, see S. Garben, 'A Taste of Its Own Medicine: Assessing the Impact of the EU Better Regulation Agenda', *European Law Journal*, 26 (2020), pp. 83–103.

Ordinary Legislative Procedure

The ordinary legislative procedure gives structure to some of the most heated political debates for the adoption of key EU acts. This procedure used to be called the co-decision procedure, because the Council can only adopt texts in agreement with the Parliament, and vice versa. While this remains the main feature of this procedure, it is now called the 'ordinary' legislative procedure, because it is intended to be the most standard way of adopting EU legislative acts. The procedure is described in Article 294 TFEU.

Main Stages

The main features of the procedure are sketched out in Figure 3.5 and consist of a back and forth between the Parliament and the Council in order to reach a joint agreement.[296] In essence, the procedure is split into three main stages after the Commission has circulated its proposals. In stage 1, each of the co-legislators examines the text and adopts a formal position. This is the Parliament to start with, and then the Council, on the basis of the Parliament's position. During this so-called 'first reading',[297] each of the two institutions may either: (1) not move forward on the text, in which case the procedure stagnates and may lead to the Commission withdrawing the proposal; (2) reject the proposal; (3) agree on the text of the (amended) draft legislative act, in which case the act is then adopted; or (4) wish to further discuss the content of the proposal. If the Council does not approve the Parliament's position at first reading but is willing to discuss further, it will adopt its own position at first reading, state its reasons and communicate all of this to the Parliament.

The latter scenario paves the way for stage 2, in which first the Parliament and then the Council will each examine the text again. During this so-called 'second reading',[298] each of the two institutions may agree – thus leading to the adoption of the act: The Parliament may agree explicitly or implicitly[299] with the Council's position at first reading; or the Parliament may suggest further amendments subsequently approved by the Council at the second reading.[300] Yet it is possible for the Parliament to reject the Council's position at first reading altogether, in which case the act is not adopted and the procedure ends.[301] It is also possible for the Council not to approve all the amendments suggested by the Parliament in its position at the second reading.

The latter scenario paves the way for stage 3. An equal number of representatives of the Parliament and the Council are convened to seek to reach an agreement on a joint text on the basis of the respective positions of these institutions at second reading. This Conciliation Committee[302] may either fail to reach an agreement, in which case the act is deemed not to have been adopted, or actually succeed in approving a joint text. If agreement is reached within the Conciliation Committee, the Parliament and the Council are invited to formally adopt the act negotiated by their representatives in what is then a 'third reading'.[303] If they fail to support the agreement reached in the Conciliation Committee, the act is deemed not to have been adopted.

[296] Note the existence of a limited number of legal bases enabling reliance on so-called 'emergency brakes' to slow down the legislative process and discussion at European Council level; see Chapter 2, Section 2.3.4.4, Qualified Majority Voting.

[297] Art. 294(3–6) TFEU. [298] Art. 294(7–9) TFEU.

[299] Art. 294(7)(a) TFEU: if the Parliament does not take a decision at its second reading, the act is deemed to be adopted.

[300] Art. 294(7)(a) and (8)(a) TFEU. [301] Art. 294(7)(b) TFEU. [302] Art. 294(10–12) TFEU.

[303] Art. 294(13–14) TFEU.

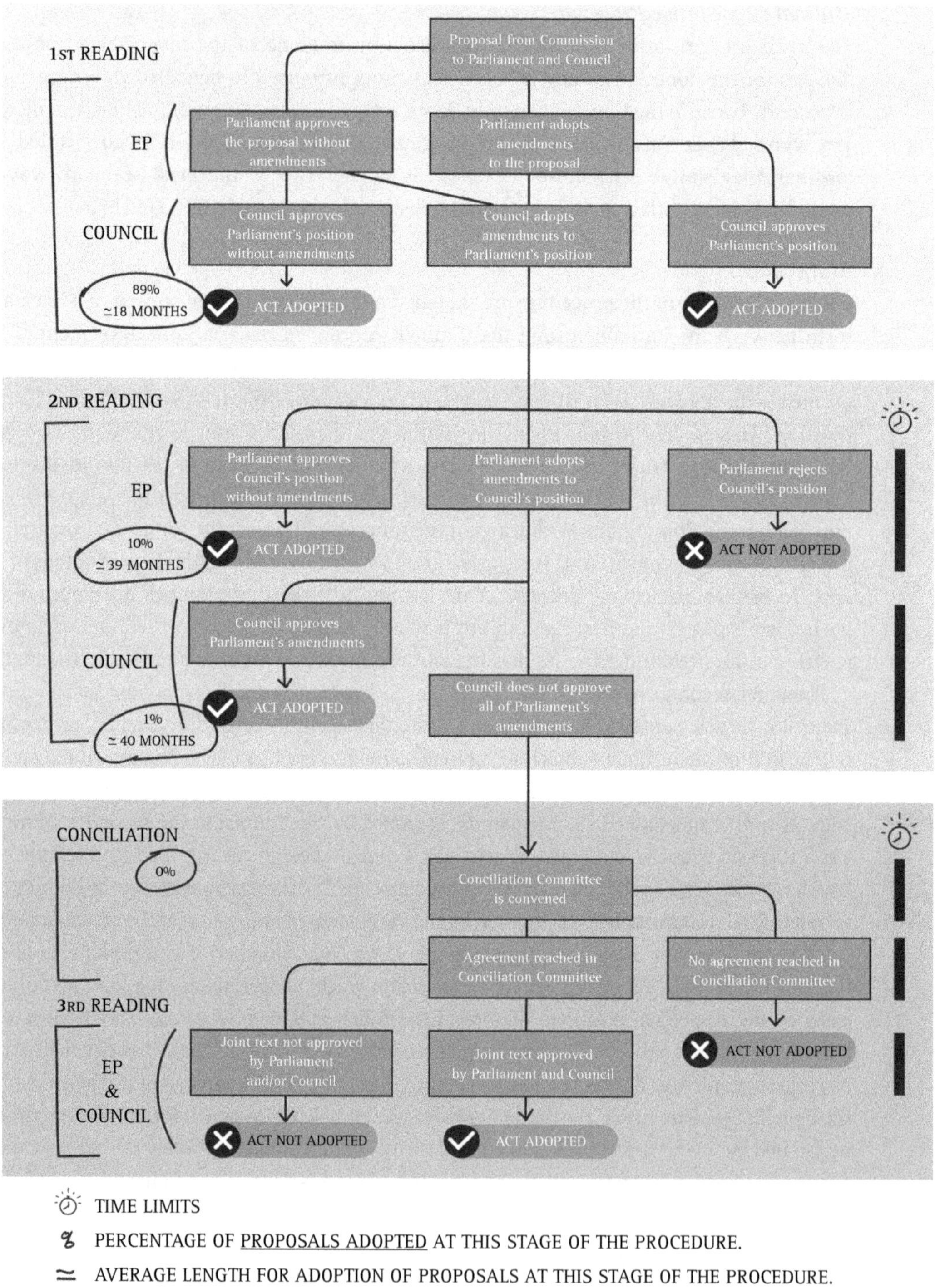

Figure 3.5 The main stages of the ordinary legislative procedure[304]

[304] This scheme is inspired from the one available on the Parliament's website europarl.europa.eu/olp and relies on data provided in Parliament, 'Activity Report: Developments and Trends of the Ordinary Legislative Procedure', 1.7.2014–1.1.2019.

Noticeable Features

This brief overview of the main stages of the procedure must be complemented by four observations. The first relates to the role of the Commission. Not only does it initiate the legislative process by submitting a proposal, it also contributes to shaping the negotiations throughout the process. As noted already, at any time up to the end of the first reading, it may alter (or withdraw) the proposal. It also issues an opinion on the Council's position if there is no agreement with the Parliament at first reading.[305] And again, it may be called upon to issue an opinion on the Parliament's amendments at second reading if there is continued disagreement between the Parliament and Council.[306] As well as those measures, the Commission shall take part in the proceedings of the Conciliation Committee, to help reconcile the positions of Parliament and Council where there is a failure to reach an agreement at second reading.[307] Some of the Commission's prerogatives are protected by means of adjustments to voting arrangements in the Council, as will now be discussed. The Commission thus plays a prominent role in steering as well as shaping the negotiation process.

The second observation relates to voting arrangements. Unless otherwise specified, the Parliament decides by a majority of the votes cast and the Council by qualified majority voting.[308] Yet the general rule is accommodated in a number of settings, illustrating the institutional implications of the process. On the one hand, the Commission's influence on the draft legislative act results in the Council having to act by unanimity both when wishing to depart from the Commission's proposal during the Council's first reading, and when acting on the Parliament's amendments at second reading if they have received a negative opinion from the Commission.[309] On the other hand, at the second reading it is easier for the Parliament to agree with the Council than to depart from the Council's position: if the Parliament disagrees with the Council's position at first reading, it must act by a majority of its component members both to reject the Council's proposal (which marks the failure of the procedure) or to propose amendments.[310]

The third observation concerns the time frame within which the institutions involved operate. As Figure 3.5 illustrates, the pressure increases as the draft legislative acts makes its way through the legislative process. While there is no obligation to adopt or negotiate at the first stage,[311] the clock starts ticking once the willingness of the Parliament and Council to negotiate is confirmed and there is no agreement at first reading. In other words: there are no time limits for the first reading; each institution ought to act within three months for the second reading;[312] a Conciliation Committee ought to be convened within six weeks after the second reading by the Council, and must come to a decision within another period of six weeks;[313] and finally, the Parliament and Council must each come to a decision

[305] Art. 294(6) TFEU. [306] Art. 294(7)(c) TFEU. [307] Art. 294(11) TFEU.

[308] Art. 231, para. 1 TFEU; Art. 16(3) TEU. The same rules apply within the Conciliation Committee.

[309] Arts. 293(1), 294(9) TFEU. [310] Art. 294(7)(b) and (c) TFEU.

[311] Save where otherwise specified in the EU Treaties. [312] Art. 294(7) and (8), first sentences TFEU.

[313] Art. 294(8)(b) and (12) TFEU.

within six weeks for the third reading.[314] These time limits of three months and six weeks may each be extended by up to one month and two weeks respectively, upon the initiative of the Parliament or Council.[315]

Finally, and importantly, the dynamics of the ordinary legislative procedure are strongly marked by the 'established practice' of informal negotiations between the three institutions at all stages of the procedure.[316] These trilogues, as they are commonly referred to, contribute to the successful adoption of the vast majority of legislative acts at first reading (see circled statistics in Figure 3.5). Representatives of the three institutions[317] are in regular contact to seek a compromise on the draft text before the Parliament and the Council each adopt their formal positions at first (or second) reading. The Commission acts as a facilitator and is expected to ensure a fair balance in the relationship between the Parliament and the Council.[318] In practice, the initial negotiating position for the Parliament usually takes the form of a 'legislative report' or 'legislative resolution', while for the Council it takes the form of a 'general approach'. Any positive outcome of trilateral negotiations, which comes in the form of a 'provisional agreement', needs to be supported by each institution adopting their formal positions in accordance with the legal requirements spelt out previously for the act to be adopted.

While the practice has the merit of facilitating the adoption of EU legislative acts, it has fervent detractors. Critics point primarily to the lack of transparency of the process.[319] The practice makes it difficult, for instance, to monitor the negotiation process and thus to know who suggests and decides on what. One of the ways for the EU institutions to (at least partially)[320] address the criticism has been to allow greater access to the joint document which forms the basis of the negotiations. It shows, in each of its four columns, the respective position of the Parliament and the Council when compared to the Commission proposal, as well as the compromise text.[321]

[314] Art. 294(13) TFEU. [315] Art. 294(14) TFEU.

[316] The importance of these trilateral negotiations is acknowledged: 'Interinstitutional Agreement between the European Parliament, the Council of the European Union and the European Commission on Better Law-Making', OJ L 123, 12.5.2016, p. 1, points 32–40; see also, for instance, T-540/15, *De Capitani*, EU: T:2018:167, paras. 70–71.

[317] Usually, these are civil servants from the Directorate-General in charge at the Commission, members of the parliamentary committee in charge at the Parliament (including the rapporteur), and members of the working party or Coreper at the Council (including representatives from the Presidency).

[318] Parliament, Council and Commission, 'Joint Declaration on Practical Arrangements for the Co-decision Procedure (Article 251 of the EC Treaty)', OJ C 145, 30.6.2007, p. 5, para. 13.

[319] See further European Ombudsman, Decision setting out proposals following her strategic inquiry concerning the transparency of Trilogues, Decision in case OI/8/2015/JAS; see also Chapter 2, Sections 2.2.2 and 2.3.4.4, Meetings, Votes and Transparency.

[320] Read further, Curtin and Leino, 'In Search of Transparency for EU Law-Making'; contrast with J. Bauerschmidt, 'The Basic Principles of the European Union's Ordinary Legislative Procedure', *ERA Forum*, 22 (2021), pp. 224–225; see also Chapter 2, Section 2.3.4.4, Meetings, Votes and Transparency.

[321] See Code of Conduct for negotiating in the context of the ordinary legislative procedure, as approved by the Conference of Presidents of the Parliament on 28.9.2017, point 3; see further case T-540/15, *De Capitani*, EU:T:2018:167, para. 84, where the General Court asserts that there is no general presumption of non-disclosure that can be upheld in relation to the fourth column of trilogue tables concerning an ongoing legislative procedure.

Special Legislative Procedures

The legislative procedure described so far is meant to illustrate the 'ordinary' state of the EU legislative process, yet exceptions are not uncommon. Several legal bases require the use of alternative, also called 'special', legislative procedures. Although the resulting legal act is also a legislative act normally adopted on a proposal from the Commission, it will be the outcome of a less balanced interaction between the Parliament and the Council. Two main scenarios can be distinguished.

Most often, the act is adopted by the Council with the participation of the Parliament. In other words, these procedures are used in areas of EU law where the Member States want to retain stronger control over the decision-making process at EU level. The Parliament may either have a right of veto when its 'consent' is necessary for the adoption of the act, or may have an advisory role when it ought to be 'consulted'. The 'consent procedure'[322] is simpler than the ordinary legislative procedure, as the Parliament only has a choice between accepting or refusing to support the instrument, and thus has much less say on the substance of the final text.[323] In contrast, in the 'consultation procedure',[324] the Council will not be bound by the opinion of the Parliament. Yet again, it is an essential procedural requirement for the Council to consult, and both the Parliament and the Council ought to comply with the principle of sincere cooperation in this context.[325]

In a second, and much less common set of cases, the Parliament is placed in the driving seat and the Council only participates through consent.[326]

Non-legislative Acts of Secondary Law

A number of ad hoc legal bases provide for the adoption of acts on the basis of the EU Treaties, but without mentioning the 'legislative' nature of the procedure.[327] There are no general rules on this matter, so that one ought to look at each legal basis individually. A noticeable example is Article 352(1) TFEU, known as the flexibility clause,[328] which requires the Council (acting by unanimity) to act on a proposal from the Commission with the consent of the Parliament (acting by a majority of the votes cast).

[322] An example may be found in Art. 19(1) TFEU for the adoption of legislation to combat discrimination on grounds of gender (other than in employment), racial or ethnic origin, religion or belief, disability, age or sexual orientation.

[323] Yet in the preliminary stages of the procedure, it can make its concerns known and put pressure on the Council to influence the final text by threatening not to grant consent.

[324] An example may be found in Art. 153(2), subpara. 4 TFEU for the adoption of legislation on social security and social protection of workers.

[325] If the duty to consult is disregarded, the act adopted is void; Case 138/79, *Roquette Frères*, EU:C:1980:249, para. 33. The Council must consult again if the draft legislative act has undergone substantial changes after the Parliament was consulted. It must also do its best to obtain an opinion in due time, wait for a reasonable time for such an opinion before adopting its final position, and formally refer to the opinion. Conversely, the Parliament may not unduly delay its opinion; C-65/93, *Parliament* v. *Council (Generalised tariff preferences)*, EU:C:1995:91, paras. 26–28.

[326] E.g. Art. 226, para. 3 TFEU on the exercise by the Parliament of its right of inquiry.

[327] On the practical implications of the distinction between legislative and non-legislative acts of secondary law, see Chapter 3, Section 3.5.3.2, Secondary Law.

[328] See Chapter 3, Section 3.2.3.3.

3.6.1.2 Acts of Tertiary Law

As explained already, an act of secondary law may constitute a 'parent act' (also known as a 'basic act') including legal bases for the adoption of a third layer of acts. Here again, each legal basis provides the specific procedural arrangements for decision-making. In the aftermath of the Treaty of Lisbon, three main scenarios to be chosen from by the EU institution(s) drafting the parent act can be distinguished, only the first two of which are explicitly foreseen in the EU Treaties.

Delegated Acts within the Meaning of Art. 290 TFEU

The first category of tertiary acts is set out in Article 290 TFEU. These 'delegated acts' result from a limited form of delegation of legislative power,[329] which explains the key features of the procedural safeguards for their adoption. The latter are indeed in the hands of the institutions responsible for adopting legislative acts.

The possibility to adopt delegated acts is entrusted to the Commission, by the legislative act itself, which ought to identify explicitly the 'objectives, content, scope and duration of the delegation of power'.[330] The parent act must also explicitly lay down the conditions of delegation. The TFEU identifies a non-exhaustive list of control mechanisms from which the EU institutions shaping the parent act may choose, or which they may combine: the Parliament (acting by a majority of its component members) or the Council (by qualified majority) may be empowered to revoke the delegation; and/or these institutions may (with the same voting arrangements) be empowered to object within a specific time frame to the entry into force of a delegated act.[331] The three institutions have developed a common understanding of how to shape the powers of the Commission to adopt delegated acts, and have agreed to refer as far as possible to pre-drafted standard clauses to serve as a legal basis in the parent act.[332] Emphasis is placed on transparency and consultation with experts and stakeholders on the part of the Commission.[333]

For example, the power of the Commission to update the list of transmissible animal diseases which are subject to specific rules for prevention and control in an annex to the Animal Health Law Regulation[334] are set for a period of five years, with possible tacit extension in the absence of opposition from the Parliament and Council. The power to adopt delegated acts requires the Commission to consult with experts (including from the Member States) and may be revoked *at any time* by the Parliament or Council. Any delegated act must be notified to these institutions and shall only enter into force if they do not object within two months or notify the Commission that they will not object.

Implementing Acts within the Meaning of Art. 291 TFEU

The second category of acts of tertiary law is set out in Article 291 TFEU. The EU legislator, departing from the principle by which the Member States are responsible for implementing

[329] See Chapter 3, Section 3.5.3.2, Tertiary Law. [330] Art. 290(1), subpara. 2 TFEU. [331] Art. 290(2) TFEU.

[332] 'Interinstitutional Agreement between the European Parliament, the Council of the European Union and the European Commission on Better Law-Making', OJ L 123, 12.5.2016, p. 1, Annex and Appendix.

[333] Ibid., point 28 and Annex, point II.

[334] 'Regulation (EU) 2016/429 of the European Parliament and of the Council of 9 March 2016 on Transmissible Animal Diseases and Amending and Repealing Certain Acts in the Area of Animal Health' (Animal Health Law, last modified 2020), OJ L 84, 31.3.2016, p. 1, Art. 5(2) and (4) read in conjunction with Art. 264.

EU law, shall empower the Commission (or, in duly justified specific cases and in the cases provided for in Articles 24 and 26 TEU on the CFSP, the Council)[335] to adopt implementing measures, where necessary, to ensure the uniformity of the conditions for implementing legally binding Union acts. Although the related procedures often create fora for highly technical discussions on the implementation of EU legislation, the latter shall not be equated with non-sensitive materials. For instance, it is through the Commission implementing decisions that the authorisation for the placing on the market of products containing certain genetically modified maize is regularly renewed, as is often hotly debated.[336]

These 'implementing acts' that are normally adopted by the Commission provide details in relation to the content of an act of secondary law, in order to ensure that the latter is implemented uniformly in all Member States.[337] Precisely because the implementing powers are exercised by EU institutions rather than Member States themselves by way of exception, the related mechanisms of control are primarily in the hands of the Member States.

Regulation 182/2011 provides guidance on how to adopt implementing acts.[338] It was adopted shortly after the entry into force of the Treaty of Lisbon to establish the rules and general principles concerning mechanisms for control by Member States of the Commission's exercise of implementing powers.[339] These mechanisms grant varying degrees of control to *committees* composed of representatives of the Member States (chaired by a representative of the Commission)[340] over the Commission. The involvement of these committees is the reason why the process is often referred to as 'comitology'.

By virtue of this Regulation, the EU institutions, when drafting the parent act (also known as the basic act), choose between two procedures. The 'examination procedure' is to be used for the adoption of implementing acts in a set of cases deemed to be of particular importance,[341] including for the adoption of implementing acts of general scope or specific policies with important implications, such as the common agricultural and fisheries policies or the common commercial policy. In this context, the committee composed of representatives of the Member State that must be involved (acting by qualified majority voting)[342]

[335] If exception is being made to the rule that it is the Commission that is responsible for exercising that power, the procedural details for the adoption of the implementing act by the Council vary, depending on the choices made in the parent act.

[336] The Parliament, for instance, regularly uses its power of scrutiny to express disagreement, e.g. Parliament resolution of 7.7.2021, finding that the draft implementing act exceeds the implementing powers of the Commission.

[337] See Chapter 3, Section 3.5.3.2, Tertiary Law.

[338] 'Regulation (EU) No. 182/2011 of the European Parliament and of the Council of 16 February 2011 Laying Down the Rules and General Principles Concerning Mechanisms for Control by Member States of the Commission's Exercise of Implementing Powers', OJ L 55, 28.2.2011, p. 13.

[339] Art. 291(3) TFEU.

[340] The chair shall not take part in the committee vote ('Regulation (EU) No. 182/2011 of the European Parliament and of the Council of 16 February 2011 Laying Down the Rules and General Principles Concerning Mechanisms for Control by Member States of the Commission's Exercise of Implementing Powers', OJ L 55, 28.2.2011, Art. 3(2)). Each committee shall adopt its own rules of procedure on the basis of the Standard rules of procedures for committees (OJ C 206, 12.7.2011, p. 11), drawn up by the Commission following consultation with Member States.

[341] 'Regulation (EU) No. 182/2011 of the European Parliament and of the Council of 16 February 2011 Laying Down the Rules and General Principles Concerning Mechanisms for Control by Member States of the Commission's Exercise of Implementing Powers', OJ L 55, 28.2.2011, Art. 2(2).

[342] As laid down in Art. 16(4) TEU and Art. 238(3) TFEU.

may issue a positive opinion on the Commission draft implementing act, and the act 'shall' be adopted.[343] The committee may also issue no opinion, in which case the Commission may, in principle, adopt the act.[344] It may finally issue a negative opinion, in which case the Commission 'shall not' adopt the act.[345] In the latter scenario, the Commission representative chairing the committee may amend the draft and resubmit, or submit to an appeal committee (also composed of representatives of the Member States and chaired by the Commission).[346]

In contrast, the 'advisory procedure' is in principle used in all cases not listed as warranting reliance on the examination procedure: it is thus the backup option.[347] The Commission adopts the implementing act, taking the 'utmost account of the conclusions drawn from the discussions within the committee [composed of representatives of the Member States] and of the opinion delivered'.[348] The Commission is not bound by this advice. In other words, the degree of control by the Member States is significantly less than in the examination procedure.

The Parliament and the Council always receive key information on proceedings in committees.[349] The Parliament and the Council also retain a power of scrutiny for the adoption by the Commission of acts implementing provisions of legislation adopted through the ordinary legislative procedure. These two institutions that are responsible for adopting jointly the said legislative acts may at any time indicate that a draft implementing act exceeds, in their view, the implementing powers set out in the parent act.[350] The Commission has a subsequent duty to review its draft and to inform both institutions of the outcome of its reflection, but it is not bound by their positions.[351]

Other Acts of Tertiary Law

The procedures examined previously and set out in the EU Treaties do not provide an exhaustive lists of acts of tertiary law and procedures for their adoption.[352] Institutional practice, supported and framed by the case law of the Court of Justice of the European

343 See statement by the Parliament, the Council and the Commission in the Annex to 'Regulation (EU) No. 182/2011 of the European Parliament and of the Council of 16 February 2011 Laying Down the Rules and General Principles Concerning Mechanisms for Control by Member States of the Commission's Exercise of Implementing Powers', OJ L 55, 28.2.2011, nuancing the obligation.

344 Ibid., Art. 5(4). Specific provisions therein further set out the procedure to follow in case the committee does not issue an opinion.

345 Ibid., Art. 5.

346 'Rules of Procedure for the Appeal Committee (Regulation (EU) No. 182/2011): Adopted by the Appeal Committee on 29 March 2011', OJ C 183, 24.6.2011, p. 13, Art. 5. Members of the appeal committee (also deciding by qualified majority) may suggest amendments to the draft; the purpose being to try to find a solution commanding the widest support within the appeal committee. If the opinion of the appeal committee is positive, the implementing act shall be adopted; if the opinion is not issued, the act in principle may be adopted; if the opinion is negative, the Commission shall not adopt the act; Regulation (EU) No. 182/2011 of the European Parliament and of the Council of 16 February 2011 Laying Down the Rules and General Principles Concerning Mechanisms for Control by Member States of the Commission's Exercise of Implementing Powers', OJ L 55, 28.2.2011, Art. 6.

347 Ibid., Art. 2(3); although exceptions may be made, in duly justified cases, to use the advisory procedure, even if the examination procedure would be applicable in principle.

348 Ibid., Art. 4. The committee does not have to take a vote, but if it does, the opinion shall be delivered by a simple majority of its component members.

349 Ibid., Art. 11(3–4). 350 Ibid., Art. 11.

351 Any remaining disagreement may be brought to the attention of the Court of Justice of the European Union in the context of an annulment action; see Chapter 4, Section 4.3.1.1.

352 See Chapter 3, Section 3.5.3.2, Tertiary Law.

Union, enables EU institutions to delegate some of their powers to actors that are not EU institutions – in contrast with what is provided for in Articles 290 and 291 TFEU discussed so far. Once again though, the decision to delegate belongs to the EU institutions drafting the act that will become the parent act. EU agencies, in particular, benefit increasingly from such delegation.

The substantive limits to such delegation have already been examined in this Chapter.[353] It suffices here to recall that a delegation of power to a public body, such as an EU agency, may enable the delegated entity to exercise a degree of decision-making power and to adopt, in strictly circumscribed circumstances, measures of general application. What matters is that the delegation is 'precisely delineated and amenable to judicial review in the light of the objectives established by the delegating authority'.[354]

In procedural terms, the conditions for the adoption of this open-ended category of acts will be defined by the parent act. There is no template for that purpose. What may be observed, however, are efforts to bring coherence to the design of EU agencies, namely their decision-making and accountability rules, as was examined in Chapter 2, Section 2.4.2. The design of decentralised agencies, in particular, brings together a limited number of persons appointed by EU institutions (often from the Commission) with a large number of persons appointed by the Member States. Furthermore, agencies are accountable to EU institutions and their acts may be reviewed by the Court of Justice of the European Union.

3.6.1.3 Institutional Cooperation, Transparency and Publication

Once the act has been adopted by the institution(s) in charge, it must be signed by the President of the said institution(s) and published in the Official Journal of the European Union.[355] The act enters into force on the date specified in it or, if there is no date, on the twentieth day following publication.[356] Subject to exceptions for acts addressed to specific entities,[357] the same holds true for legislative as well as non-legislative acts (whether they are acts of secondary or tertiary law) adopted in the form of regulations, directives or decisions.[358]

It may be recalled here that the Official Journal is available online and for free in all twenty-four official languages of the EU.[359] The related website provides an ever-growing amount of information on EU acts of secondary as well as tertiary law.[360] The timing of the various stages of the decision-making process prior to adoption of the act can be identified, as well as the main positions of relevant EU organs.[361] Similarly, one may track whether an act has been subsequently amended or subject to judicial interpretation by the Court of

353 See Chapter 3, Section 3.2.3.4.

354 C-270/12, *UK* v. *Parliament and Council (Short Selling)*, EU:C:2014:18, paras. 44–55.

355 Art. 297(1) TFEU.

356 Note that directives addressed to Member States enable them to benefit from a 'transposition period' after their entry into force; see Chapter 3, Section 3.5.3.2, Nature of EU Internal Acts.

357 These shall be notified to the addressee and take effect upon such notification.

358 Art. 297(2) TFEU.

359 See eur-lex.europa.eu; see also Chapter 2, Section 2.2.2.

360 Other useful online tools to monitor EU decision-making processes are the Parliament's legislative train, europarl.europa.eu/legislative-train, and legislative observatory, europarl.europa.eu/oeil.

361 In order to do so, one only has to enter the details of a Commission proposal or final act in the search box; once on the page showing the document, click on 'procedure'.

Justice of the European Union, and access information on the main national transposition measures communicated by Member States when relevant.[362]

Throughout the processes described previously, EU organs ought to comply with higher-ranking norms of EU law, which include the principles of conferral, institutional balance and sincere cooperation.[363] More specifically, the Parliament, the Council and the Commission shall consult each other and make arrangements for their cooperation in the form of interinstitutional agreements which may be of a binding nature.[364] This has indeed resulted in the adoption of agreements such as the above-mentioned one on Better Law-Making between the three institutions, or that on relations between Parliament and Commission.[365]

Attention is devoted to improving the flow of information between EU organs as well as transparency, to enable engagement by stakeholders and to know which stakeholders are engaging with EU organs. It may be recalled that the Parliament shall meet in public, as shall the Council when considering and voting on a draft legislative act.[366] As noted previously in relation to trilogues, which are an informal – yet currently inherent – part of the ordinary legislative procedure, much attention continues to be devoted to addressing the limits of transparency in the EU legislative process.[367] The Parliament has revised its rules of procedures to enhance transparency and political accountability,[368] the Council has committed to enhance access to key preliminary documents,[369] and the President of the Commission has committed to working towards more transparency through the legislative process.[370]

Beyond the legislative process, the three institutions also reached an agreement on a mandatory register to enhance transparency concerning interested representatives and awareness of their potential influence.[371] There is now also a joint functional register including both delegated and implementing acts to enhance 'transparency, facilitate planning and enable traceability' in the lifecycle of these acts.[372] Furthermore, the rules on public access to documents also apply to the committees involved in the adoption of Commission implementing acts within the meaning of Article 291 TFEU;[373] the

[362] Similarly, click on 'document information', and so on. [363] See Chapter 3, Section 3.2.1.

[364] Art. 295 TFEU.

[365] 'Framework Agreement on Relations between the European Parliament and the European Commission', OJ L 304, 20.11.2010, p. 47 (as amended 17.2.2018). Reflecting on the legal effects of the interinstitutional agreement on Better Law-Making, see Opinion of Advocate General Sharpston, C-482/17, *Czech Republic* v. *Parliament and Council*, EU:C:2019:321, para. 93 *et seq.*

[366] Art. 15(2) and (3) TEU.

[367] See, for instance, European Ombudsman, Recommendation on the Transparency of the Council legislative process, case OI/2/2017/TE.

[368] E.g. Parliament, 'Rules of Procedure', Rule 74 on the conduct of negotiations (in particular, in the context of trilogues).

[369] Presidency/General Secretariat of the Council, Strengthening legislative transparency, Brussels, 9.7.2020.

[370] von der Leyen, *Political Guidelines for the Next European Commission 2019–2024*.

[371] 'Interinstitutional Agreement of 20 May 2021 between the European Parliament, the Council of the European Union and the European Commission on a Mandatory Transparency Register', OJ L 207, 11.6.2021, p. 1.

[372] 'Interinstitutional Agreement between the European Parliament, the Council of the European Union and the European Commission on Better Law-Making', OJ L 123, 12.5.2016, p. 1, point 29; see webgate.ec.europa.eu/regdel.

[373] Regulation (EU) No. 182/2011 of the European Parliament and of the Council of 16 February 2011 Laying Down the Rules and General Principles Concerning Mechanisms for Control by Member States of the Commission's Exercise of Implementing Powers', OJ L 55, 28.2.2011, Art. 9(2).

Commission also keeps a register of committee proceedings.[374] While these recent efforts remain to be evaluated and may not be perfect, there is little doubt that EU institutions are devoting increasing attention to enhancing transparency at EU level.

3.6.2 External Action

3.6.2.1 (Ordinary) Procedure for the Adoption of International Agreements

The procedure for the adoption of international agreements between the EU and third countries or international organisations gives a decisive role to the Council (composed of representatives of the Member States), an important agency role to the Commission, and increasing weight to the Parliament.[375] Unless otherwise specified in the EU Treaties,[376] the ordinary procedure for the negotiation and conclusion of international agreements is set out in Article 218 TFEU. This procedure also applies to the negotiation and conclusion of international agreements in the context of the CFSP.

The procedure is triggered by the Council. The latter acts on a recommendation from the Commission, or from the High Representative for Foreign Affairs and Security Policy 'where the agreement envisaged relates exclusively or principally to the common foreign and security policy'.[377] On this basis, the Council decides to open the negotiations. To that effect, the Council adopts negotiating instructions.[378] It decides, depending on the subject matter of the agreement envisaged, to nominate the EU negotiator (usually the Commission, or the High Representative for CFSP matters) or the negotiating team who will be the face of the EU during the negotiations (these are both the Commission and High Representative, where an agreement relates both to CFSP and non-CFSP matters without one being incidental to the other). In the latter case, the Council identifies the Commission or the High Representative as the head of the team. It is for the Commission or the High Representative to designate the specific individuals who will be in charge on the ground.

Negotiations that have been commenced are carried out between representatives of third countries or international organisations, on the one hand, and representatives of the EU designated for that purpose, on the other hand. This latter category of actors often develop informal contacts with experts from the Member States and regularly report to Council working groups themselves under the authority of Coreper and the Council itself. The Council may – or must, as in the case of trade negotiations – also designate a special committee for the negotiators to consult.[379] On the side of the EU, the negotiations thus

[374] Ibid., Art. 10.

[375] Specific provisions apply for the suspension of the application of an agreement, the establishment of the positions to be adopted on the EU's behalf by a body set up by agreement, as well as for the authorisation, at the time of concluding an agreement, of the negotiator to approve modifications to the agreement by simplified means; Art. 218(9) and (7) TFEU.

[376] Compare, for instance, the procedure set out for the negotiation of an agreement on the exchange rate of the euro in relation to the currencies of third states; Art. 219(1) TFEU.

[377] Art. 218(3) TFEU; there may also be joint proposals. See Arts. 22(2), 30(1) TEU.

[378] Art. 218(2) and (4) TFEU. The instructions are known as 'directives', but ought not to be confused with directives within the meaning of Art. 288 TFEU that result from decision-making procedures for the adoption of internal acts.

[379] Art. 218(4) TFEU; on the collaboration between the Commission and Council during the negotiation process, see further C-425/13, *Commission* v. *Council*, EU:C:2015:483. As regards trade agreements, see Art. 207(3) TFEU.

result in a regular back and forth between the Commission and the Council, until agreement is found on a draft.

The negotiator proposes to the Council the adoption of a decision authorising the signature of the agreement, and if necessary that it apply provisionally 'before entry into force'.[380] A recent example is the post-Brexit Trade and Cooperation Agreement that was concluded between the EU and the UK: it applied provisionally as of 1 January 2021, and entered into force later on 1 May 2021.[381] Provisional application is common in practice for certain types of international agreements, such as mixed agreements. This mechanism results in certain international agreements being applied before the Parliament has formally given its consent when empowered to do so, as we shall see subsequently, although the Commission and the Council ought then to ensure sincere cooperation with the Parliament.[382]

The negotiator also proposes to the Council, often in the same document as that regarding signature, the adoption of the decision that results in the conclusion of the agreement (and thus ratification by the EU). The decision to conclude is made by the Council. Yet since the Treaty of Lisbon, a vast majority of agreements have also required prior consent from the Parliament. This is so, in particular, regarding agreements with major institutional implications (such as association agreements[383] with third countries or accession to the ECHR), agreements with major budgetary implications, and agreements covering fields to which legislative procedures giving the Parliament a strong role apply for the adoption of acts in the same field internally – procedures requiring its consent or procedures where it is an equal player with the Council, as in the ordinary legislative procedure.[384] As was explained previously, the latter legislative procedure is now common and places the Parliament on an equal footing with the Council for the adoption of acts internally. To ensure a clearer parallel between internal and external decision-making procedures, the procedure applicable for the conclusion of international agreements thus increasingly often requires the consent of the Parliament, as in the field of trade for instance.[385] Where the consent of the Parliament is not specifically requested, it ought however to be consulted.[386] The Parliament's consent or opinion are not required for the conclusion of agreements relating exclusively or predominantly to the CFSP, where the Parliament plays a lesser role.[387]

The Council normally acts by qualified majority throughout the procedure. Exceptions exist, however, in settings with major institutional implications (such as association

[380] Art. 218(5) TFEU.
[381] 'Trade and Cooperation Agreement between the European Union and the European Atomic Energy Community, of the one part, and the United Kingdom of Great Britain and Northern Ireland, of the other part', OJ L 149, 30.4.2021, p. 10, Art. 783.
[382] Art. 13(2) TEU and Art. 218(10) TFEU. The Parliament may also make its position known and, for instance, call on other institutions not to (recommend to) provisionally apply the envisaged agreement.
[383] Association agreements create particularly close relations with third States; some of them even help with preparation for accession to the EU.
[384] See further Art. 218(6)(a) TFEU. The Parliament and Council may, in urgent situations, agree upon a time limit for consent.
[385] Art. 207 TFEU.
[386] Art. 218(6)(b) TFEU for standard external action. The Parliament must act within a time limit set by the Council and depending on the urgency of the matter. In the absence of an opinion within that time limit, the Council may act. See also Art. 218(10) TFEU that also applies to the CFSP; also Chapter 3, note 390.
[387] C-263/14, *Parliament* v. *Council (Pirates II)*, EU:C:2016:435, para. 55.

agreements with third countries or accession to the ECHR), and when the agreement covers a field for which unanimity is required for the adoption of acts in the same field internally;[388] as well as where specifically requested by provisions of the EU Treaties other than Article 218 TFEU.[389] To ensure sound collaboration with the Parliament, the latter must be kept 'immediately and fully informed at all the stages of the procedure'.[390] The Parliament itself, in response, may designate parliamentary committees entrusted with following up on specific sets of negotiations, such as the Committee on International Trade, which, in particular, monitors the process related to trade agreements.[391]

It may be recalled that, in order to limit tensions between international agreements (that will be binding on the EU under international law once they enter into force) and higher norms of EU law, Article 218(11) TFEU provides for an *ex ante* control mechanism. This enables the Court of Justice to issue an opinion on the matter, and prevents the entry into force of the envisaged agreement as such, in case incompatibilities are discovered.[392]

3.6.2.2 Acts in the Context of the CFSP

International agreements related to the CFSP are adopted through the standard procedure set out previously, and subject to specific arrangements mentioned thereupon.[393] The latter arrangements results in a less involved Commission in favour of the High Representative, an overall less involved Parliament,[394] and greater reliance on unanimity at the Council.

In contrast, procedures for the adoption of other acts of EU law in the CFSP field are clearly distinct. They continue to be tainted by a strong intergovernmental logic.[395] For the adoption of such acts, which are listed in Article 25 TEU, it all depends on the specific legal basis. Yet in general terms, decision-making processes are dominated by the European Council and the Council, usually acting by unanimity, with the High Representative putting the policy into effect and at times taking initiatives.[396] The Commission and Parliament are left with a lesser role.[397] This domain of EU law is also marked by the visible role of Member States – for instance, to make proposals to the Council.[398]

[388] See further Art. 218(8), subpara. 2 TFEU. Note that the decision concluding an agreement on accession to the ECHR will only enter into force after it has been approved by the Member States in accordance with their respective constitutional requirements.

[389] As in relation to certain types of trade agreements; see Art. 207(4) TFEU.

[390] Art. 218(10) TFEU. This includes settings in which the Parliament has no formal role in the final adoption of the international agreement because it is adopted on a legal basis related to the CFSP; C-658/11, *Parliament* v. *Council (Mauritius)*, EU:C:2014:2025, paras. 84–86.

[391] Parliament, 'Rules of Procedure', Annex VI, para. III.

[392] See Chapter 3, Section 3.5.3.1, Secondary Law in the Form of International Agreements. It may be recalled that the Court has limited jurisdiction in relation to the CFSP; see Chapter 4, Section 4.4.1.

[393] Art. 37 TEU and Art. 218 TFEU.

[394] As noted already, however, the Parliament must be kept informed; see C-658/11, *Parliament* v. *Council (Mauritius)*, EU:C:2014:2025, para. 86.

[395] See Art. 24 TEU.

[396] See, in particular, Arts. 24(1), subpara. 1, and 26, 31 TEU. Note that Art. 31, subpara. 2 TEU relates to 'constructive abstention': a Member State that abstains does not prevent adoption of an act requiring unanimous support, but the said State may 'qualify' its abstention to the effect that the measure adopted will be legally binding on the EU, but that State will not be obliged to apply it.

[397] See, for instance, Arts. 22(2), 30 TEU, on initiatives with or supported by the Commission; Art. 36 TEU, on interactions with the Parliament.

[398] Art. 30(1) TEU.

It may be recalled that the jurisdiction of the Court of Justice of the European Union with respect to the provisions relating to the CFSP is limited, yet the case law on the matter has been evolving fast. [399]

3.6.3 Financial Provisions

The procedures for the adoption of the rules that relate to EU finances stand out from what has been examined so far. The importance of the EU budget cannot be overestimated, it deals with much more than the financial needs of EU institutions and organs – it also supports EU policies overall.[400] The sensitivity of attracting resources at EU level and allocating these resources among various entities and interests, explains why the related decision-making processes are peculiar. Despite long-standing efforts to assert the important role of the Parliament in this field, the latter remains characterised, in practice, by a remarkably strong role for the Council or, actually, the European Council, and even the Member States in their sovereign capacities, as we shall see subsequently. While it would be beyond the scope of this book to set out the substantive rules of EU financial law,[401] the main features of decision-making in the field deserve attention, to shed light on their importance in shaping EU action.

3.6.3.1 Own Resources Decision

The EU finances the functioning of the organs and staff running it, as well as its policies, through its financial resources – funding which, until recently, originated from several main sources:[402] traditional own resources, such as customs, agricultural duties and a contribution calculated in relation to the value added tax collected in the Member States, as well as a uniform percentage levy on Member States' gross national income. This system of resources is the outcome of decades of negotiations at the highest level. Today, the details are further elaborated upon in a decision on the own resources of the EU (Own Resources Decision) which has been adopted in accordance with Article 311 TFEU.

Within this framework, it is for the Council acting (by unanimity) on a proposal from the Commission, and after consultation of the Parliament, to lay down the details of this system of own resources; it may thereby abolish or create new resources. The Own Resources Decision resulting from this special legislative procedure is peculiar, in that it shall not enter into force until it is approved by all the Member States, acting in accordance with their respective constitutional requirements. The combination of the requirements of unanimity at the Council, and of Member States' individual support before entry into force, makes the procedure more akin to

[399] Arts. 24(1), subpara. 2, and 275, para. 1 TFEU. On judicial review in the CFSP, see further Chapter 4, Section 4.4.1.

[400] Specific provisions apply for expenses related to the CFSP; Art. 41 TEU.

[401] See, for instance, European Union, *Public Finance*, 5th ed. (Publications Office of the European Union, 2014).

[402] Art. 311, para. 2 TFEU; for an overview of historical developments in that regard, see Chapter 1, Section 1.3, and see subsequently on more recent developments.

a reform of the EU Treaties[403] than to the procedures for making standard secondary law. The Council may further adopt related implementing measures.[404]

The current Own Resources Decision[405] serves as a good example of the high stakes of the related decision-making process. It was adopted in the midst of the COVID-19 crisis, with high-level political tensions ultimately addressed at the level of the European Council in December 2020.[406] The Decision was swiftly ratified by all the Member States and entered into force on 1 June 2021. It attracted much attention because it allows extraordinary and temporary additional means to address the consequences of the COVID-19 crisis, as well as to steer policy reforms in the coming years. For that purpose, the Commission is empowered to borrow up to EUR 750,000 million on capital markets on behalf of the EU.[407] Another novelty is the creation of a (permanent) own resource, added to the three identified earlier, and charged on non-recycled plastic packaging waste.[408]

3.6.3.2 Multiannual Financial Framework

Closely related to the Own Resources Decision, another EU act must be adopted to organise the EU's expenditure within the limits of the EU's own resources. This is done in accordance with Article 312 TFEU, planning a period of at least five years – in practice, seven years – in the form of the so-called Multiannual Financial Framework Regulation (often referred to as MFF or MFF Regulation).[409] This document sets out the ceilings of amounts of expenditure for major sectors of activity of the EU on an annual basis, as well as provisions for the annual budgetary procedure to run smoothly. For instance, the current MFF foresees EUR 3,164 million in commitment appropriations – the upper limit of expenditure which can be committed from the EU budget – for migration and border management purposes in 2023.

The MFF is also adopted by a special legislative procedure. The Council acts (by unanimity) on a proposal from the Commission, and with the consent of the Parliament. Yet again, an atypical mechanism enables the European Council, acting by unanimity, to decide to authorise the Council to act by qualified majority.[410] As the related negotiations may be difficult, the Treaty foresees a mechanism to enable the continuation of the previous MFF ceilings until adoption of a new one.[411]

[403] Chapter 1, Section 1.4.4.
[404] Art. 311, para. 4 TFEU. The procedure is very atypical (special legislative procedure, in so far as provided for in the Own Resources Decision, after obtaining consent of the Parliament).
[405] 'Council Decision (EU, Euratom) 2020/2053 of 14 December 2020 on the System of Own Resources of the European Union and Repealing Decision 2014/335/EU, Euratom', OJ L 424, 15.12.2020, p. 1.
[406] See Chapter 2, Sections 2.3.3.1 and 2.3.3.2.
[407] 'Council Decision (EU, Euratom) 2020/2053 of 14 December 2020 on the System of Own Resources of the European Union and Repealing Decision 2014/335/EU, Euratom', OJ L 424, 15.12.2020, Art. 5.
[408] 'Council Decision (EU, Euratom) 2020/2053 of 14 December 2020 on the System of Own Resources of the European Union and Repealing Decision 2014/335/EU, Euratom', OJ L 424, 15.12.2020, Art. 2.
[409] For an overview of historical developments in that regard, see Chapter 1, Section 1.3.
[410] There is uncertainty as to whether this would enable a permanent switch (or passerelle) to qualified majority voting in this field, or only an ad hoc solution to address a specific political deadlock.
[411] Art. 312(4) TFEU.

The latest MFF Regulation[412] was adopted alongside the Own Resources Decision, also in the midst of the COVID-19 crisis and high political tensions. The sequence of events confirmed observers' views to the effect that in practice, much of the negotiation on the MFF actually takes place within the European Council, thus creating the risk of marginalising the Parliament.[413]

3.6.3.3 Annual Budget

An annual budget is furthermore adopted every year in compliance with the MFF,[414] to decline the said multiannual planning into annual revenue and expenditure authorisations. Here, the decision-making process is, in principle, more straightforward, as key political decisions are already made in the relevant Own Resources Decision and MFF Regulation – yet as we shall see, discussions may also be heated at this level.

The applicable provision is Article 314 TFEU, which sets outs yet another special legislative procedure. This one is akin to a simplified version of the ordinary legislative procedure, accompanied by a set of very tight deadlines.[415] The time frame seeks to ensure that this annual decision-making process is not perpetually slowed down, which would defeat the purpose of annual cycles. A system of provisional monthly budgets is also foreseen to address circumstances in which the budget is not adopted on time for the new financial year.[416]

In brief, the Commission submits a proposal containing a draft budget (estimate of revenues and expenditures), the Council adopts its position and forwards it to the Parliament. Action by the latter institution may take several forms: approval or absence of a decision, in which case the budget is (deemed to have been) adopted; or, adoption of amendments. In this latter scenario, a Conciliation Committee, composed of an equal number of representatives of the Parliament and the Council, is convened and the Commission takes part to steer the process towards an agreement. If agreement is reached within the Committee, the Parliament and the Council must formally approve the text. In case of failure, the Commission puts forward a new draft budget.[417]

In practice, the procedure gives rise to political and interinstitutional tensions. In the decade following the entry into force of the Treaty of Lisbon, there have been several examples of annual cycles in which the Parliament and the Council could not find agreement within the time frame set for conciliation, thus necessitating a second round of 'crisis negotiations' in December so that a budget could be adopted before the end of the financial year.[418]

[412] 'Council Regulation (EU, Euratom) 2020/2093 of 17 December 2020 Laying Down the Multiannual Financial Framework for the Years 2021–2027' (MFF Regulation), OJ L 433I, 22.12.2020, p. 11.

[413] European Council, Conclusions on the recovery plan and multiannual financial framework for 2021–2027, 17–21.7.2021, and Conclusions on the MFF and Next Generation EU, COVID-19, climate change, security and external relations, 10–11.12.2021. See Crowe, 'The European Budgetary Galaxy', p. 438.

[414] Art. 312(1), subpara. 3 TFEU.

[415] On the specifics of the time frame, see further 'Interinstitutional Agreement between the European Parliament, the Council of the European Union and the European Commission on Budgetary Discipline, on Cooperation in Budgetary Matters and on Sound Financial Management, as well as on New Own Resources, Including a Roadmap towards the Introduction of New Own Resources', OJ L 433I, 22.12.2020, p. 28, Annex II.

[416] Art. 315 TFEU. [417] The complex set of options is detailed at Art. 314(7–8) TFEU.

[418] Crowe, 'The European Budgetary Galaxy', p. 437.

3.6.3.4 Institutional Cooperation and Transparency

Interinstitutional collaboration is particularly warranted throughout all aspects of decision-making on the EU's finances, as illustrated by the latest Interinstitutional Agreement on budgetary discipline, on cooperation in budgetary matters and on sound financial management, as well as on new own resources.[419]

This interinstitutional agreement is remarkable in that, alongside the 2020 Own Resources Decision and MFF Regulation, the three institutions agreed on a roadmap towards the introduction of new own resources in the coming years.[420] The Commission was thus expected to make proposals in 2021 for new own resources, based on a carbon border adjustment mechanism, a digital levy and a revised Emissions Trading System, and, by June 2024, potentially submitting additional proposals on a Financial Transaction Tax and a financial contribution linked to the corporate sector, or a new common corporate tax base.[421] The three institutions have agreed that this coordinated roadmap should result in a limited number of revisions of the Own Resources Decision.[422]

Along with seeking to enhance cooperation between the three institutions to facilitate decision-making in this sensitive field, emphasis is also placed on transparency and institutional balance. The rules and dilemmas applicable to transparency in legislative procedures are equally applicable to the related legislative procedures. Furthermore, the Commission shall also report annually on several aspects of the EU's finances.[423] Yet overall institutional imbalances, with the prominent role played by the European Council in MFF negotiations, as well as the multiplication of atypical instruments to ensure funding, have raised concerns among observers that the control mechanisms set out in the EU Treaties may be stretched to their limits.[424]

[419] 'Interinstitutional Agreement between the European Parliament, the Council of the European Union and the European Commission on Budgetary Discipline, on Cooperation in Budgetary Matters and on Sound Financial Management, as well as on New Own Resources, Including a Roadmap towards the Introduction of New Own Resources', OJ L 433I, 22.12.2020, p. 28. Note also that cooperation is particularly warranted in the context of the MFF negotiations; Art. 312(5) TFEU. Furthermore, the Presidents of the three institutions meet to facilitate decision-making in this field; Art. 324 TFEU; see also Chapter 6 TFEU.

[420] 'Interinstitutional Agreement between the European Parliament, the Council of the European Union and the European Commission on Budgetary Discipline, on Cooperation in Budgetary Matters and on Sound Financial Management, as well as on New Own Resources, Including a Roadmap towards the Introduction of New Own Resources', OJ L 433I, 22.12.2020, p. 28, Annex II.

[421] The Commission proposed three new own resources (the first based on revenues from emissions trading, the second drawing on the resources generated by the proposed EU carbon border adjustment mechanism, and the third based on the share of residual profits from multinationals that will be reallocated to EU Member States under the OECD/G20 agreement on a reallocation of taxing rights): see Commission, Communication, 'The Next Generation of Own Resources for the EU Budget', COM(2021) 566, 22.12.2021.

[422] 'Interinstitutional Agreement between the European Parliament, the Council of the European Union and the European Commission on Budgetary Discipline, on Cooperation in Budgetary Matters and on Sound Financial Management, as well as on New Own Resources, Including a Roadmap towards the Introduction of New Own Resources', OJ L 433I, 22.12.2020, Annex II, point K.

[423] Ibid., points 16–17; Art. 318 TFEU. See also the Commission's implementing powers, Chapter 2, Section 2.3.5.7.

[424] See P. Leino-Sandberg, 'New Generation EU: A Constitutional Change without Constitutional Change' (blog), reconnect-europe.eu (13.1.2021); and contrast with A. De Gregorio Merino, 'The Recovery Plan: Solidarity and the Living Constitution', *European Papers*, 50 (2021), p. 1.

3.6.4 The Institutional History of an EU Act

Before closing this chapter, it should be observed that the publication of an act in the Official Journal of the EU, its title and the first lines of its preamble and final provisions provide a wealth of information on the position of the instrument in the EU system of legal norms. As illustrated in Box 3.2, for acts of secondary or tertiary law, information includes: (1) whether the act is a legislative act or not, (2) the nature of the act, (3) the author(s) of the act, (4) the legal basis (or legal bases), (5) the organs that have been consulted, (6) the procedure for adoption, (7) the date for the expiry of transposition (in the case of directive) and (8) the date of entry into force.

Box 3.2 Rough guide to EU legal acts

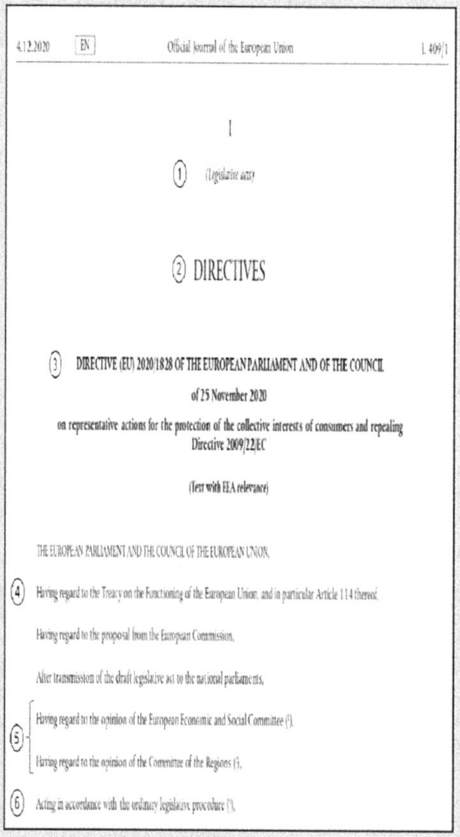

4.12.2020 EN Official Journal of the European Union L 409/1

I

(1) *(Legislative acts)*

(2) DIRECTIVES

(3) DIRECTIVE (EU) 2020/1828 OF THE EUROPEAN PARLIAMENT AND OF THE COUNCIL

of 25 November 2020

on representative actions for the protection of the collective interests of consumers and repealing Directive 2009/22/EC

(Text with EEA relevance)

THE EUROPEAN PARLIAMENT AND THE COUNCIL OF THE EUROPEAN UNION,

(4) Having regard to the Treaty on the Functioning of the European Union, and in particular Article 114 thereof,

Having regard to the proposal from the European Commission,

After transmission of the draft legislative act to the national parliaments,

(5) Having regard to the opinion of the European Economic and Social Committee (1),

Having regard to the opinion of the Committee of the Regions (2),

(6) Acting in accordance with the ordinary legislative procedure (3),

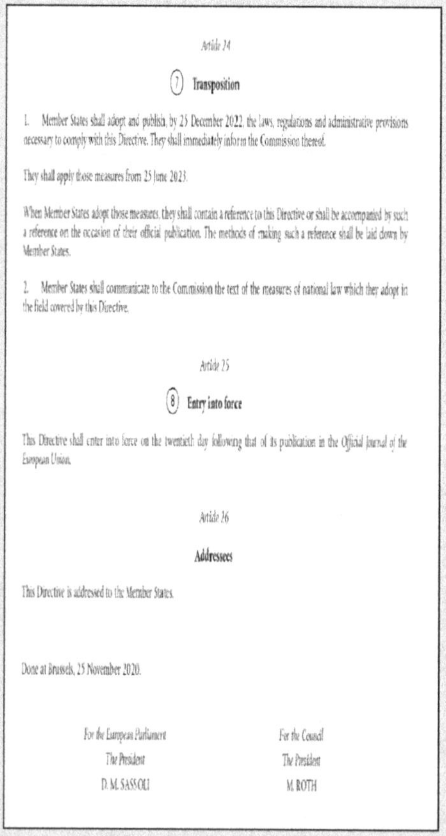

Article 24

(7) **Transposition**

1. Member States shall adopt and publish, by 25 December 2022, the laws, regulations and administrative provisions necessary to comply with this Directive. They shall immediately inform the Commission thereof.

They shall apply those measures from 25 June 2023.

When Member States adopt those measures, they shall contain a reference to this Directive or shall be accompanied by such a reference on the occasion of their official publication. The methods of making such a reference shall be laid down by Member States.

2. Member States shall communicate to the Commission the text of the measures of national law which they adopt in the field covered by this Directive.

Article 25

(8) **Entry into force**

This Directive shall enter into force on the twentieth day following that of its publication in the *Official Journal of the European Union*.

Article 26

Addressees

This Directive is addressed to the Member States.

Done at Brussels, 25 November 2020.

For the European Parliament / *The President* / D. M. SASSOLI

For the Council / *The President* / M. ROTH

4

The Unique Nature of the EU Legal Order

The legal order of the European Union can be distinguished from other international law systems because its legal acts have autonomous effects that are independent of the specific laws of its members. These effects result in EU law being integrated with the laws of its Member States (Section 4.1), and this is also enabled by the particularly sophisticated machinery put in place at European level for the appropriate implementation and enforcement of EU law across the Member States of the EU (Section 4.2). To ensure adherence to its founding values, as well as its perennity, the powerful legal order that results is itself subject to the rule of law (Section 4.3), as well as to ongoing reflections on its limitations (Section 4.4).

4.1 AN 'INTEGRATED' LEGAL ORDER

The EU Treaties, and the law deriving therefrom, are integrated with the law of the Member States in a uniquely sophisticated and powerful way, combining reliance on the principles of primacy and direct effect, as largely shaped by the Court of Justice of the European

Union.[1] This integrated legal system is heavily anchored, and dependent upon, national procedural law.

4.1.1 Primacy of EU Law

4.1.1.1 The Principle of Primacy

Origins and Definition

The first foundational principle showing such integration is that of primacy, as set out in the *Costa* v. *ENEL* case. It establishes the pre-eminence of EU law over national law. To give a sense of the implications of that ruling, which dates back to the early 1960s, it is best to provide a brief overview of its facts.

Mr Costa, an Italian citizen, owned shares of the Edison Volta company, and being opposed to Italy's nationalisation of the production and distribution of electric energy in 1962 and the creation of the ENEL company, he refused to pay one of his bills. In ensuing proceedings initiated against him by ENEL for non-payment, Mr Costa asked the Giudice Conciliatore (an Italian court) to refer a preliminary question[2] to the Court of Justice to interpret several provisions of the treaty preceding the TFEU, the Treaty establishing the European Economic Community. Mr Costa argued that the nationalisation of 1962 was contrary to that Treaty.[3] Although the Court of Justice gave a ruling related to EU law in an abstract manner only, when applying the solution at national level, the Italian judge found in favour of Mr Costa.[4]

The *Costa* v. *ENEL* case[5]

[1] See Chapter 1, Section 1.4.2. [2] This procedure is explained subsequently; see Chapter 4, Section 4.2.3.
[3] To what is now Art. 37 TFEU.
[4] M. Hilf (ed.), 'Costa v. ENEL Case', *Max Planck Encyclopedias of International Law* (Oxford University Press, online resource).
[5] Cartoon by Malt © Pascal Hansens, Brussels, 2021.

In answer to the question from the Italian court, the Court of Justice examined how the Treaty should be interpreted to enable the national judge to assess the compatibility of the nationalisation process with it, and, more importantly, it explained its vision of how that Treaty interacted with national law – essentially, that there had been an agreed transfer of powers and limitation of sovereign rights:

> By creating a Community [now, 'Union'] of unlimited duration, having its own institutions, its own personality, its own legal capacity and capacity of representation on the international plane and, more particularly, real powers stemming from a limitation of sovereignty or a transfer of powers from the States to the Community ['Union'], the Member States have limited their sovereign rights, albeit within limited fields, and have thus created a body of law which binds both their nationals and themselves.
>
> [. . . T]he law stemming from the Treaty, an independent source of law, could not, because of its special and original nature, be overridden by domestic legal provisions, however framed, without being deprived of its character as Community ['Union'] law and without the legal basis of the Community ['Union'] itself being called into question.
>
> The transfer by the States from their domestic legal system to the Community ['Union'] legal system of the rights and obligations arising under the Treaty carries with it a permanent limitation of their sovereign rights, against which a subsequent unilateral act incompatible with the concept of the Community ['Union'] cannot prevail.[6]

In this foundational ruling, the Court of Justice thus adopted a teleological reading of the initial version of what has become the TFEU. The Court of Justice observed the creation of a uniquely ambitious new legal order, and was concerned with not letting the Member States jeopardise the attainment of its objectives. The Court of Justice concluded that, after the entry into force of the Treaty, a national rule that is inconsistent with EU law cannot be tolerated. EU law thus takes precedence – or has primacy – over national law; and this as a matter of EU law itself. From the perspective of EU law, EU law takes primacy over national law irrespective of whether the Member State concerned is dualist or monist.[7] The practical consequences were further spelt out a few years later in *Simmenthal*,[8] as will be elaborated upon subsequently.

Scope and National Perspectives

The highest courts in the Member States expressed concerns in response to this bold assertion of the Court of Justice: To what extent would EU law also prevail on the highest norms of the Member States? In particular, how would national constitutional courts, as the guardians of the constitutions of their States, articulate the requirement spelt out by the

[6] Case 6/64, *Costa* v. *ENEL*, EU:C:1964:66.

[7] In other words, from the perspective of EU law, the primacy of EU law is independent of the specificities of national law and there is no possibility for the Member States to add conditions to the primacy of EU law over national law. This results from the fact that such primacy is inherent in EU law itself, which the Member States adhere to of their own will through accession and treaty ratification.

[8] Case 106/77, *Simmenthal*, EU:C:1978:49, para. 24.

Court of Justice to accept the unconditional primacy of EU law over their own primary norms, national constitutional law?

This was the subject matter of another foundational ruling by the Court of Justice, *Internationale Handelsgesellschaft.*[9] In that case, a German import-export undertaking contested the legality of two [EU] regulations setting out rules requiring a deposit before an export licence for maize meal could be obtained before a national court. The national court asked the Court of Justice for guidance in the form of a preliminary question,[10] considering that the deposit system was contrary to certain German constitutional law principles, which should have prevailed over European law. The Court of Justice stated that the validity of an EU measure cannot be affected by allegations that it runs counter to 'either fundamental rights as formulated by the constitution [. . .] or the principles of a national constitutional structure'.[11] The undertaking would thus have to comply with EU law.

Yet the Court of Justice also stated that respect for fundamental rights must be ensured within the EU legal system, and that it forms an integral part of the general principles of law that it will itself protect.[12] It noted that the protection of such rights is in fact inspired by the constitutional traditions common to the Member States. The Court of Justice then assessed whether [EU] fundamental rights could be interpreted as precluding the deposit system in question, and concluded in the negative.

In *Internationale Handelsgesellschaft*, the Court of Justice thus did two things simultaneously: it asserted that the primacy of EU law goes as far as to also apply to its relationship with national constitutional law; and it acknowledged that gaps in protection of constitutional principles at European level could be filled in by seeking inspiration from national constitutional traditions common to the Member States. It combined the primacy of EU law, in a reflexive process, with an openness to learn from the common features of the Member States' constitutional systems.[13]

The highest courts of the Member States have accepted this quid pro quo overall, but they articulate it in their own terms. This approach is sometimes referred to as setting counter-limits to the primacy of EU law, in particular in countries with a dualist tradition, which are less at ease with accepting the unconditional primacy of EU law.[14] Examples may be taken from the case law of the BVerfG, which combines traits of the approaches of several other courts. In the early years, the BVerfG refused the primacy of EU law, 'so long as' no sufficient safeguards for the protection of fundamental rights were ensured in the EU legal order (*Solange I*, 1974).[15] The Court of Justice, however, developed its approach to the protection of fundamental rights through general principles, and later the BVerfG reversed the 'so long as', or 'Solange', doctrine.[16] The primacy of EU law would be accepted

[9] Case 11/70, *Internationale Handelsgesellschaft*, EU:C:1970:114. [10] Explained in Chapter 4, Section 4.2.3.

[11] Case 11/70, *Internationale Handelsgesellschaft*, EU:C:1970:114, para. 3. [12] Ibid., para. 4.

[13] For a more recent example, see Case C-42/17 *M.A.S. and M.B. (Taricco II)*, EU:C:2017:936, para. 53.

[14] See further A. Arena, 'The Twin Doctrines of Primacy and Pre-emption', in Schütze and Tridimas (eds.), *Oxford Principles of European Union Law*, pp. 318–322; R. Schütze, *European Union Law*, 2nd ed (Cambridge University Press, 2018), pp. 130–138.

[15] BVerfG, 2 BvL 52/71, *Solange I*, 29.5.1974. A point was also made on the lack of a democratically legitimate elected Parliament; that point was addressed a few years later through institutional reform at EU level; see Chapter 1, Section 1.3.2.2.

[16] In German, 'solange' means 'so long as'.

under the presumption that EU law complied with EU fundamental rights, but only as long as there was no evidence to the contrary (*Solange II*, 1986).[17]

With the expansion of EU competences, notably since the Treaty of Maastricht, the BVerfG added to this fundamental rights' review of claims to the primacy of EU law, a second one. The BVerfG noted that the EU does not have the competence to decide on its own competences. This is often referred to as the 'kompetenz-kompetenz' doctrine.[18] As a consequence, in the exceptional event of a manifest and structurally significant exceeding of competences by EU organs, national constitutional organs may take steps to restore legality. In particular, although the BVerfG acknowledges that the interpretation and application of EU law primarily falls to the Court of Justice of the European Union, the BVerfG may control EU action so that it does not manifestly exceed the authorisation given to it by the Member States in the framework of the EU Treaties. In that context, the BVerfG ensures that the EU does not act beyond the scope of the competences conferred upon it by its component members in a serious way – in other words, in an ultra vires way. This form of control is exercised with restraint.[19]

Finally, in recent years and like many other national constitutional courts, the BVerfG has developed another type of counter limit, to ensure the protection of national (constitutional) identity.[20] Although each Member State's highest court may have a different approach, for the BVerfG, the identity review examines the respective EU act in a substantive sense, as to whether the inviolable principles of the German Constitution identified in its Article 79(3) have been affected or not.[21] This article then refers back to several other provisions of the German Constitution that may not be amended: on the safeguarding of the core of human dignity in fundamental rights, as well as the fundamental principles upon which the principles of democracy, the rule of law, the social state and the federal state are based.[22]

The unconditional primacy of EU law on all national norms, including constitutional norms, is a long-standing feature of the EU legal system. As EU law continues to evolve, the Member States' highest courts constantly adjust their own way of articulating this feature with their own national constitutional mandates. In recent years, and unlike in the first

[17] BverfG, 2 BvR 197/83, *Solange II*, 22.10.1986.

[18] The doctrine relates to who has the competence to monitor compliance with the rules on the allocation of competences.

[19] BverfG, 2 BvR 2134/92, 2 BvR 2159/92, Decision on the Treaty on European Union, 12.10.1993. Such a review recently led to a highly exceptional and much discussed finding that EU institutions had been acting ultra vires: BverfG, 2 BvR 859/15, 5.5.2020; see Chapter 3, Section 3.3.1. Note that the French Council of State promptly distinguished its approach from that adopted by the BverfG: Nos 393099, 394922, 397844, 397851, 424717, 424718, French Data Network et autres, Décision du 21.4.2021, para. 8.

[20] BverfG, 2 be 2/08, 2 BvE 5/08, 2 BvR 1010/08, 2 BvR 1022/08, 2 BvR 1259/08, 2 BvR 182/09, *Lisbon ruling*, 30.6.2009; see also Chapter 1, Section 1.1.2. For a critical analysis of the doctrine of constitutional identity, see F. Fabbrini and A. Sajó, 'The Dangers of Constitutional Identity', *European Law Journal*, 25 (2019) 25, pp. 457–473. In the view of the Court of Justice though, if a national court considers that a provision of secondary EU law infringes the obligation to respect the national identity of that Member State, that court must ask for guidance from the Court of Justice; C-430/21, *RS*, EU:C:2022:99, para. 71; on the related procedure, see Chapter 4, Section 4.2.3.

[21] See also Art. 23(1) of the German Basic Law that recalls the importance of Art. 79(3) in the context of the development of the EU.

[22] BVerfG, 2 BvR 2728/13, 2 BvE 13/13, 2 BvR 2731/13, 2 BvR 2730/13, 2 BvR 2729/13, *Constitutional Complaints and Organstreit Proceedings Against the OMT Programme of the European Central Bank*, 21.6.2016, extracts from paras. 153, 138.

decades of the process of European integration when they used to avoid doing so, those highest courts have more frequently made their views known to the Court of Justice on these questions by means of the preliminary ruling procedure.[23] While divergences of approach between these various courts on the primacy of EU law attract much attention in specialised circles, as well as occasionally in the press or parliamentary debates,[24] it must be noted that they remain the exception.[25]

In practice, conflicts between EU law and national norms are resolved by giving precedence to the former and are overall unproblematic. Even in the more sensitive case of conflicts between EU law and national constitutional norms, these are usually anticipated and resolved by the States concerned before accession, or before changes to the EU Treaties, through constitutional reform. As a testament to the delicate encounter between the primacy of EU law and national constitutional law, the authors of the Treaties have so far decided not to explicitly assert the primacy of EU law in the EU Treaties. What we currently have is Declaration 17 annexed to the final act which adopted the Treaty of Lisbon, according to which:

> in accordance with well settled case law of the Court of Justice of the European Union, the Treaties and the law adopted by the Union on the basis of the Treaties have primacy over the law of Member States, under the conditions laid down by the said case law. [. . .][26]
>
> The fact that the principle of primacy will not be included in the future treaty shall not in any way change the existence of the principle and the existing case-law of the Court of Justice.

4.1.1.2 Consequences of the Primacy of EU Law over National Law

General Principles

A first practical consequence of the primacy of EU law is that the authorities of a Member State may not adopt, and must render inapplicable, rules or practices that would run contrary to EU law. This results from the ruling in *Simmenthal*, by which the Court of Justice further specified that a national court which is called upon to apply provisions of EU law is under a duty

> to give full effect to those provisions, if necessary refusing of its own motion to apply any conflicting provision of national legislation, even if adopted subsequently, and it

[23] The procedure is introduced subsequently, Chapter 4, Section 4.2.3. The BVerfG, used as an example previously, asked its first ever preliminary question to the Court of Justice in 2014. See further, A. Dyevre, A. Atanasova and M. Glavina, 'Who Asks Most? Institutional Incentives and Referral Activity in the European Union Legal Order', *Journal of European Public Policy*, 27 (2019), pp. 912–930.

[24] E.g. M. Sandbu, 'German Court Has Set a Bomb under the EU Legal Order', *Financial Times* (5.5.2020). On the related divergences of views between the Court of Justice and the German Constitutional Court, see further Chapter 3, Section 3.3.2, note 123. See also Parliament, 'Poland: Constitutional Tribunal Is Illegitimate, Unfit to Interpret Constitution', press release, 21.10.2021; on the related tensions between EU institutions and the Polish Constitutional Tribunal, see Chapter 4, Section 4.3.2, in particular, note 320.

[25] B. De Witte, 'Direct Effect, Primacy and the Nature of the Legal Order', in P. Craig and G. de Búrca (eds.), *The Evolution of EU Law*, 3rd ed. (Oxford University Press, 2021), pp. 187–227, at 221.

[26] Declaration 17 concerning primacy annexed to the Treaty of Lisbon. Note that the expression 'the law adopted by the Union on the basis of the Treaties' covers both secondary and tertiary EU law.

is not necessary for the court to request or await the prior setting aside of such provision by legislative or other constitutional means.[27]

The Court of Justice of the European Union will not normally itself – and nor will any other EU organ – annul or declare void an act of national law.[28] This would be beyond the scope of EU competences conferred upon them in the EU Treaties. Instead, it is for the national authorities – public organs, including all courts, irrespective of their level in the national judicial system[29] – before which an act or a practice inconsistent with EU law is at stake to disapply it, and then for the competent national authorities to further annul or repeal the act,[30] or to correct the practice. The duty to disapply national law that is in conflict with EU law may very exceptionally be lifted, if such dis-application would lead to a breach of a fundamental right protected at national level and if the lifting of the duty does not hinder the primacy, the unity and the effectiveness of EU law; although the national authorities and the legislature, in particular, will be reminded of their duty to take the necessary measures to bring national law in line with EU law.[31] If the national authorities' duty to ensure compliance with EU law is not respected, the Member State in question may be held liable for damages, or infringement proceedings may be commenced against them before the Court of Justice.[32]

The duty to set aside may relate to national rules or practices that directly and explicitly conflict with the substance of EU requirements. In this context, the setting aside of the conflicting national rule often amounts to actually directly applying EU law. This will be further elaborated upon when we discuss the direct effect of EU law.[33] Yet the duty to set aside also extends to national rules or practices that hinder the effectiveness – also referred to as full effect or *effet utile* – of EU law in more indirect ways. Indeed, rules or practices on procedures and remedies may impair the ability of national courts to ensure the effectiveness of directly applicable EU rules, and thus also ought to be set aside by the said national court.[34]

The facts of the case in *Factortame* illustrate the point. In that case, certain companies challenged the compatibility with EU law of a UK rule that, if applied, would have deprived them of fishing rights. They also requested interim relief (in the form of suspension of the effects of the said rule, and thus authorisation to fish) until the final judgment. The House of Lords asked for guidance by sending a request for a preliminary ruling to the Court of Justice. The House of Lords explained that it could not grant interim relief: this was made impossible by an old common-law rule precluding interim injunctions against an act adopted by the Crown – that is to say, against the government – in conjunction with the presumption that an Act of the national parliament is presumed to be in conformity with EU law, until such time as a decision on its compatibility with that law has been given.

[27] Case 106/77, *Simmenthal*, EU:C:1978:49, para. 24; see also para. 17.

[28] This may be possible in very exceptional cases, however, as shown in recent case law; see Chapter 4, Section 4.4.1, especially note 333.

[29] C-118/00, *Larsy*, EU:C:2001:368, paras. 51–53.

[30] Case 159/78, *Commission* v. *Italy*, EU:C:1979:243, para. 22.

[31] Case C-42/17, *M.A.S. and M.B. (Taricco II)*, EU:C:2017:936, paras. 47–55, read in conjunction with para. 61.

[32] See Chapter 4, Sections 4.1.3.3 and 4.2.2.

[33] See Chapter 4, Sections 4.1.2 and 4.1.4.

[34] This was reiterated in C-378/17, *Minister for Justice and Equality and Commissioner of An Garda Síochána*, EU:C:2018:979, para. 36. National rules or practices on procedures and remedies are increasingly understood to come into immediate conflict with the fundamental right to an effective remedy enshrined in Art. 47 CFEU. As this provision has direct effect, national rules or practices conflicting with it thus also ought to be set aside: C-30/19, *Braathens Regional Aviation*, EU:C:2021:269, paras. 56–58.

In response, the Court of Justice stated that if a national court considers that the sole obstacle to granting interim relief is a national rule, it must set aside that rule.[35] To give full effect to EU law, national courts must be able to grant interim protective measures, irrespective of the sensitivity of the matter at national level.[36]

Duty of Consistent Interpretation in Light of EU Law

Before further discussing fully fledged conflicts between a national rule and an EU rule, we ought to stress that these can most often be avoided owing to an interpretative technique. National law indeed may be worded, or structured, in such a way that national authorities can change their interpretation of the relevant provisions. This avoids the emergence of a conflict, and instead reconciles the national and EU layers of norms.

The Court of Justice, in *von Colson and Kamann*, has made clear that national authorities are under a duty, by virtue of the principle of sincere cooperation enshrined in Article 4(3) TEU, to use this technique to ensure that national rules are interpreted in conformity with EU law.[37] This shall be done wherever and whenever possible. For instance, the duty of consistent interpretation applies in disputes between a private party and public authorities, whereby the latter ought itself to make use of the interpretative technique under the control of reviewing courts.[38] As confirmed by the Court in *Marleasing*, the duty also applies in disputes between private parties, whereby national courts ought to ensure consistent interpretation of national rules in light of relevant EU rules.[39] The date on which the national rule was adopted, whether it is before or after the entry into force of the relevant EU rule, is, in principle, irrelevant.[40] For instance, where national law prohibits the advertising of products which promote the consumption of nicotine without mentioning electronic cigarettes, the silence of national law must be interpreted in light of the EU directive regulating the sale of tobacco and related products (including nicotine). That directive requires the Member States to prohibit commercial communications on electronic cigarettes, to the effect that the national ban must also encompass advertising for electronic cigarettes.[41]

On the subject of directives, the Court of Justice of the European Union has specified that there is (only) a fully fledged duty of consistent interpretation *after* expiry of their transposition period. In between the entry into force of a directive and the expiry of its transposition period,[42] the duty is accommodated to reflect the specific nature of directives and the margin of manoeuvre left to the Member States by Article 288(3) TFEU. In *Adeneler*, the Court of Justice

[35] Case C-213/89, *Factortame*, EU:C:1990:257, para. 23.

[36] For another example, see Joined Cases C-188/10 and C-189/10, *Melki and Abdeli*, EU:C:2010:363, para. 57 on national legislation which establishes an interlocutory procedure for the review of the constitutionality of national laws. It would be against EU law for such a rule to give priority to the interlocutory procedure and to thereby prevent – both before the submission of a question on constitutionality to the national court responsible for reviewing the constitutionality of laws and, as the case may be, after the decision of that court on that question – all the other national courts or tribunals from exercising their right or fulfilling their obligation to refer questions to the Court of Justice for a preliminary ruling.

[37] Case 14/83, *von Colson and Kamann*, EU:C:1984:153, para. 26. [38] Ibid., para. 26.

[39] C-106/89, *Marleasing*, EU:C:1990:395, paras. 2, 6–9. [40] Ibid., para. 8.

[41] 'Directive 2014/40 of the European Parliament and of the Council of 3 April 2014 on the Approximation of the Laws, Regulations and Administrative Provisions of the Member States Concerning the Manufacture, Presentation and Sale of Tobacco and Related Products and Repealing Directive 2001/37/EC', OJ L 127, 29.4.2014, p. 1, Art. 20(5).

[42] See Chapter 3, Section 3.5.3.2, Nature of EU Internal Acts.

specified that national courts 'must refrain as far as possible from interpreting domestic law in a manner which might seriously compromise, after the period for transposition has expired, attainment of the objective pursued by [the] directive'.[43] The national courts' duty is thus formulated negatively and is forward-looking. The concern is to prevent future damage to EU law obligations, rather than to instantly eliminate conflict. In contrast, after expiry of the transposition period, the Court noted that the national court ought 'to do whatever lies within its jurisdiction'. In *Pfeiffer*, the Court of Justice stressed that the national court ought to have regard not only to national rules transposing EU obligations, but also to 'the whole body of rules of national law', with a view to ensuring that consistent interpretation can be achieved.[44]

The duty of consistent interpretation is perhaps the least visible way of bringing national law in line with EU law obligations, precisely because clashes are avoided. Nevertheless, it is a common mechanism used to ensure the primacy of the latter over the former. The duty of consistent interpretation does suffer two important limitations. Firstly, and this is inherent in the nature of this technique, it may be that the wording of the provision of national law does not lend itself to consistent interpretation. As the Court of Justice confirmed in *Wagner Miret*, there can be no duty to interpret a provision against its own wording, or *contra legem*.[45] Second, consistent interpretation may not be used to determine or aggravate the criminal liability of a person. Such an outcome would indeed constitute a breach of the general principles of EU law, in particular of the principles of legal certainty and non-retroactivity which protect individual liberties in the area of criminal law.[46]

4.1.2 Direct Effect of EU Law

The mechanisms introduced previously, such as the prohibition to adopt rules conflicting with EU law and the duty of consistent interpretation, are distinct as well as complementary principles that ensure the primacy of EU law over national law. In addition to these expressions of the primacy of EU law, attention turns to the principle of direct effect. Direct effect refers to the ability of a provision of EU law to confer rights to and obligations on individuals which may be enforced directly at the national level, and which national courts ought to protect. Direct effect ensures that provisions of EU law prevail over national provisions,[47] even in the case of a direct conflict between the two layers of norms that cannot be addressed through consistent interpretation: a directly effective provision of EU law acts as a shield against conflicting national law that must be set aside. It can also grant an autonomous substantive EU right when national law fails to grant that right: a directly effective provision of EU law acts as a sword.

4.1.2.1 Origins and Definition

Direct effect was first asserted in the early 1960s in the *Van Gend en Loos* case.[48] The case arose from the reclassification of a chemical, by the Benelux countries, into a customs category that

[43] Case 212/04, *Adeneler*, EU:C:2006:443, para. 123.
[44] Joined Cases, C-397/01 to C-403/01, *Pfeiffer and others*, EU:C:2004:584, paras. 118–119.
[45] C-334/92, *Wagner Miret*, EU:C:1993:945, para. 22.
[46] Case 80/86, *Kolpinghuis Nijmegen*, EU:C:1987:431, para. 13.
[47] Joined Cases C-46/93 and C-48/93, *Brasserie du Pêcheur and Factortame*, EU:C:1996:79, para. 20. See further C. Hilson and A. Downes, 'Making Sense of Rights: Community Rights in EC Law', *European Law Review*, 24 (1999), pp. 121–138.
[48] Case 26/62, *Van Gend en Loos*, EU:C:1963:1.

was subject to higher customs charges. Preliminary questions were asked by the Dutch Tariefcommissie in a dispute between Van Gend en Loos, a transport company, and the Dutch tax authorities with regard to import duties. The Court of Justice held that this should be read by the national judge as constituting a breach of the Treaty provision that prohibits Member States from introducing or increasing custom duties in their commercial relations with each other. It continued to rule that the breach could be litigated by individuals bringing claims before national courts, and thus not just by the Member States, reasoning as follows:

> To ascertain whether the provisions of an international treaty extend [to enabling nationals of Member States to lay claim to rights which the national court must protect] it is necessary to consider the spirit, the general scheme and the wording of those provisions.
>
> The objective of the EEC Treaty [now TFEU], which is to establish a common market, the functioning of which is of direct concern to interested parties in the Community [now 'Union'], implies that this Treaty is more than an agreement which merely creates mutual obligations between the contracting states.
>
> [. . . T]he [EU] constitutes a new legal order of international law for the benefit of which the states have limited their sovereign rights, albeit within limited fields, and the subjects of which comprise not only Member States but also their nationals. Independently of the legislation of Member States, [EU] law therefore not only imposes obligations on individuals but is also intended to confer upon them rights which become part of their legal heritage.

The *Van Gend en Loos* case: a small tax with a big impact[49]

[49] Malt © Pascal Hansens, Brussels, 2021.

In this other foundational ruling, as in *Costa* v. *ENEL*, the Court of Justice also adopted a teleological reading of the initial version of what has become the TFEU. The Court's approach is particularly interesting in so far as it understands the role of individuals as guardians of the EU legal order, alongside representatives of the public interest – the Commission and the Member States. Indeed, the Court of Justice explained that while the EU Treaties enable the Commission and the Member States to bring a State before the Court of Justice for failure to fulfil its obligations,[50] that does not mean that individuals cannot also plead these obligations, should the occasion arise, before national courts. Quite to the contrary, the Court of Justice emphasised:

> [T]he vigilance of individuals concerned to protect their rights amounts to an effective supervision in addition to the supervision entrusted by Articles [258] and [259 TFEU] to the diligence of the Commission and of the Member States.

This idea of dual vigilance (private and public actors side by side) is central to the current system of judicial remedies for the enforcement of EU law. The preliminary ruling procedure (which will be introduced later) acts as a bridge between national courts – before which private actors, in particular, may bring claims to enforce their EU rights – and the Court of Justice, to ensure the uniform interpretation and application of EU law.

4.1.2.2 Criteria and Types of Direct Effect

Over the years, the Court of Justice of the European Union has developed *general criteria* providing guidance to identify provisions of EU law capable of being relied upon directly before national courts, and thus having direct effect. The provision of EU law must be: (1) intended to confer rights on or impose obligations on individuals; (2) sufficiently clear and precise; and (3) unconditional. Although the Court of Justice continues to refer to these criteria regularly, and to the last two in particular, which provide useful methodological support, in practice the Court does not always rigorously check that each one has been satisfied. The Court's primary underlying concern is that, in the situation in question, the national court is in a position to establish how to apply the relevant provision of EU law to its case.[51]

One ought to distinguish between different types of direct effect depending on the setting in which the EU norm is relied upon. A provision of EU law may be relied upon, as such, in a dispute between private parties and public authorities: in this context, the national judge is invited to assess the ability of the provision of EU law to produce *vertical* direct effect.[52] A provision of EU law may also be relied upon, as such, in a dispute between private parties: the national judge is here seeking to assess the ability of the provision to produce *horizontal* direct effect.[53] While it is inherent in EU norms, which are intended to be legally binding and have been produced at supranational level, that they create obligations on States in 'vertical disputes' if the necessary criteria are met, it is often less clear that provisions of EU law are intended to create obligations on private parties in 'horizontal disputes', as will now be illustrated.

[50] See Chapter 4, Section 4.2.2. [51] E.g. Case 43/75, *Defrenne* v. *Sabena*, EU:C:1976:56, para. 23.
[52] This pictures private parties at the bottom and public authorities above them.
[53] This pictures groups of private parties side by side on a horizontal plan.

4.1.2.3 Direct Effect of the Various Instruments of EU Law

Before analysing individual provisions of EU law in detail, which is necessary to test the ability of a national court to establish if there is a directly effective right, one ought to look at the overall nature of the instrument of EU law at stake. This may indeed impact on the respective importance of the various criteria above, as well as on the type of direct effects that may result from the relevant provision of EU law.

EU Treaties

The EU Treaties are addressed to the Member States, the contracting parties. If the criteria identified previously are fulfilled, Treaty provisions may thus be relied upon before national courts in disputes between private parties and public authorities (vertical direct effect), as was the case in *Van Gend en Loos*. In *Defrenne* v. *Sabena*, the Court of Justice swiftly added that, depending on their ultimate objective, which may be to create rights for individuals and to impose obligations on them, certain provisions of what has now become the TFEU may also be relied upon before national courts against private parties (horizontal direct effect).[54] Ms Defrenne could thereby bring a claim alleging breach of the rules on equal pay for equal work between men and women against her private employer. Ms Defrenne argued before the national court that female air hostesses must be paid the same as male cabin stewards performing identical work, a right protected by Article 157(1) TFEU, which is directly effective and could thus be relied upon before the national court. This approach to horizontal direct effect has now been confirmed for several other provisions of the TFEU, including Article 45, on the free movement of workers in the EU; Article 18, on the prohibition of discrimination on grounds of nationality; and Article 49, on the right of establishment.[55]

General Principles of EU Law

It is inherent in the unwritten nature and gap-filling function of general principles of EU law that there is little guidance on their use. These principles are primarily intended to regulate action by public authorities. They may have direct effect if the national court or tribunal is in a position to establish how to apply the principle to a specific case. In recent years, the Court of Justice has more specifically accepted, in a situation covered by the prohibition of discrimination on grounds of age in employment enshrined in Directive 2000/78, that the general principle to which the Directive gives expression may have horizontal direct effect.[56] As we shall now see, much of the debate that this approach has triggered now revolves around the question of the horizontal direct effect of the CFEU, which is a more recent source for the protection of fundamental rights in the EU.

[54] Case 43/75, *Defrenne* v. *Sabena*, EU:C:1976:56, para. 39.

[55] See, respectively, C-281/98, *Angonese*, EU:C:2000:296, paras. 33–36; C-411/98, *Ferlini*, EU:C:2000:530, para. 50; C-438/05, *International Transport Workers' Federation and Finnish Seamen's Union*, EU: C:2007:772, paras. 57–61. Note that in the last two examples, the private parties against which EU law obligations were imposed had collective regulatory powers (e.g. as do trade unions). See further L. Gormley, 'Private Parties and the Free Movement of Goods: Responsible, Irresponsible, or a Lack of Principles?', *Fordham International Law Journal*, 28 (2015), pp. 993–1016.

[56] 'Council Directive 2000/78/EC Establishing a General Framework for Equal Treatment in Employment and Occupation', OJ L 303, 2.12.2000, p. 16; Case C-555/07, *Kücükdeveci*, EU:C:2010:21, paras. 50–51.

Charter of Fundamental Rights of the EU

It is clear from Article 51(1) of the CFEU that the provisions of the Charter are addressed, among others, to the Member States when they are acting within the scope of EU fundamental rights law.[57] The provisions of the Charter are thus an instrument that can produce vertical direct effect if the criteria above are fulfilled. In that respect, it shall be recalled that Article 52(5) CFEU distinguishes between principles and rights – and the former 'shall be judicially cognisable only in the interpretation of such acts and in the ruling on their legality'. This could suggest that principles protected by the CFEU may not produce direct effect. But the CFEU is unclear as to which of its provisions protect rights, and which protect principles. As things stand currently, the three standard criteria identified previously remain the best tool to distinguish provisions of the CFEU that may produce direct effect from those that may not.

Until fairly recently, there has been uncertainty as to whether the provisions of the CFEU may have horizontal direct effect. Indeed, Article 51(1) CFEU does not identify private parties as possible entities to whom the Charter is addressed. In a recent series of cases, however, the Court of Justice has clarified that certain provisions of the CFEU can have horizontal direct effect.[58] In the *Egenberger* case, involving the prohibition of discrimination on grounds of religion in employment covered by Directive 2000/78, the corresponding right in Article 21(1) CFEU could be granted horizontal direct effect.[59] Similarly, in *Bauer and Willmeroth*, a case involving the right to annual paid leave within the meaning of Directive 93/104, the corresponding right in Article 31(2) CFEU could be granted horizontal direct effect.[60] Article 47 CFEU has also been said to be directly effective in horizontal disputes.[61]

International Agreements between the EU and Third States or International Organisations

International agreements to which the EU is a party are primarily intended to create obligations for public authorities, and may thus have vertical direct effect. Yet special attention will be devoted to examining 'the wording and the purpose and nature of the agreement itself' to ensure that the international agreement is indeed intended to confer rights on individuals.[62] For instance, it is understood that in principle certain international agreements, such as the General Agreement on Tariffs and Trade (GATT), are not intended to create rights and obligations. The Court of Justice noted that this is so due to the 'the spirit, the general scheme and the terms of the General Agreement', which is based on reciprocity and characterised by the great flexibility of its provisions.[63] Such agreements, therefore, do not have direct effect.

[57] See Chapter 3, Sections 3.1.3.2 and 3.1.3.5.

[58] It may be noted that, in the key paragraphs of the rulings discussed subsequently, the criteria applied for the said provisions of the CFEU to be granted direct effect were formulated in different terms than the traditional criteria for direct effect introduced previously.

[59] 'Council Directive 2000/78/EC Establishing a General Framework for Equal Treatment in Employment and Occupation', OJ L 303, 2.12.2000, p. 16; C-414/16, *Egenberger*, EU:C:2018:257, para. 76.

[60] 'Council Directive 93/104/EC of 23 November 1993 Concerning Certain Aspects of the Organisation of Working Time', OJ L 307, 13.12.1993, p. 18; Joined Cases C-569/16 and C-570/16, *Bauer and Willmeroth*, EU:C:2018:871, para. 85.

[61] C-414/16, *Egenberger*, EU:C:2018:257, para. 78; see further Chapter 4, note 34.

[62] Case 12/86, *Demirel*, EU:C:1987:400, para. 14.

[63] Joined Cases 21 to 24-72, *International Fruit Company*, EU:C:1972:115, paras. 19–21.

In contrast, certain provisions related to the Association Agreement with Turkey, for example, do have vertical direct effect.[64] Depending on the nature and purpose of the international agreement some of their provisions, such as those of an Association Agreement, may also have horizontal direct effect.[65] Decisions adopted by an international body created by an international agreement, such as the latter, may also have direct effect.[66]

Regulations

Article 288 TFEU specifies that regulations shall be 'directly applicable' in all Member States. This means that application of regulations in favour of, or against, those subject to it do not depend on any additional enacting measure in national law. Furthermore, Member States have the duty not to obstruct, through the adoption of national measures, their applicability.[67] They may, however, adopt measures to enhance their implementation spontaneously, or where a regulation itself so requires. The 'direct effect' of a regulation relates to the ability of individuals to invoke it, or rely on it, directly before national courts.[68] Because regulations are binding in their entirety and directly applicable in national legal orders, in principle they may create rights and obligations that can be relied upon in courts against both public authorities as well as other private parties, as illustrated by the ruling in *Muñoz*, and this as long as the general criteria for direct effect are met.[69]

Directives

It may be briefly recalled here, too, that a directive is binding 'as to the result to be achieved, upon each Member State to which it is addressed'.[70] As a consequence, in the normal state of things, directives that are properly transposed by the Member States in their legal order take effect through national transposition measures. It is only if that is not the case that the autonomous legal effects of the directive need to be examined.

That a directive would create legal effects against the State itself, as envisaged by the doctrine of direct effect, is only possible after the expiry of the transposition period of a directive. Indeed, until that stage, it is inherent in the design of directives and transposition periods that Member States cannot be faulted for not having yet adopted measures transposing them into national law.[71] After the entry into force and during the transition period, it follows from Article 4(3), paragraph 2 TEU, in conjunction with Article 288, paragraph 3 TFEU, that the only duty of the Member States to which the directive is

[64] E.g. the standstill clause in Art. 41(1) of the Additional Protocol to the Agreement establishing an Association between the European Economic Community and Turkey (Ankara Agreement) prohibiting the contracting parties from introducing new restrictions on the freedom of establishment; C-37/98, *Savas*, EU:C:2000:224, paras. 46–48.

[65] C-438/00, *Deutscher Handballbund*, EU:C:2003:255, paras. 19, 32, 37.

[66] E.g. Art. 7 of Decision 2/76 of the Association Council on the implementation of Art. 12 of the Ankara Agreement and Art. 13 of Decision 1/80 of the Association Council on the development of the Association as regards the introduction of new restrictions on the access to employment of workers legally resident and employed in the territory of the contracting State; C-192/89, *Sevince*, EU:C:1990:322, paras. 18, 26.

[67] Case 34/73, *Variola*, EU:C:1973:101, para. 10.

[68] E.g. A. McDonnell, 'Application and Enforcement of EU Law in the Member States', in Kuijper et al. (eds.), *The Law of the European Union*, p. 428.

[69] C-253/00, *Muñoz*, EU:C:2002:497, para. 30. Note that not all provisions of every regulation meet these criteria; it is necessary to check on a case-by-case basis.

[70] Art. 288, para. 3 TFEU.

[71] C-129/96, *Inter-Environnement Wallonie*, EU:C:1997:628, para. 43.

addressed is a negative and forward-looking one: to refrain from taking any measures liable to seriously compromise the attainment of the result prescribed by it.[72]

After expiry of the transposition period though, directives that have not been (properly) implemented may produce direct effect against the State to which they are addressed ('ascending' vertical direct effect). Directives being addressed to and binding on States, the State cannot avail itself of its own wrongdoing – in the form of a failure to ensure appropriate transposition – to escape its obligations towards individuals under EU law.[73] The facts of the key ruling on the matter illustrate the point. In *Van Duyn*, a Dutch national challenged a decision by the Home Office in the UK to refuse her leave to enter the UK to take up employment as a secretary with the Church of Scientology. She was able, for the purpose of seeking entry, to rely on the requirement established by Article 3(1) of Directive 64/221,[74] according to which measures restricting the free movement of workers on grounds of public policy shall be based exclusively on the personal conduct of the individual.[75]

In contrast, even after expiry of the transposition period, directives may not be relied upon to create obligations against a private party.[76] As a consequence, directives may not have horizontal direct effect, nor can they be relied upon by the State against a private party (no 'descending' vertical direct effect). The reasoning of the Court of Justice leading to that conclusion was made clear in *Faccini Dori*, as follows:

> The effect of extending [the case law on the ascending vertical direct effect of directives] to the sphere of relations between individuals would be to recognize a power in the [EU] to enact obligations for individuals with immediate effect, whereas it has competence to do so only where it is empowered to adopt regulations.[77]

The Court of Justice is thus concerned to maintain the distinction between regulations and directives, the latter creating only obligations in terms of the results to be achieved by States. In *Faccini Dori*, for instance, in the absence of measures transposing the Directive on the protection of consumers in respect of contracts negotiated away from business premises,[78] a consumer (private party) could not derive from the directive a right of cancellation against traders (also a private party) with whom they had concluded such a contract. It shall be noted that, although directives may not be relied upon directly against a private party, in the way they may be relied upon

[72] Ibid., para. 45; see also Chapter 4, note 43. [73] Case 148/78, *Ratti*, EU:C:1979:110, para. 22.

[74] 'Council Directive 64/221/EEC of 25 February 1964 on the Co-ordination of Special Measures Concerning the Movement and Residence of Foreign Nationals which Are Justified on Grounds of Public Policy, Public Security or Public Health', OJ 56, 4.4.1964, p. 850, now replaced by 'Directive 2004/38 of the European Parliament and of the Council of 29 April 2004 on the Right of Citizens of the Union and their Family Members to Move and Reside Freely within the Territory of the Member States Amending Regulation 1612/68 and repealing Directives 64/221, 68/360, 72/194, 73/148, 75/34, 75/35, 90/364, 90/365 and 93/96', OJ L 158, 30.4.2004 (last amended 2011), Art. 27.

[75] Case 41/74, *Van Duyn*, EU:C:1974:133, paras. 13–15. [76] Case 152/84, *Marshall*, EU:C:1986:84, para. 48.

[77] C-91/92, *Faccini Dori*, EU:C:1994:292, para. 24.

[78] 'Council Directive 85/577/EC of 20 December 1985 to Protect the Consumer in Respect of Contracts Negotiated Away from Business Premises', OJ L 372, 31.12.1985, p. 31.

against the State, the ascending vertical direct effect of the directive can have adverse repercussions on private third parties.[79]

The asymmetry between the existence of ascending vertical direct effect of directives on the one hand, and the absence of horizontal or descending vertical direct effect on the other hand, has resulted in a challenge of definition: What is a 'public authority' for the purpose of allowing ascending vertical direct effect? The Court of Justice adopts a broad definition of the notion, thus allowing ascending vertical direct effect of directives in a vast array of settings. For instance, a public authority acting in an employer's capacity (such as a local health authority, as in the *Marshall* case), will be deemed to be acting on behalf of the State for the purpose of having to comply with the obligations contained in a directive.[80] In *Foster*, the Court of Justice specified that:

> a body, whatever its legal form, which has been made responsible, pursuant to a measure adopted by the State, for providing a public service under the control of the State and has for that purpose special powers beyond those which result from the normal rules applicable in relations between individuals is included in any event among the bodies against which the provisions of a directive capable of having direct effect may be relied upon.[81]

As a result, the British Gas Corporation, a statutory corporation responsible for developing and maintaining a system of gas supply in Great Britain, which had a monopoly of the supply of gas and whose members were appointed by the competent Secretary of State (who also had the power to give directions in relation to matters affecting the national interest and instructions concerning its management), would be an entity against which the direct effect of a directive could be relied upon. The so-called *Foster* criteria are not exhaustive.[82] A directive may also be relied upon against 'a private law body on which a Member State has conferred a task in the public interest, such as that inherent in the obligation imposed on the Member States [by a directive], and which, for that purpose, possesses, by statute, special powers, such as the power to oblige insurers carrying on motor vehicle insurance in the territory of the Member State concerned to be members of it and to fund it'.[83]

This case law, providing a generous definition of the organs against which the ascending vertical direct effect of directives may be used, tempers the detrimental effects of their lack of horizontal direct effect. It must be recalled that a set of other

[79] C-201/02, *Delena Wells*, EU:C:2004:12, para. 57. Here, a private party relied on the provisions of a directive against the State to obtain an environmental assessment of works carried out by another private party, the owners of a quarry. The Court of Justice noted here that 'the obligation on the Member State [. . .] to ensure [. . .] an assessment of the environmental effects of the working of the quarry is not directly linked to the performance of any obligation which would fall, pursuant to Directive 85/337, on the quarry owners. The fact that mining operations must be halted to await the results of the assessment is admittedly the consequence of the belated performance of that State's obligations. Such a consequence cannot, however, [. . .], be described as inverse [horizontal or descending] direct effect of the provisions of that directive in relation to the quarry owners'. Such *incidental* effects ought to be distinguished from a situation where a private party would rely on the direct effect of a directive against the State, and where the State's duty would be *directly* linked to the performance of another obligation by a private third party (para. 56) – for instance, for the payment of a fine that would be imposed on the owners.

[80] Case 152/84, *Marshall*, EU:C:1986:84, para. 4.

[81] C-188/89, *Foster and others*, EU:C:1990:313, para. 20.

[82] C-413/15, *Farrell*, EU:C:2017:745, paras. 26, 29.

[83] C-413/15, *Farrell*, EU:C:2017:745, para. 42.

legal effects, deriving from the primacy of EU law, may also be used for that purpose.[84] Furthermore, recent developments empowering the Commission to chase Member States for failure to notify measures for the transposition of directives reduce the risk that the latter do not take full effect through national transposition measures.[85] This is all the more important given that directives are commonly used in EU law, in particular in areas which regulate interpersonal relationships, such as EU social law or consumer law.

Decisions

Decisions are binding in their entirety by virtue of Article 288 TFEU, and may thus both create rights and obligations.[86] This depends on their precise content, to whom they are addressed, and subject to compliance with the traditional criteria.

4.1.3 National Procedural Law at the Service of the EU Legal Order

On a daily basis, it is for *national* authorities – and courts, in particular – to breathe life into the doctrines of primacy and direct effect of EU law as they have just been spelt out. This results from Article 4(3) TEU on Member States' duty of sincere cooperation. Member States 'shall take any appropriate measure, general or particular, to ensure fulfilment of the obligations arising out of the Treaties or resulting from the acts of the institutions of the Union'. They shall 'facilitate the achievement of the Union's tasks and refrain from any measure which could jeopardize the attainment of the Union's objectives'. The Member States are also specifically requested to provide remedies sufficient to ensure effective legal protection in the fields covered by EU law (Article 19(1), subparagraph 2 TEU). As a consequence, and unless otherwise specified by EU law, the implementation, enforcement and judicial monitoring of EU law obligations is primarily in the hands of the Member States.

4.1.3.1 National Procedural Autonomy

This decentralised system comes with an autonomous power for the Member States which was formulated by the Court of Justice as follows:

> in the absence of [. . .] measures of harmonization [at EU level] the right conferred by [EU] law must be exercised before the national courts in accordance with the conditions laid down by national rules.[87]

By virtue of the duty of sincere cooperation, it is thus for each national legal system to decide which courts have jurisdiction, and to determine procedural conditions to ensure the protection of the rights which citizens derive from EU law. This principle was asserted in the dual cases of *Rewe* and *Comet*,[88] and is now commonly referred to as the principle of national procedural autonomy.

[84] See Chapter 4, Section 4.1.4.
[85] See Chapter 4, Section 4.2.2.3, Failure to Notify Measures Transposing a Legislative Act that Is a Directive.
[86] Illustrating vertical direct effect: Case 9/70, *Grad*, EU:C:1970:78, para. 5.
[87] Case 33/76, *Rewe*, EU:C:1976:188, para. 5. [88] Case 45/76, *Comet*, EU:C:1976:191, para. 15.

4.1.3.2 Limits to National Procedural Autonomy

National procedural autonomy is not unlimited. As is clear from the quote above, it only exists in the absence of specific EU law requirements. In recent years, EU law has become increasingly detailed on such specific requirements, as illustrated by the provisions on legal presumptions and burden of proof in the directive on transparent and predictable working conditions.[89] National procedural autonomy shall therefore not be mistaken for a principle that governs the allocation or exercise of EU competences.[90] It cannot be used to object to EU intervention on procedural matters. It merely designates the logic that governs Member States' margin of manoeuvre when ensuring fulfilment of their EU Treaty obligations to ensure the protection of EU rights and where there are no harmonised EU rules of procedure.

Furthermore, even in the absence of specific EU rules of procedure, national procedural autonomy is not absolute. Because of the risks that different national rules can create for the correct application of EU law, the Court of Justice has conditioned the application of national procedural rules on two twin requirements also asserted in *Rewe* and *Comet*.[91]

Firstly, national law ought to afford equivalent protection to rights derived from EU law when compared to rights derived from national law. For instance, a time limit to bring a claim based on an EU right cannot be less favourable than time limits relating to comparable legal actions based on national law only. There are multiple examples of national procedural rules that have been tested for compliance with the requirement of equivalent protection: these may relate to the burden of proof, the duty for courts to raise a matter of EU law of their own motion, interim relief and so on.

Second, national procedural law must ensure the effectiveness of EU law – it cannot make it 'virtually impossible or excessively difficult'[92] to exercise EU rights. By way of example, national law must provide for reasonable time limits – excluding particularly short ones – to enable claimants to bring a legal action. It must also be possible for private parties to effectively rely upon EU law before national courts.[93]

Finally, national rules giving effect to rights and obligations enshrined in EU law ought to comply with fundamental rights. In *Åkerberg Fransson*, the Court of Justice noted that tax penalties and criminal proceedings for tax evasion related to the VAT, which is addressed by a directive on the common system of value added tax[94] and relates to the financial interests of the EU protected by Article 325 TFEU, falls within the scope of EU fundamental rights law – the facts of the case constituted a threat to the *ne bis in idem* principle protected by EU law.[95] Among EU fundamental rights, Article 47 CFEU on the right to an effective remedy and to a fair trial is playing an increasingly important role in assessing the compatibility of national measures giving effect to EU law with the Charter.[96]

89 'Directive (EU) 2019/1152 of the European Parliament and of the Council of 20 June 2019 on Transparent and Predictable Working Conditions in the European Union', OJ L 186, 11.7.2019, p. 105, Arts. 15, 18. See further, M. Eliantonio and E. Muir, 'Legitimacy, Rationale and Extent of the Incidental Proceduralisation of EU Law', *Review of European Administrative Law*, 8 (2015), pp. 175–204.

90 See Chapter 3, Sections 3.3 and 3.4.

91 Case 33/76, *Rewe*, EU:C:1976:188, para. 5.

92 Case 199/82, *San Giorgio*, EU:C:1983:318, para. 14.

93 Case 222/84, *Johnston*, EU:C:1986:206, para. 17.

94 In that case, 'Council Directive 2006/112/EC of 28 November 2006 on the Common System of Value Added Tax', OJ L 347, 11.12.2006, p. 1.

95 C-617/10, *Åkerberg Fransson*, EU:C:2013:105, para. 27.

96 See Chapter 4, note 34 and see further, R. J. G. M. Widdershoven, 'National Procedural Autonomy and General EU Law Limits', *Review of European Administrative Law*, 2 (2019), pp. 5–34.

4.1.3.3 State Liability in Damages for Breaches of EU Law

Among the obligations imposed on the Member States to ensure that they take all appropriate measures to ensure the fulfilment of their obligations, one of the most advanced is the obligation of Member States to provide a mechanism to remedy loss and damage caused by the Member States' breaches of EU law. The doctrine of State liability for damages dates back to the early 1990s. In *Francovich*, the Court of Justice asserted that a State 'must be liable for loss and damage caused to individuals as a result of breaches of [EU] law for which the State can be held responsible'. This, the Court added, is 'inherent in the system of the Treaty':[97] it is another way of ensuring the primacy of EU law.[98]

This option does not result in the right protected by EU law actually being granted as such, as may result from the direct effect of a provision of EU law, or consistent interpretation of national law in light of EU law. It is often understood as a fallback option, used when other attempts to rely on EU law have failed, although it can be used in conjunction with, as well as independently from, other mechanisms.[99] The facts in the ruling in *Francovich* illustrate the point. Mr Francovich claimed to be entitled to obtain, from the Italian State, guarantees that unpaid wages would be paid to him as provided for by Directive 80/987,[100] which was intended to protect employees if their employer were to become insolvent. In the alternative, he claimed compensation. Italy had not implemented the Directive, even though the time limit to do so had expired. The Court of Justice held that where the full effectiveness of EU rules is subject to prior action on the part of the State, and where, in the absence of such action, individuals cannot enforce EU law rights before national courts,[101] it is a principle of EU law that the individual must be able to obtain redress from the State.

The conditions to succeed in obtaining damages from the State varied considerably at the national level across Europe at the time of this foundational ruling, in particular as regards liability for acts of the legislature that was not accepted in several Member States.[102] The doctrine was asserted by the Court of Justice owing to a teleological interpretation of EU law, and in the absence of specific textual guidance. Further case law thus had to clarify the criteria to be met to trigger liability for damages, in light of the fundamental principles of the EU legal system[103] and, where necessary and possible, general principles common to the

[97] Joined Cases C-6/90 and C-9/90, *Francovich and others*, EU:C:1991:428, para. 35. The Court of Justice referred, in particular, to the duty of sincere cooperation; see para. 36.

[98] See further T. Lock, 'Is Private Enforcement of EU Law through State Liability a Myth? An Assessment 20 Years after Francovich', *Common Market Law Review*, 49 (2012), pp. 1675–1702.

[99] Joined Cases C-46/93 and C-48/93, *Brasserie du Pêcheur and Factortame*, EU:C:1996:79, paras. 18–20, 22.

[100] 'Council Directive 80/987/EEC of 20 October 1980 on the Approximation of the Laws of the Member States Relating to the Protection of Employees in the Event of the Insolvency of Their Employer', OJ L 283, 28.10.1980, p. 23.

[101] Joined Cases C-6/90 and C-9/90, *Francovich and others*, EU:C:1991:428, para. 34. Here, the provisions of the directive were not sufficiently precise and unconditional to be relied upon for the purpose of triggering the direct effect of the directive: paras. 11, 26 (even though the provisions of the directive are sufficiently precise and unconditional as regards the determination of the persons entitled to the guarantee and as regards the content of that guarantee, those provisions do not identify the person liable to provide the guarantee).

[102] Joined Cases 83 and 94/76, 4, 15 and 40/77, *HNL* v. *Council and Commission*, EU:C:1978:113, para. 5; Opinion of Advocate General Léger, C-5/94, *Hedley Lomas*, EU:C:1995:193, paras. 96–100.

[103] Such as drawing a parallel with the conditions for non-contractual liability of the EU for damage caused by its institutions.

legal systems of the Member States. In *Brasserie du Pêcheur and Factortame*,[104] the Court of Justice refined its approach. The three conditions, which are both necessary and sufficient,[105] can now be summarised as follows:

1. The provision of EU law infringed must be intended to confer rights on individuals.[106]
2. There must be a sufficiently serious breach of EU law. The key question is whether the Member State manifestly and gravely disregarded the limits on its discretion. The less discretion that was left to the Member State, the easier it would be to show that the threshold for a sufficiently serious breach has been met. For instance, failure to take any measure to transpose a directive in order to achieve the result it prescribes within the period laid down for that purpose constitutes a sufficiently serious breach.[107]
3. There must be a direct causal link between the breach of the obligation resting on the State – which could result from an act or an omission – and the damage sustained by the injured parties.

The Court of Justice specified that the doctrine of State liability for damages holds good 'for any case in which a Member State breaches [EU] law, whatever be the organ of the State whose act or omission was responsible for the breach'.[108] As a consequence, the doctrine applies in case of a breach caused by the administration as well as by the national legislative branch.[109] This also includes liability for loss or damage caused by a decision of a national court adjudicating at last instance.[110] The Court of Justice has explained the rationale for this ambitious approach to State liability for damages in *Köbler*. The Court also clarified that the conditions for State liability in the context of loss or damage caused by the judiciary remain the same, although, as regards the condition of a sufficiently serious breach of EU law:

> regard must be had to the specific nature of the judicial function and to the legitimate requirements of legal certainty [. . .]. State liability for an infringement of [. . .] law by a decision of a national court adjudicating at last instance can be incurred only in the exceptional case where the court has manifestly infringed the applicable law.[111]

In *Köbler*, for instance, the Supreme Administrative Court of Austria was in breach of its duty to refer a preliminary question on the interpretation of EU law to the Court of Justice – but in this case it was deemed *not* to constitute a sufficiently serious breach to trigger State

[104] Joined Cases C-46/93 and C-48/93, *Brasserie du Pêcheur and Factortame*, EU:C:1996:79, para. 51 *et seq.*

[105] Member States may not add conditions such as a requirement of 'fault' going beyond that of a sufficiently serious breach; Joined Cases C-46/93 and C-48/93, *Brasserie du Pêcheur and Factortame*, EU:C:1996:79, para. 79.

[106] This requirement is distinct from the ones for the direct effect of provisions of EU law, as will be discussed subsequently, and as exemplified by the ruling in *Francovich*; see Chapter 4, note 101 and see further paras. 34, 40–41.

[107] Joined Cases 178-9 and 188-90/94, *Dillenkofer and others*, EU:C:1996:375, para. 29. Similarly, a breach is sufficiently serious if it has persisted despite a judgment finding the infringement in question to be established, or a preliminary ruling or settled case law of the Court on the matter from which it is clear that the conduct in question constituted an infringement; Joined Cases C-46/93 and C-48/93, *Brasserie du Pêcheur and Factortame*, EU:C:1996:79, para. 57.

[108] Joined Cases C-46/93 and C-48/93, *Brasserie du Pêcheur and Factortame*, EU:C:1996:79, para. 32.

[109] Ibid., paras. 32–36. [110] C-224/01, *Köbler*, EU:C:2003:513, paras. 33–34. [111] Ibid., paras. 52–53.

liability.[112] Despite the theoretical possibility of a finding of State liability for the acts of the judiciary as just described, the mechanism is not used much in practice.[113] This is understandable in light of the high threshold that has to be met. Furthermore, it is remarkable that lower courts may thereby be expected to assess the consequences of breaches of EU law by higher courts within the same judicial system.

While the criteria identified previously are set out by the Court of Justice of the European Union, the factual evaluation and procedural consequences of a finding of State liability for damages are left for the Member States. The latter are autonomous in that regard, as long as they ensure effective protection of EU rights and a protection equivalent to national rights. It is also for each internal legal order to designate the competent courts.[114] It may be added that case law, as well as legislation, have developed EU-level mechanisms to allow compensation for breaches of certain provisions of EU competition law by private parties.[115]

4.1.4 Primacy, Direct Effect and National Procedural Law Together

The primacy and the direct effect of EU law work hand in hand[116] to ensure the full effect of the latter in national legal orders, through national procedural law. The interplay between the various concepts is briefly recalled here.

Primacy results in the prohibition for Member States to adopt measures or practices contravening EU law, as well as in the duty to brush away inconsistencies. Such inconsistencies may be eliminated by national authorities invalidating or repealing conflicting measures as well as (to the extent possible) by interpreting national law in conformity with EU law.

It may be, however, that a national rule cannot be interpreted in conformity with EU law and is in direct conflict with a rule of EU law, or that national law is silent on a right granted by EU law. Depending on the nature of the instrument of EU law at hand, and of the vertical or horizontal nature of the dispute, a provision of EU law that fulfils the general criteria for *direct effect* may be directly relied upon before national courts. This can result in the duty of the national court to grant the right enshrined in a directly effective provision of EU law (here, EU law is used as a sword); or in a duty for the national authority to set aside the

[112] It may be recalled that the Member States may not add stricter conditions for liability in damages to those listed previously. This holds true in claims of liability for damages caused by the judiciary; C-173/03, *Traghetti del Mediterraneo*, EU:C:2006:391, paras. 45–46 (national legislation may not limit liability solely to cases of intentional fault and serious misconduct on the part of the court).

[113] Z. Varga, 'Why Is the Köbler Principle Not Applied in Practice?', *Maastricht Journal of European and Comparative Law*, 23 (2016), pp. 984–1008.

[114] Respectively, Joined Cases C-46/93 and C-48/93, *Brasserie du Pêcheur and Factortame*, EU:C:1996:79, para. 67; Joined Cases C-6/90 and C-9/90, *Francovich and others*, EU:C:1991:428, para. 42.

[115] C-453/99, *Courage and Crehan*, EU:C:2001:465, para. 26 and Joined Cases C-295/04 to C-298/04, *Manfredi and others*, EU:C:2006:461, para. 63 (as regards breaches of Art. 101 TFEU); and 'Directive 2014/104/EU of the European Parliament and of the Council of 26 November 2014 on Certain Rules Governing Actions for Damages under National Law for Infringements of the Competition Law Provisions of the Member States and of the European Union', OJ L 349, 5.12.2014, p. 1.

[116] It must be stressed that the relationship between primacy and direct effect remains subject to much academic debate, and is not always clear from the case law of the Court of Justice. See further M. Dougan, 'When Worlds Collide: Competing Visions of the Relationship between Primacy and Direct Effect', *Common Market Law Review*, 44 (2007), pp. 931–963; E. Muir, 'Of Ages in – and Edges of – EU Law', *Common Market Law Review*, 48 (2011), pp. 39–62.

contravening rule of national law in the dispute at hand, if there is rule contravening a directly effective provision of EU law (here, EU law is used a shield). The Court of Justice specified in *Popławski II* that, conversely, a provision of EU law which does *not* have direct effect may *not* be relied on, as such, in order to disapply a provision of national law that conflicts with it.[117]

By virtue of the duty of *sincere cooperation*, the Member States ought to ensure that EU rights receive effective protection in the national legal system, and that this protection is equivalent to that afforded to rights originating in national law. In particular, national courts ought to make good the damage caused by the State's non-compliance with EU law subject to the *Francovich* line of cases. Furthermore, national courts ought to set aside national rules of procedure that hinder the effective protection of EU rights. The ruling by the Court of Justice in *Országos* provides a concrete example of the far-reaching implications of this approach: where national law absolutely prevents a court from ruling on respect for EU rights in relation to detention of an applicant for international protection, the national court ought to declare that it has jurisdiction to examine the lawfulness of such detention, disapplying, where necessary, any national provision which prohibits it from proceeding in that way. The duty thereby imposed on the national judge results from the conjunction of the primacy of EU law and sincere cooperation, on the one hand, and the need to ensure effective judicial protection of EU rights as requested by the Directive laying down standards for the reception of applicants for international protection and Article 47 CFEU, on the other hand.[118]

In all the settings mentioned, the vigilance of individuals in protecting their EU rights is crucial, alongside that of public organs, to ensure the good operation of EU law. This private prong of the 'dual vigilance' system set out in *Van Gend en Loos* works before national courts irrespective of their level in the national judicial system, thus making these courts key agents of the EU system of judicial remedies, as forcefully illustrated in *Országos*.

4.2 CENTRALISED COMPONENTS OF THE EU'S DECENTRALISED ENFORCEMENT MACHINERY

EU institutions may decide themselves to specify how to achieve the effective protection and even enforcement of EU rights. This was exemplified previously with reference to EU legislation on legal presumptions and burden of proof for predictable working conditions.[119] In certain policy areas, EU organs also have advanced enforcement powers, as illustrated by those of the Commission in the field of antitrust. The Commission may, for instance, conduct inquiries into a particular type of agreements between undertakings, as well as inspect the premises of undertakings and impose

[117] C-573/17, *Popławski*, EU:C:2019:530, paras. 61–62; see also Chapter 4, note 34.

[118] 'Directive 2013/33/EU of the European Parliament and of the Council of 26 June 2013 Laying Down Standards for the Reception of Applicants for International Protection' (recast), OJ L 180, 29.6.2013, pp. 96–116, Art. 9(3); Joined Cases C-924/19 PPU and C-925/19 PPU, *Országos*, EU:C:2020:367, paras. 290–291. See further Chapter 4, note 34.

[119] See Chapter 4, note 89.

fines.[120] Unless such specific rules exist though (as noted previously in Section 4.1.3.1), the main characteristic of the EU legal order is that it relies on implementation and enforcement at the national level – a decentralised model. Yet this is also a model that relies on a sophisticated system of centralised monitoring to ensure the smooth functioning of the EU legal order.

4.2.1 Who Is in Charge of Centralised Monitoring?

The European Commission is the 'Guardian of the EU Treaties'. As observed previously, according to Article 17(1) TEU, it:

> shall promote the general interest of the Union and take appropriate initiatives to that end. It shall ensure the application of the Treaties, and of measures adopted by the institutions pursuant to them. It shall oversee the application of Union law under the control of the Court of Justice of the European Union.

While the Commission monitors, reports and engages in dialogue with national authorities on the implementation of EU law, it may also commence legal proceedings against them before the Court of Justice. The Court of Justice of the European Union shall, for its part, 'ensure that in the interpretation and application of the Treaties the law is observed' (Article 19(1), subparagraph 1 TEU).[121]

As will be explained subsequently, Member States may also monitor each other by commencing legal proceedings before the Court of Justice. Furthermore, and most importantly, national courts before which private parties are litigating can also benefit from the guidance of the Court of Justice.

Along with the procedures provided for in the EU Treaties, as will be elaborated upon subsequently, it shall be noted that there are a multitude of non-judicial problem-solving mechanisms to enhance compliance with EU law. Once may, for instance, refer to the compliance dialogues and EU pilot projects created by the Commission,[122] SOLVIT[123] or the European Network of Ombudsmen.[124] Ultimately though, the last word on any dispute related to the interpretation and application of EU law will be given by the Court of Justice of the European Union.

4.2.2 Infringement Action

The Commission and the Member States monitor compliance with EU law and may trigger legal action before the Court of Justice of the European Union – more specifically, the Court of Justice in such settings – in case of infringement of EU law by a Member State. The

[120] 'Council Regulation (EC) No. 1/2003 of 16 December 2002 on the Implementation of the Rules on Competition Laid Down in Articles 81 and 82 of the Treaty', OJ L 1, 4.1.2003 (last amended 2009), Arts. 17, 20, 23.

[121] For an in-depth overview of the institution and its work, see Lenaerts et al., *EU Procedural Law*.

[122] Commission, Communication, 'EU Law: Better Results through Better Application', OJ C 18, 19.1.2017, pp. 11–12.

[123] A service provided by the national administration in each EU country, free of charge, and mainly online, it aims to find solutions within ten weeks; https://ec.europa.eu/solvit.

[124] It facilitates cooperation between ombudsmen, with a view to safeguarding the rights of EU citizens and individuals under EU law; www.ombudsman.europa.eu/en/european-network-of-ombudsmen/about/en.

procedure has changed significantly over time, gaining more bite against recalcitrant Member States. The mechanism is set out in what are now Articles 258, 259 and 260 TFEU.[126] The infringement procedure is remarkable in that it allows a Member State to be brought before supranational judges in a fairly routine manner.

4.2.2.1 Procedure Initiated by the Commission

Article 258 TFEU can be usefully reproduced here (Box 4.1) while emphasising the various stages of the procedure, to which we return subsequently.

Box 4.1 Rough guide to the Commission initiating an infringement action[125]

Article 258 TFEU

If the Commission considers that a Member State has failed to fulfil an obligation under the Treaties [1], it shall deliver a reasoned opinion on the matter [3] after giving the State concerned the opportunity to submit its observations [2].

If the State concerned does not comply with the opinion within the period laid down by the Commission, the latter may bring the matter before the Court of Justice of the European Union [4].

Administrative versus Judicial Phases

1. The Commission can only initiate the procedure if it considers that there has been an infringement of EU law.[127] The Commission may become aware of such problems through a multitude of sources of information, such as individual complaints addressed to it, petitions submitted to the Parliament and parliamentary questions to the Commission, and failure by the Member States to notify measures for the transposition of directives that they are usually requested to communicate. Despite the peremptory tone of the first sentence of Article 258 TFEU, the Commission is not bound by the Treaty to pursue all findings of infringement; this in fact would not be feasible. The Commission thus decides which problems to treat as a matter of priority, and regularly seeks to shed light on its approach, as in its latest Communication on 'Better results through better application'. The Commission indeed announces a focus on the most important infringements. These are understood to be those which obstruct the implementation of important EU policy objectives, or which risk undermining the four fundamental freedoms, failures to communicate transposition measures, or where those measures have incorrectly transposed directives.[128]

[125] Bracketed numbering added.

[126] See further L. Prete, 'Enforcement Actions', in Schütze and Tridimas (eds.), *Oxford Principles of European Union Law*, pp. 942–980.

[127] See further L. Prete and B. Smulders, 'The Age of Maturity of Infringement Proceedings', *Common Market Law Review*, 58 (2020), pp. 289–294.

[128] Commission, Communication, 'EU Law: Better Results through Better Application', OJ C 18, 19.1.2017, p. 10, Section 3. The extent to which the Commission actually follows these priorities is subject to controversy.

When assessing the existence of an infringement of EU law by a Member State, the Commission can adopt a generous approach to the entities that may trigger liability on the part of the State. This is quite straightforward if the infringement results from the act of the national administration, or the legislator. Article 258 TFEU, however, may also be triggered by acts of the national highest courts,[129] or where action on the part of the government is insufficient to address frequent and serious incidents caused by private parties in breach of EU law.[130] An example of the latter scenario is known as the *Angry farmers*' case: the free movement of fruit and vegetables in the EU was obstructed by violent and recurrent protest movements of private farmers based in France and directed against agricultural products from other Member States, involving, for instance, intercepting lorries and destroying their loads. France could be held liable for the actions of the farmers, for having failed to bring them to an end.

2. If the Commission decides to initiate the first stages of an infringement procedure, it shall first of all give the Member State concerned an opportunity to submit observations. The Commission does so by informally approaching the Member State and thereby privileging voluntary compliance. If the Member State is not responsive, this may lead to issuing a first formal document known as the 'letter of formal notice', which establishes the scope of the infringement and requests further information from the country concerned, within a specified period, usually two months.[131]

3. It is only if the letter of formal notice has been unsuccessful that the Commission may decide to issue a 'reasoned opinion', which is the second formal document. The reasoned opinion explains in detail why the Commission considers that the Member State is breaching EU law[132] and requests compliance. It also demands that the Member State inform the Commission of the measures taken, within a specified period, also usually two months.[133]

The letter of formal notice and reasoned opinion are important because they set out the legal scope and time frame for the procedure that may lead to litigation before the Court of Justice.[134] They are thus procedural requirements[135] ensuring that the Member State has been given a fair opportunity to adjust its position or to prepare its defence.[136]

[129] E.g. C-416/17, *Commission* v. *France (Advance payment)*, EU:C:2018:811, paras. 106–114. Here, the French Council of State had wrongfully failed to make a reference to the Court of Justice, in accordance with the procedure provided for by Art. 267(3) TFEU, in order to clarify the interpretation of EU law.

[130] C-265/95, *Commission* v. *France (Angry farmers)*, EU:C:1997:595, para. 52.

[131] Commission, 'Infringement procedure', ec.europa.eu/info/law/law-making-process/applying-eu-law/infringement-procedure_en.

[132] There must be a sufficient statement of reasons; Case 301/81, *Commission* v. *Belgium (Credit institutions)*, EU:C:1983:51, para. 8.

[133] Commission, 'Infringement procedure', ec.europa.eu/info/law/law-making-process/applying-eu-law/infringement-procedure_en.

[134] The subject matter of an action under Art. 258 TFEU is established by the reasoned opinion, and even when the fault has been remedied after the time limit prescribed therein, there is still a subject matter for the action if the Commission decides to pursue the case. This may, for instance, subsequently help, in the context of distinct legal proceedings, to establish a breach of EU law for the purpose of forming the basis of State liability for damages; Case 39/72, *Commission* v. *Italy (Premiums for slaughtering cows)*, EU:C:1973:13, paras. 9, 11.

[135] The opportunity for the Member State to submit its observations constitutes an essential formal requirement; Case 51/83, *Commission* v. *Italy*, EU:C:1984:261, para. 5.

[136] The reasoned opinion may not extend beyond the scope of the letter of formal notice (Case 51/83, *Commission* v. *Italy*, EU:C:1984:261, paras. 6–8) and the application for the judicial phase must be based on the same grounds as the reasoned opinion (Case 211/81, *Commission* v. *Denmark*, EU:C:1982:437, para. 14). The reasoned opinion,

4. In the event of continued non-compliance, the Commission may commence legal proceedings against the Member State in question before the Court of Justice. It is only then that the judicial phase of the infringement action, in contrast to the pre-litigation or administrative phases described so far, begins.

Figures usefully illustrate the relative use of the various phases above, and the prevalence of the non-judicial phase: in 2020, the Commission launched 903 new procedures by sending a letter of formal notice, but only 152 reasoned opinions, and the Court rendered only twenty-eight judgments in the context of infringement proceedings brought before it.[137]

Discretion of the Commission

The key feature of all four stages is the Commission's discretion on the decision to start, pursue or interrupt the procedure. The Commission often decides not to initiate, or to interrupt the procedure, because the State is deemed to have complied with EU law. Member States indeed make serious efforts to address their infringements. For instance, in 2020 again, the Commission closed nine cases *after* deciding to refer the case to the Court of Justice, but *before* submitting the actual application. This was because the relevant Member States had taken the necessary measures to comply with the requests of the Commission, and the latter did not deem it useful to pursue the case.[138] In practice, the Commission may also decide not to move forward because the problem is not a priority (any longer), or because it deems the matter too sensitive and/or better addressed through other means.

The Commission is also free, if it takes action, to decide on the timing of such an action. It sometimes takes several years before the Commission sends a reasoned opinion or refers a matter to the Court of Justice. Importantly, such delays or a lack of action is not necessarily, or not systematically, a weakness or a failure on the part of the Commission – it may be a wise choice. The purpose of the procedure is to ensure compliance with EU law, which at times requires lengthy exchanges between the Commission and the Member State concerned – for instance, if the matter is highly technical. Furthermore, it shall be remembered that the infringement action is remarkable in that it allows a State to be brought before a supranational jurisdiction, and this may require careful prioritising on the part of the institution in charge, as explained in the Communication on 'Better results through better application' mentioned previously.[139]

The Commission's discretion has important legal consequences, as made clear in *Star Fruit*.[140] One may not seek the annulment of a decision by which the Commission makes it clear that it will *not* make use of Article 258 TFEU. Nor may one bring an action against the

and then the application, however, might be more detailed than previous letters. The scope of the claim might be narrowed down (C-279/94, *Commission* v. *Italy*, EU:C:1997:396, paras. 24–25).

137 Commission, 'Commission Staff Working Document. Part I: General Overview', *Monitoring the Application of European Union Law: 2020 Annual Report*, 23.07.2021, pp. 21, 22, 24 (the data include judgments under both Arts. 258 and 260(2) TFEU).

138 Ibid., p. 24. Note that the subject matter of an action under Art. 258 TFEU is established by the reasoned opinion, and even when the fault has been remedied after the time-limit prescribed therein, there is still a subject matter for the action if the Commission decides to pursue the case. See Chapter 4, note 134.

139 Commission, Communication, 'EU Law: Better Results through Better Application', OJ C 18, 19.1.2017, p. 10.

140 Case 247/87, *Star Fruit*, EU:C:1989:58, paras. 10–13.

Commission for failure, and thus omission, to initiate a procedure under Article 258 TFEU. The EU also cannot be held liable for damages in that context.[141]

4.2.2.2 Procedure Initiated by a Member State

Although the Commission is seen as the primary organ responsible for initiating infringement actions, it is also possible for a Member State to take another Member State before the Court of Justice for breach of EU law. The sensitivity of this approach makes it a rare phenomenon. The related procedure is adjusted to enable the Commission to take the matter into its own hands if it so wishes, and if the interested Member State does not insist on taking action itself.

Indeed, Article 259 TFEU requires that, before a Member State brings an action against another Member State for an alleged infringement of an obligation under the Treaties, it shall bring the matter before the Commission. The Commission must then deliver a reasoned opinion after each of the States concerned has been given the opportunity to submit its observations.

Once again though, the Commission has discretion. Article 259 TFEU thus foresees that, if the Commission has not delivered a reasoned opinion observing an infringement within three months of the date on which the matter was brought before it, the absence of such opinion shall not prevent the Member State in question from bringing the case before the Court of Justice itself. In fact, the Member State may decide to take action even if the Commission issues a reasoned opinion observing an infringement of EU law.[142]

To date, there are only a handful of examples of litigation brought before the Court of Justice by a Member State against another one, and these are typically of a highly political nature.[143] Examples are a dispute between Spain and the UK related to the voting rights of residents in Gibraltar,[144] and between Hungary and the Slovak Republic in relation to a refusal to allow the President of Hungary to enter Slovak territory to celebrate a sensitive historical event between the two countries.[145] More recently, a high profile case was triggered by the Czech Republic against Poland on matters raising important issues of compliance with EU environmental law.[146]

4.2.2.3 Judicial Phase

Infringement Actions before the Court of Justice

Once the case is brought before the Court of Justice, on the basis of either Article 258 or 259 TFEU, the Court will examine the claim. In practice, after what are often extensive exchanges between the Commission – as the applicant (rather than another Member State) in the vast majority of cases – and the Member State, the judicial part of the procedure

[141] C-72/90, *Asia Motor France* v. *Commission*, EU:C:1990:230, para. 13. One may, however, have a claim against the Member State.

[142] Case 141/78, *France* v. *UK (Sea fisheries)*, EU:C:1979:225, para. 2.

[143] C-457/18, *Slovenia* v. *Croatia*, EU:C:2020:65, decided in January 2020, was the eighth case in the history of the Court of a Member State bringing infringement proceedings against another Member State; CJEU, Press release 131/12, 18.6.2018.

[144] C-145/04, *Spain* v. *UK*, EU:C:2006:543. [145] C-364/10, *Hungary* v. *Slovak Republic*, EU:C:2012:630.

[146] C-121/21, *Czech Republic* v. *Republic of Poland*, EU:C:2022:82. Interim measures were granted by Order C-212/21 R. The case was ultimately withdrawn after an amicable settlement between the parties.

often results in a finding against the State. It was so in twenty-seven out of twenty-eight cases in 2020.[147] Importantly, the legal dispute primarily revolves around what may be the appropriate interpretation of EU obligations. The Commission bears the burden of proof and will argue in favour of what it believes to be in the EU's interest. The Court of Justice may find not only the existence of a breach of EU law, but also the existence of a 'repeated and persistent' or 'systemic and persistent' breach, as found, in particular, in certain environmental protection cases.[148]

Member States have often tried to use a vast array of arguments to claim exceptional treatment and thereby escape their EU obligations. Yet the Court of Justice is very reluctant to accept these lines of defence tailored to individual Member States. Instead, it reasserts that EU law unconditionally takes precedence over national law. It refuses to accept as a valid defence that an EU institution, or another Member State, also failed to fulfil its obligations.[149] The dissolution of the national parliament and even a bomb attack against a data-processing centre, making it very difficult to process EU requirements, were not deemed to be acceptable defences.[150] Finally, infringement proceedings are still possible even when an EU law obligation has ceased to exist at the time of the ruling, which was recently illustrated in a case against Poland, Hungary and the Czech Republic for failure to relocate applicants for international protection, as required under a temporary obligation that had ceased to exist.[151] The alleged infringement of EU law is indeed assessed at the expiry of the deadline set in the reasoned opinion.[152]

Failure to Comply with a Ruling on Infringement

When the Court of Justice rules that the Member State has infringed EU law and requires it to take the necessary measures to comply with its judgment, this is purely declaratory. The Court of Justice does not have the power to modify national law. This leaves open the possibility that the Member State will not correct its failure, as indeed sometimes happens. Various reforms of the EU Treaties have sought to improve the functioning of the infringement procedure on that point. What may the Commission do if it finds that the State concerned has not taken the necessary measures to comply with the judgment? Well, it may, with the same discretionary power observed previously,[153] decide to initiate another infringement procedure.

[147] Commission, 'Commission Staff Working Document. Part I: General Overview', *Monitoring the Application of European Union Law: 2020 Annual Report*, 23.07.2021, p. 24 (the data include judgments under both Arts. 258 and 260(2) TFEU).

[148] C-494/01, *Commission* v. *Ireland (Waste management)*, EU:C:2005:250, paras. 27, 47; C-644/18, *Commission* v. *Italy (Ambient air quality)*, EU:C:2020:895, paras. 71–76, 146.

[149] Joined Cases 90 and 91/63, *Commission* v. *Luxembourg and Belgium*, EU:C:1964:80, para. 2; Case 52/75, *Commission* v. *Italy*, EU:C:1976:29, para. 11.

[150] Case 77/69, *Commission* v. *Belgium*, EU:C:1970:34, para. 15; Case 28/81, *Commission* v. *Italy*, EU:C:1985:330, para. 16 (the effects of the bomb attack could only have lasted a certain time).

[151] Joined Cases C-715/17, C-718/17 and C-719/17, *Commission* v. *Poland, Hungary and Czech Republic*, EU:C:2020:257, para. 57.

[152] See also Chapter 4, note 133.

[153] Illustrating the discretion of the Commission on the time frame, see C-328/16, *Commission* v. *Greece (Urban waste-water treatment)*, EU:C:2018:98, paras. 23, 26. Here, a Directive had to be implemented by 1998, the first ruling finding an infringement came in 2004, and the second in 2018.

In this second round, however, the procedure can be fast-tracked to a certain extent. According to Article 260(2) TFEU, there is no need for a reasoned opinion. It is enough to allow the State to submit its observations by means of a letter of formal notice. The second action is also more powerful: the Commission can propose a lump sum and/or a penalty payment to be paid by the State concerned. Whether to impose such measures is ultimately to be decided by the Court of Justice if it finds there was a failure to comply with the first judgment.[154] The function of the lump sum, which is a defined amount to be paid, is to act as a sanction for the continued infringement after the first ruling, as well as to reflect on the effects of such infringement on public and private interests – and at times to deter similar infringements from being repeated.[155] The lump sum may be combined with a penalty payment, a sum to be paid per day of additional delay, to bring national law into compliance with the first ruling finding an infringement. The penalty payment thus comes as an incentive to comply quickly.[156] In practice, the Commission systematically asks for both the lump sum and the periodic penalty payment.[157]

Member States often take the measures necessary to comply with a Court judgment promptly though.[158] In 2020, the Court of Justice only gave three judgments under Article 260(2) TFEU in a second infringement action.[159] Member States are reported to normally pay lump sums and penalty payments if ordered to do so by the Court of Justice.[160]

Failure to Notify Measures Transposing a Legislative Act that Is a Directive

The current EU Treaties provide for a specific tool to challenge infringements of EU law flowing from a failure to notify measures requested for the transposition of a directive adopted through a legislative procedure. Such infringements have a number of characteristics: they are frequent, they may be easier to identify (if they do not require detailed qualitative analysis) and they are a political priority for the Commission so as to ensure the effectiveness of directives.[161]

[154] The proposals by the Commission on a lump sum and penalty payment are not binding on the Court, but are treated as 'a useful point of reference'; C-387/97, *Commission* v. *Greece (Waste)*, EU:C:2000:356, para. 89.

[155] C-328/16, *Commission* v. *Greece (Urban waste-water treatment)*, EU:C:2018:98, para. 118.

[156] C-304/02, *Commission* v. *France (Fisheries conservation)*, EU:C:2005:444, paras. 80–83.

[157] Commission, Communication, 'EU Law: Better Results through Better Application', OJ C 18, 19.1.2017, p. 15. Further information on the policy of the Commission on the matter is provided by the Commission itself: Commission, Communication, 'Application of Article 228 of the EC Treaty' (today, Art. 260 TFEU), SEC(2005)1658, para. 10.3 *et seq.*; and regular updates on data used to calculate lump sum and penalty payments, e.g. taking into account the impact of the COVID-19 pandemic, see Commission, Communication, 'Updating of Data Used to Calculate Lump Sum and Penalty Payments to Be Proposed by the Commission to the Court of Justice of the European Union in Infringement Proceedings', OJ C 74, 15.2.2022, p. 2.

[158] Commission, 'Commission Staff Working Document. Part I: General Overview', *Monitoring the Application of European Union Law: 2020 Annual Report*, 23.07.2021, p. 24.

[159] Ibid., p. 23.

[160] Alternatively, the sums due by the Member States could be deducted from financial support granted by the EU to the Member State in question; see further 'Regulation (EU, Euratom) 2018/1046 of the European Parliament and of the Council of 18 July 2018 on the Financial Rules Applicable to the General Budget of the Union', OJ L 193, 30.7.2018 (last amended 2021). For an example of payment problems, see M. Brion, 'European Commission to Withhold EU Funds Allocated to Poland over Turów Mine Case', *Europe Daily Bulletin* 12886 (Agence Europe, 9.2.2022).

[161] There were 599 new late transposition infringements in 2020. Commission, 'Commission Staff Working Document. Part I: General Overview', *Monitoring the Application of European Union Law: 2020 Annual Report*, 23.07.2021, p. 27.

Article 260(3) TFEU sets out a simplified and more efficient version of the infringement procedure to address these breaches of EU law. The Commission may propose a lump sum and penalty payment[162] to apply from the date of the *first* infringement action brought before the Court of Justice under Article 258 TFEU.[163] The Court of Justice will ultimately decide on whether to award the measures, but they may not decide on an amount that exceeds what the Commission has asked for.

In its first cases on the matter, the Court of Justice has asserted that it would use this mechanism to enhance the effects of directives:

> the obligation to adopt the national measures for the purposes of ensuring that a directive is transposed in full and the obligation to notify those measures to the Commission are fundamental obligations incumbent on the Member States in order to ensure optimal effectiveness of EU law and that failure to fulfil those obligations must therefore be regarded as undoubtedly serious.[164]

The failure to comply with EU law for the purpose of triggering Article 260(3) TFEU may therefore result from a failure to notify to the Commission all, but also parts only, of the transposition measures, as well as from the provision of insufficiently clear and precise information on the matter. Member States are required to specify, for each provision of the directive, the national provision or provisions ensuring its transposition.[165] The objective of this demanding approach is to ensure that the Commission has all the necessary information to examine the content of the transposition measures. The Commission may thereby subsequently decide on whether to trigger an infringement action for 'incorrect' transposition of the directive (within the meaning of Article 258, in conjunction with Article 260(2) TFEU) – rather than 'non-communication' and 'non-transposition' (Article 258, in conjunction with Article 260(3) TFEU).[166]

Furthermore, the Court has indicated that the amount to be paid as part of a lump sum, thus with a punitive and possibly dissuasive effect, would be calculated from the date of the expiry of the transposition period of the directive concerned – rather than at the expiry of the reasoned opinion, as for other types of infringement action, and which would have been more favourable to the defendant State.[167] By way of example, and although the Member States had ultimately notified their transposition measures before the judgment,[168] in 2020 the Court of Justice ordered Romania and Ireland to pay lump sums of 3 million euros and 2 million euros respectively. These States had failed to transpose in full, within the period

[162] Subject to specificities introduced subsequently, the case law on lump sums (C-549/18, *Commission* v. *Romania*, EU:C:2020:563, para. 72) and penalty payments (C-543/17, *Commission* v. *Belgium (High Speed Networks)*, EU:C:2019:573, para. 61) in relation to Art. 260(2) TFEU applies by analogy to Art. 260(3) TFEU.

[163] In practice, the Commission systematically asks for both; Commission, Communication, 'EU Law: Better Results through Better Application', OJ C 18, 19.1.2017, p. 15. The Commission is under no obligation to motivate its decision to propose these, but ought to motivate its decision on the nature and amount of what is requested; C-549/18, *Commission* v. *Romania*, EU:C:2020:563, paras. 48, 51. The Court of Justice, on the other hand, must state reasons when imposing penalties or lump sums.

[164] C-543/17, *Commission* v. *Belgium (High Speed Networks)*, EU:C:2019:573, para. 85. [165] Ibid., para. 59.

[166] Ibid., paras. 51–59. [167] C-549/18, *Commission* v. *Romania*, EU:C:2020:563, paras. 69, 79–83.

[168] Ibid., para. 67.

prescribed, the directive on the prevention of the use of the financial system for the purposes of money laundering or terrorist financing.[169]

4.2.3 Preliminary Ruling Procedure

The preliminary ruling procedure, set out in Article 267 TFEU (reproduced in Box 4.2), is an instrument allowing national courts, seised of disputes related to EU law, to seek interpretative guidance from the Court of Justice. As noted already,[170] the doctrines of primacy and direct effect of EU law may be activated before national judges of any level. The latter are thus understood as the ordinary judges of EU law, and may liaise with the Court of Justice through the preliminary ruling procedure to ensure consistency in the EU legal order. Public authorities, as well as individuals, may benefit from this procedure to ensure the correct application of EU law before national courts.

Box 4.2 **Rough guide to the preliminary ruling procedure**

Article 267 TFEU

The Court of Justice of the European Union shall have jurisdiction to give preliminary rulings concerning:

(a) the interpretation of the Treaties;
(b) the validity and interpretation of acts of the institutions, bodies, offices or agencies of the Union;

Where such a question is raised before any court or tribunal of a Member State, that court or tribunal may, if it considers that a decision on the question is necessary to enable it to give judgment, request the Court to give a ruling thereon.

Where any such question is raised in a case pending before a court or tribunal of a Member State against whose decisions there is no judicial remedy under national law, that court or tribunal shall bring the matter before the Court.

If such a question is raised in a case pending before a court or tribunal of a Member State with regard to a person in custody, the Court of Justice of the European Union shall act with the minimum of delay.

In the foundational ruling *Costa* v. *ENEL*, the Court of Justice made it clear that Article 267 TFEU 'is to be applied regardless of any domestic law, whenever questions relating to the interpretation of the Treaty arise'.[171] This procedure is the keystone of the system of judicial remedies precisely because it allows the enforcement of EU law at national level to blossom for a better application of EU law, while ensuring consistency across the EU legal

[169] 'Directive (EU) 2015/849 of the European Parliament and of the Council of 20 May 2015 on the Prevention of the Use of the Financial System for the Purposes of Money Laundering or Terrorist Financing', OJ L 141, 5.6.2015, p. 73; C-549/18, *Commission* v. *Romania*, EU:C:2020:563, para. 86; C-550/18, *Commission* v. *Ireland*, EU:C:2020:564, para. 98.

[170] See Chapter 4, Sections 4.1.1 and 4.1.2.

[171] Case 6/64, *Costa* v. *ENEL*, EU:C:1964:66.

order.[172] This is reflected in the fact that the procedure represents, in practice, around 75 per cent of the workload of the Court of Justice, and it is used intensively in sensitive areas such as the AFSJ and taxation.[173] The importance of the procedure is illustrated by the fact that the Court of Justice itself, by opposition to the General Court, is so far retaining jurisdiction to answer questions from national judges.[174]

4.2.3.1 Who May Ask for a Preliminary Ruling

In accordance with Article 267 TFEU, 'any court or tribunal of a Member State' before which a question of EU law is raised may make use of the preliminary ruling procedure. To determine whether the organ making contact is such a court or tribunal, the Court of Justice has developed its own set of criteria. In particular, it looks at 'whether the body is established by law, whether it is permanent, whether its jurisdiction is compulsory, whether its procedure is *inter partes*, whether it applies rules of law and whether it is independent'. These are known as the *Dorsch Consult* criteria.[175] The concern of the Court of Justice is to ensure a dialogue between genuine judicial organs, to the exclusion of an attempt, in particular, by administrative bodies to obtain clearance in case of doubts on the interpretation of EU law.[176]

In recent years, the Court of Justice has devoted specific attention to ensuring that organs making use of the preliminary ruling are 'independent': they must be autonomous from external influence (notably, judges must, in principle, be irremovable) and be impartial.[177] The Court, for instance, rejected the admissibility of questions from the Central Tax Tribunal in Spain, notably because national legislation did not provide particular safeguards in respect of the removal or the termination of the appointment of its members.[178] Note, however, that challenges against decisions of the said Tribunal, before genuine courts or tribunals within the meaning of Article 267 TFEU could be admissible in due course.[179]

4.2.3.2 Types of Preliminary Questions

The preliminary ruling procedure enables national courts or tribunals to ask the Court of Justice a question on the interpretation of EU law – these are the most common questions asked. The national court or tribunal may also ask a question on the validity of acts of EU institutions, bodies, offices or agencies. This second type of question is less common, and opens up the possibility for both public and private parties involved in litigation before national courts to call into question the validity of EU acts that may affect them. This possibility is all the more important given that, as will be seen subsequently, it is particularly difficult for these private parties to challenge the validity of EU acts by bringing a case directly before the organs of the

[172] C-284/16, *Achmea*, EU:C:2018:158, para. 37. See further N. Wahl and L. Prete, 'The Gatekeepers of Article 267 TFEU: On Jurisdiction and Admissibility of References for Preliminary Rulings', *Common Market Law Review*, 55 (2018), pp. 511–547.

[173] Court of Justice of the European Union, 'Annual Report 2020: Judicial Activity', 2021, p. 208.

[174] Court of Justice, 'Report Submitted Pursuant to Article 3(2) of Regulation (EU, Euratom) 2015/2422 of the European Parliament and of the Council Amending Protocol (No 3) on the Statute of the Court of Justice of the European Union', December 2017, p. 7. This may change in the future though.

[175] C-54/96, *Dorsch Consult*, EU:C:1997:413, para. 23.

[176] E.g. the Bulgarian Commission for Protection against Discrimination was deemed not to qualify to initiate the preliminary ruling procedure; C-394/11, *Belov*, EU:C:2013:48, paras. 41–54.

[177] C-274/14, *Banco de Santander SA*, EU:C:2020:17, paras. 57–63. [178] Ibid., para. 69. [179] Ibid., para. 79.

Court of Justice of the European Union (without going through a national court).[180] A claim raised before national courts may thus, through the means of a preliminary ruling request from a national court, be put before the Court of Justice indirectly.

In *Schecke*, for instance, the applicants disputed the Land of Hesse's decision to publish personal data relating to them as recipients of EU agricultural funds before national courts. The applicants argued that the provisions of EU law creating a duty to publish information on each of the beneficiaries of such funds were in breach of their fundamental right to data protection protected by EU primary law. The national court asked for a preliminary ruling to the Court of Justice, which agreed on the invalidity of the EU law provisions in question.[181]

Importantly, a question on interpretation, as well as a question on validity, may relate to any type of EU act, as long as the question is necessary to enable the national court to give a judgment; there is no strict requirement that the act shall be 'intended to produce legal effects *vis-à-vis* third parties', as in the context of the procedure for annulment of an EU act.[182] For instance, in *Florescu*, the Court of Justice reviewed a Memorandum of Understanding between the EU and Romania. The Memorandum gave specific form to an agreement between them on an economic programme under which Romania undertook to comply with economic objectives in order to be able to benefit from financial assistance from the EU.[183]

4.2.3.3 Possibility versus Duty to Refer a Preliminary Question

As a matter of principle, national courts are free to request or not to request a preliminary ruling from the Court of Justice.[184] This means that even if one of the parties, or both sides, request that the national court make a reference to the Court of Justice, EU law does not create an obligation for the national judge to do so. Conversely, a national court or tribunal may make a reference even if this has not been suggested, or requested, by the parties. In any case, national rules of procedure may not hinder the effectiveness of the preliminary ruling procedure, and must create conditions for its use that are equivalent to those for comparable mechanisms at national level.[185] The possibility for any national court, and in particular lower courts, to engage in direct contact with the Court of Justice, with a view to asserting the primacy, the unity and the effectiveness of EU law, is thus a very powerful and dynamic way for EU law to interact with national legal orders.[186]

The freedom to refer is limited by two important exceptions. Firstly, as made clear by the wording of Article 267, paragraph 3 TFEU, where a question on the interpretation of EU law is raised before a court or tribunal 'against whose decisions there is no judicial remedy under national law', there is an obligation to refer the preliminary question. This is to ensure that the judicial organ that is last in the judicial hierarchy to examine a question of EU law

[180] See Chapter 4, Section 4.3.1.1, Categories of Applicants.

[181] Joined Cases C-92/09 and C-93/09, *Schecke*, EU:C:2010:662, para. 89.

[182] C-322/88, *Grimaldi*, EU:C:1989:646, para. 8; see also Chapter 4, Section 4.3.1.1, Reviewable Acts. Calling for reform of the EU system of judicial remedies to allow for control of the legality of soft law: Opinion of Advocate General Bobek, C-911/19, *Fédération bancaire française (FBF)* v. *Autorité de contrôle prudentiel et de résolution (ACPR)*, EU:C:2021:294.

[183] C-258/14, *Florescu and Others*, EU:C:2017:448, paras. 29–36. See further Wahl and Prete, 'The Gatekeepers of Article 267 TFEU'.

[184] Art. 267, para. 2 TFEU. [185] See Chapter 4, Section 4.1.3.2, note 36.

[186] See further K. Alter, *Establishing the Supremacy of European Law: The Making of an International Rule of Law in Europe* (Oxford University Press, 2001).

will seek guidance from the Court of Justice, with a view to enabling the latter to ensure that the uniform interpretation and application of EU law.[187] In recent years, the highest courts in the Member States have been intensifying dialogue with the Court of Justice through this channel;[188] meanwhile, the mechanisms of accountability of the State for failure of its judiciary to make references have been used more often, though that remain rare.[189]

This obligation for last-instance courts or tribunals to make a reference was mitigated by the Court of Justice in the *CILFIT* case. The Court indeed acknowledged that the correct interpretation of EU law may have been clarified already (*acte éclairé*), or be particularly clear (*acte clair*).[190] As further elaborated upon in subsequent case law, that may be the case either because the interpretation of EU law has been clarified by earlier case law, or because it 'may be so obvious as to leave no scope for any reasonable doubt as to the manner in which the question raised is to be resolved'.[191] Then last-instance courts are exempted from the duty to refer. Before it comes to the conclusion that such is the case, the national court or tribunal must be convinced that the matter is equally obvious to the courts or tribunals of last instance of the *other Member States* as well as to the Court of Justice, and account must be taken of the characteristic features of EU law as well as the particular difficulties to which its interpretation gives rise. If a national court or tribunal against whose decisions there is no judicial remedy under national law takes the view that it is relieved of its obligation to make a reference to the Court of Justice, that national court must state the reasons enabling it to come to that conclusion.[192]

The second limitation to the principle according to which national courts or tribunals are free to make a reference is where the point of EU law raised in a dispute before them calls into question the validity of an EU act. If national judges consider that the validity of the EU act is dubious, they are under a duty to refer.[193] Although this is not explicit in the wording of Article 267 TFEU, the Court of Justice explained its approach in *Foto-Frost*. It is in the interest of the uniformity of EU law, as well as the coherence of the system of judicial protection established by the EU Treaties,[194] that the Court of Justice shall have exclusive jurisdiction to declare EU acts invalid.[195]

[187] Art. 19(1), subpara. 1 TEU.

[188] See further A. Dyevre, A. Atanasova and M. Glavina, 'Who Asks Most? Institutional Incentives and Referral Activity in the European Union Legal Order', *Journal of European Public Policy*, 27 (2019), pp. 912–930.

[189] See Chapter 4, note 111 on State liability for damages for the acts of the judiciary, and note 128 on infringement actions.

[190] Case 283/81, *CILFIT*, EU:C:1982:335, paras. 14, 16. An answer to the question of interpretation also ought to be necessary to enable the national court to give judgment (Art. 267 TFEU).

[191] Ibid. The Court of Justice further clarified its approach in C-561/19, *Consorzio Italian Management, Catania Multiservizi SpA* v. *Rete Ferroviaria Italiana SpA*, EU:C:2021:799.

[192] In the view of the European Court for Human Rights, the refusal by a court against which there is no judicial remedy under national law to refer a question to the Court of Justice must be duly reasoned to ensure compliance with Art. 6(1) ECHR on the right to a fair hearing; ECtHR, *Ullens de Schooten et Rezabek* v. *Belgium*, Application Nos. 3989/07 and 38353/07, CE:ECHR:2011:0920JUD000398907, para. 60. The Court of Justice adopted a similar approach in light of Art. 47 of the Charter; C-561/19, *Consorzio Italian Management, Catania Multiservizi SpA* v. *Rete Ferroviaria Italiana SpA*, EU:C:2021:799, para. 51.

[193] There is no duty to refer if the national court or tribunal finds that the claim of invalidity is unfounded; Case 314/85, *Foto-Frost*, EU:C:1987:452, para. 14.

[194] As noted previously, the preliminary ruling procedure allows private parties to call into question the validity of EU acts even where the annulment action (Art. 263 TFEU, examined subsequently) may not do so.

[195] Case 314/85, *Foto-Frost*, EU:C:1987:452, paras. 15–17.

4.2.3.4 The Preliminary Ruling

Before giving its answer, the Court of Justice may check not only that the referring entity is a court or a tribunal within the meaning introduced previously, but also that its answer would be 'necessary in order to enable the national court or tribunal to give judgment'.[196] As a corollary, the national court or tribunal making the reference must provide the factual and legal context of the questions it is asking or, at the very least, explain the factual circumstances on which those questions are based, with a view to enabling the Court of Justice to give a useful answer.[197] The national court or tribunal may, and often, interestingly, does, state its views on the answer to be given by the Court of Justice.

It is thus for the national court or tribunal to assess the relevance, timing and wording of the preliminary question(s) it asks – so that they have a presumption of relevance, as recently shown in the *Wightman* case in the context of Brexit.[198] Yet the Court of Justice may – and often does – reformulate the question to ensure that its answer will be useful. Furthermore, the Court of Justice exercises a degree of control in order to ensure that preliminary questions do not distort the preliminary ruling procedure from its original purpose. It will hold the question to be inadmissible if it deems that its ruling on the matter would not be useful to solve a pending dispute. For instance, in *Foglia*, the Court held that it would decline to answer if the parties to the main action are in agreement as to the result to be attained, and have inserted a clause in their contract in order to induce judicial guidance on that point.[199] The Court also declines to provide an answer to purely hypothetical questions.[200]

Importantly, it is not the role of the Court of Justice to solve the dispute pending before national courts, to address questions of facts or to interpret national law. Instead, the national judge suspends the proceedings pending before it to ask for guidance from the Court of Justice on the interpretation or validity of EU law *before* being able to finally apply EU law to the facts of the case. That explains the name *preliminary* ruling attributed to the contribution by the Court of Justice to the procedure pending before the national court. It may be observed, however, that the Court of Justice may decide to be very prescriptive when answering questions from national judges on EU law, at times considerably limiting the margin of manoeuvre of national authorities. For instance, in *AGET Iraklis*, the Court of Justice first explained in a fair degree of detail which type of mechanisms imposing a legal framework on collective redundancies could comply with EU law. It then observed that Article 49 TFEU on the freedom of establishment had to be interpreted so as to preclude a mechanism such as the one at hand.[201]

The legal value of the preliminary ruling is equivalent to that of the measure of EU law interpreted by the Court of Justice (more specifically, primary law, secondary law, tertiary

[196] Art. 267(2) TFEU.

[197] Joined Cases C-320/90 to C-322/90, *Telemarsicabruzzo*, EU:C:1993:26, para. 5. See further Court of Justice, 'Rules of Procedure', Art. 94; Court of Justice, 'Recommendations to National Courts and Tribunals in Relation to the Initiation of Preliminary Ruling Proceedings', OJ C 381, 8.11.2019, p. 1.

[198] The Court of Justice agreed to answer a preliminary question from a lower Scottish court, raised before it by Parliamentarians seeking a declaration specifying whether, when and how the notification referred to in Art. 50 TEU on the intention of a Member State to withdraw from the EU can unilaterally be revoked; C-621/18, *Wightman*, EU:C:2018:999, paras. 26–31.

[199] Case 104/79, *Foglia*, EU:C:1980:73, paras. 10–11.

[200] Case 244/80, *Foglia II*, EU:C:1981:302, para. 18.

[201] C-201/15, *AGET Iraklis*, EU:C:2016:972, paras. 92–94, 95–104.

law), and it takes primacy over national law. The national judge is thus bound to follow the interpretation of EU law provided by the Court of Justice. If the Court of Justice concludes that an act of EU law is invalid, no national court may apply it anymore, and the competent EU organs will have to take the necessary steps to address the illegality by amending or repealing the act.[202] Furthermore, the authority of the ruling is not limited to the case from which it originates (*inter partes*). The interpretation or validity of EU law holds good across the EU legal order (*erga omnes*) from the date of the ruling by the Court of Justice. Importantly, the decision of a court or tribunal to refer a case to the Court of Justice will have been notified to all Member States and to the Commission, as well as to the EU organ which adopted the act that is the subject of the validity or interpretation dispute. These actors will have been given two months to submit observations to the Court of Justice and to share their understanding of the relevant point of EU law.[203]

It takes, on average, around fifteen to sixteen months for the Court of Justice to answer questions from national courts or tribunals in the context of Article 267 TFEU.[204] Yet its last paragraph now specifies that, if the question is raised in a case regarding to a person in custody – which is not uncommon, since the Court of Justice has jurisdiction in the AFSJ – the Court shall minimise any delay. There is also, more generally, the possibility of an expedited procedure if the nature of the case requires that it be dealt with within a short time.[205]

4.3 THE EU IS SUBJECT TO THE RULE OF LAW

The EU legal order is thus characterised by a sophisticated implementation and enforcement machinery, contributing to the primacy, the unity and the effectiveness of EU law *within the Member States*. Precisely because the design of the EU is so powerful and advanced, it requires two sets of safeguards at EU level.[206] Firstly, EU organs themselves, as key players in the production of EU norms, ought to be accountable for their actions by those being subject to judicial review under EU law. Second, the legal systems of the Member States, from which the EU system originates and on which it relies, ought to be fundamentally sound to ensure the perennity of the EU legal system. As we shall see, a set of mechanisms enable EU organs to review compliance with the rule of law within the Member States.

[202] Case 66/80, *SpA International Chemical Corporation* v. *Amministrazione delle finanze dello Stato*, EU:C:1981:102, paras. 12, 16.

[203] Statute of the Court of Justice of the European Union (Consolidated version, 1 May 2019), Art. 23. In specific circumstances, the questions referred may also be communicated to non-EU Member States, giving them the opportunity to submit observations. See also Court of Justice, 'Rules of Procedure', Art. 96.

[204] Court of Justice of the European Union, 'Annual Report 2020: Judicial Activity', 2021, p. 220; see further Chapter 2, Section 2.3.7.4, Judicial Procedure.

[205] Statute of the Court of Justice of the European Union, Art. 23a, and Court of Justice, 'Rules of Procedure', Arts. 105–114. On the distinction between the two, see further Court of Justice, 'Report on the use of the urgent preliminary ruling procedure by the Court of Justice', January 2012, pp. 1–2. Note that the urgent preliminary ruling in the context of the AFSJ is not necessarily limited to situations of custody: Court of Justice of the European Union, 'Recommendations to National Courts and Tribunals in Relation to the Initiation of Preliminary Ruling Proceedings', OJ C 380/1, 8.11.2019, p. 1, point 36. See also Chapter 2, Section 2.3.7.4, Judicial Procedure.

[206] For an in-depth overview of the role of the Court of Justice of the European Union in that respect, see Lenaerts et al., *EU Procedural Law*.

4.3.1 Judicial Enforcement of EU Law against EU Organs

It may be recalled that each source of EU law below EU primary law originates in EU primary law, thus resulting in several layers of norms.[207] Actions by EU institutions, bodies, offices or agencies (together referred to as EU organs) thus have to comply with the layer(s) of norm(s) on which their action is based, as well as higher ones within the family tree described in Chapter 3. Several mechanisms are set out in the EU Treaties to ensure such compliance. We have already mentioned the *ex ante* control mechanism set out in Article 218(11) TFEU, allowing clashes between international agreements and EU primary law to be prevented.[208] We will focus here on mechanisms that allow action or lack of action by EU organs to be challenged before the Court of Justice *ex post*.

4.3.1.1 Action for Annulment

The direct way to challenge the validity of an EU act is the annulment action set out in Articles 263 (reproduced in part subsequently) and 264 TFEU.[209] The competence to deal with such cases is shared between the General Court and the Court of Justice.[210] Annulment procedures constitute close to a third of the total number of cases brought directly before the General Court – which is often the competent court in practice.[211]

Reviewable Acts

The acts that may be reviewed in the context of this procedure are specified in Article 263, paragraph 1 TFEU. Firstly, only acts emanating from specific EU organs may be challenged. The list of authors of reviewable acts has evolved over time to reflect the increasingly broad range of entities shaping EU law. Today, the list consists of the Parliament,[212] the Council, the European Council,[213] the Commission, the Central Bank and bodies, offices or agencies of the EU. The latter allow judicial review in the context of the EMU,[214] as well as judicial review of the growing regulatory powers of agencies.[215]

Second, the acts that may be reviewed must be 'intended to produce legal effects vis-à-vis third parties'.[216] This is understood as establishing a requirement that the act challenged

[207] See Chapter 3, Section 3.5.1.1.

[208] See Chapter 3, Section 3.5.3.1, Secondary Law in the Form of International Agreements.

[209] See also Art. 19(3)(a) TEU.

[210] Art. 256 TFEU; Statute of the Court of Justice of the European Union, Art. 51; see also Chapter 2, Section 2.3.6.2. In brief, the General Court deals with cases that are normally primarily of an administrative nature, while the Court of Justice has exclusive competence on matters that are more likely to raise sensitive institutional questions.

[211] Court of Justice of the European Union, 'Annual Report 2020: Judicial Activity', 2021, p. 349; see also Chapter 2, Section 2.3.6.2.

[212] Previously resulting from an amendment of the relevant legal provision as a result of the Maastricht Treaty, the Court of Justice started treating the Parliament as others within the meaning of Art. 263, para. 1 TFEU in its seminal ruling in Case 294/83, *'Les Verts'*, EU:C:1986:166, paras. 23–25.

[213] Conversely, acts adopted by the Heads of State or Government of the EU are not reviewable within the meaning of Art. 263, para. 1 TFEU; Cases T-192/16, T-193/16 and T-257/16, *NF, NG and NM* v. *European Council (EU-Turkey statement)*, EU:T:2017:128, para. 69. See also Chapter 2, Section 2.1.1.

[214] The Court of Justice will review, for instance, acts of the Central Bank, in the exercise of its exclusive decision-making powers, to which national authorities have contributed, and the later contributions may not be reviewed at national level as they are covered by the jurisdiction of the Court of Justice; C-219/17, *Berlusconi and Fininvest*, EU:C:2018:1023, paras. 42–44, 47–51.

[215] See Chapter 2, Section 2.3.7 and Chapter 3, Section 3.2.3.4.

[216] Art. 263, para. 1 TFEU.

produces binding legal effects.[217] This characterisation is not based on the form of the act. It is therefore not enough for the defendant to argue that the act was a recommendation to escape judicial review, for instance. Instead, the legal effects are assessed in accordance with objective criteria looking at the contents of that measure, taking into account, as appropriate, the context in which it was adopted and the powers of the institution which adopted the measure, as well as the intention of the author of the act in question.[218] As an example, Air France was entitled to bring a claim against a statement made by the Commission's spokesman declaring that the Commission had no power to consider, under a regulation on the control of concentrations between undertakings, the merger between British Airways and Dan Air. This was so because the legal effects of the contested statement could be adequately established.[219]

Time Limit

The annulment action must be filed within two months of the official publication of the measure or of its notification to the applicant.[220] This requirement results in protecting EU acts against late direct challenges. It shall be noted, however, that in practice, applicants – in particular, privileged applicants, such as key EU institutions and Member States – are aware of the act while it is in the process of being adopted, as well as its possible weaknesses, before the trigger of the two-month time limit. Note that non-privileged applicants, and applicants who could not clearly have triggered an annulment action within the two-month time limit, might, under certain conditions, be able to challenge the validity of the EU act indirectly after the said time limit.[221]

Categories of Applicants

The various paragraphs of Article 263 TFEU distinguish between three sets of applicants, starting with the 'lucky' ones in paragraph 2, and ending with the 'significantly less lucky' ones in paragraph 4.[222]

Privileged Applicants

A first set of applicants does not have to show any specific interest in the annulment action in order to be able to commence such proceedings. It is assumed that they have a legitimate interest in bringing the action. These applicants are: the Member States, the Parliament,[223] the Council and the Commission. This list is remarkably shorter than the one for organs that may be the author of an act that can be reviewed in the context of an annulment action. For instance, the European Council is not included on the list.

[217] This requirement is stricter than for questions on EU acts raised by national courts or tribunals in the context of the preliminary ruling procedure; see Chapter 4, Section 4.2.3.2. For an in-depth criticism of this narrow approach and the specific concerns it creates in the context of the rise of soft law, see Opinion of Advocate General Bobek, C-16/16 P, *Belgium* v. *Commission (online gambling services)*, EU:C:2017:959, paras. 122–154.

[218] E.g. T-283/15, *Esso Raffinage* v. *ECHA*, EU:T:2018:263, paras. 49, 51.

[219] T-3/93, *Air France* v. *Commission*, EU:T:1994:36, para. 52.

[220] Or, in the absence thereof, of the day on which it came to the knowledge of the latter: Art. 263, para. 6 TFEU.

[221] See further Chapter 4, Section 4.3.1.3.

[222] And, to a lesser extent, para. 5. See Chapter 4, note 229.

[223] Previously resulting from Treaty change introduced by the Maastricht Treaty – when the Parliament became a quasi-privileged applicant – and the Treaty of Nice – with the Parliament as a privileged applicant – the Court started treating the Parliament as a quasi-privileged applicant since its seminal ruling in C-70/88, *Parliament* v. *Council (Chernobyl)*, EU:C:1990:217, paras. 26–28.

Quasi-privileged Applicants

A second set of applicants only needs to show that the annulment action is brought for the purpose of protecting their prerogatives. These organs indeed have a more specific mandate than the ones listed previously. They are: the Court of Auditors, the Central Bank and the Committee of the Regions.[224] For instance, before the Parliament became a privileged applicant, and when it was treated as a quasi-privileged applicant,[225] it brought annulment actions seeking to challenge the use of a decision-making procedure in which it had been given a lesser role than expected in light of its reading of the various legal bases available.[226] It could thus show that its prerogatives had been negatively impacted.

Non-privileged Applicants

The third set of applicants are those who have to overcome the greatest hurdle. These are natural and legal persons. This would include individuals like you and me, undertakings or legal entities such as regions.[227] As for associations for the protection of the collective interests of a category of persons, such as non-governmental organisations (NGOs), they may only have standing to commence legal proceedings if their members can do so. The same applies to NGOs acting to protect the environment.[228] The relevant legal framework is set out in Article 263, paragraph 4 TFEU (reproduced in Box 4.3). These non-privileged applicants may institute proceedings in three settings - identified below as options 1, 2 and 3 - that can be singled out in the text of the Treaty itself, and on which we will elaborate in turn.[229]

Box 4.3 **Rough guide for private applicants seeking to bring an annulment action[230]**

Article 263, paragraph 4 TFEU

Any natural or legal person may [. . .] institute proceedings against [1] an act addressed to that person or [2] which is of direct and individual concern to them, and [3] against (a) a regulatory act (b) which is of direct concern to them and (c) does not entail implementing measures.

[224] On the possibility of the Committee of Regions to bring an annulment action on grounds of infringement of the principle of subsidiarity, see Protocol 2, Art. 8, para. 2.

[225] See Chapter 4, note 223.

[226] C-70/88, *Parliament* v. *Council (Radioactive contamination of foodstuffs)*, EU:C:1991:373, para. 7.

[227] For instance, when seeking the annulment of an EU act renewing the approval of the active substance 'glyphosate', in the context of the placing of plant protection products on the market, the Brussels Capital Region is treated as a non-privileged applicant; C-352/19 P, *Région de Bruxelles-Capitale* v. *European Commission*, EU:C:2020:978, paras. 19, 26. A State with international legal personality, must also be regarded as a 'legal person' within the meaning of Art. 263, para. 4 TFEU; C-872/19 P, *Bolivarian Republic of Venezuela* v. *Council*, EU:C:2021:507, para. 53. Note that the Court has accepted that an organisation which did not have legal personality had to have standing to contest the restrictive measures imposed on it; C-229/05 P, *PKK and KNK* v. *Council*, EU:C:2007:32, para. 112.

[228] C-321/95 P, *Stichting Greenpeace Council* v. *Commission*, EU:C:1998:153, paras. 27–34. See further Chapter 4, note 251.

[229] Note that acts establishing bodies, offices and agencies of the EU may lay down specific conditions and arrangements concerning actions brought by natural or legal persons against acts of these bodies, offices or agencies intended to produce legal effects in relation to them; Art. 263, para. 5 TFEU.

[230] Bracketed numbering/letters added.

1. If the act being challenged is addressed to the applicant, the said person is entitled to bring the case. It seems only logical that a person shall be entitled to call into question the validity of an act addressed to them. For instance, when the Commission finds that a specific undertaking has abused its dominant position on a given market and accordingly imposes a financial penalty for breach of EU competition rules, that undertaking can challenge the decision.[231]

2. If the act is not addressed to the applicant, the latter shall, in principle, establish that the act is of 'direct and individual concern' to them. These terms have traditionally been interpreted by the Court of Justice restrictively, thus placing a heavy burden on applicants.

Firstly, the applicant must show that they are directly concerned by the act. In other words, the applicant shall establish that the act 'directly affects the legal position of the parties concerned', as established in *International Fruit*.[232] This is commonly understood as requiring a direct causal link between the contested EU act and the altered legal situation of the applicant. This excludes situations where the intervention of a third party – such as a national authority – may have broken the link by exercising a discretionary power. In the latter case, the applicant ought to challenge the act which constitutes the exercise of such a discretionary power.

Second, and this is often most difficult, the applicant must establish that they are individually concerned by the act that they seek to challenge. Since its early ruling in the *Plaumann* case, the Court has consistently interpreted this requirement as follows:

> persons other than those to whom an [EU act] is addressed may only claim to be individually concerned if that [act] affects them by reason of certain attributes which are peculiar to them or by reason of circumstances in which they are differentiated from all other persons and by virtue of these factors distinguishes them individually just as in the case of the person addressed.[233]

In the case at hand, an importer of clementines was not concerned in any more specific way than any other person engaged, or wishing to engage, in that commercial activity. As a consequence, the undertaking did not fulfil the requirement of individual concern to be able to challenge a Commission Decision refusing to authorise Germany to suspend some customs duties on clementines imported from third countries. An act formulated in abstract terms, as opposed to acts addressed to a specific entity, is thus most unlikely to be of individual concern to natural or legal applicants.

The number of persons impacted by the act under challenge, even if small or identifiable in advance, is *not* in itself sufficient to establish individual concern if the act is worded in generalised terms and applies to objectively determined situations. For instance, a regulation

231 Similarly, when the Commission addresses a decision of rejection to a natural or legal person who can show a legitimate interest in alleging a breach of competition law within the meaning of 'Council Regulation (EC) No. 1/2003 of 16 December 2002 on the Implementation of the Rules on Competition Laid Down in Articles 81 and 82 of the Treaty', OJ L 1, 4.1.2003 (last amended 2009), Art. 7(2), that person or entity can bring an action for annulment against the rejection; e.g. T-193/02, *Piau* v. *Commission*, EU:T:2005:22, para. 38.

232 Joined Cases 41 to 44/70, *International Fruit*, EU:C:1971:53, para. 28; for a more detailed and recent overview of the case law on the matter, see Opinion of Advocate General Bobek, C-352/19 P, *Région de Bruxelles-Capitale* v. *Commission*, EU:C:2020:588, paras. 46–56.

233 Case 25/62, *Plaumann*, EU:C:1963:17.

limiting the granting of production aid for producers, defined in abstract and objective terms, in relation to a particular agricultural product is not of individual concern to specific producers merely because it would be possible to count them, or even identify them.[234]

As a consequence of the narrow interpretation by the Court of Justice of the notion of 'individual concern', enshrined in the *Plaumann* formula, it is difficult for natural or legal persons to challenge EU acts not addressed to them. Examples of applicants having succeeded in convincing the Court of their individual situation, however, do exist.[235]

A first set of examples relates to situations where the individual applicant belonged to a group that was not only identifiable in advance, but was also fixed – in the sense that it could not change – for instance, because a new person would meet the criteria when the measure came into force. Members of such closed groups have been able to show individual concern in a number of cases where the author of the act had a special duty of care towards the said group. For instance, in *Piraiki-Patraiki*, the applicant could challenge a Commission Decision authorising France to take protective measures with regard to imports of cotton yarn from Greece. The applicant was part of a group that had already concluded a contract for such imports before the adoption of the Decision, and towards which the Commission had a duty of care in the context of Greece's process of accession to the EU.[236]

A second set of examples relate to applicants who had a specific procedural right in the process leading to the adoption of the act. There are specific lines of cases in sectors of EU law, such as anti-dumping, State aid and competition law.[237] These fields are characterised by procedural arrangements allowing undertakings to contribute more or less directly to the adoption of an EU act.

A final group gathers a variety of exceptional circumstances. Two illustrations are provided here. In *Codorníu*, the provisions of an act laying down general rules restricting the use of the term 'crémant' to certain sparkling wines from France and Luxembourg could be challenged by an applicant that had established the existence of a protected graphic trade mark for the use of the expression 'Gran *Cremant* de Codorníu' in Spain since 1924.[238] In *UEAPME*, the principle of democracy on which the EU is founded required – in the absence of the participation of the Parliament in the relevant legislative process – that parties representative of management and labour which had been consulted in the adoption of EU social legislation, and whose particular representation would have been necessary in order to raise the collective representativity of its content, even if they were not signatories of the agreement turned into legislation.[239]

These examples of successful applications by a natural or legal person, however, remain the exception. It is very difficult for private applicants to challenge an act addressed to another person or entity, or an act of general application. Legislative acts, in particular, are remarkably rarely challenged through this channel. Until the Treaty of Lisbon, annulment

[234] Joined Cases 789 and 790/79, *Calpak*, EU:C:1980:159, para. 9.

[235] For a more in-depth overview, see Lenaerts et al., *EU Procedural Law*, pp. 323–364.

[236] Case 11/82, *Piraiki-Patraiki*, EU:C:1985:18, paras. 19, 28, 31. See also, for instance, on goods in transit, C-152/88, *Sofrimport* v. *Commission*, EU:C:1990:259, para. 11.

[237] E.g. Case 169/84, *COFAZ*, EU:C:1986:42, paras. 22–23; Case 26/76, *Metro*, EU:C:1977:167, para. 13. See also Chapter 4, note 251, on environmental law.

[238] C-309/89, *Codorníu*, EU:C:1994:197, paras. 21–22.

[239] T-135/96, *UEAPME*, EU:T:1998:128, paras. 89–90.

actions were only possible for natural and legal persons under the conditions set out previously. In response to the Court of Justice's narrow approach to the notion of individual concern, the General Court, as well as advocates general, have called for greater access to judicial review of EU acts in the famous *UPA* and *Jégo-Quéré* saga.[240] In response, the Court of Justice reasserted its approach to the *Plaumann* formula, and called on the authors of the EU Treaties themselves to make changes to Article 263 TFEU, should they deem it necessary.[241] It is in this context that a third limb was added to that article by the Treaty of Lisbon.

3. Indeed, it is now also possible for applicants to commence proceedings disputing an act characterised by three cumulative features: it must be (a) a regulatory act, (b) which is of direct concern to them, and (c) does not entail implementing measures.

In this context, the requirement of 'direct concern' (c) has been interpreted in the same way as under the second limb of Article 263, paragraph 4 TFEU, as already introduced (under option 2).[242] Compared to option 2, option 3 thus merely eliminates the demanding requirement of individual concern for a specific type of acts: (a) regulatory acts that (c) do not entail implementing measures.

Attention thus turned to the definition of 'regulatory act' and the notion of 'not entailing implementing measures', which became the gateway for easier access to the annulment action for natural and legal persons challenging an act not addressed to them. In a challenge against restrictions to the trade in seal products brought by Inuit Tapiriit Kanatami and others, the notion of regulatory act (a) was defined by the Court of Justice as 'acts of general application other than legislative acts'.[243] They are thus acts of general application that have *not* been adopted through a legislative procedure.[244]

As to the requirement that the regulatory act 'does not entail implementing measures' (c), it shall be assessed by reference to the position of the applicant – it is irrelevant whether the act entails implementing measures with regard to others – and to the subject matter of the action.[245] In *Microban*, for instance, the General Court found that a decision by the Commission prohibiting the marketing of materials and articles containing triclosan intended to come into contact with foodstuffs had automatic effects and thus entailed no implementing measures.[246]

Option 3 in Article 263, paragraph 4 TFEU thus allows (some of) the concerns expressed by the General Court and advocates general on the limits of access to judicial review for

240 See, in particular, Opinion of Advocate General Jacobs, C-50/00 P, *Unión de Pequeños Agricultores (UPA)*, EU:C:2002:197 and T-177/01, *Jégo-Quéré*, EU:T:2002:112.

241 C-263/02 P, *Jégo-Quéré*, EU:C:2004:210 and C-50/00 P, *Unión de Pequeños Agricultores (UPA)*, EU:C:2002:462, para. 45.

242 C-274/12 P, *Telefónica*, EU:C:2013:204, para. 59.

243 C-583/11 P, *Inuit Tapiriit Kanatami*, EU:C:2013:625, para. 60.

244 See Chapter 3, Section 3.5.3.2. Legislative acts are thus excluded from option 3, even if they do not entail implementing measures; they may only be challenged if the demanding criteria set out in option 2 are fulfilled. This creates a risk of lack of protection of non-privileged applicants unable to show direct and individual concern when challenging a legislative act that does not entail implementing measures.

245 C-274/12 P, *Telefónica*, EU:C:2013:852, paras. 30–31. Distinguishing for that purpose between the perspective of producers and traders of phytopharmaceutical products on the one hand, and that of consumers and agricultural producers on the other, in the context of a challenge against an EU regulatory act renewing the authorisation to place on the market the said products: C-313/19 P, *Associazione GranoSalus v. Commission*, EU:C:2020:869, paras. 37–43. In that case, the EU regulatory act was deemed not to entail implementing measures from the perspective of consumers and agricultural producers.

246 T-262/10, *Microban*, EU:T:2011:623, paras. 33–34.

natural and legal persons under option 2 to be addressed. In the view of the Court, the fundamental right to a judicial remedy against EU acts is now ensured, along with the three options just examined, because where the implementation of an EU act is the responsibility of a subset of actors, the implementing act itself may be challenged. Indeed, where responsibility for the implementation of EU acts lies with EU organs, the validity of the parent act may be called into question, pursuant to Article 277 TFEU on the plea of illegality, as will be examined subsequently.[247] Alternatively, where implementation is for the Member States as is often the case, applicants may plead the illegality of the act being implemented before national courts and tribunals: a challenge to the validity of the act being implemented is possible through the preliminary ruling procedure.[248] Building on that last point, the Court of Justice has repeatedly asserted that, for persons who do not fulfil the requirements of Article 263, paragraph 4 TFEU to bring an action directly before the Court of Justice, it is for the Member States to establish a system of legal remedies and procedures which ensure respect for the fundamental right to effective judicial protection.[249]

Nevertheless, many observers[250] continue to argue that the conditions for private applicants to be able to challenge the validity of EU acts directly before the Court of Justice should be more flexible, and should make judicial review less dependent on the diversity and limitations of national legal systems. This could be achieved without the need for a Treaty amendment, should the Court of Justice decide to depart from the *Plaumann* formula. The problem has been particularly acute in the context of litigation for the protection of the environment where litigants often are NGOs seeking to give a voice to the environment, yet struggling to fulfil the requirements under Article 263, paragraph 4 TFEU. A recent reform of the legislative framework on access by NGOs or members of the public to internal review (within the Commission), as well as judicial review (at the Court of Justice of the European Union), of administrative acts in the field of the environment is expected to appease these concerns.[251]

Grounds for Annulment

Once it is established that the claim fulfils admissibility requirements – it has been brought against a reviewable act, within the time limit and by an applicant entitled to bring the case – the General Court or Court of Justice will turn to its substance. Applicants may rely on four grounds for annulment identified in Article 263, paragraph 2 TFEU.

Firstly, the applicant may argue that the author of the act lacks competence. As noted already, the EU is bound by the principle of conferral.[252] Its organs may only act within the

[247] See Chapter 4, Section 4.3.1.3. [248] See Chapter 4, Sections 4.3.1.3 and 4.2.3.

[249] E.g. C-456/13 P, *T & L Sugars*, EU:C:2015:284, paras. 49–50. The overall approach of the Court of Justice on the matter is recalled and explained from para. 29 onwards.

[250] For a valuable overview, see A. Hinarejos, 'Action for Annulment: Direct Review of EU Measures', in Schütze and Tridimas (eds.), *Oxford Principles of European Union Law*, pp. 887–909.

[251] 'Regulation (EC) No. 1367/2006 of the European Parliament and of the Council of 6 September 2006 on the Application of the Provisions of the Aarhus Convention on Access to Information, Public Participation in Decision-making and Access to Justice in Environmental Matters to Community Institutions and Bodies', OJ L 264, 25.9.2006, pp. 13–19 (last amended 2021); G. C. Leonelli, 'Access to EU Courts in Environmental and Public Health Cases and the Reform of the Aarhus Regulation: Systemic Vision, Pragmatism, and a Happy Ending', *Yearbook of European Law*, 40 (2021), pp. 230–264.

[252] See Chapter 3, Section 3.2.

limits of the competences conferred upon them. The absence or wrongful use – for instance, in the case of delegated powers – of a legal basis is a ground for annulment of the act.

Second, there may have been an infringement of an essential procedural requirement. This is so if the authority in charge does not follow key steps required under the legal basis and applicable EU principles, such as sincere cooperation or institutional balance,[253] for the adoption of an act. In the 1980s and early 1990s, for instance, the Parliament successfully challenged the failure to allow it to exercise its consultative role against the Council, when the latter did not consult it[254] or did not consult it on a new version of the draft act.[255]

Third, there may have been an infringement of the Treaties, or of any rule of law relating to their application. Such a challenge requires a detailed analysis of the norm challenged to check compliance with the substance of higher-ranking norms of EU law. An argument could be made that an EU act is in breach of the fundamental rights enshrined in the CFEU, for instance.

Finally, and more rarely, the applicant may argue that the author of the act has misused its power. For that purpose, it must be shown that, 'on the basis of objective, relevant and consistent evidence', the act has been taken 'with the exclusive or main purpose of achieving an end other than that stated or evading a procedure specifically prescribed by the Treaty for dealing with the circumstances of the case'.[256] For instance, by organising an internal competition for the sole purpose of promoting a specific official and of appointing him to the post declared vacant, the appointing authority misuses its powers.[257]

Effects of the Ruling

In accordance with Article 264 TFEU, if the Court of Justice or the General Court deems the action to be well-founded, it shall declare the act concerned to be void. The act is thereby considered null as from its entry into force (*ex tunc*), and across the EU legal order (*erga omnes*). An act may be declared fully or partially void, depending on the nature of the breach of higher-ranking norms, and of the relationship that a specific provision in breach of EU law may have with the main body of the instrument it belongs to. Furthermore, the Court may, if necessary, state which of the effects of the act that it has declared void shall be considered as definitive nevertheless. The Court may also adopt interim measures, and decide to temporarily maintain the legal effects of an act pending adoption of a new act. The author of the act who has been declared void shall take the necessary measures to comply with the judgment.[258]

As a reminder,[259] certain types of annulment actions – in particular, those brought by natural and legal persons – are filed before the General Court, while others – such as those brought by a Member State against a legislative act or by EU institutions – are brought

[253] See Chapter 3, Sections 3.4 and 3.6; e.g. Case 817/79, *Buyl and others* v. *Commission*, EU:C:1982:36, para. 16.
[254] Case 138/79, *Roquette Frères* v. *Council*, EU:C:1980:249, para. 33
[255] C-65/90, *Parliament* v. *Council*, EU:C:1992:325, para. 16.
[256] C-491/01, *The Queen* v. *Secretary of State, ex parte British American Tobacco*, EU:C:2002:741, para. 189.
[257] E.g. Case 105/75, *Franco Giuffrida* v. *Council*, EU:C:1976:128.
[258] Art. 266 TFEU.
[259] See Chapter 2, Section 2.3.6.2.

directly before the Court of Justice. In so far as the first categories of annulment actions are concerned, rulings by the General Court may form the subject matter of an appeal on points of law before the Court of Justice.

4.3.1.2 Action for Failure to Act

The action for annulment of EU *acts* is complemented by a procedure that allows for *inaction* by EU organs to be tackled: the action for failure to act is provided for in Article 265 TFEU. The two procedures 'merely prescribe one and the same method of recourse'.[260] Most of what was said in relation to the action for annulment is thus applicable to the action for failure to act, with a few adjustments reflecting the difficulty of holding an EU organ accountable for the absence of action.

A failure to act occurs at the expiry of a period of two months, after the applicant has called upon the EU organ to define its position, and the action must be taken within a further period of two months.[261] The failure must relate to an omission to adopt any act with legal effects, or to a refusal to act.[262] The EU organ whose failure has been declared in breach of EU law shall take the necessary measures to comply with the judgment within a reasonable time.[263] Conversely, if the EU organ adopts the requested act, or another act,[264] the action for failure to act loses its purpose. The applicant may instead consider seeking the annulment of the newly adopted measure. Furthermore, a finding of a breach of EU law in the context of Article 265 TFEU can only result from the preliminary finding of a duty to act.[265] For instance, one may not bring an action against the Commission for failure to initiate an infringement action, as the Commission is under no obligation to initiate infringement actions.[266]

The procedure may be initiated by a Member State or an EU institution without them having to demonstrate any specific interest.[267] As for natural or legal persons, they may 'complain to the Court that an institution, body, office or agency of the Union has failed to address to that person any act other than a recommendation or an opinion'.[268] The Court of Justice has confirmed, after the Treaty of Lisbon and the changes to Article 263, paragraph 4 TFEU on annulment actions, its case law to the effect that natural or legal persons may only bring an action for failure to adopt an act if it would be admissible to challenge its validity through an annulment action.[269]

[260] Case 15/70, *Chevalley*, EU:C:1970:95, para. 6. [261] Art. 265, para. 2 TFEU.

[262] A refusal to act, however explicit it may be, can be brought before the Court of Justice under Art. 265 TFEU, since it does not put an end to the failure to act; Case 302/87, *Parliament* v. *Council*, EU:C:1988:461, para. 17.

[263] Art. 266 TFEU. By analogy with the notion of 'reasonable time': Case 266/82, *Turner*, EU:C:1984:3, para. 5. The failure to execute the judgment can incur the liability of the EU. See, by analogy, T-84/91, *Meskens*, EU:T:1992:103, paras. 89–92.

[264] Illustrating that the position of an EU organ may be defined by the adoption of an act other than the one requested: Case 8/71, *Deutscher Komponisterverband*, EU:C:1971:82, para. 3.

[265] T-32/93, *Ladbroke Racing Ltd*, EU:T:1994:261, para. 35.

[266] See Chapter 4, Section 4.2.2.1, Discretion of the Commission.

[267] There is no mention of the Committee of Regions, unlike in Art. 263 TFEU. [268] Art. 265, para. 3 TFEU.

[269] C-130/16 P, *Anastasia-Soultana Gaki*, EU:C:2016:731, para. 17.

4.3.1.3 Indirect Challenges to the Validity of EU Acts

Plea of Illegality

The plea of illegality allows the validity of an EU act (EU act A) to be called into question in a dispute involving another related EU act (EU act B) – it is thus a parasitical claim – before the Court of Justice or the General Court. The plea of illegality is available to any party, notwithstanding the expiry of the two-month period laid down to bring annulment actions against the act (EU act A), and can relate to the same grounds for annulment as the annulment action.[270] This parasitical claim is provided for in Article 277 TFEU. A finding by the Court of Justice of the illegality of an EU act, in light of higher-ranking norms of EU law, will only result in the inapplicability of the act in the dispute at hand (*inter partes*). The author of the act then ought to take appropriate steps to restore legality.[271]

For instance, an applicant may challenge the legality of an act of secondary law of general application (EU act A) in the context of an annulment action against an act of tertiary law based thereupon and for which they have standing (EU act B).[272] This enables an applicant who would not have had standing to bring an annulment action under Article 263(4) TFEU against EU act A to nevertheless call into question its validity in the context of proceedings against the legal act based thereupon, EU act B: EU act B is invalid because there is a direct legal link with EU act A, which is itself in breach of a higher-ranking norm of EU law, as illustrated in Figure 4.1 (on the left-hand side of the pyramid).[273]

The plea of illegality thus contributes to compensating for the restricted possibility for natural and legal persons to bring an annulment action against EU acts. The Court of Justice, however, asserted in *TWD* that the plea of illegality is not available to an applicant who could undoubtedly have brought proceedings directly against EU act A and did not do so within the two-month time limit prescribed by Article 263 TFEU.[274]

Preliminary Question on Validity

Doubts as to the validity of an EU act (EU act A) may also arise in the context of litigation before national courts or tribunals. This creates a duty on them to refer a preliminary question to the Court of Justice. This mechanism, set out in Article 267(b) TFEU and already introduced, is very similar to the plea of illegality in that it is also a parasitical claim allowing the validity of an EU act to be called into question, notwithstanding the expiry of the two-month period laid down to bring annulment actions against that act (EU act A).

Nevertheless, important differences exist. The procedural framework for preliminary rulings is clearly distinct from the plea of illegality.[275] Unlike the latter, the preliminary ruling procedure is not initiated in the context of a procedure against an EU act (EU act B, see previous section). It instead emerges in a dispute involving an act

[270] See Chapter 4, Section 4.3.1.1, Time Limit and Grounds for Annulment. [271] Art. 266 TFEU, by analogy.

[272] The conditions to be admissible to challenge the validity of EU act B are those set out previously: Chapter 4, Section 4.3.1.1.

[273] For a recent synthesis of the approach of the Court of Justice to the matter, see, for instance, T-764/16, *Paulini*, EU:T:2018:101, paras. 28–32.

[274] C-188/92, *TWD* v. *Bundesrepublik Deutschland*, EU:C:1994:90, para. 23 (by analogy) and Joined Cases T-244/93 and T-486/93, *TWD* v. *Commission*, EU:T:1995:160, para. 103. For an application of the test in light of the new wording of Art. 263, para. 4 TFEU post-Lisbon: C-207/17, *Rotho Blaas*, EU:C:2018:840, paras. 28–40.

[275] See Chapter 4, Section 4.2.3.

related to EU act A,[276] but *within the national legal system*, and therefore before the national judiciary, as illustrated in Figure 4.1 (on the right-hand side of the pyramid).

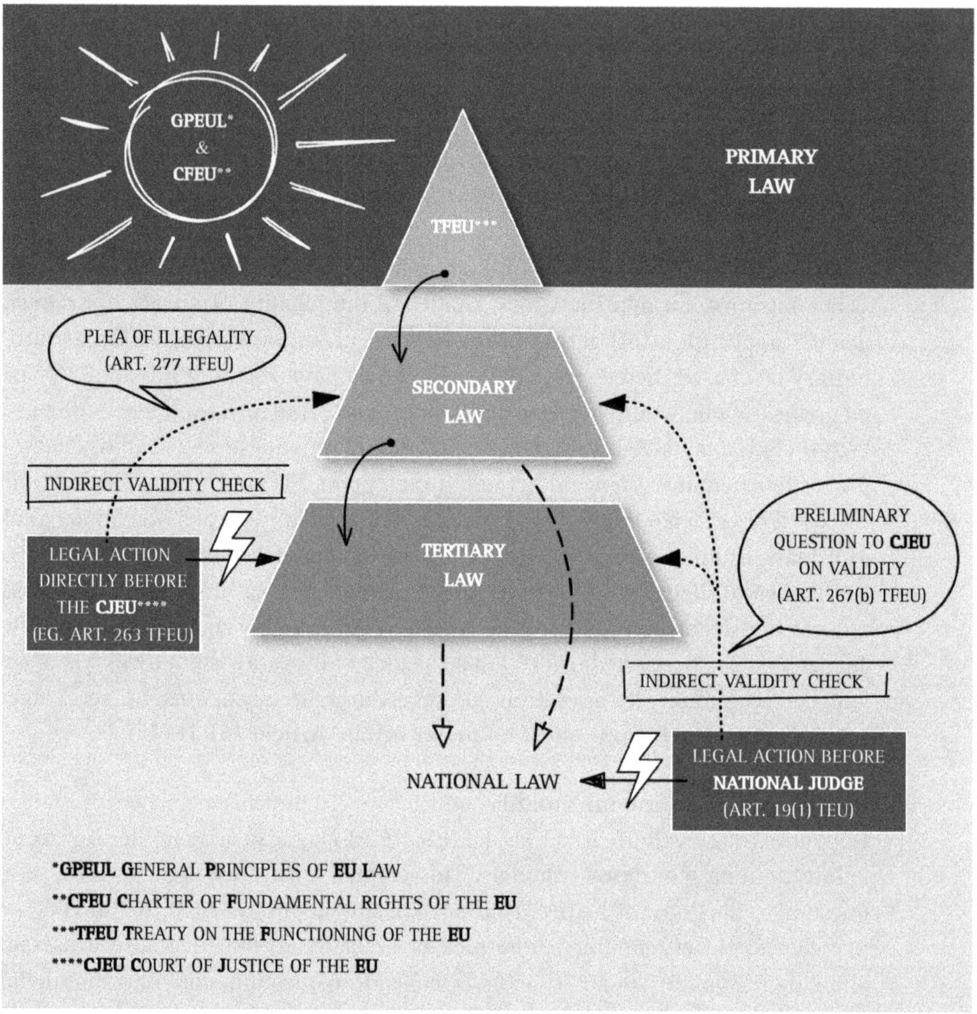

Figure 4.1 Indirect avenues to challenge the validity of EU acts

Like the plea of illegality, the possibility for national courts or tribunals to ask a question about the validity of EU act A contributes to compensating for the strict rules on standing for natural and legal persons to bring an annulment action against it.[277] This has led the Court of Justice to (controversially) assert that Articles 263 (on annulment actions) and 277 (on the plea of illegality), on the one hand, and Article 267 (on preliminary ruling), on the other hand, the TFEU established:

[276] For instance, a national measure implementing an EU act A.

[277] The preliminary question on validity may not be used by applicants who could undoubtedly have brought an annulment action against EU act A; see Chapter 4, note 274.

> *a complete system of legal remedies and procedures* designed to permit the Court of Justice to review the legality of measures adopted by the institutions. Natural and legal persons are thus protected against the application to them of general measures which they cannot contest directly before the Court by reason of the special conditions of admissibility laid down in Article [263, paragraph 4 on non-privileged applicants,] of the TFEU.[278] (Emphasis added)

4.3.1.4 EU Non-contractual Liability in Damages

As well as these possibilities to call into question the legality of EU action or inaction, EU law provides for a possibility to claim compensation for harm or damage arising due to breaches of EU law caused by EU organs. In 2020, such cases constituted less than 2 per cent of all actions brought before the General Court.[279] The latter indeed has jurisdiction in disputes relating to the non-contractual liability of the EU.[280] In accordance with Article 340 TFEU, the EU shall make good 'any damage caused by its institutions or by its servants in the performance of their duties', in accordance 'with the general principles common to the laws of the Member States'.[281]

The Court of Justice has for a long time, since the ruling in *Brasserie du Pêcheur and Factortame*, sought to ensure that the protection of the rights which individuals derive from EU law does not vary depending on whether a national authority or an EU organ is responsible for the damage resulting from a breach of EU law.[282] This was made particularly clear in *Bergaderm*.[283] The conditions under which the State may incur liability for damages caused to individuals thus do not differ, in principle, from those governing the liability of the EU in like circumstances. The three cumulative conditions for Member States' liability for damages, as well as the related explanations, also apply to EU liability in damages:[284]

1. The provision of EU law infringed must be intended to confer rights on individuals.
2. There must be a sufficiently serious breach of EU law. The Court of Justice has confirmed, in *Bergaderm*, that the decisive test is whether the EU organ 'manifestly and gravely disregarded the limits on its discretion'.[285]

[278] Case 294/83, *'Les Verts'*, EU:C:1986:166, para. 23; see also Chapter 4, Section 4.3.1.1, Categories of Applicants. Calling into question the completeness of the system, see previously: on the difficulty of challenging legislative acts that do not entail implementing measures (Chapter 4, note 244); on the difficulties for environmental organisations to bring cases (Chapter 4, note 251); controversies on the need and possibility to challenge the validity of soft law (Chapter 4, note 182); and for a synthesis, see reference in Chapter 4, note 251.

[279] Court of Justice of the European Union, 'Annual Report 2020: Judicial Activity', 2021, p. 349.

[280] Arts. 256(1), 268 TFEU. We leave aside, for the purpose of this introductory handbook, the contractual liability of the EU and the personal liability of its servants; see Art. 340, paras. 1, 3 TFEU.

[281] Art. 340, para. 2 TFEU; see also Art. 41(3) CFEU. The liability of the EU may be concurrent with that of the Member State: it will all depend on whether and at which level there is discretionary power.

[282] Joined Cases C-46/93 and C-48/93, *Brasserie du Pêcheur and Factortame*, EU:C:1996:79, para. 42.

[283] C-352/98 P, *Bergaderm*, EU:C:2000:361.

[284] See Chapter 4, Section 4.1.3.3. Joined Cases C-46/93 and C-48/93, *Brasserie du Pêcheur and Factortame*, EU:C:1996:79, para. 51. See further D. Hanf, 'EU Liability Actions', in Schütze and Tridimas (eds.), *Oxford Principles of European Union Law*, pp. 910–941.

[285] C-352/98 P, *Bergaderm*, EU:C:2000:361, para. 43.

3. There must be a direct causal link between the breach (which could result from an act or a failure to act) of the obligation resting on the EU and the damage sustained by the injured parties.

The action for compensation is primarily designed to enable compensation of natural or legal persons who have shown an individual interest in the claim.[286] An action for damages against the EU does not necessitate, but may be facilitated by, the prior existence of a challenge to the legality of an EU act or failure to act. Furthermore, an action for damages may be admissible even if the applicant does not fulfil the conditions to bring an annulment action under Article 263 TFEU. In any case, the action for damages ought to be brought within a time limit of five years from the occurrence of the event giving rise to the damage.[287]

It shall be noted that the nature of the EU act triggering liability is irrelevant as long as the conditions above are fulfilled.[288] Similarly, the author of the EU act that may trigger liability is not specified in Article 340, paragraph 2 TFEU.[289] As a result, it may be an institution, a body, an office, an agency or even another type of organ 'established by the Treaties and [. . .] intended to contribute to the achievement of the Union's objectives'.[290] For example, there is a set of interesting cases on actions against the EU for damage caused by delays in the issuing of a ruling by the General Court.[291] In contrast, and disagreeing on this point with the General Court, in the context of an appeal the Court of Justice ruled in *Chrysostomides* that the Eurogroup[292] is not an organ of the EU within the meaning of Article 340 TFEU. The Court of Justice thus refused to examine the substance of an action for damages against the Eurogroup. The Court instead stressed that cases could be brought against EU institutions in respect of the acts or conduct that those EU institutions adopt following a political agreement within the Eurogroup.[293]

4.3.2 The EU Legal Order Is Dependent on Sound National Legal Systems

The EU legal order, as powerful and sophisticated as it has been described, requires EU organs to be accountable for breaches of the rule of EU law. Yet EU organs do not operate in a vacuum. As shown, they largely depend on national legal infrastructures: national

[286] T-259/03, *Nikolaou*, EU:T:2007:254, para. 44. In principle, it could also be brought by a Member State, but there are few elements to confirm this to date.

[287] Statute of the Court of Justice of the European Union, Art. 46.

[288] For an example of an act that qualifies, in the context of the adoption of the Memorandum of Understanding from 26.4.2013, on Specific Economic Policy Conditionality concluded between the Republic of Cyprus and the European Stability Mechanism, the Commission acting on behalf of the European Stability Mechanism had the general task of overseeing the application of EU law and ensuring compliance with EU law; Joined Cases C-8/15 P to C-10/15 P, *Ledra Advertising*, EU:C:2016:701, paras. 55, 67.

[289] Art. 340, para. 3 TFEU further specifically refers to the Central Bank: it shall also make good any damage caused by it or by its servants in the performance of their duties.

[290] T-209/00, *Lamberts* v. *Ombudsman*, EU:T:2002:94, para. 49.

[291] E.g. C-150/17 P, *Kendrion*, EU:C:2018:1014 and Joined Cases C-138/17 P and C-146/17 P, *Gascogne Sack*, EU:C:2018:1013; see also Chapter 2, Section 2.3.6.2.

[292] See Chapter 2, Section 2.3.4.7.

[293] Joined Cases C-597/18 P, C-598/18 P, C-603/18 P and C-604/18 P, *Council* v. *Chrysostomides et al.*, EU: C:2020:1028, paras. 90, 93, 97. The Court of Justice further recalled the Commission's duties as Guardian of the Treaties, to ensure compliance with EU law, in the context of its participation in the activities of the Eurogroup (para. 96).

authorities – and courts in particular – breathe life into the doctrines of primacy and direct effect of EU law on a daily basis, allowing EU law to be integrated in the legal orders of the Member States. The latter thus ought to be fundamentally healthy for the EU legal system to function normally. This has been usefully recalled by the Court of Justice in *Achmea*, as follows:

> EU law is thus based on the fundamental premiss that each Member State shares with all the other Member States, and recognises that they share with it, a set of common values on which the EU is founded, as stated in Article 2 TEU. That premiss implies and justifies the existence of mutual trust between the Member States that those values will be recognised, and therefore that the law of the EU that implements them will be respected. It is precisely in that context that the Member States are obliged, by reason inter alia of the principle of sincere cooperation set out in the first subparagraph of Article 4(3) TEU, to ensure in their respective territories the application of and respect for EU law, and to take for those purposes any appropriate measure, whether general or particular, to ensure fulfilment of the obligations arising out of the Treaties or resulting from the acts of the institutions of the EU [. . .][294]

Member States have a duty anchored in EU law, that transcends the specific regulatory competences conferred on the EU by the Treaties, to ensure that their legal systems are fundamentally sound.[295] This translates, in legal terms, as a duty to abide by the values listed in Article 2 TEU with which we started this book.[296] Such obedience is a precondition for accession to the EU.[297] Furthermore, compliance with the rule of law, which features prominently in Article 2 TEU, plays a particularly important role in ensuring the perennity of the EU legal order, in which law has such a structuring function that respect for the law is existential. Yet Article 2 TEU is formulated in too broad terms to constitute a self-standing basis for legal action (such as an infringement action) against the Member States not complying with its content. How does EU law, then, ensure that Member States, after accession to the EU, continue to abide by the values listed in Article 2 TEU and, in particular, with the rule of law?

4.3.2.1 Political Monitoring of Compliance with the Values in Article 2 TEU

Since the Treaty of Amsterdam, and as strengthened by the Treaty of Nice, the EU Treaties include a mechanism for political institutions to make decisions in case of threats, in

294 C-284/16, *Achmea*, EU:C:2018:158, para. 34.

295 The principle of sincere cooperation (Art. 4(3) TEU) requires from the Member State that it uses its entire apparatus to ensure the full effectiveness of EU law (see Case 33/76, *Rewe*, EU:C:1976:188, para. 5; Case 45/76, *Comet*, EU:C:1976:191, paras. 12–13). There is furthermore a general duty to 'provide remedies sufficient to ensure effective legal protection in the fields covered by Union law' (Art. 19(1), subpara. 2 TEU). See, for instance, C-896/19, *Repubblika*, EU:C:2021:311, paras. 36–39: the Court of Justice observed that it has jurisdiction, within the meaning of Art. 19(1), subpara. 2 TEU to review a situation whereby a national court is seeking a ruling on the conformity with EU law requirements on judicial independence of national provisions governing the procedure for the appointment of members of the judiciary of the Member State to which that court belongs, and who may be called upon to rule on questions relating to the interpretation or application of EU law.

296 See Chapter 1, Section 1.1.3.

297 Art. 49(1) TEU; see also Chapter 2, Section 2.1.2.

a Member State, to the values listed in Article 2 TEU. The mechanism is enshrined in Article 7 TEU and can be summarised as follows.

Firstly, Article 7(1) TEU institutionalises possibilities to respond to a '*clear risk* of a serious breach' by a Member State of the values referred to in Article 2 TEU. The procedure may be triggered by a reasoned proposal from one third of the Member States, the Parliament or the Commission. The Council, acting by a special majority of four-fifths of its members, and with the consent of the Parliament, 'may determine' that there is such a clear risk of a serious breach. The Council must have heard the Member State,[298] may address its recommendations and ought to regularly verify that the grounds on which such a determination was made continue to apply.

Second, and without there being any explicit mention of a possible interdependence with Article 7(1) TEU, Article 7(2) TEU provides for a tool to react to 'the *existence* of a serious and persistent breach' by a Member State of the values referred to in Article 2 TEU. As can be seen from the choice of words, as well as the subsequent procedural requirements, the gravity of the situation that is the subject matter of this second limb of Article 7 TEU is more acute. This mechanism may be triggered, by a proposal from one third of the Member States or by the Commission – to the notable exclusion of the Parliament. It is then the European Council, deciding by unanimity, with the consent of the Parliament, that 'may determine' that there exists such a serious and persistent breach. The Member State must have been invited to submit its observations.

While the finding of a 'clear risk' (Article 7(1) TEU) does not have specific procedural consequences, the determination of the 'existence of a serious and persistent breach' (Article 7(2) TEU) enables the Council to decide on the suspension of certain EU rights of the Member State.[299] The Council then decides by qualified majority and may, for instance, suspend the voting rights of the representatives of the Member State concerned in the Council. In the meantime, EU law in its entirety continues to be binding on the Member State concerned.[300]

The voting arrangements within EU institutions are adjusted to the specific purpose and seriousness of Article 7 TEU procedures. The Member State in question does not take part in votes at the Council or European Council.[301] The Parliament votes by a two-thirds majority of the votes cast, representing the majority of its components.[302] Furthermore, for decisions on the suspension of certain rights of the Member State, special rules on a higher qualified majority at the Council apply.[303] The Court of Justice shall have jurisdiction to decide on the

[298] See General Secretariat of the Council, Note with regard to the standard modalities for hearings referred to in Art. 7(1) TEU, 10641/2/19, 9.7.2019.

[299] Art. 7(3) TEU. The measures can subsequently be adjusted or revoked, depending on the evolution of the situation; Art. 7(4) TEU.

[300] The Court of Justice has indicated that a determination of the existence of a serious and persistent breach by the European Council, within the meaning of Art. 7(2) TEU, would contribute to enabling other Member States to automatically refuse to implement EU law on the European Arrest Warrant in relation to the Member State concerned by the determination; C-216/18 PPU, *LM*, EU:C:2018:586, paras. 72–73.

[301] Art. 7(5) TEU and Art. 354 TFEU. The Member State concerned by the procedure does not count in the calculation of the one-third of the Member States referred to in Art. 7(1–2) TEU; and abstentions by members present in person or represented shall not prevent the adoption of decisions referred to in Art. 7(2) TEU.

[302] Elaborating on recent case law on the calculation of the relevant thresholds, see Chapter 2, Section 2.3.2.5, Voting Arrangements.

[303] Seventy-two per cent of the members of the Council, comprising at least 65 per cent of the population of these States; Art. 7(5) TEU; Arts. 354, 238(3)(b) TFEU.

legality of an act adopted by the European Council or by the Council pursuant to Article 7 TEU solely at the request of the Member State concerned, and in respect solely of the procedural stipulations contained in that Article (and thus to the exclusion of a review of the level of the risks posed to the values referred to in Article 2 TEU).[304]

Article 7 TEU has gained attention in recent years due to vivid concerns expressed by selected European institutions as regards risks of serious breaches of Article 2 TEU in Poland, and in Hungary in particular.[305] As things currently stand, the Commission has issued a reasoned proposal within the meaning of Article 7(1) TEU against Poland regarding the rule of law, and the Parliament has done the same in relation to Hungary for threats to the values on which the EU is founded.[306] This illustrates the existence of very serious concerns about compliance with the founding values of the EU within certain Member States. These are the first and only examples to date of the procedure being initiated. Although these initiatives date back to 2017 and 2018 respectively, and the Council has heard the Member States in question, the Council has not, at the time of writing, made a determination on whether there is a clear risk of a serious breach.

The use of Article 7 TEU is highly disputed for several reasons. On the one hand, the Commission and the Parliament have been deemed to react too slowly, and the Council is accused of inaction. Furthermore, there are concerns in relation to several (other) Member States, and questions of fair and equal treatment among them. On the other hand, it is often feared that several Member States targeted by EU action may rally to hinder the functioning of Article 7 TEU. It is also argued that attacks on the rule of law, or founding values more generally, warrant sophisticated legal and political responses, based on dialogue rather than isolation. Furthermore, it is at times recalled that the EU does not have competence to actually regulate the internal political or judicial organisation of its Member States – while another European organisation, in the form of the Council of Europe, with its Venice Commission, may be better placed to monitor the matter.[307] These debates point to a paradox: Article 2 TEU acts as a gateway to the EU, as compliance with its content is a condition for accession,[308] but the EU has limited means to actually control compliance

[304] Art. 269 TFEU; T-337/03, *Bertelli Gálvez* v. *Commission*, EU:T:2004:106, para. 15. Such a request must be made within one month from the date of such an act. The Court shall rule within one month from the date of the request. Note that the Court of Justice accepted the admissibility of a legal challenge brought against the Resolution of the Parliament, adopted under Art. 7(1) TEU, in relation to Hungary (C-650/18, *Hungary* v. *Parliament*, EU:C:2021:426, paras. 33, 39–40); the case was dismissed on the merits.

[305] Concerns have also been expressed in relation to other Member States; see, for instance, 'European Parliament Resolution of 8 October 2020 on the Rule of Law and Fundamental Rights in Bulgaria', 2020/2793(RSP); 'European Parliament Resolution of 18 December 2019 on the Rule of Law in Malta Following the Recent Revelations Surrounding the Murder of Daphne Caruana Galizia', 2019/2954(RSP). See, more generally, Commission, '2021 Rule of Law Report: The Rule of Law Situation in the European Union', COM (2021) 700 final, 20.7.2021.

[306] Commission, 'Proposal for a Council Decision on the Determination of a Clear Risk of a Serious Breach by the Republic of Poland of the Rule of Law', COM(2017) 835 final, 20.12.2017; 'European Parliament Resolution of 12 September 2018 on a Proposal Calling on the Council to Determine, Pursuant to Article 7(1) of the Treaty on European Union, the Existence of a Clear Risk of a Serious Breach by Hungary of the Values on which the Union Is Founded', 2017/2131(INL), 12.09.2018. Note that an annulment action against the latter was dismissed; C-650/18, *Hungary* v. *Parliament*, EU:C:2021:426.

[307] More information is available at venice.coe.int.

[308] Art. 49(1) TEU. The Court of Justice recently stated that a Member State cannot amend its legislation in such a way as to bring about a reduction in the protection of the value of the rule of law. Member States are required to ensure that, in the light of that value, any regression of their laws on the organisation of justice

and continued commitments to the said values once a State has become a member of the club.

It shall be kept in mind that Article 7 TEU does not exist in a vacuum. Complementary mechanisms and initiatives have been mushrooming within the EU legal order in the past years. For instance, the Commission has created a pre-Article 7 TEU procedure to act as an intermediary between 'the "soft power" of political persuasion and the "nuclear option" of Article 7 TEU', and it has been used in the case of Poland.[309] The Commission has also issued Rule of Law Reports since 2020 to review the situation in the EU on a yearly basis and country by country – the intention is to prevent problems from emerging or deepening.[310] A specific instrument was created to follow up on the relatively recent accession to the EU by Romania and Bulgaria, and is still in place.[311] The Parliament itself has proposed the creation of a more comprehensive mechanism for the protection of democracy, the rule of law and fundamental rights,[312] while the Council developed a rule of law dialogue, recently adjusted in response to the Commission's latest initiative on yearly country by country review.[313]

4.3.2.2 Is Compliance with the Rule of Law at National Level Judicially Enforceable?

One tool recently activated to tackle threats to the rule of law, through judicially enforceable means this time, is Article 19 TEU. It is the article of the EU Treaties that shapes the decentralised system for judicial protection in the EU legal order.[314] In the now well-known *ASJP* ruling, the Court of Justice reasoned as follows:

> The European Union is a union based on the rule of law in which individual parties have the right to challenge before the courts the legality of any decision or other national measure relating to the application to them of an EU act [. . .]. Article 19 TEU, which gives concrete expression to the value of the rule of law stated in Article 2 TEU, entrusts the responsibility for ensuring judicial review in the EU legal order not only to the Court of Justice but also to national courts and tribunals [. . .]. The

is prevented, by refraining from adopting rules which would undermine the independence of the judiciary. See C-896/19, *Repubblika*, EU:C:2021:311, paras. 61–64.

309 Commission, 'A New EU Framework to Strengthen the Rule of Law', COM(2014) 158 final, 11.3.2014, Preamble; see also Commission, Communication, 'Further Strengthening the Rule of Law within the Union: State of Play and Possible Next Steps', COM(2019) 163 final, 3.4.2019.

310 Commission, '2021 Rule of Law Report: The Rule of Law Situation in the European Union', COM(2021) 700 final, 20.7.2021. See also the Parliament's critical response: 'European Parliament Resolution of 7 October 2020 on the Establishment of an EU Mechanism on Democracy, the Rule of Law and Fundamental Rights', 2020/2072(INI), points N and 4–7 in particular.

311 'Commission Decision of 13 December 2006 Establishing a Mechanism for Cooperation and Verification of Progress in Bulgaria to Address Specific Benchmarks in the Areas of Judicial Reform and the Fight against Corruption and Organised Crime', OJ L 354, 13.12.2006, p. 58; 'Commission Decision of 13 December 2006 Establishing a Mechanism for Cooperation and Verification of Progress in Romania to Address Specific Benchmarks in the Areas of Judicial Reform and the Fight against Corruption', OJ L 354, 13.12.2006, p. 56. See further C-83/19, *Asociația 'Forumul Judecătorilor din România'*, EU:C:2021:393.

312 'European Parliament Resolution of 14 November 2018 on the Need for a Comprehensive EU Mechanism for the Protection of Democracy, the Rule of Law and Fundamental Rights', 2018/2886(RSP), 14.11.2018.

313 Council, 'Presidency Conclusions: Evaluation of the Annual Rule of Law Dialogue', 14173/19, 19.11.2019; see further General Affairs Council, 13 October 2020: 'The presidency has developed a new approach to the Council's annual rule of law dialogue'.

314 See Chapter 4, Section 4.1.3.

> Member States are therefore obliged, by reason, *inter alia*, of the principle of sincere cooperation, set out in the first subparagraph of Article 4(3) TEU, to ensure, in their respective territories, the application of and respect for EU law [. . .]. In that regard, as provided for by the second subparagraph of Article 19(1) TEU, Member States are to provide remedies sufficient to ensure effective judicial protection for individual parties in the fields covered by EU law. [. . .] The very existence of effective judicial review designed to ensure compliance with EU law is of the essence of the rule of law [. . .]. It follows that every Member State must ensure that the bodies which, as 'courts or tribunals' within the meaning of EU law, come within its judicial system in the fields covered by that law, meet the requirements of effective judicial protection. In that regard, the Court notes that the factors to be taken into account in assessing whether a body is a 'court or tribunal' include, *inter alia*, whether the body is established by law, whether it is permanent, whether its jurisdiction is compulsory, whether its procedure is *inter partes*, whether it applies rules of law and whether it is independent [. . .][315]

In this seminal ruling, the Court of Justice thereby shaped the duty built into Article 19(1), subparagraph 2 TEU on Member States to provide sufficiently sound remedies to better ensure effective judicial protection in the fields covered by EU law.[316] This gives the Court of Justice authority to exercise a degree of control on particularly serious threats to the soundness of the justice system of the Member States of the EU, in addition to the requirements to ensure an effective protection of EU rights, equivalent to that granted to national rights, as introduced previously (Chapter 4, Section 4.1.3.2).[317] This approach, in recent years, has enabled the Commission to bring infringement actions against Poland for reforms threatening the independence of its judges,[318] and has enabled national courts to raise related preliminary questions.[319] In this context, the Court of Justice has treated

[315] C-64/16, *Associação Sindical dos Juízes Portugueses (ASJP)*, EU:C:2018:117, paras. 31–38.

[316] See Chapter 4, Section 4.1.3. Art. 19(1), subpara. 2 TEU has direct effect so that if it is not possible to interpret the national provisions in a manner consistent with the second subparagraph of Article 19(1) TEU, national courts must disapply those national provisions of their own motion; C-430/21, *RS*, EU:C:2022:99, paras. 58–89.

[317] C-497/20, *Randstat Italia*, EU:C:2021:1037, paras. 56–59.

[318] Eg. the Court of Justice found Poland to be in violation of Art. 19(1), subpara. 2 TEU, by providing that the measure consisting of lowering the retirement age of the judges of the Sąd Najwyższy (Supreme Court) is to apply to judges in post who were appointed to that court before 3 April 2018, and by granting the President of the Republic the discretion to extend the period of judicial activity of judges of that court beyond the newly fixed retirement age; C-619/18, *Commission* v. *Poland (Independence of the Supreme Court)*, EU: C:2019:531. The Court has also ruled against Poland on the right of the Minister for Justice to decide whether or not to authorise judges of the ordinary Polish courts to continue to carry out their duties beyond the new retirement age of those judges, as lowered; C-192/18, *Commission* v. *Poland (Independence of ordinary courts)*, EU:C:2019:924.

[319] Note that for the Court of Justice to answer such questions, there ought to be a connecting factor between the dispute pending before the referring court and Art. 19(1), subpara. 2 TEU, whose interpretation is sought, by virtue of which that interpretation is objectively required for the decision to be taken by the referring court; C-558/18 and C-563/18, *Miasto Łowicz and Prokuratura Okręgowa w Płocku*, EU: C:2018:923, para. 48. If there is such a connecting factor, the question of whether Art. 19(1), subpara. 2 TEU has been infringed may relate to the substance of the case; C-896/19, *Repubblika*, EU:C:2021:311, paras. 29–30, 33. For an example of a preliminary question that was found admissible, see C-824/18, *A.B., et al.* v. *Krajowa Rada Sądownictwa (Appointment to a position as judge at the Supreme Court)*, EU: C:2021:153. The Court of Justice noted, among other things in a very lengthy ruling, that Art. 19(1), subpara. 2 TEU must first be interpreted as enabling review of the system of judicial protection in place at

certain cases as a matter of priority, and adopted interim measures as well as penalty payments for non-compliance with these interim measures.[320] These cases are both highly important for the EU legal order, and highly delicate for the Court of Justice: there is a fine line between ensuring the good functioning of the EU legal order through the scrutiny of national judicial systems and intruding unduly into national decisions on the organisation of justice.[321]

4.3.2.3 When the Rule of Law Meets the Rule of EU Law

Article 7 TEU and Article 19(1), subparagraph 2 TEU (as employed by the Court of Justice in the case law introduced previously), are instruments specifically developed to address threats to EU values, and to the rule of law in particular. It shall not be forgotten, however, that threats to the rule of law, or to the values listed in Article 2 TEU more broadly, are often directly entangled with direct conflicts with specific EU law requirements.[322] In such cases, the traditional machinery of EU law may be relied upon, and even modernised, to address related challenges.

For instance, the Commission may initiate infringement proceedings – sometimes in a coordinated manner – for the unjustified restrictions on foreign donations to civil society organisations, in breach of EU rules on the free movement of capital. The Commission may also rely on other provisions, such as the CFEU itself in situations falling within the scope of EU law.[323] Similarly, OLAF detects and investigates misuse of EU public funds. In this

the level of the Supreme Court, in particular in relation to its Civil and Commercial Chambers, which are fields covered by EU law (para. 114). Second, the said provision requires review of whether the said judicial organ is independent, as this is essential to ensure adjudication within the EU system of legal remedies (para. 116). Third, it demands that the rules governing the appointment of judges, read in their broader national, factual and historical context, do not 'give rise to systemic doubts in the minds of individuals as to the independence and impartiality of the judges appointed at the end of that process' (para. 129; this criterion is further developed at paras. 157–164). The Court is overall concerned with not 'prejudicing the trust which justice in a democratic society governed by the rule of law must inspire in subjects of the law' (para. 139). Ultimately, the final assessment is for the national court to make (paras. 96, 139). Where it is established that Art. 19(1), subpara. 2 TEU has been infringed, 'the principle of primacy of EU law must be interpreted as requiring the referring court to disapply the amendments at issue, whether they are of a legislative or constitutional origin, and, consequently, to continue to assume the jurisdiction previously vested in it to hear disputes referred to it before those amendments were made' (paras. 142–149).

[320] See, for instance, on giving the case priority treatment: C-824/18, *A.B., et al.* v. *Krajowa Rada Sądownictwa (Appointment to a position as judge at the Supreme Court)*, EU:C:2021:153, paras. 49–53; on interim measures: C-204/21 R, *Commission* v. *Poland*, EU:C:2021:593; on the addition of periodic penalty payment: C-204/21 R, *Commission* v. *Poland*, EU:C:2021:878. The line of case law from the Court of Justice on the interpretation of Art. 19(1) TEU, and on interim measures to protect the right to effective judicial review by an independent and impartial tribunal established by law, has been the subject of tensions with the Polish Constitutional Tribunal's rulings of 14.7.2021 and 7.10.2021. On 22.12.2021, the Commission initiated the first (non-judicial) phases of an infringement action against Poland for violation of EU law by its Constitutional Tribunal. See further Chapter 4, Section 4.1.1.1, Scope and National Perspectives, note 24.

[321] See further C-619/18, *Commission* v. *Poland (Independence of the Supreme Court)*, EU:C:2019:531, para. 52; A. Torres Pérez, 'From Portugal to Poland: The Court of Justice of the European Union as Watchdog of Judicial Independence', *Maastricht Journal of European and Comparative Law*, 27 (2020), pp. 105–119.

[322] This may, for instance, affect mutual trust in the context of the AFSJ in particular; see C-216/18 PPU, *Minister for Justice and Equality (Deficiencies in the system of justice)*, EU:C:2018:586. See further Editorial comments, 'The Rule of Law in the Union, the Rule of Union Law and the Rule of Law by the Union: Three Interrelated Problems', *Common Market Law Review*, 53 (2016), pp. 597–605.

[323] E.g. C-78/18, *Commission* v. *Hungary (Transparency of Associations)*, EU:C:2020:476, paras. 110–134, 139–142; as well as C-235/17, *Commission* v. *Hungary (Usufruct over Agricultural Land)*, EU:C:2019:432, paras. 123–129; C-66/18, *Commission* v. *Hungary (Higher Education)*, EU:C:2020:792, paras. 222–234,

function, it will be supported increasingly by the newly created European Public Prosecutor's Office.[324] In the context of European economic policy, and more specifically of the European Semester, recommendations may also steer sound institutional reform within the Member States. The 2020 recommendations to Hungary, for instance, noted the need to strengthen judicial independence and recalled the existence of systemic deficiencies in this country's system of public procurement.[325]

Examples of engagement with the rule of law through mainstream mechanisms thus abound and should be used in conjunction to address systemic threats to the rule of law; such a strategic and targeted use of EU tools remains a considerable challenge.[326] The latest instrument to date is the hotly debated regulation on a general regime of conditionality for the protection of the EU budget.[327] It seeks to connect the sound management of the budget of the EU, and thus the allocation and use of EU funds at the level of the Member States, to compliance with principles of the rule of law enshrined in Article 2 TEU. The Commission, in collaboration with the Council, is primarily in charge of implementing the mechanism thereby created. If, how and when this mechanism will start being used remains unclear at the time of writing.[328]

4.4 EUROPEAN INTEGRATION IS A PROCESS

To close this chapter on the unique nature of the EU legal order, and, more generally, this book introducing the foundations, actors and system of norms of this legal order, it shall be humbly recalled that the EU, just like the present attempt to introduce it, has limitations and is imperfect.

4.4.1 Focus: Legal Design of the EMU, the AFSJ and the CFSP

When introducing the main stages of the evolution of the EU legal order, I opted to shed light on three policy areas that have come to take centre stage in EU affairs in recent years, together

239–242. See further M. Bonelli, 'Infringement Actions 2.0: How to Protect EU Values before the Court of Justice', *European Constitutional Law Review* 18 (2022), pp. 30–58.

324 'Council Regulation (EU) 2017/1939 of 12 October 2017 Implementing Enhanced Cooperation on the Establishment of the European Public Prosecutor's Office', OJ L 283, 31.10.2017 (last amended 2020). Note, however, that the EPPO represents enhanced cooperation among twenty-two Member States only – Denmark, Ireland, Hungary, Poland and Sweden are not taking part.

325 'Council Recommendation of 20 July 2020 on the 2020 National Reform Programme of Hungary and Delivering a Council Opinion on the 2020 Convergence Programme of Hungary', OJ C 282, 26.8.2020, pp. 107–115, Preamble recitals (27) and (29).

326 See further Commission, 'Further Strengthening the Rule of Law within the Union: State of Play and Possible Next Steps', COM(2019) 163 final, 3.4.2019.

327 'Regulation (EU, Euratom) 2020/2092 of the European Parliament and of the Council of 16 December 2020 on a General Regime of Conditionality for the Protection of the Union Budget', OJ L 433I, 22.12.2020, pp. 1–10.

328 In a remarkable institutional imbroglio (see Chapter 2, Section 2.3.3.2), the European Council has stated that the Commission intends to develop and adopt guidelines on the way that it will apply the regulation; such guidelines would be developed in close consultation with the Member States. The European Council added that should an action for annulment be introduced, the guidelines will be finalised after the judgment (expected in March 2022) so as to incorporate any relevant elements stemming from such judgment. Until such guidelines are finalised, the Commission would not propose measures under the Regulation; European Council Conclusions, 10–11 December 2020, on the MFF and Next Generation EU, COVID-19, climate change, security and external relations, point I.2.c. Annulment actions against the instrument have indeed been initiated and dismissed; C-156/21, *Hungary* v. *Parliament and Council*, EU:C:2022:97; C-157/21, *Poland* v. *Parliament and Council*, EU:C:2022:98.

with the foundational project of market integration: monetary policy, home affairs and foreign affairs.[329] Today, these are commonly referred to in the context of the EMU, the AFSJ and the CFSP. The specific trajectory of these EU policies, and the nature of the related competences,[330] help us to understand the ongoing challenges that relate to their institutional design.

The considerable increase in the political as well as legal relevance of the EMU in the first two decades of the twentieth century has brought to the fore a number of key challenges, several of which have been highlighted in this book. In terms of judicial protection, many norms take the shape of soft law, which is not always easy to fit into the traditional procedures for judicial review examined in this chapter, despite their potentially far-reaching implications.[331] The rising powers of the Eurogroup are difficult to grasp for the purpose of judicial review,[332] as well as for the understanding of how decisions are made in the EU.[333] The multi-layered, sophisticated and powerful structure on which the Central Bank relies also raises novel challenges.[334]

It may be recalled that for the AFSJ in EU law, the institutional framework has been redesigned by the Treaty of Lisbon. Yet the legal effects of EU acts adopted prior to Lisbon through atypical instruments shall be preserved until those acts are repealed, annulled or amended in the implementation of the Treaties.[335] This results in anachronisms such as the continued existence of 'framework decisions' – an old and odd instrument of EU law! – such as that on the European Arrest Warrant that regularly attracts media attention.[336] We know from the ruling of the Court of Justice in *Pupino* that national judges are under a duty to interpret national law in conformity with framework decisions adopted in the context of EU criminal law, which was located in the Third Pillar that existed before the Treaty of Lisbon.[337] Framework decisions have primacy over national law, but they may not produce direct effect – they can neither be used as a sword nor as a shield.[338] Thankfully though, other acts of EU law related to the AFSJ are now subject to standard judicial procedures discussed in this chapter,[339] with the possibility of an urgent preliminary ruling procedure

329 See Chapter 1, Section 1.3.2. 330 See Chapter 1, Section 1.3.2 and Chapter 3, Section 3.3, respectively.

331 See further on the challenges with the Court of Justice of the European Union reviewing the validity of soft law, Chapter 4, note 181; on the absence of a possibility to bring infringement actions in response to excessive government deficit, see Art. 126(10) TFEU.

332 See Chapter 4, note 292.

333 See, for example, the interesting request for proposals from the European Council to the Eurogroup in search for an appropriate response to the COVID-19 crisis: Eurogroup, 'Report on the Comprehensive Economic Policy Response to the COVID-19 Pandemic', press release, 9.4.2020; and subsequent statement by the President of the European Council, 'Conclusions of the President of the European Council Following the Video Conference of the Members of the European Council', press release, 23.4.2020.

334 See Chapter 2, Section 2.3.7. See, for instance, the jurisdiction of the Court of Justice to review actions brought against a *national* act entailing definitive or temporary prohibition on performing the duties of governor of a national central bank (Joined Cases C-202/18 and C-238/18, *Ilmārs Rimšēvičs*, EU: C:2019:139); and the possibility for the Governing Council of the European Central Bank to initiate infringement actions against national central banks before the Court of Justice of the European Union (Art. 271(d) TFEU).

335 Protocol 36 on Transitional Provisions, Title VI, Art. 9.

336 'Council Framework Decision of 13 June 2002 on the European Arrest Warrant and the Surrender Procedures between Member States: Statements Made by Certain Member States on the Adoption of the Framework Decision', OJ L 190, 18.7.2002, p. 1 (last amended 2009). See also Chapter 1, Section 1.3.2.3 and Chapter 3, Section 3.5.3.2, Nature of EU Internal Acts.

337 C-105/03, *Pupino*, EU:C:2005:386, paras. 35–43.

338 C-573/17, *Popławski*, EU:C:2019:530, paras. 69–71. See also Chapter 4, Sections 4.1.2 and 4.1.4.

339 Protocol 36 on Transitional Provisions, Title VI, Art. 10.

being employed when a person whose liberty is at stake because they are in custody.[340] A notable feature of this field of law is that it 'shall not affect the exercise of the responsibilities incumbent upon Member States with regard to the maintenance of law and order and the safeguarding of internal security'.[341] Yet the Court has so far rejected attempts to read limits on its jurisdiction into that provision.[342]

The picture is different if we turn to the CFSP, which is still subject to a distinct institutional framework.[343] In terms of judicial protection, the rules described in the present chapter hardly apply in this field, resulting in a much weaker set of safeguards. Article 24(1) TEU, introducing the Treaty chapter on the CFSP, makes it clear that the Court of Justice 'shall not have jurisdiction in the field'.[344] This comes with two sets of notable exceptions. The Court retains jurisdiction to monitor compliance with Article 40 TEU on the relationship between the CFSP and mainstream EU competences.[345] The Court also retains jurisdiction to review the legality of decisions providing for restrictive measures against natural or legal persons adopted by the Council, in proceedings brought in accordance with Article 263, paragraph 4 TFEU corresponding to the procedure for annulment actions against EU acts, by virtue of Article 275, paragraph 2 TFEU. In recent years, the Court of Justice has rendered a number of rulings in which it makes a very narrow reading of the limitations to its jurisdiction over the CFSP and thereby actually asserts, in limited but significant ways, its jurisdiction in the field.[346] For instance, in *Rosneft*, the Court asserted that its jurisdiction to review the validity of restrictive measures against natural or legal persons through annulment actions entails jurisdiction to do so also in the context of the preliminary ruling procedure.[347]

4.4.2 Epilogue

These oddities in the institutional design of certain areas of EU law are but illustrations that the process of European integration is constantly in need of adjustment. Next to the three

[340] See Chapter 4, note 205.

[341] Art. 72 TFEU; see also Art. 276 TFEU on the limited jurisdiction of the Court of Justice of the European Union over such matters.

[342] E.g. Joined Cases C-715/17, C-718/17 and C-719/17, *Commission* v. *Poland, Hungary and Czech Republic* (*Temporary mechanism for the relocation of applicants for international protection*), EU:C:2020:257, paras. 142–147.

[343] See Chapter 2, Section 2.3.6 and Chapter 3, Section 3.5.3.1, Acts Adopted in the Context of the Common Foreign and Security Policy.

[344] See also Art. 275, para. 1 TFEU.

[345] As listed in Arts. 3–6 TFEU.

[346] The Court of Justice is thereby, to some extent, limiting the gap in judicial protection that was one of the arguments against the draft agreement on accession by the EU to the ECHR: Opinion 2/13, Accession of the European Union to the European Convention for the Protection of Human Rights and Fundamental Freedoms, EU:C:2014:2454, paras. 249–257. See further P. Van Elsuwege, 'Judicial Review and the Common Foreign and Security Policy: Limits to the Gap-Filling Role of the Court of Justice', *Common Market Law Review*, 58 (2021), pp. 1731–1760.

[347] C-72/15, *Rosneft*, EU:C:2017:236, paras. 65–81. The General Court and, in the case of an appeal, the Court of Justice also have jurisdiction to hear a claim for damages allegedly suffered by a person or entity as a result of restrictive measures against natural or legal persons pursuant to CFSP Decisions, in accordance with Art. 215 TFEU; C-134/19 P, *Bank Refah Kargaran*, EU:C:2020:793, para. 44. See also C-439/13 P, *Elitaliana*, EU:C:2015:753, paras. 41–50 (jurisdiction to interpret and apply the provisions of the Financial Regulation – related to the EU budget – with regard to public procurement in the context of the CFSP); C-455/14 P, *H* v. *Council and others*, EU:C:2016:569, paras. 39–62 (jurisdiction in relation to staff members seconded by the Member States to an EU Police Mission in the context of the CFSP and redeployed to meet the needs of that mission at theatre level).

salient policy areas chosen to illustrate the point, several other challenges are currently high on the agenda. We have mentioned the difficulties for EU organs to grapple with serious threats to EU values in several of its Member States, for the EU to comply with its duty to accede to the ECHR, the process of maintaining good relations with the UK after Brexit, the response to the COVID-19 crisis, the dilemmas related to differentiated integration and the latest Russian military aggression against Ukraine. The list could be long, but as the reader will have understood, the objective here is not to be exhaustive. It is, more modestly, to invite critical and constructive thinking on a process which aims to promote peace, the values of the EU and the well-being of its peoples.[348]

[348] Art. 3(1) TEU.

Index

For EU product safety concerns, contact us at Calle de José Abascal, 56–1°, 28003 Madrid, Spain or eugpsr@cambridge.org.

www.ingramcontent.com/pod-product-compliance
Lightning Source LLC
LaVergne TN
LVHW081934200926
848484LV00009B/2428

* 9 7 8 1 1 0 8 4 8 5 6 0 9 *